PRONOUNCING ENGLISH:
A Stress-Based Approach
with CD-ROM

Richard V. Teschner
and
M. Stanley Whitley

Georgetown University Press
Washington, D.C.

Georgetown University Press, Washington, D.C.
© 2004 by Georgetown University Press. All rights reserved.
Printed in the United States of America

10 9 8 7 6 5 4 3 2 1   2004

This volume is printed on acid-free paper meeting the requirements of the American National Standard for Permanence in Paper for Printed Library Materials.

Library of Congress Cataloging-in-Publication Data

Teschner, Richard V.
     Pronouncing English : a stress-based approach, with CD-Rom / Richard
V. Teschner and M. Stanley Whitley.
        p. cm.
Includes bibliographical references (p.   ) and index.
     ISBN 1-58901-002-7 (pbk. : alk. paper)
        1. English language—Pronunciation.   I. Whitley, Melvin Stanley, 1948–
     II. Title.

PE1137.T44   2004
428 .3—dc22   2003019467

This book is dedicated by Richard V. Teschner to the memory of his father, Richard Rewa Teschner (1908–97), germanophone by birth and an avid learner of English, and to the memory of his mother, Dorothea Joy Griesbach Teschner (1909–2003), model speaker, writer, and editor of her native tongue.

It is dedicated by M. Stanley Whitley to his family—Mary Jo, Steven, and Philip—for their love and support, and to his students for what they continue to teach him in their efforts to master the pronunciation of a second language.

CONTENTS

Preface   xi

List of Symbols   xiii

Chapter 1   The Metric Foot   1

  1.1   The notion of stress: Present stress and absent/null stress   1

  1.2   Metricalism   3

  1.3   The five major metric feet: Spondees, trochees,
iambs, dactyls, and anapests   5

  1.4   Weak stress, null stress, and vowels   12

  1.5   The English drive toward monosyllabicity   19

  1.6   Teaching the topics of chapter 1 to students of ESOL   21

Notes   23

Wrap-Up Exercises   24

**Chapter 2   Strong Stresses and Weak:
How to Know Where They Go**   27

  2.1   Strong stress moves leftward, but only so far   27

  2.2   Three main factors in strong-stress position   31

    2.2.1   Syllable structure   31

    2.2.2   Part of speech   32

    2.2.3   Affixation   32

  2.3   Strong-stress retention on the same base vowel   33

  2.4   Word families with shifting stress   33

  2.5   The effect of suffixation on strong-stress position   36

  2.6   The shiftless, stress-free life of the prefix   40

  2.7   Applying strong-stress rules to bisyllabic words   42

2.8	Applying strong-stress rules to trisyllabic words	44
2.9	Strong-stressing words of four, five, and more syllables	45
2.10	Weak stress: Placing the strong, locating the weak	47
2.11	Weak stress on bisyllabic words	47
	2.11.1 Bisyllabics that strong-stress the ult	47
	2.11.2 Bisyllabics that strong-stress the pen	48
2.12	Weak-stressing trisyllabic words	49
2.13	Weak-stressing "four-plus" words	50
	2.13.1 Ult stress patterns	50
	2.13.2 Pen stress patterns	50
	2.13.3 Ant(epenultimate) stress patterns	51
	2.13.4 Pre(antepenultimate) stress patterns	53
	2.13.5 Qui stress patterns	54
2.14	Vowel reduction: The price we pay for shifting stress	55
2.15	Teaching the topics of chapter 2 to students of ESOL	57
Notes		58

Chapter 3 Intonation—The Melodic Line		**61**
3.1	"Peak" stress for contrast and emphasis	61
3.2	Some analogies with music	64
3.3	Stressing compound words and phrases	66
	3.3.1 Two-word compounds and phrases	66
	3.3.2 Multiple-word compounds and phrases	71
	3.3.3 Pitch adjustment in compounds' post-peak words	73
3.4	Peak stresses and info units	75
3.5	Melodic lines long and short, falling and rising, and so on	79
	3.5.1 Falls and rises, statements and questions	79
	3.5.2 Fall-rise and rise-fall	82
	3.5.3 Some other melodies	82
3.6	Melodic lines and compound melodies	84
	3.6.1 Enumeration	84
	3.6.2 Selection questions	84
	3.6.3 Tags	85
	3.6.4 Complex sentences	86

3.7   Approaches to intonation   88

3.8   Teaching the topics of chapter 3 to students of ESOL   90

Notes   91

Wrap-Up Exercises   92

Chapter 4   From Orthography to Pronunciation   **95**

4.1   Even *English* spelling can be reduced to rules   95

4.2   Consonants: The (somewhat) easy part   100

   4.2.1   The fairly easy equivalencies: Phonemes /tʃ h ŋ θ ð w j/   104

   4.2.2   The tough equivalencies: Phonemes /k s z ʃ ʒ dʒ/   108

   4.2.3   Grapheme 'i' and the consonants that precede it   111

   4.2.4   When is 's(s)' /s/ and when is it /z/, /ʃ/, or even /ʒ/?   113

   4.2.5   Grapheme 's' and /s/, /z/, and /ʒ/   114

   4.2.6   Grapheme 'x' and the five things it renders   116

4.3   Vowels: Which are easy and which are tough to spell   117

   4.3.1   Vowels that are fairly easy to spell   121

   4.3.2   Vowels that are tough to spell   123

      4.3.2.1   The four tense vowels /i e o u/   123

      4.3.2.2   Diphthong /ai/   125

      4.3.2.3   The mid lax vowels /ɔ/ and /ʌ/   125

   4.3.3   Vowel phonemes and graphemes:
        An encapsulated review   126

4.4   Vowel reduction redux   127

   4.4.1   General guidelines for spelling the schwa   128

   4.4.2   How to spell unstressed final /ər/   128

   4.4.3   The three ways to spell stressed /ər/   129

4.5   Teaching the topics of chapter 4 to students of ESOL   130

Notes   131

Wrap-Up Exercises   132

Chapter 5   Vowels   **135**

5.1   Vowels, broadly and narrowly   135

5.2   How to make vowels: Tongue and lip position   136

5.3   Other vowels, other languages   137

	5.4	Stressed vowels	139
		5.4.1 Low /ɑ/ and /æ/	140
		5.4.2 Mid and high vowels: Tense /i e o u/ versus lax /ɪ ɛ ʊ ɔ/	141
		5.4.3 Full diphthongs: /ai oi au/	145
		5.4.4 Uh, er . . . : The lax vowels /ʌ/ and /ər/	147
	5.5	Unstressed vowels: The schwa zone	150
	5.6	Shifting vowels make the dialect	152
		5.6.1 Low back problems	152
		5.6.2 Vowel breaking	153
		5.6.3 Diphthongs on the move	154
		5.6.4 Smoothed diphthongs	154
		5.6.5 Lexical incidence: "You say *tomayto* and I say *tomahto* . . ."	155
	5.7	Rules and regularities	156
	5.8	Other analyses of English vowels	159
	5.9	Teaching pronunciation: Vowels and consonants	161
Notes			163
Wrap-Up Exercises			164
Chapter 6	**Consonants**		**169**
	6.1	Consonants and syllable position	169
	6.2	Types of consonants	171
		6.2.1 Voicing	171
		6.2.2 Place of articulation	172
		6.2.3 Manner of articulation	175
		6.2.4 Secondary modifications	176
	6.3	English consonant phonemes	177
	6.4	Consonants that can behave like vowels	178
		6.4.1 Liquids: *l*s and *r*s	178
		6.4.2 Nasals	182
		6.4.3 Goin' s'llabic	184
	6.5	Stops	185
		6.5.1 Stops and VOT	186
		6.5.2 Stops that flap	189

6.6	All those sibilants	191
6.7	Slits up front	194
6.8	/h/: A sound that can get lost	196
6.9	Glides /j/ and /w/	197
6.10	Syllable reprise: How to build an English word	201
6.11	Teaching pronunciation: Error analysis	205
Notes		208
Wrap-Up Exercises		208

Chapter 7	**Sounds and Forms That Change and Merge**	**211**
7.1	English phonemes in (con)text	211
7.2	When words change their pronunciation	212
7.3	Changes due to word linkage	213
7.4	Changes due to stress	215
	7.4.1 Speaking metrically	215
	7.4.2 Crushed words: Weak forms and contractions	217
7.5	Changes due to grammar: Morphemes and allomorphs	221
7.6	Phonology in grammar	223
	7.6.1 Inflectional morphology	223
	7.6.2 A case study: English plural formation	224
7.7	The phoneme exchange	229
	7.7.1 Vowel alternations	230
	7.7.2 Consonant alternations	232
	7.7.3 Rules, constraints, alternations: How deep does phonology go?	236
7.8	English spelling revisited	240
7.9	Teaching pronunciation: Sounds in context	241
Notes		243
Wrap-Up Exercises		244

Chapter 8	**Appendix**	**251**
8.1	Acoustic phonetics	251
8.2	The International Phonetic Alphabet	257
8.3	*PEASBA*'s CD: Recordings and Corpus	259
Notes		261

Glossary 263

References 273

Index 277

PREFACE

Pronouncing English: A Stress-Based Approach (henceforth *PEASBA*) is a college text-book designed for upper-level undergraduate or beginning-level graduate courses in English phonetics and phonology. It does not presuppose prior linguistic training; fundamental concepts are introduced as they arise. It is suitable for majors in English or linguistics in general, and it is addressed in particular to those who plan to be instructors in the various fields of English as a Foreign Language (EFL), English as a Second Language (ESL), and multilingual education involving English.

Like other major languages, English is *multinational* (used natively in many countries) as well as *international* (used for intercommunication by people from different countries around the globe, in addition to whatever languages they may use locally). Even in the earliest times, the English of England showed multiple varieties, and its spread over the centuries to other countries produced many more of these. Today, the more than 400,000,000 speakers of the language show such diversity in their speech patterns that they are sometimes referred to as a community of "Englishes."

It is nonetheless the case that media, education, and reference materials are dominated by two historically acknowledged standards: Southern British English (with Received Pronunciation, or RP), and General American. Neither one corresponds to any one local dialect, or is as homogeneous as it may seem, or differs greatly from the other; but both are fairly coherent norms that are regarded as regionally neutral for overall communication and are worthwhile models to learn and teach. Other local standards, such as those of Australia or Canada, are more or less similar to these two. In *PEASBA* we focus on the prevailing pronunciation of General American English, and we also point out the major characteristics of RP when different, as well as local variants where these seem important for analysis and teaching.

Each language has its idiosyncrasies, and those of English are well known. However, years of teaching a wide variety of students of English have convinced us that its pronunciation must be approached on the basis of the powerful role of stress in the language. This aspect of its phonology receives relatively little attention in pedagogy in part, perhaps, because it is ignored in the writing system. Yet we have found that virtually all aspects of English pronunciation—from the vowel system (the language's main *bête noire*) to the articulation of syllables, words, and sentences—are determined by the presence or absence of stress. This is the reason that English can seem more complicated than it is when analysis and presentation begin with the segmental units and work upward. Thus many textbooks describe the schwa sound, point out that "some" vowels become schwa and that this depends on absence of stress, and then move on to a description of stress, stress assignment, and the stress patterns and intonation of phrases and sentences.

PEASBA's approach turns all this around: it starts with an analysis of the cause—the role of stress in the language—and then proceeds to its effects on pronunciation. In particular, we first prepare a solid foundation in English metricality at the word and phrase level and then expand in three directions: "upward" toward an appreciation of the interfaces between stress and intonation, "sideward" in the complex relationships between graphemes and phonemes in an orthographically conservative and form-focused language, and "downward" in a thorough analysis of individual vowels and consonants and their stress-based variation in context.

In addition, numerous observations on English stress patterns, phonemes, and orthography are based on original research, as explained in the appendix; *PEASBA* is in fact the first work of its kind to be based to a large extent on an exhaustive statistical analysis of all the lexical entries of an entire dictionary. Our goal, however, is not just an improved linguistic description of English pronunciation; it is also the improvement of how it is taught, and each of the seven chapters points out useful pedagogical generalizations and ends in a section specifically devoted to teaching techniques.

Other special features of *PEASBA* include the following:

- Frequent exercises, not only at the end of the chapters but after each major point, to promote analysis, application, and discussion.
- A list of symbols and glossary of key terms for easy reference.
- A CD-ROM containing the data files, called "Corpus," on which many of *PEASBA*'s statistical observations were based, as well as recordings of many of the exercises. (Exercises in the book with a listening component are cued by a headphones symbol, ∩.)
- An appendix that provides an introduction to acoustic phonetics, a chart of the International Phonetic Alphabet, and further information on the CD's files and tracks and on the use of the data in the Corpus.

PEASBA is a textbook that devotes itself exclusively to examining the pronunciation of English. In courses that also cover additional areas (e.g., grammar and lexicography) or in programs promoting multileveled language development, *PEASBA* can be combined effectively with textbooks that have different focuses.

Special thanks go to Gail Grella, Deborah Weiner, and Hope Smith of the Georgetown University Press for their support and assistance with this project, and to Bakhit Kourmanov, Mary Jo Whitley, and Héctor Enríquez for their help in recording the CD. We also acknowledge the kind permission of the International Phonetic Association to reprint their current chart in this book.

LIST OF SYMBOLS

The symbols used in this book are summarized by the following list, in roughly alphabetical order. Phonetic symbol names are generally those of the International Phonetic Alphabet (IPA). For the full set of IPA symbols, see figure 8h in the appendix. Phones marked with a double-dagger, ‡, do not normally occur in standard American or British varieties of English.

symbol	name(s)	meaning
ɑ	script *a*	low (or open) back unrounded vowel
ɒ	turned script *a*	low (or open) back-rounded vowel
a	lowercase *a*	low (or open) central-to-front unrounded vowel
æ	ash, ae ligature	low (or near-open) front unrounded vowel
b	*b*	voiced bilabial stop
β	beta	‡ voiced bilabial fricative
ç	curly-tail *c*	‡ voiceless prepalatal (alveolo-palatal) sibilant fricative
C	uppercase C	consonants; any consonant
č	*c* wedge (hachek)	= [tʃ]
d	*d*	voiced alveolar stop
dʒ	*d* with ezh	voiced alveopalatal affricated stop
ɖ	right-tail *d*	‡ voiced retroflex stop
D	small capital D	= [ɾ]
ð	eth	voiced (inter)dental fricative
e	*e*	tense-mid (or close-mid) front unrounded vowel
ə	schwa (turned *e*)	lax mid-central unrounded vowel
ɚ	right-hook schwa	retroflex (*r*-colored) lax mid-central vowel
ɛ	epsilon	lax mid (or open-mid) front unrounded vowel
ɜ	reversed epsilon	mid (or open-mid) central unrounded vowel
ɞ	closed reversed epsilon	mid (or open-mid) central rounded vowel
f	*f*	voiceless labiodental fricative
ɸ	phi	‡ voiceless bilabial fricative
g	open-tail *g*	voiced velar stop
G	uppercase G	glides; any glide (semivowel)

ɣ	gamma	‡ voiced velar fricative
h	*h*	voiceless glottal fricative
ʰ	superscript (raised) *h*	aspirated
i	*i*	tense high (or close) front unrounded vowel
ɨ	barred *i*	‡ tense high (or close) central unrounded vowel
ɪ	small capital *i*	lax high (or near-close) front unrounded vowel
ɪ̵	barred small capital *i*	lax high (or near-close) central unrounded vowel
j	*j*	palatal glide (semivowel)
ʲ	superscript (raised) *j*	‡ palatalized
ʝ	curly-tail *j*	‡ voiced palatal fricative
ɟ	barred dotless *j*	‡ voiced palatal stop
ǰ	*j* wedge (hachek)	= [dʒ]
k	*k*	voiceless velar stop
l	*l*	voiced alveolar lateral
L	uppercase L	liquids; any liquid
ɭ	right-tail *l*	voiced retroflex lateral
l̦	*l* with left hook	clear *l*
ɫ	*l* with tilde through	velarized (dark) alveolar lateral
ɬ	belted *l*	‡ voiceless lateral fricative
ɮ	*l*-ezh ligature	‡ voiced lateral fricative
m	*m*	voiced bilabial nasal
ɱ	left-tail *m*	voiced labiodental nasal
n	*n*	voiced alveolar nasal
N	uppercase N	nasals; any nasal
ŋ	eng	voiced velar nasal
ɳ	right-tail *n*	‡ voiced retroflex nasal
o	*o*	tense mid (or close-mid) back rounded vowel
ɵ	barred *o*	tense mid (or close-mid) central rounded vowel
Ø	null (slashed zero)	null, nothing, dropped, deleted
ɔ	open *o* (turned *c*)	lax mid (or open-mid) back rounded vowel
p	*p*	voiceless bilabial stop
r	*r*	any rhotic (*r*-sound)
r̄	*r* with macron	‡ voiced alveolar trill
ʀ	small capital R	‡ voiced uvular trill
ʁ	inverted small capital R	‡ voiced uvular fricative
ɾ	fishhook (turned small *J*)	voiced alveolar flap
ɹ	turned *r*	voiced alveolar approximant
ɻ	turned *r* right tail	voiced retroflex approximant
s	*s*	voiceless alveolar sibilant fricative
σ	lowercase sigma	syllable
$	dollar sign	syllable boundary

ʃ	esh (elongated *s*)	voiceless alveopalatal (postalveolar) sibilant fricative
š	*s* wedge (hachek)	= [ʃ]
t	*t*	voiceless alveolar stop
tʃ	*t* with esh	voiceless alveopalatal affricated stop
ʈ	*t* with long tail	‡ voiceless retroflex stop
θ	lowercase theta	voiceless (inter)dental fricative
u	*u*	tense high (or close) back rounded vowel
ʉ	barred *u*	tense high (or close) central rounded vowel
ɯ	turned *m*	‡ tense high (or close) back unrounded vowel
ʊ	upsilon	lax high (or near-close) back rounded vowel
ʌ	turned *v*	lax mid (or open-mid) back unrounded vowel
v	*v*	voiced labiodental fricative
V	uppercase V	vowels; any vowel
w	*w*	rounded labiovelar glide (semivowel)
ʍ	turned *w*	voiceless labiovelar fricative, = [hw]
ʷ	superscript (raised) *w*	rounded (labialized)
x	*x*	‡ voiceless velar fricative
y	*y*	‡ tense high (close) front rounded vowel
z	*z*	voiced alveolar sibilant fricative
ʑ	curly-tail *z*	‡ voiced prepalatal (alveolo-palatal) sibilant fricative
ʐ	right-tail *z*	‡ voiced retroflex sibilant fricative
ʒ	ezh (tailed *z*)	voiced alveopalatal (postalveolar) sibilant fricative
ž	*z* wedge (hachek)	= [ʒ]
ʔ	glottal stop	glottal stop
→	right arrow	becomes, changes to
↘	down diagonal arrow	fall (intonation)
↗	up diagonal arrow	rise (intonation)
↘↗	down-up arrow	fall-rise (intonation)
↗↘	up-down arrow	rise-fall (intonation)
	low right arrow	low flat (intonation)
↓	down vertical arrow	falling terminal (intonation)
↑	up vertical arrow	rising terminal (intonation)
~	tilde (between symbols)	varying with
≈	double tilde (congruence)	majority (in summarizing stress patterns)
<	raised left-wedge	fronted
˺	corner	unreleased
˭	raised equals	unaspirated
ˈ	raised vertical stroke	primary (strong) stress
ˌ	lowered vertical stroke	secondary (weak) stress

ː	length mark	long (lengthened)
/ /	slashes	phonemic representation
[ ]	square brackets	phonetic (narrow) representation; feature
.	period	syllable boundary
#	pound sign, cross-hatch	word boundary
|	single vertical bar	foot boundary; (chap. 3) info-unit boundary
||	double vertical bar	pause or phrase boundary
{	brace	or
*	asterisk	ungrammatical, wrong, violation; peak stress
+	plus	morpheme boundary; positive marking of feature
>	right angled bracket	greater than (in a hierarchy or scale)
§	section	see section ___ (cross-reference in book)
☊	earphones	see corresponding recording on CD
☞	right-pointing hand	optimal output

Diacritics (over or under another symbol)

´	acute accent	strong-stressed, primary-stressed
`	grave accent	weak-stressed, secondary-stressed
~	superscript tilde	nasalized
⌢	top tie bar	pronounced together
˘	breve	unstressed (null stressed); short
+	subscript plus	fronted, advanced
˳	under-ring	voiceless
ˌ	syllabicity mark (tick)	syllabic
˄	subscript arch	nonsyllabic
‿	bottom tie bar	linked
ˑ	subscript bridge	dental
ˌ	inverted subscript bridge	apical
ˍ	subscript square (box)	laminal
<u><u>aaa</u></u>	double underline	peak stress

CHAPTER 1

The Metric Foot

1.1 The notion of stress: Present stress and absent/null stress. A word's strong stress either falls or does not fall on a particular vowel. Strong stress can be defined simplistically as 'the greater prominence or loudness that a vowel or syllable exhibits within a word.' A vowel is the nucleus of a syllable; a word contains as many syllables as it contains separate vowel sounds. When a two-syllable word is pronounced alone, one syllable or the other must receive strong stress. In a word like *begin*, strong stress is ultimate, falling on the right-most syllable: *begín* (*"be-GIN"*). In a word like *cotton*, strong stress is penultimate, falling on the second syllable leftward: *cótton* (*"COT-ton"*). In *animal* (*"AN-i-mal"*), strong stress is antepenultimate, falling on the third syllable leftward. (As this makes clear, English syllables are counted from the end of the word—from right to left—for the purpose of telling where strong stress falls.)

When analyzing a language like English, it is quite important that you learn to hear exactly where a word's strong stress actually falls. One of the ways you can train your ear to hear where strong stress falls is to pronounce a word incorrectly: **begín, *cottón, *aní-mal/*animál*. (Words are preceded by asterisks when linguists want to mark them as ungrammatical or otherwise wrong.) A two-syllable word like *begin* can be wrongly stressed in just one place: **bégin*. But a three-syllable word like *animal* can be wrongly stressed in two different places: **anímal/*animál*. And a four-syllable word like *anticipate* can be wrongly stressed in three different places: **ánticipate, *anticípate, *anticipáte*.

A STRONG-STRESSED vowel—*begín, cótton, ánimal, antícipate*—is more prominent than the other vowels in the word: it is **louder** in volume and **longer** in duration/length and/or **differently pitched** on the musical scale than the rest of the vowels in the word. A strong-stressed vowel has a louder volume, has a longer duration, and/or has a different pitch ("higher" or "lower" on a musical scale) than a weak vowel, let alone a null-stressed

Figure 1.a. The relationship between terms that are used to classify stress

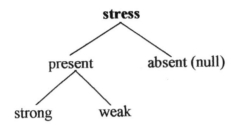

vowel. We say that stress is PRÉSENT on any syllable with strong stress or weak stress, but ÁBSENT from any unstressed syllable. (Absent stress is also known as NULL STRESS.)

As noted, English has two types of present stress: STRONG (or primary) and WEAK (or secondary). One common way to indicate a strongly stressed syllable is to write an acute accent mark (´) atop the strong-stressed vowel, just as we did earlier: *begín, cótton*. If a syllable is weakly stressed, the grave accent mark (`) is used: *màgníficent*. When a syllable is null-stressed, as is the ultimate syllable of *cót<u>ton</u>*, nothing is written atop its vowel.

A STRONG-STRESSED vowel—*begín, cótton, ánimal, antícipate*—is the most prominent one: it is louder in volume and tends to be longer in duration and higher in pitch than the rest of the vowels in the word. A WEAK-STRESSED vowel is less prominent than a strong-stressed one, but still more prominent than an UNSTRESSED one. Strong and weak stress are also called primary and secondary stress and are generally marked by an acute and grave accent, respectively; null stress (the lack of stress) is left unmarked. Thus in the word *màgníficent*, the second syllable is most prominent, the first is also prominent but less so than the second, and the last two syllables are totally unstressed (null stressed) and thus lack prominence. We say that stress is PRÉSENT on any syllable with strong or weak stress, but ÁBSENT from any unstressed syllable. The tree in figure 1.a summarizes the relationship between these terms.

Note on symbols

American dictionaries traditionally show stress with accents (heavier for strong stress) *after* a syllable: *mag´nif´icent*. The International Phonetic Association prefers to use vertical ticks *before* syllables, a raised one for strong (primary) stress and a lowered one for weak (secondary) stress: *beˈgin, ˈcotton, ˌmagˈnificent*. In this book, we use accent marks on vowels because these do not require knowledge of syllable divisions, which are often unclear in English (see chapters 6–7). In all transcription systems, unstressed syllables are generally left unmarked, although a breve (˘) may be used to call attention to a syllable's null stress: *begĭn, cóttŏn*.

Exercise 1.1

(A) Write the acute accent atop the vowel of each strong-stressed syllable in the words below. Follow the example. (And remember: if you're having trouble hearing where the strong stress falls, try pronouncing the word in as many different ways as there are syllables in the word—thus *cápital, *capítal, *capitál.*)

Example: capital (You write the acute accent atop the first vowel, *a*, thus: cápital.)

1. pencil	7. student	13. instructor
2. uncle	8. adore	14. doctor
3. prefer	9. constitution	15. architect
4. interest	10. substitute	16. Alabama
5. bottle	11. substitution	17. Michigan
6. demand	12. nothing	18. Minneapolis

(B) Two-way dictation: You and your partner each make a list of twenty words that have more than one syllable. Read your list to your partner, telling him/her to put an acute accent atop each word's strongest-stressed syllable. Now reverse the roles, with you writing down your partner's words. Each of you should now correct the other's list and then discuss the corrections you have made.

(C) Read these ten sentences out loud. Pay close attention to the acute-accented syllables and make sure that you are strong-stressing them.

1. Bétter láte than néver.
2. Évery róse hás its thórns, and évery dóg hás his dáy.
3. Gód hélps thóse who hélp themsélves.
4. If thís is téa, gíve me cóffee; if thís is cóffee, gíve me téa.
5. Cábbage twíce sérved is déath.
6. Stríke while the íron is hót.
7. You can léad a hórse to wáter but you cánnot máke it drínk.
8. Dówn and óut and góne to pót; nóthing léft is whát he's gót.
9. Óut of síght, óut of mínd.
10. Íf at fírst you dón't succéed, trý, trý agáin.

1.2 Metricalism. Earlier approaches such as Chomsky and Halle (1968) treated stress as a feature assigned by a series of complex rules to individual sounds or SEGMENTS—and to vowels in particular. More recent theories treat properties such as stress and pitch as SUPRASEGMENTALS ('above the segment'), assigned to syllables that are organized into higher-level groupings. Thus METRICALISM or METRICAL(IST) THEORY (Liberman and Prince 1977) examines the relative strength of a syllable at successively higher levels of organization. To do so, it uses terms such as FOOT and SYLLABLE for analytical purposes. This analysis can be illustrated with a branching diagram or TREE. Figure 1.b depicts a hierarchy of syllable strength for the word *extérminàtor*. In this tree, *extérminàtor* is seen to contain a structure of two METRIC FEET (F). The first metric foot is "stronger" (*s*) than the second, which is "weak" (*w*). And **within** each foot, one syllable is stronger (*s*) than the other, which is weak (*w*). *Extérminàtor* thus consists of two feet—one stronger, one weaker—and each foot has two syllables (one stronger, one weaker). The initial unstressed syllable, *ex*, is analyzed as being EXTRAMETRICAL, that is, lying outside the foot structure, rather like a pickup beat in music.

How do we know where the metric foot starts? We assume that each foot begins with a strong syllable unless the analyzed word starts with a weak syllable—in which case that weak syllable attaches to the following strong syllable. These words begin with a STRONG SYLLABLE: *éxtra, cónvent, márried, állegory, álligàtor, pórcupìne*. These words begin with a WEAK SYLLABLE: *annóunce, discúss, rejéct, engáge, alígn, retúrn*.

Metric feet are either unbounded or bounded; languages themselves are described that way: UNBOUNDED LANGUAGES or BOUNDED LANGUAGES. In an UNBOUNDED language, each metric foot embraces the entire word, no matter how many syllables it has. In unbounded languages, stress always falls on the same syllable of the word; thus French always stresses the right-most syllable, whereas Czech always stresses the left-most. Right-most stressing is known as RIGHT-HEADEDNESS (because the 'head' or main-stressed syllable is at the right end of the foot), whereas left-most stressing is called LEFT-HEADEDNESS. In a BOUNDED language such as English, longer words typically have two or more stresses, one that is strong and one or more that are weak; therefore longer words may have two or more feet—as many strong/weak feet as there are combinations of strong/weak stresses. Thus *néighbor* and *néighborly* consist of just one foot each, whereas *màthemátics* consists of two (*màthe | mátics*) and *còunterrèvolútion* consists of three (*còunter | rèvo | lútion*). English manifests both left- and right-headedness in its metrical patterning, as the following words will show: *áddress, óbject* (both left-headed) but *addréss, objéct* (both right-headed).

There are many excellent sources for more information on metricalism, in particular Hayes (1981, 1985), Hogg and McCully (1987), and Gussenhoven and Jacobs (1998, chapters 13–14).

Figure 1.b. A metricalist analysis of a word's feet and syllables

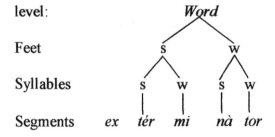

Exercise 1.2

Following are all the words we have just finished citing plus a few more. Take each one and analyze it with a tree as in figure 1.b, showing strength at syllable, word, and foot.

1. extra	6. porcupine	11. engage
2. convent	7. announce	12. algebraic
3. married	8. emancipator	13. mathematics
4. allegory	9. reject	14. investigation
5. alligator	10. discuss	15. anticipate

1.3 The five major metric feet: Spondees, trochees, iambs, dactyls, and anapests. All English words can be analyzed in terms of their metric feet. For our purposes, a metric foot is any combination of syllables that either begins with a strong-stressed syllable and includes the non-strong-stressed syllable(s) that follow it, or begins with one or more non-strong-stressed syllables and includes the strong-stressed syllable that follows them. If any given metric foot is just two syllables long and both syllables are strong-stressed, that foot is called a SPONDEE or a spondaic foot. Here are two SPONDEES, each one forming its own foot: _Téll Jóan ríght nów!_ Multisyllabic combinations beginning with a strong-stressed syllable are known as TROCHEES, which have two syllables per trochaic foot (_Káren tríed to téll_ her), or else as DACTYLS, which have three syllables per dactylic foot: _Tímothy Gárrison wánted_ to _símplify._ Metricalism might describe each third syllable as extrametrical. Combinations ending with a strong-stressed syllable are either IAMBS, which have two syllables per iambic foot (_I wánt to gó to sléep_), or ANAPESTS, which have three syllables per anapestic foot: _I woke úp on a bóat that was stárting to flóat_). Once again, metricalism might describe each first syllable as extrametrical. Review these terms by looking at figure 1.c.

English is the kind of language that constructs feet around regularly recurring stresses. Indeed, English **never** allows five or more null-stressed syllables to appear in sequence, and four null-stressed syllables will only appear consecutively if the word is

Figure 1.c. The terms that are used to describe metric feet

	Number of syllables per foot				
	1	2		3	
syllable where strong stress falls:	(sequential syllables) _(DA-DA)_	first _(DA-da)_	second _(da-DA)_	first _(DA-da-da)_	third _(da-da-DA)_
name of this metrical pattern:	spondee ′ ′ — —	trochee ′ ′ — — —	iamb ′ ′ — — —	dactyl ′ ′ —— ——	anapest ′ —— ——
examples	_Téll Jóan!_	_Káren tried to téll her._	_I wánt to gó to sléep._	_Timothy Gárrison._	_I woke úp on a bóat._

very long or if several unstressed determiners, prepositions, conjunctions, or pronouns come together. But in the typical English sentence, some sort of present stress—strong or weak—will fall on every third syllable, on every second syllable, or even on every single syllable. Here are examples of what is meant:

- Each syllable is strong-stressed (i.e., a sequence of spondees):
  Pát tóld Súe thrée bád líes.
- Nearly every syllable is strong-stressed (several feet are spondees):
  Súe tóld Pát that friénds néver téll líes.
- Most syllables are strong-stressed (several feet are trochees):
  Pát ánswered by télling Súe to gó to héll.
- Half the syllables are strong-stressed (all feet are trochees):
  Pát and Súe no lónger tálk to óne anóther.

In natural speech, strong-stress variation—and thus any variation in foot formation—is dependent on factors such as spoken tempo and informational focus, an important point that is explored later (§1.4, §3.4, §7.3). Nowhere is the English preference for recurring stresses and regular feet more apparent than in traditional poetry, songs, chants, and proverbs. English poetry has long been analyzed in terms of metric feet. Here again are the five most frequently used metric feet—the spondee, the trochee, the iamb, the dactyl, and the anapest. Studying them one more time will help us review the terms we've just finished learning. When analyzing poetry and when undertaking the preliminary analyses of prose that this chapter provides, an underline (_), a dash (–), or a breve (˘) will represent weak-stressed or null-stressed vowels. (See chapter 2 for further details on weak and null stress.) The acute accent (′) always indicates that a vowel and its syllable are strong-stressed. (Poetry, of course, exaggerates stress patterns in ways that are not always found in naturalistic speech, though it is precisely **because of** poetic exaggeration that we highlight it here, the better to clarify the degree to which spoken prose reveals these stress patterns too.)

- The SPONDEE. In a line of spondaic feet, every syllable is strong-stressed, and two adjacent strong stresses equal one spondee. The following example contains three spondees:
  Pát tóld Súe thrée bád líes.

Spondees are represented by acute accent marks as follows: ′ ′ (etc.).

- The TROCHEE. A trochaic foot contains two syllables. Every **odd** syllable is strong-stressed, starting with the first syllable of the line:
  Jóe and Sándy léft todáy for Dállas, hóping thére to fínd a hóuse they'd fáll for.

Here is the representation of the trochaic metric pattern: ′ _ ′ _ ′ _ ′ _ (etc.).

- The IAMB. An iambic foot contains two syllables. Every **even** syllable is strong-stressed, starting with the second syllable of the line:

    What's míne is míne, what's yóurs is yóurs, so dón't be gréedy áll the tíme.

Here is the representation of the iambic metric pattern: _ ′ _ ′ _ ′ _ ′ (etc.).

- The DACTYL. A dactylic foot contains three syllables. The first, the fourth, the seventh, the tenth, and so on receive strong stresses:

    Thómas and Chárlie had bétter stop smóking in tíme to avóid a most hórrible déath without médical bénefits.

Dactyls are represented like this: ′ _ _ ′ _ _ ′ _ _ ′ _ _ (etc.).

- The ANAPEST. An anapestic foot contains three syllables. Every third syllable is strong-stressed starting with syllable number three. That is to say, the third, the sixth, the ninth, the twelfth, and so forth take strong stresses:

    In a rúsh came the stórm off the tóp of the péak, and we rán for our ténts with the spéed of a wólf.

Anapests are represented like this: _ _ ′ _ _ ′ _ _ ′ _ _ ′ (etc.).

Each of the following poems illustrates one or more of these five metric foot types. Again, only strong stresses are marked, and always with acute accents. When analyzing the metric patterns of poems we must bear in mind that poetry often exaggerates those patterns to enhance an artistic effect. It is also the case that in order to maintain a metrical pattern, a poem will sometimes strong-stress a syllable that would seldom take a strong stress in prose. Here is an example of what we mean: *If ónly Í could sée the tópmost bránches óf a tree!* (poem) versus *If ónly I could sée the tópmost bránches of a tree!* (prose). The poem strong-stresses two syllables—"I" and "of"—that the prose version doesn't. The poem does so in order to maintain a strict iambic metricality throughout: _ ′ _ ′ _ ′ _ ′ _ ′ _ ′ _ ′. The prose version has no need to maintain any sort of strict metricality and therefore it doesn't do so.

The first poem, Robert Herrick's *The Argument of His Book*, nicely exemplifies IAMBIC metricality. (We have used examples from the seventeenth and the eighteenth centuries to show how far back these phenomena go in the English language.)

Robert Herrick (1591–1674), *The Argument of His Book*
I síng of bróoks, of blóssoms, bírds, and bówers,
Of Ápril, Máy, of Júne, and Júly flówers
I síng of Máypoles, hóck carts, wássails, wákes,
Of brídegrooms, brídes, and óf their brídal cákes.
I wríte of yóuth, of lóve, and háve accéss
By thése to síng of cléanly wántonnéss.

I síng of déws, of ráins, and, píece by píece,
Of bálm, of óil, of spíce, and ámbergrís.
I síng of tímes trans-shífting, ánd I wríte
How róses fírst came réd and lílies whíte.
I wríte of gróves, of twílights, ánd I síng
The cóurt of Máb and óf the fáiry kíng.
I wríte of héll; I síng (and éver sháll)
Of héaven, and hópe to háve it áfter áll.

As is typical of poetry, even the best, not every word's natural stress pattern conforms perfectly to the metric feet that the poem's rhythm imposes. Thus *Julý* is stressed on its last syllable in ordinary discourse, but the demands of the iambic meter of this poem have changed its stress to *Júly*. In similar fashion, the same poem's *wantonness*, which would normally receive just one strong stress (*wántonness*), here receives two (*wántonnéss*), given the need to conserve iambic meter throughout. Likewise, Herrick's *heaven*, normally bisyllabic, becomes a monosyllable here to fit the meter. Although a certain amount of poetic "license" of this sort is permitted, no traditional poem can long overlook the demands that are placed on it by the usual stress pattern of each multisyllabic word. So while an occasional **Júly* is tolerated, multiple instances of this sort of thing would not be viewed with a favorable eye; for example, **blossóms, *bowérs, *cleanlý, *lilíes, *fairý*.

Our second poem, George Herbert's "Discipline," illustrates two types of metric feet: the TROCHAIC (lines one, two, and four of each stanza) and the SPONDAIC (line three of every stanza).

George Herbert (1593–1633), *Discipline* (excerpts)
Thrów awáy thy ród,
Thrów awáy thy wráth:
    Ó mý Gód,
Táke the géntle páth.

Nót a wórd or lóok
Í afféct to ówn,
    Bút bý bóok
Ánd thy bóok alóne.

Thóugh I fáil, I wéep:
Thóugh I hált in páce,
    Yét Í créep,
Tó the thróne of gráce.

Thén let wráth remóve;
Lóve will dó the déed:
    Fór wíth lóve
Stóny héarts will bléed.

Thrów awáy thy ród;
Thóugh man fráilties háth,
    Thóu árt Gód:
Thrów awáy thy wráth.

Our third poem illustrates meters that have **three** syllables per foot—both the ANAPESTIC meter (_ _ ′) and the DACTYLIC (′ _ _) meter.

Lady Mary Wortley Montagu (1689–1762), *The Lover: A Ballad* (excerpts)
But I háte to be chéated, and néver will búy
Long yéars of repéntance for móments of jóy.
Oh wás there a mán (but whére shall I fínd
Good sénse and good náture so équally jóined?)
Would válue his pléasure, contríbute to míne,
Not méanly would bóast, nor would léwdly desígn,
Not óver sevére, yet not stúpidly váin,
For I wóuld have the pówer though nót give the páin.
. . . .

But whén the long hóurs of públic are pást
And we méet with champágne and a chícken at lást,
May évery fond pléasure that hóur endéar,
Be bánished afár both discrétion and féar,
Forgétting or scórning the áirs of the crówd
He may céase to be fórmal, and Í to be próud,
Till lóst in the jóy we conféss that we líve,
And hé may be rúde, and yet Í may forgíve.

And thát my delíght may be sólidly fíxed,
Let the friénd and the lóver be hándsomely míxed,
In whóse tender bósom my sóul might confíde,
Whose kíndness can sóothe me, whose cóunsel could guíde.
From súch a dear lóver as hére I descríbe
No dánger should fríght me, no míllions should bríbe;
But tíll this astónishing créature I knów,
As I lóng have lived cháste, I will kéep myself só.

Exercise 1.3

(A) Indicate whether each metric pattern is spondaic, trochaic, iambic, dactylic, or anapestic. Mark each strong-stressed syllable with an acute accent and, below the line, indicate the stress pattern (′ for strong stress or _ for weak or null stress). Follow the example:

Example: As I lóng have lived cháste I will kéep myself só.
_ _ ′ _ _ ′ _ _ ′ _ _ ′: *This sentence's metrical pattern is consistently anapestic.*

1. Once upon a time you see / Long ago he came to me

2. That age is best which is the first / When youth and blood are warmer.

3. Then be not coy, but use your time / And while ye may, go marry;
    For, having lost but once your prime / You may forever tarry.

4. Piping down the valleys wild / Piping songs of pleasant glee
    On a cloud I saw a child / And he laughing said to me . . .

5. Flow gently, sweet Afton, among thy green braes,
    Flow gently, I'll sing thee a song in thy praise;
    My Mary's asleep by thy murmuring stream,
    Flow gently, sweet Afton, disturb not her dream.

6. Truth fails not; but her outward forms that bear
    The longest date do melt like frosty rime,
    That in the morning whitened hill and plain
    And is no more; drop like the tower sublime . . .

7. Humpty Dumpty sat on a wall,
    Humpty Dumpty had a great fall.
    All the king's horses and all the king's men
    Couldn't put Humpty together again.

8. I think that I shall never see
    A poem lovely as a tree.
    A tree whose hungry mouth is prest
    Against the sweet earth's flowing breast.

(B) ♠ Read these ten sentences out loud and compare to the corresponding recording on the CD. Pay attention to the accented syllables and make sure you are strong-stressing them. Then identify their metric patterns. (Not all patterns will be consistent; extrametricality may occur.)

1. Her éyes are as bíg as sáucers.
2. Húnger néver sáw bád bréad.
3. Néver lóok a gíft horse in the móuth.
4. Éarly to béd, éarly to ríse, mákes a màn héalthy, wéalthy and wíse.
5. Pút your trúst in Gód and kéep your pówder drý.
6. Gíve him an ínch and he'll táke a míle.

7. "Whát a dúst I've trúly ráised," said the flý to the gálloping hórse.
8. Ás the twíg is bént, the trée is bówed.
9. Just a hóp, a skíp, and a júmp awáy.
10. A sáint abróad and a dévil at hóme.

How can we apply to the rhythms of English **prose** what we just finished learning about the metric feet of English poetry? Let's start by analyzing an old keyboard practice sentence:

Nów is the tíme for áll góod mén to cóme to the áid of their párty.

′ _ _ ′ ′ ′ ′ _ ′ _ _ ′ _ _ ′ _

The first metric foot is a dactyl: ′ _ _. But then, the metricality changes briefly to a trochee (′ _) before changing to an expanded spondee (′ ′). There follow two dactyls, the first of which is extrametrical. The sentence ends in a trochee. An analysis of the feet of the sentence produces the following:

/ Nów is the / tíme for / áll / góod / mén / (to) cóme to the / áid of their / párty

dactyl   trochee expanded spondee   dactyl   dactyl   trochee

Here's another keyboard practice sentence with an interesting meter.

The quíck brówn fóx júmped óver the lázy sléeping dóg.

_ ′ ′ ′ ′ ′ _ _ ′ _ ′ ′

In this example, two consecutive spondaic feet appear, to be followed by a trochee and three iambs. Only the null-stressed syllable (*The . . .*) at the start of the sentence is extrametrical.

Exercise 1.4

(A) Use the diagonal line (/) to delineate metric feet in the following sentences. Write in the acute accent mark atop all strong-stressed syllables. Follow this example:

Example: John was not at all aware that Mary had a little lamb.

/ Jóhn was / nót at / áll a-/-wáre that / Máry / hád a / líttle / lámb /

The example sentence contains seven consecutive trochaic feet followed by an extrametrical beat. Note that feet do not always coincide with words and that the trochaic meter forces us to divide one of the words between separate feet: *aware* "a-/-wáre."

1. Tammy and Teddy will never be ready.
2. Get that dog out of here!
3. Try and get some sleep tonight.
4. Upon whose bosom snow has lain; who intimately lives with rain.
5. Poems are made by fools like me, but only God can make a tree.
6. What's mine is mine, and don't you forget it.
7. On the top of the tree sat a fat buzzing bee.
8. Astonishing results reluctantly emerged from the experiment.
9. Nowhere is it written that a victim enjoys being victimized.
10. If Alice doesn't phone, be sure to write her a note, okay?
11. Go to the store and buy bananas, avocados, apples and pears.
12. If I've told you once, I've told you twice: Haste makes waste!
13. A penny saved is a penny earned, and a stitch in time saves nine.
14. Little Miss Muffet sat on a tuffet eating her curds and whey.
15. Along came a spider who sat down beside her and frightened Miss Muffet away.
16. We just can't stand that Pat!

(B) Using the five metric feet—spondaic, trochaic, iambic, dactylic, and anapestic—create a brief poetic summary of your life. The lines can rhyme if you want, but they do not have to do so.

1.4 Weak stress, null stress, and vowels. Sometimes hard to hear without training is the difference between weak stress and null stress. The null-stressed vowel is often a special kind of vowel that is called "schwa." The schwa, represented by the symbol /ə/, is the "uh" sound we hear in the underlined vowels of words like *abóut, agáinst, impóssible, abóminable, àmplificátion, àllegórical, cèremónial,* and *commúnicàte.* But before we further discuss the schwa, we will first take a quick look (see figure 1.d) at something we'll devote more time to in chapter 5: the English vowel system. Study the symbols shown in the trapezoid diagram, associating them with the sounds that are shown in the "Key" box.

As seen in figure 1.d, all high vowels and nearly all mid vowels are divided into tense/lax pairs: /i ɪ, e ɛ, u ʊ, o ɔ/. The tense vowels are /i e o u/, and the lax vowels are /ɪ ɛ ʌ ɔ ʊ ə/; this distinction is important when assigning stress, as chapter 2 will show.[1] (Low vowels /ɑ æ/ do not make a tense/lax distinction.) Another relevant distinction for stress assignment is the difference between CHECKED and FREE vowels. Checked vowels—/ɪ ɛ æ ʌ ʊ/—generally cannot end a syllable, whereas free vowels—the tense vowels /i e o u/ along with /ə ɔ ɑ/ and /oi ai au/—can end a syllable.

Figure 1.d. The English vowel trapezoid

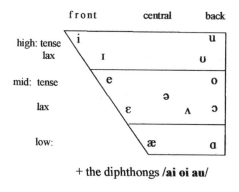

+ the diphthongs /**ai oi au**/

Key:
/i/ = *me, feat, feet*   /u/ = *food*
/ɪ/ = *fit*   /ʊ/ = *foot*
/e/ = *fate*   /o/ = *foe, foal, fold*
/ɛ/ = *fed*   /ɔ/ = *fall, fought*
/æ/ = *fat*   /ə/ = *sofa, fanatic*
/ɑ/ = *far, fodder*   /ʌ/ = *fun*
/ai/ = *fight, fine*   /au/ = *found, fowl*
/oi/ = *foist*

The symbols in figure 1.d come from a transcriptional system called the INTERNA-TIONAL PHONETIC ALPHABET (**IPA**).[2] It was developed in the late nineteenth century to enable any linguist anywhere to use the same symbol when transcribing ('writing down') a particular sound. The IPA is especially useful for linguists working with languages whose speakers have no writing system, or with languages such as English whose orthography is irregular. By using IPA symbols (and regardless of what language a linguist is analyzing), a mid-front tense vowel sound, for example, will always be transcribed with the symbol /e/. (The diagonals indicate that we're referring to a sound, not a letter or spelling symbol; thus "/e/" means the vowel sound in *fate*, not the letter 'e'.)

Without going into chapter 5's details, we can now state one of the most important general rules about English: **When English vowels are null stressed, they tend to be pronounced as schwa.** One way to prove this is by examining some of this book's 357 pairs of closely related words. (See the "families" files in the Corpus on the book's CD.) In these word pairs, stress shifts from one vowel to another when you go from one word to another word. When you do that, you bring about an alternation between a "full" vowel—/i ɪ e ɛ æ ɑ ɔ o ʊ u ʌ ai au oi/—and the schwa vowel /ə/. Here are just twenty-five of those pairs, whose most salient schwa/nonschwa vowel alternations have been underlined:

ábdomen	áble	accláim	abólish	catástrophe
àbdóminal	abílity	àcclamátion	àbolítion	càtastróphic
abérrant	acádemy	ácid	áddict	cátegorìze
àberrátion	àcadémic	acídic	addíction	càtegórical
admíre	admónish	adóre	ágile	cértifỳ
àdmirátion	àdmonítion	àdorátion	agílity	certíficate

állergy	altérnative	ánalògue	anátomy	chronólogy
allérgic	àlternátion	análogous	ànatómical	chrònológical
applỳ	béllicòse	béstial	botánic	sátìre
àpplicátion	bellígerent	bèstiálity	bótanist	satírical

In the pair *catástrophe/càtastróphic*, for example, shifting the strong stress from the syllable *tas* to the syllable *troph* creates the following changes in vowel pronunciation, which are best understood by lining up each word's transcription:

1. *catástrophe* /kətǽstrəfi/
2. *càtastróphic* /kæ̀təstrɑ́fək/

In evidence here, the /æ/ in *catástrophe* changes to schwa in *càtastróphic* because the strong stress has changed syllables. In similar fashion, the schwa of the first syllable of *catástrophe* appears as /æ/ in *càtastróphic* because that syllable now carries a weak stress, and therefore ceases to be a schwa. And the same comments can be made about the switch from schwa to /ɑ́/ in the pair's third and fourth syllables. Another well-known example of schwa/nonschwa alternation is the pair *phótogràph/photógraphy*. Though the words are obviously related, **not one vowel** of *phótogràph* is the same as the corresponding vowel of *photógraphy*. In sum, a thorough knowledge of metric feet and stress patterning is fundamental to knowing how the vowels of English are pronounced.

Unlike strong stress, weak stress is more difficult to identify and locate; that is, distinguishing weak from null stress is not always easy. One problem is that choosing one or the other may depend on REGISTER. REGISTER is a technical term that linguistics has borrowed from the world of music. In linguistics, register refers to the TEMPO of speech and to the CARE with which one speaks. Both tempo and care cover a wide range or continuum of possibilities, but the two continua are commonly described in terms of three main points each, as is shown in figure 1.e.[3]

The two endpoints often go together: people speaking in slow tempo tend to speak with great care, and people speaking in rapid tempo tend to speak with minimal care. "Medium (tempo and) average (care)" fall somewhere in between. HIGH-REGISTER speech is typically slow tempo (and shows great care), LOW-REGISTER speech is typically rapid tempo (and shows minimal care), and MIDDLE-REGISTER speech is typically medium tempo/average care, that is, between low and high. Social custom expects us to use high-register speech in the more formal domains of our lives, such as when giving a lecture in a class or a eulogy at a funeral. High-register speech often contains cautious articulation that is closer to the written language. Low-register speech often contains rapid articulation that has reductions and deletions (see chapter 7). Here is an example: *He has done something different* in shifting to a lower register would render *He's done sump'm diff'rnt.* Low-register speech would be entirely appropriate—even expressly

Figure 1.e. Register and the terms that describe it

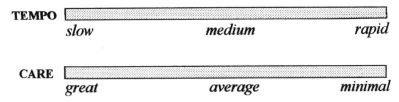

expected—in such settings as a get-together in a bar, an exchange at a gas station, a fight, an amorous encounter, and so forth. It's important to know that **low-register speech is <u>not</u> "bad" speech** but simply the sort of language that is perfectly right for a whole series of situations in which high-register speech would sound affected, stilted, and pompous.

A useful though hardly faultless rule of thumb for weak stress versus null stress is this: the higher the register, the more you will hear the weak stresses and the less you will hear the null. Likewise, the lower the register, the less you will hear the weak stresses and the more you will hear the null. The weak/null selection process, then, is register-dependent, at least in part; but because registers form part of a continuum on a sliding scale (rather than discrete levels), the weak/null distinction can vary. Nonetheless there are five helpful ways to predict and identify weak/null stress. We ask ourselves the following:

(1) Do we hear the "uh" sound—the schwa /ə/—in the syllable? If so, it may be null stressed.

(2) Have there now appeared more than two null-stressed syllables in a row? If so, there's a good probability of another stress appearing soon. (Recall that in traditional English poetry, strong stress typically falls on every second or third syllable.)

(3) How many syllables does the word contain? English is a bounded language with stress-based feet, so the greater the number of syllables we produce, the more strong (and weak) stresses we end up producing, at least in higher registers.

(4) Is a tense vowel /i e o u/ or diphthong /oi ai au/ the nucleus of the syllable? If so, that tense vowel (or diphthong) readily takes null stress without having to change to a schwa.

(5) What is the word's part of speech (noun, verb, adjective, etc.)? The main content-bearing words such as nouns, adjectives, verbs, and adverbs are more likely to be strong-stressed or at least weak-stressed than are the function words (determiners, pronouns, prepositions, conjunctions, and such).

What follows—the prose sample titled "My Car"—is a letter of complaint that was sent to a corporation by *PEASBA*'s first author, who has changed all proper nouns to protect the guilty. Listen to the recording of the letter on the CD, then read the analysis that follows the letter.

☊My Car

Thánk yòu for sénding mè a remínder, recéived yésterdày, thàt ìt will sóon bè tíme to táke mý Húpmobìle sedán to the déaler Ì bóught it fròm for its néxt schéduled máintenance. Whén Ì dó sò, Ì will ónce agáin attémpt to gét the déaler, Schlépp Mótors, to acknówledge thàt Ì háve a próblem wìth mý àutomátic trànsmíssion. Ì bóught the cár òn Fébruàry síxth. Sìnce the cár hàd bèen úsed for a wéek or só às a démonstràtor, Ì was áble to dríve ìt befóre púrchase, ànd thús becáme awáre of the óne próblem the cár hád: sóme sórt of a défèct ìn the clútch assémbly. (Whèn the cár ìs fácing dównward òn a slópe, ány mánual shíft from Párk to Revérse ór, espécially, from Néutral to Dríve prodúces a lóud slápping sóund regardless of whéther my fóot is ón or óff the bráke pèdal òr the gás pèdal; thís sóund is léss lòud when the cár is ón a lével súrface, ànd álmòst ìmpercéptible but stíll áudible when the cár fáces úpward òn a slópe.) Ì tóld mỳ sálesman Ì wánted thìs próblem fíxed befóre Ì tóok delívery. Ìt wàs nót. Ì tóok the càr báck to the déaler ìn Máy and máde the sáme rèquést of the héad of Sérvice. Hìs assístant tóld mè that áll néw Húpmobìles máde an ìdéntical nóise under símilar círcumstànces ánd, to próve hìs póint, procéeded to démonstràte that thìs was só bỳ pútting mè behínd the whéel of anóther néw Húpmobìle with jùst thírtèen míles on ìt, whìch indéed behávèd júst líke mỳ ówn hàd dóne. "Só whát?" Ì respónded. "Júst becáuse áll nèw Húpmobìles háve thís próblem dóesn't méan ìt's nót a próblem, ànd thàt it shóuldn't bè fíxed." Hìs ánswer to thát was to thánk mè for stópping bý, ànd to wísh mè a níce dáy.

The first point to make about the sample in "My Car" is that before its author could record it, he had to decide on a register: high, middle, or low. (He chose middle.) Certain key words bear this out. Take the word *démonstràtor*. In high-register speech it might be pronounced *démonstràtòr*, with a weak stress on the last syllable as well as on the penult, whereas in middle- or low-register speech, the word's last syllable is null-stressed: *démonstràtor*. Five other words—*acknówledge, prodúces, procéeded, respónded, regárdless*—also reflect the fact that the recording is middle-registered. These words' stress patterns classify the recording as middle registered as opposed to **high** registered. In a high-registered rendition, all would probably carry a weak stress on their initial syllables, thus: *àcknówledge, pròdúces, pròcéeded, rèspónded, règárdless*.

The metric feet of the passage are essentially dactylic/anapestic, but with frequent switches into trochaic/iambic plus the occasional spondee. Figure 1.f contains a sentence that nicely illustrates the passage's meter (recall that the underline _ can indicate either weak or null stress).

Figure 1.f. Analyzing a sentence for metric patterns

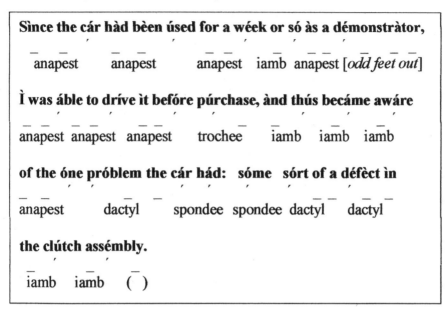

An analysis of the 307 words of "My Car" reveals that 228 are monosyllabic (74.27%), 51 are bisyllabic (16.61%), 20 are trisyllabic (6.51%), 7 are four syllable (2.28%), and one is five syllable (.33%). Three out of four of "My Car's" words, then, are monosyllabic, and slightly more than nine out of ten (90.88%) are either monosyllabic or bisyllabic. These facts are very important, as we will shortly see.

Additional information about whether a syllable is weak- or null-stressed is given in chapter 2, which also deals at length with where to put strong stress. But even here it is useful to offer some preliminary information about the stress patterns of the twenty-four words[4] of "My Car" that contain three or more syllables. They are as follows:

- **Left-headed items strong-stressed on the left-most syllable**: *áudible, círcum-stànces, démonstràte, démonstràtor, Fébruàry, Húpmobìle(s), máintenance, mánual, símilar, yesterday*

These ten words are noteworthy because once it is established that the strong stress will fall on the left-most syllable, no weak stress appears on the next syllable (at least not in a middle-register rendition). Instead, weak stress either skips a syllable, waiting until the next to fall—*círcumstànces, démonstràte, démonstràtor, Fébruàry, Húpmobìle(s), yés-terdày*—or else weak stress does not appear at all in the rest of the word: *áudible, máin-tenance, mánual, símilar*. Recall the low frequency of spondaic metric feet, both in traditional poetry and in this letter's prose. Although English is fond of frequent stresses, that fondness usually doesn't extend to many consecutive spondees. So for weak stresses as well as strong, the preferred English metrical pattern is either trochaic/iambic (two syllables per foot) or dactylic/anapestic (three syllables per foot). Consecutive spondees rub against the grain of English metrics. (Prove that by imposing spondees on any line from "My Car"; when read out loud, it will sound robotlike: *Í tóok thé cár báck tó thé déalér ín Máy ánd máde thé sáme réquést óf thé héad óf Sérvíce.*)

- **Items strong-stressed on the second-last syllable or on the third-last syllable**: *acknówledge, anóther, assémbly, assístant, delívery, espécially, ìdéntical, ìmpercéptible, procéeded, prodúces, regárdless, rèmínder, respónded, transmission*

What makes **these** words noteworthy is that in the middle register, a few—*ìdéntical, rèmínder, trànsmíssion*—carry weak stress on the left-most syllable, whereas the majority have null stress there: *acknówledge, anóther, assémbly, assístant*. However, of the ten that are null-stressed on the left-most syllable, at least eight (*acknówledge, anóther, delívery, espécially, procéeded, prodúces, regárdless, respónded*) could carry weak stress there in high-register speech: *àcknówledge, ànóther, dèlívery, èspécially, pròcéeded, pròdúces, règárdless, rèspónded*. Only the highest register would assign weak stress to **all** the non-strong-stressed syllables of some words (*àcknówlèdge, pròcéedèd, pròdúcès, rèspóndèd*), but not others (thus **ànóthèr, *assémblỳ, *assístànt, *règárdlèss*). What's more, four-syllable words hardly ever take weak stresses on all non-strong-stressed syllables; thus *dèlívery* but not **dèlívèry, èspécially* but not **èspéciàlly*.

Longer words, of which *àutomátic* and *ìmpercéptible* are the only examples in "My Car," follow similar patterns: once the strong syllable is identified, it isn't hard to predict that weak stress will fall two syllables away because it skips a syllable. Thus once we know that the penultimate syllable ("mát") of four-syllable *automátic* is strong-stressed, we can predict with confidence that the weak stress will fall on the pre-antepenultimate syllable ("àu").

In sum, the rhythm of English tends to alternate strong stress and null or weak stress. This means that many long English words generally follow an ALTERNATING STRESS RULE (or "skip-a-syllable" rule) that assigns weak stress to every other syllable. An example of this is the trisyllabic word *nòminée*, which is strong-stressed on the last syllable and thus likely to weak-stress the antepenult but not the penult. This even/odd skip-a-syllable rule will be put to the test in chapter 2, which examines in depth the whole matter of stress placement on individual words.

Exercise 1.5

(A) Use acute accent marks to identify strong stress in the sentences below. Assume their register to be middle. Follow this example: *His assístant tóld me that áll néw Húpmobiles máde an idéntical nóise under símilar círcumstances.*

1. The twelve apostles passed along the apostolic succession.
2. Right after the demobilization they will demobilize all troops.
3. Because his voice is monotonous, he always sings in a monotone.
4. In general, generalities are true, but there have been a few exceptions to that generalization.
5. Circumstantial evidence was evidently part of the circumstances surrounding that crime.
6. Circus clowns frighten little children and grownups alike by wearing outrageous clothing.
7. Several dozen elephants climbed aboard the gigantic truck, forcing the driver to flee in panic.
8. The observers observed the observance observantly.

(B) Read these ten sentences out loud. Pay attention to the acute-accented syllables and make sure you are strong-stressing them. Once you have done so, identify all metric patterns—spondaic, trochaic, iambic, dactylic, or anapestic.

1. The róad to héll is páved with góod inténtions.
2. The bígger they cóme, the hárder they fáll.
3. There's mány a slíp 'twixt the cúp and the líp.
4. Whý bólt the stáble door, ónce the hórse is góne?
5. Óne líe cálls for anóther.
6. Stícks and stónes can bréak my bónes, but wórds will néver húrt me.
7. We néver knów the wórth of wáter tíll the wéll is drý.
8. Éast, Wést, hóme is bést.
9. Állison Pátterson háppily chánted the frívolous póetry tíme after tíme at the féstival.
10. I would thínk you could téll that the mán with the stíck is the pártner of Dónovan Ánderson.

(C) Two-way dictation: In thirty words or less, dictate to your partner what you did this morning. He/she will then mark the dictation for metric patterns. Next, the two of you together will determine whether his/her decisions about metric patterns were correct or not.

1.5 The English drive toward monosyllabicity. As the "My Car" letter has shown, about 75 percent of the words in an ordinary business letter are monosyllabic, and an additional 16 percent are bisyllabic, which, combined, equal more than nine out of every ten words in the sample. On the other hand, in a dictionary corpus of 25,108 entries,[5] only 14.84 percent of them are monosyllabic and 39.26 percent bisyllabic, totaling a slight majority of 54.10 percent; 26.40 percent, 13.57 percent, 4.93 percent, .90 percent, .09 percent, and .01percent are three-, four-, five-, six-, seven-, and eight-syllable words respectively. So how do we explain the discrepancy between the sample letter's ordinary English prose and the entire corpus of a dictionary? The answer lies in the history of the English language and its speakers.

In the fifth and sixth centuries England was conquered by the Angles and the Saxons, Germanic-speaking peoples whose ancestral lands lay in what is now extreme north-western Germany. Thus English is a Germanic language as are German, Dutch, Low German, Swiss German, Danish, Swedish, Norwegian, Icelandic, Yiddish, Faroese, and Frisian, English's closest relative, a tongue still spoken in far northern Holland and on the North Sea islands of Germany. As of the eleventh century, dialects of Old English (i.e., Anglo-Saxon) were spoken throughout most of England by everyone from kings to commoners. But in 1066, the Norman French ruler William the Conqueror changed all that, defeating the Anglo-Saxons and imposing on England a French-speaking nobil-ity, clergy, and legal system that would hold sway for 300 years. During that time, thou-sands of French words entered English, and English itself underwent radical simplification, losing or reducing most of the endings that had made Old English as morphologically complex as Latin. By the end of the fourteenth century, the English dialects of the area surrounding London, which formed the basis of the modern lan-guage, contained a large number of French loanwords, many of which were polysyl-labic; but these English dialects still retained most of the words of the Old English stock, which, largely shorn of endings, now tended to be monosyllabic. And to all these medieval French loanwords were added—from the fourteenth century onward but espe-cially in the eighteenth century with its great advances in scholarship and learning—thousands upon thousands of polysyllabic words that were imported directly from Latin and/or Greek, classical antiquity's two most prestigious languages whose study was the hallmark of every educated person.

Since 1066, then, English has been a language at war with itself—the largely mono-syllabic base of Anglo-Saxon words that are used in ordinary speech versus the French/Latin/Greek borrowings that constitute the polysyllabic majority of all the words that appear in a typical dictionary such as this textbook's source. And in this "war," the native English tendency toward monosyllabicity attacks the French/Latin/Greek borrowings' polysyllabicity, doing its best to pare them down into monosyllables or at least to reduce the number of syllables they have, but never fully managing to do so. Further proof of this tendency is the ongoing popularity of CLIPPING polysyllables into monosyllables such as *bi* (*bisexual*), *chem* (*chemistry*), *con* (*convict*), *gym* (*gymnasium*), *mike* (*microphone*), *lab* (*laboratory*), *libe* (*library*), *math* (*mathematics*), *phys ed* (*physi-cal education*), *sosh* (*sociology*), *sub* (*submarine*), *tarp* (*tarpaulin*), and many more.

Take, for example, the Latin-origin word family *separate* (verb), *separate* (adj.), and *separately* (adv.). The Latin etymon ('source') is the four-syllabled, right-headed, penult-stressed verbal infinitive *separare*. Whereas the English verb *séparàte* /sɛ́pərèt/ is tri-syllabic, the adjective *séparate* /sɛ́prət/ is always bisyllabic except in the highest of registers. Students are often exasperated by this state of affairs, reasoning that what's syl-labic in the verb should be syllabic in the adjective. But it's not, and the history of the

English language is to blame for it. Another of the many examples of this sort of thing is the fate of the word *laboratory*. It was originally pronounced as spelled, with five syllables that subsequently lost one of them depending on where the strong stress was fixed:

American: → *láboratòry* → /lǽbrətɔ̀ri/ (loss of the underlined pre-antepenultimate vowel)
British: → *labóratory* /ləbɔ́rətri/ (loss of the underlined penultimate vowel)

In sum, knowing where to put the strong stress in English would be easy—if only the language hadn't borrowed such a large number of lengthy words from French, Latin, and Greek. It is precisely those many thousands of multisyllabic French/Latin/ Greek borrowings that make English such a difficult language to stress. Stress assignment in English is thus a loanword problem that exists today because of all the words that English has been borrowing for more than a thousand years—and has never given back! The loanwords, then, are the ones whose stress-assignment problems we will concentrate on in chapter 2, for they are the words that will always give us trouble. Stress in English is therefore "only" a loanword problem—but it is such a large problem because English has borrowed such a large number of words.

Exercise 1.6

☊ The following paragraph is a continuation of the letter that began in "My Car" (it is also on the CD). Make a list of all of its words that are monosyllabic, all that are bisyllabic, and all that have three, four, five, or more syllables. Then use acute accents to identify strong stress in the sentences.

In any event, my car will hit seven thousand five hundred miles sometime next month, and at that time I will once again attempt to get Schlepp Motors to do something about the clutch assembly. I suspect that the problem is the clutch assembly and nothing else because that was the phone diagnosis of the Department of Transportation's National Highway Traffic Safety Administration folks, whom I called in July. They then sent me a "Vehicle Owner's Questionnaire," which I filled out and returned; in it, I described the problem in full. (As you no doubt know, the point of these questionnaires is that if enough owners of a given car complain about the same thing, the government eventually issues a recall, ordering the manufacturer to fix the problem free of charge.)

1.6 Teaching the topics of chapter 1 to students of ESOL. As Dalton and Seidlhofer point out (1994, 72):

Pronunciation, more than any other aspect of a foreign language, will always be influenced by very personal factors such as the learner's attitude to the target language and to the speakers of that language, by individual differences in ability and motivation to learn, etc. This may be the most important reason why, especially in pronunciation, there can never be a one-to-one relationship between what is taught and what is learnt. It would be self-defeating for the teacher to think or hope that there ever could be.

Nevertheless, techniques do exist that can help students become more sensitive to pronunciation. A useful volume on classroom applications of English phonology is Celce-Murcia, Brinton, and Goodwin 1996; special attention should be drawn to that work's summation (290–318) of things to do in the ESOL classroom. One of the goals of the "teaching" sections of this textbook is to supplement Celce-Murcia, Brinton, and Goodwin by concentrating on activities which present pronunciation concepts that are strictly linguistic as opposed to those that are language developmental.

There are several ways to teach English metrical patterns to ESOL students. One highly effective technique is known as DRUMSTICKS. The only tools you need are a pair of sticks, rods, pens, pencils, or any other long and narrow object that can make a noise when you beat it against a solid object. Here is what you do: take up one pencil (pen, stick, rod, etc.) in each hand. Pretend that you are about to beat on a drum. Take any multisyllabic word in the English language and use the two pencils to beat out its rhythm against a desk, a chair, or any other solid object. Here is an example: the word whose rhythm you want to present is *ánimal*. It has three syllables and thus three beats. With one hand, strike the solid object very hard just one time; then with your other hand, strike the solid object softly twice. The hard strike represents the strong-stressed syllable of *ánimal*; the two soft strikes represent the two null-stressed syllables of that word. Now take all the words in Exercise 1.1 (A) and do the same with them. Then have your students take up their own pencils and replicate the activity right there at their desks. You will find how much they enjoy being "drummers in a band," and how effective DRUMSTICKS is at getting them to **feel** the metrical patterns of English. And it goes without saying that you can also apply the drumsticks activity to consecutive words and entire sentences. Poetry, songs, chants, and proverbs lend themselves very nicely to DRUMSTICKS.

Another effective way to teach English metrical patterns to ESOL students is WHISTLING. The only problem with whistling is that in some cultures it is considered inappropriate or even offensive. In that case, humming can be substituted with equal effectiveness. If whistling is taboo in some of your students' homeland cultures (e.g., Mexican), you can do one of two things: avoid whistling as a classroom activity or explain to your students that **this** whistling is being used for linguistic purposes only and is not being done to offend anybody. In any event, here is how you use WHISTLING to teach English metrical patterns: make sure you lips are wet and limber, for you don't want your whistles to come across as weak. Now practice whistling the metrical patterns. Try to whistle (or hum) the stress pattern of a word such as *ánimal*. When you do so, you will find that your loud whistle on the strong-stressed syllable will also come across as higher pitched. Don't worry about this, because in English, many strong-stressed syllables are also higher pitched. Once you feel you're ready to whistle or hum *ánimal* in front of your class, do so repeatedly. Then have your students repeat the whistling/humming pattern after you. Proceed to model other examples from Exercise 1.1 (A). The same technique also works with several words in sequence and even with entire sentences and lines from poems, songs, chants, and proverbs.

NOTES

1. Because it will soon be necessary to recognize tense vowels, the following is a quick preview of how to do so from the spelling: the sound /i/ is often spelled "ee"—*need, feed, greed*—, "ea"—*please, meal, flea*—or "y," usually at the end of words: *happy, sloppy, lazy*; however, "e" or "i" alone or in combination also render /i/: *region, cereal, machine, routine, piece, seize*. The sound /e/ is typically spelled any one of four ways: "ei" (*weigh, neighbor*), "a" (*gate, grave*), "ai" (*wait, straight*), and "ay" (*play, gray*), but in some words is rendered as "ea" (*great, steak*) or "ey" (*they, grey*). The sound /o/ almost always includes an "o" somewhere: "o" alone (*go, vote*), "ow" (*know, show*), "oa" (*soap, road*), "oe" (*foe, woe*), and, rarely, "ou" (*dough, mould*); annoyingly, though rarely, /o/ can even be spelled "ew" (*sew*) and "au" (*mauve, gauche*). The orthography of /u/ is even worse: "u" (*brute, flute*) and "oo" (*loop, troop*) are the most common, but /u/ can also be rendered "o" (*do, who*), "ou" (*through, soup*), "ue" (*true, blue*), "ui" (*suit, fruit*), "ew" (*chew, Jew*), and even—though rarely—"eu," "oe," or "wo" (*sleuth, shoe, two*). Obviously, much more information about the relationship between spelling and pronunciation is needed, and chapter 4 will provide it.

2. We will gradually introduce IPA symbols for showing pronunciation with fuller information on articulation and transcription in chapters 5 and 6; meanwhile, do not worry about terms such as "mid vowel" and focus on learning symbols for the limited purposes that are shown in the text. For more information on the International Phonetic Association, see the appendix.

3. TEMPOS of articulation are sometimes described with musical labels, from LARGO, or ultra-slow, through ANDANTE to ALLEGRO, and what we are calling relative CARE(FULNESS), or deliberateness of speech, is often described in terms of contextually determined STYLES (from FORMAL through COLLOQUIAL to CASUAL)—terms that we also use later. Although there are several sociolinguistic theories of register, we are simply focusing here on factors that may affect the appearance or audibility of weak (or secondary) stress.

4. The discrepancy between the number of words containing three or more syllables (27) and the number cited here has stemmed from the fact that one, *Húpmobile(s)*, appears four times in the sample.

5. These entries comprise the 655-page "English-Spanish" section (pp. 679–1433) of Carvajal and Horwood (1996), a bilingual dictionary chosen because of the length of its English corpus, which was deemed neither too long to permit its manual entry into a database nor too short to properly represent the lexicon of English.

Wrap-Up Exercises

🎧 STIDA—Spondaic, trochaic, iambic, dactylic, or anapestic? Tell which metric pattern(s) are exhibited by each of the following nursery rhymes. (Bear in mind that poems and rhymes exaggerate the stress patterns that are also found in naturalistic nonpoetic speech.)

Example: Metric pattern(s):

Old McDonald had a farm   *trochaic*
Ee eye ee eye oh.
On that farm he had some ducks
Ee eye ee eye oh.

1.   Metric pattern(s):
Humpty Dumpty sat on a wall
Humpty Dumpty had a great fall
All the king's horses and all the king's men
Couldn't put Humpty together again.

2.   Metric pattern(s):
Little Miss Muffet
Sat on a tuffet
Eating her curds and whey.
Along came a spider
And sat down beside her
And frightened Miss Muffet away.

3.   Metric pattern(s):
Mary had a little lamb
Its fleece was white as snow.
Everywhere that Mary went
The lamb was sure to go.

4.   Metric pattern(s):
Baa, baa, black sheep, have you any wool?
Yes sir, yes sir, three bags full.
One for my master, one for my dame,
And one for the little boy who lives in the lane.

5.   <u>Metric pattern(s):</u>

Hey diddle diddle, the cat and the fiddle
The cow jumped over the moon.
The little dog laughed to see such sport
And the dish ran away with the spoon.

6.   <u>Metric pattern(s):</u>

There was an old woman who lived in a shoe.
She had so many children, she knew not what to do.
She gave them some broth, without any bread
Then whipped them all soundly and sent them to bed.

7.   <u>Metric pattern(s):</u>

Jack Sprat would eat no fat
His wife would eat no lean
And so between the two of them
They licked the platter clean.

8.   <u>Metric pattern(s):</u>

Twinkle twinkle little star
How I wonder what you are.
Up above the world so high
Like a diamond in the sky.

9.   <u>Metric pattern(s):</u>

Pat-a-cake, pat-a-cake, baker's man
Bake me a cake as fast as you can
Pat it and prick it, and mark it with B
And put it in the oven for baby and me.

CHAPTER 2

Strong Stresses and Weak: How to Know Where They Go

2.1 Strong stress moves leftward, but only so far. As we already know from figure 1.e, and as the analysis of any sample of ordinary English prose will show, a clear majority—about 75 percent—of commonly used words are monosyllabic and thus can only be strong-stressed on their single syllable. Some of these are common FUNCTION WORDS such as articles (*the*), auxiliary verbs (*be, can*), prepositions (*at*), and pronouns (*her*) that usually lose their stress in the stream of speech (§7.4.2). The challenge begins with the words that are two syllables long and continues through the rest of the multisyllabled lexicon of the language.

Chapter 1 has already pointed out the disparity between what the dictionary contains and what the average person says, hears, reads, and writes in a typical day. On the one hand, only about 15 percent of the 25,108 entries in our middle-sized dictionary corpus are monosyllabic and 39 percent bisyllabic, totaling a slight majority of 54 percent. (About 26%, 14%, 5%, 1%, .10%, and .01% are three-, four-, five-, six-, seven-, and eight-syllabled. For a list of all 25,108 entries, see the Corpus file on the CD.) On the other hand, and as chapter 1 also shows, 75 percent of words in a typical sample of ordinary English prose are monosyllabic and thus trouble-free when pronounced alone. In any event, to handle the eleven thousand polysyllabic words that appear in our corpus—mostly loanwords from French, Latin, or Greek—we must acquire a lot of information about where strong stress goes and where it does not.

If only the rules of English stress placement were as simple as those of languages with unbounded feet such as Czech, Hungarian, French, Polish, and Serbian/Croatian! In Czech and Hungarian (both left-headed), strong stress always falls on the word's first syllable, no matter how long the word is; in French (which is right-headed), strong stress is oxytonic,

Figure 2.a. Technical terms that describe where strong stress falls

Position of stress	Name of that syllable	Our abbrev.	Term for words with that stress pattern
last syllable	ultimate	**ult**	oxytone (or "ult-stressed")
next to the last syllable	penultimate	**pen**	paroxytone (or "pen-stressed")
3rd from the last syllable	antepenultimate	**ant**	proparoxytone (or "ant-stressed")
4th from the last syllable	pre-antepenultimate	**pre**	
5th from the last syllable	quintultimate	**qui**	
6th from the last syllable	sexultimate	**sex**	

falling on a word's last syllable, or "ult"; in Polish all words are paroxytones, stressed penultimately on the word's next-to-the-last, or "pen" syllable; and in Serbian/Croatian all words are proparoxytones, stressed antepenultimately on the third syllable from the last, or "ant." Such easy regularity and predictability of stress placement is not the case with English. English words can be OXYTONES (stressed on the ult), PAROXYTONES (stressed on the penult), PROPAROXYTONES (stressed on the third-from-last syllable, or antepenult), and can even be stressed pre-antepenultimately (fourth-from-the-last) and on the fifth-from-the-last syllable. (It is next to impossible for an English word to be stressed on the sixth-from-the-last syllable—our corpus contains just two that are—and strong stress **never** falls any further to the left than syllable six, regardless of the word's length.) Figure 2.a summarizes the technical terms that we use to describe where strong stress falls.

Based on the classification of words by stress position, Figures 2.b–c present important statistics that were compiled from our corpus. Figure 2.b's classification by n.o.s. shows that a majority—54.1 percent—of the words in the corpus are either monosyllabic or bisyllabic. Sizeable numbers of words, though, are three-, four-, or five-syllabled. Figure 2.b's classification by s.s.p. shows that a vast majority of the corpus entries, 95.34 percent—nineteen out of twenty—are strong-stressed on the ult/pen/ant. Therefore pre/qui/sex stress is a rarity. This fact, together with the statistics that are presented in figure 2.c, will lead to some important generalizations.

Figure 2.c shows that nearly 82 percent of all bisyllabic words are paroxytones (penultimately strong-stressed). This proves that the longer the word, the more likely strong stress will fall leftward. Figure 2.c shows that six out of every ten trisyllabic words are proparoxytones (antepenultimately strong-stressed); this too indicates a leftward trend in the positioning of stress. Figure 2.c tells us that only 21.67 percent of all four-syllable words are strong-stressed on the fourth syllable from the right. This proves that **the leftward trend usually stops at the antepenult** rather than advancing to the pre-antepenult. Statistics for figure 2.c's five-syllabled words (and also the six-syllabled words that appear below them) show the same tendencies that four-syllabled words do: a plurality or majority is antepenultimately strong-stressed, so **the leftward movement tends to stop at the antepenult**.

Figure 2.b. Classification of words in the corpus

By number of syllables (n.o.s.)			By strong stress placement (s.s.p.)		
n.o.s.	totals	percentage	s.s.p.	totals	percentage
01	3,725	14.84	ult	6,000	23.90
02	9,858	39.26	pen	11,561	46.05
03	6,629	26.40	ant	6,375	25.39
04	3,406	13.57	pre	1,094	4.36
05	1,237	4.93	qui	76	.30
06	227	.90	sex	2	.00
07	23	.09		25,108	100.00
08	3	.01			
	25,108	100.00			

Figure 2.c. Classification by number of syllables and strong stress placement

Classification group: n.o.s. plus s.s.p.	Total count	Percentages . . .		
		of each classification group	of the entire corpus (__ / 25,108)	
01-ult	3,725	100.00	14.84 (= 3,725/25,108)	
02-ult	1,813 ⎫	18.39 ⎫	7.22 (= 1,813/25,108, et seq.)	
02-pen	8,045 ⎬ 9,858	81.61 ⎬ 100.00	32.04	
03-ult	423 ⎫	6.38 ⎫	1.68	
03-pen	2,228 ⎬ 6,629	33.61 ⎬ 100.00	8.87	
03-ant	3,978 ⎭	60.01 ⎭	15.84	
04-ult	38 ⎫	1.12 ⎫	.15	
04-pen	954 ⎬ 3,406	28.01 ⎬ 100.00	3.80	
04-ant	1,676	49.20	6.67	
04-pre	738 ⎭	21.67 ⎭	2.94	
05-ult	1 ⎫	.01 ⎫	.004	
05-pen	281	22.72	1.12	
05-ant	591 ⎬ 1,237	47.78 ⎬ 100.00	2.35	
05-pre	308	24.90	1.23	
05-qui	56 ⎭	4.53 ⎭	.22	
06-pen	51 ⎫	22.47 ⎫	.20	
06-ant	115	50.66	.46	
06-pre	44 ⎬ 227	19.38 ⎬ 100.00	.18	
06-qui	15	6.61	.06	
06-sex	2 ⎭	.88 ⎭	.001	
07-pen	3 ⎫	13.04 ⎫	.001	
07-ant	14 ⎬ 23	60.87 ⎬ 100.00	.06	
07-pre	2	8.70	.001	
07-qui	4 ⎭	17.39 ⎭	.001	
08-ant	1 ⎫	33.33 ⎫	.001	
08-pre	1 ⎬ 3	33.33 ⎬ 100.00	.001	
08-qui	1 ⎭	33.33 ⎭	.001	
Total:	**25,108**		**100.00**	

The various tables of figures 2.b and 2.c show us two important things:

- the more syllables a word contains, the more it is likely that strong stress will appear to the left, away from the end of the word. However,
- strong stress will appear only so far to the left, for as these tables have also shown, relatively few words are strong-stressed on the pre-antepenult and even fewer are strong-stressed on the fifth or sixth syllable from the rear.

And to repeat what we already know, an overwhelming majority of the words in our corpus—95.34 percent—are stressed on the ult, the penult, or the antepenult. Knowing this makes it a lot easier to learn the rules of strong stress placement in English.

Let's review what we know about strong stress placement:

- Three of every four words are monosyllabic in ordinary prose, so strong stress can only fall on their single syllable.
- More than nine of every ten words are either mono- or bisyllabic in ordinary prose, so most ordinary words have just two syllables.
- Nineteen of every twenty words in the dictionary corpus strong-stress the ult, the penult, or the antepenult, no matter how many syllables the words contain.
- More than eight of every ten bisyllabic words will strong-stress the penult, which shows that stress moves leftward.
- **While strong stress moves to the left, it rarely appears more leftward than the antepenult**.

These five generalizations are very useful, for they help us clear away a lot of the underbrush from the forest of English stress placement. But no forest can be fully described without paying at least some attention to its trees, and that is what we will do in §2.2.

Exercise 2.1

(A) Tell which syllable-length-and-stress category (see figure 2.a) each of the following words belongs to. To do this, count each word's syllables and then locate its strong stress. If you don't know where a word's strong stress falls, see the several Corpus files on the CD. To refresh your memory, here are all the length and stress categories that we have used. (Note that some categories have no examples: 06-ult, 06-sex, and many seven- or eight-syllable groups.)

01-ult
02-ult, 02-pen
03-ult, 03-pen, 03-ant
04-ult, 04-pen, 04-ant, 04-pre
05-ult, 05-pen, 05-ant, 05-pre, 05-qui
06-pen, 06-ant, 06-pre, 06-qui
07-pen, 07-ant, 07-pre, 07-qui
08-ant, 08-pre, 08-qui

Example: *encounter*. **03-pen**. (*Encounter* has three syllables, and its strong stress falls on the pen)

1. integrity	8. December	15. ascertain
2. stand	9. tragic	16. condemn
3. deliver	10. tragedy	17. condemnation
4. delivery	11. constitution	18. dutiful
5. deliverance	12. constitutional	19. duty
6. astonish	13. anticonstitutional	20. anthropology
7. astonishing	14. defy	

(B) The following are nonsense words, invented for this exercise. Guess where each word's stress falls, describe its stress pattern, and then tell if that pattern is typical of the language as a whole.

1. ferping	5. ractonic	9. sorbocentrism
2. congrinjulation	6. rejabulate	10. predepressionicity
3. sligrescent	7. defractible	
4. avunculable	8. frumplusciousness	

(C) ESOL students from various backgrounds have incorrectly pronounced the following words. The main mistake involves stress. You will figure out the student's native language by looking at where he/she has wrongly stressed the word. Recall: Czech and Hungarian always stress words' first syllables; Serbian/Croatian always stress words' antepenultimate syllables; Polish always stresses words' penultimate syllables, and French always stresses words' last ("ult") syllables.

1. *ácceptable	7. *amphibían	13. *cómputational
2. *affíxation	8. *marvélous	14. *Englísh
3. *envý	9. *kitchén	15. *fantastíc
4. *insólence	10. *undérlining	16. *antíquated
5. *mágnificent	11. *ínstructions	
6. *tremendóus	12. *anímal	

2.2 Three main factors in strong-stress position. There are three main factors in English that affect the placement of strong stress in a word: syllable structure, part of speech, and affixation. Let's examine each one now.

2.2.1 Syllable structure. One general rule about English stress is based on types of syllable structure (see §6.1). A CLOSED syllable ends in one or more consonants and contains a checked or free vowel (§1.4); an OPEN syllable ends in a (free) vowel sound. The rule is this: while the stress of open syllables varies (*féllow* but *belów*, *préview* but *revíew*), a closed syllable tends to attract stress: *abóard, abóut, abrúpt, accláim*.

2.2.2 Part of speech. Another general rule is this: words that are **verbs** are more likely to be right-headed, that is, strong-stressed on the **ult**. The reason is that most of these verbs' first syllables were originally unstressed prefixes in French, Latin, or Greek (see §2.2.3). Here are some examples of the phenomenon: *abhór, abjúre, abscónd, abstáin, acquáint, acquíre, acquít, adhére*.

The part-of-speech rule often combines with the syllable-structure rule, because some ult-stressed bisyllabic words function as verbs **and** end in a closed syllable; examples of this are the words just presented. As is well known, English is full of word pairs that are strong-stressed on the ult as **verbs** but are strong-stressed on the penult or (pre)antepenult when used as **nouns and/or adjectives**. Figure 2.d gives samples of such pairs from our corpus. Most of these pairs' components are bisyllabic; the noun/adjective form appears first and the verb second.

2.2.3 Affixation. Yet another general rule states that affixes—prefixes and especially suffixes—play a major role in determining where strong stress will fall. Consider the difference between words bearing either one of the following two **prefixes**: *un-* and *tele-*. Words beginning with the prefix *un-* will never strong-stress it in noncontrastive speech; thus *unáble, uncánny, unconvéntional, undecíded, unéasy, unháppy*, and so on. However, words beginning with the prefix *tele-* almost always strong-stress it: *télecast, télecommuting, télegram,*

Figure 2.d. Pairs of words that change part of speech when changing stress

ábstract/abstráct	éxploit/exploít	recáll/recáll
áddress/addréss	éxport/expórt	récap/recáp
áttribute/attríbute	éxtract/extráct	récord/recórd
cómmune/commúne	ímplant/implánt	réfuse/refúse
cómpound/compóund	ímprint/imprínt	réhash/rehásh
cónflict/conflíct	íncrease/incréase	réject/rejéct
cónduct/condúct	ínsert/insért	rélay/reláy
cónscript/conscrípt	ínsult/insúlt	réplay/repláy
cónstruct/constrúct	ínvalid (n.)/inválid (adj.)	réprint/reprínt
cóntent/contént	óbject/objéct	rérun/rerún
cóntract/contráct	óverflow/overflów	rétard/retárd
cóntrast/contrást	óverwork/overwórk	rétread/retréad
cónvert/convért	pérfume/perfúme	réwrite/rewríte
cónvict/convíct	pérvert/pervért	súbject/subjéct
défect/deféct	présent/presént	súrvey/survéy
désert/desért	próduce/prodúce	súspect/suspéct
dígest/digést	prógress/progréss	tórment/tormént
díscharge/dischárge	próject/projéct	tránsfer/transfér
díscount/discóunt	prótest/protést	tránsport/transpórt
éscort/escórt	rébel/rebél	úpdate/updáte

télemarketing, téléphone, télesales, téléscope, télevision. Of much greater importance in determining stress placement is the large number of English **suffixes**. Consider these two: *-ness* and *-tion.* Adding *-ness* to a word does not cause the position of its stress to change; thus *discontínuous → discontínuousness, schólarly → schólarliness, páinstaking → páinstakingness.* On the other hand, adding *-tion* to a word does change the position of its stress; thus *detérmine → determinátion, adjúdicate → adjudicátion, accómmodate → accomodátion, certíficate → certificátion, stágnate → stagnátion.* There's a useful generalization here: *-ness* is like most other native Anglo-Saxon suffixes, which don't alter where stress falls on the stem, whereas *-tion* is like most other Romance suffixes, which typically do alter stress position.

2.3 Strong-stress retention on the same base vowel. Once strong stress has been assigned to a vowel in a base word, the rest of the words in that base word's family usually keep the strong stress on that very same vowel. Corpus information shows that in 3,822 of our word families—almost 72 percent of them—stress does not shift from one vowel to another: it stays on the same base vowel. This means that nearly three out of every four word families behave like *achíeve, admít,* and *cáre,* where stress remains on the same base vowel, regardless of the suffix. Let's take a look at the base forms *achíeve, admít,* and *cáre* plus their lexical families:

achíeve	admít	cáre	cárelessly
achíevable	admíssible	cárefree	cárelessness
achíevement	admíssion	cáreful	cárer
achíever	admíttance	cárefully	cáretaker
	admíttedly	cáreless	cáring

Regardless of whatever expansion occurs, strong stress continues to fall on the very same syllable's vowel—the 'i' or the 'a'—that it fell on in the base word *achíeve, admít,* and *cáre.*

It is very helpful to know that a word belongs to a family whose strong stress always falls in the same place, for once you learn where strong stress falls on **one** word in a family, you know where strong stress will fall on all the **rest** of the words in that family. Our corpus contains more than 3,800 word families like *achíeve, admít,* and *cáre.* These families constitute 72 percent of the word-family corpus. This shows that **English is a language that prefers *not* to shift the position of a strong stress once it has been established**.

2.4. Word families with shifting stress. Strong stress **does** shift from place to place in the remaining 1,498 (28%) of our lexical families, and they are the ones that may give trouble. In these families, strong stress shifts whenever a "shifter" suffix is attached to the base form. Nonetheless, in most cases only **one** word in the family reveals a shifted stress, which means that strong stress does **not** shift in the rest of the family. What is more, about 90 percent of all shifts in strong stress can be accounted for by just these four shifters: *-al, -ity, -tion,* and *-ic(s).* (The remaining 10% are accounted for by a very large number of additional shifter suffixes—seventy-four in all; see figure 2.e.) There follow four lexical families, each illustrating one of the four shifter suffixes. The stress-shifted word appears in boldface; all the other words in each family retain the stress position of the base word.

árchitect	accóunt	appréciable	cháracter
architéctural	**accountabílity**	appréciably	**characterístic**
árchitecture	accóuntable	appréciate	cháracterize
	accóuntancy	**appreciátion**	cháracterless
	accóuntant	appréciative	
		appréciatively	

In the case of many families where strong stress shifts, it does so just once, but it affects two or more words (in boldface). This is also not a major problem for the student of English.

astrónomer, **astronómical, astronómically,** *astrónomy*
óptimism, óptimist, **optimístic, optimístically**
lócal, **locále, locálity,** *lócalize, lócally*

Figure 2.e. The four most important shifter suffixes

suffix	*effect*	*examples*
-al	shifts strong stress to the **antepenult**; 97 instances of shifted stress in the corpus	ágriculture → agricúltural állegory → allegórical anátomy → anatómical anthropólogy → anthropológical árchitecture → architéctural
-ity	shifts strong stress to the **antepenult**; 185 instances of shifted stress in the corpus	accóuntable → accountabílity ácid → acídity áctual → actuálity ágile → agílity anónymous → anonýmity
-tion	shifts strong stress to the **penult**; 537 instances of shifted stress in corpus (includes three instances of *-sion* and two of *-xion*)	abbréviate → abbreviátion abérrant → aberrátion abólish → abolítion ábrogate → abrogátion absólve → absolútion
-ic(s)	shifts strong stress to the **penult**; 177 instances	ácrobat → acrobátics (a)ésthete → (a)esthétic álcohol → alcohólic állergy → allérgic álphabet → alphabétic

But major problems **can** arise when strong stress shifts not once but twice (or, rarely, thrice). In our corpus there are 188 families—about 12.5 percent of the 1,498—in which stress shifts more than once. (See file "families-2" in the Corpus on the CD; in that file, the multishifting families are boldfaced.) Here are three examples of that type of family:

Family	1	2	3
	áccess	adápt	**appendéctomy**
	accessibílity	**adaptabílity**	**appendicítis**
	accéssible	adáptable	appéndix
	accéssion	**adaptátion**	appéndices
	accéssory	adápter/adáptor	

But even in families like these it is usually possible to tell which stress pattern typifies the **base word** that the others derive from. The base word is typically a noun or a verb and is shorter than the others. Thus in family 2 the base is *adápt* (from which *adáptable* and *adápter/adáptor* derive), and in family 3 the base is *appéndix*. Only family 1 might not use the noun/verb *áccess* as its base, probably preferring the adjective *accéssible* or the noun *accéssory*. Some of these 188 families' stress patterns get quite complicated, as the examples from the following family show:

subsíde
subsídence
subsidiárity
subsídiary
súbsidize
súbsidy

Yet even in this messy family, patterns arise. Thus the first two words—*subsíde, subsídence*—as well as the last two—*súbsidize, súbsidy*—are respectively stressed alike (the first pair right-headed, the second pair left-headed) because each pair constitutes a subfamily of its own. (*Subsíde* means 'to sink to a lower level,' and *subsídence* is its noun; *súbsidize* is 'to grant or contribute money,' so a *súbsidy* is that contribution.) Only the middle two—*subsídiary, subsidiárity*—resist classification.

Exercise 2.2

Tell where the strong stress falls on the following words by writing an acute accent atop the strong-stressed vowel. Then give as many of the remaining members of the word's family as you can think of, writing an acute accent atop each one's strong-stressed vowel as well.

Example: *differ*. This word is **02-pen** and is strong-stressed as *díffer*. The remaining members of its family are: *dífference, dífferent, differéntial, differéntiate, differentiátion, dífferently.*

1. value	8. rapid	15. record (two possibilities)
2. universe	9. pure	16. magnify
3. tempt	10. origin	17. legal
4. statistic	11. object (two possibilities)	18. institute
5. satisfy	12. modern	19. infinite
6. respect	13. method	20. history
7. repeat	14. liberate	21. horror

2.5. The effect of suffixation on strong-stress position. As we already know, four of the shifter suffixes are highly important, for we can add them to thousands of base words, and together they account for around 90 percent of all shifts in stress. Two of these shifters (*-al, -ity*) shift stress to the antepenult, whereas the two others (*-tion, -ic(s)*) shift it to the penult. Figure 2.e provides some examples of each of these four shifter suffixes, together with the number of instances in which the suffix has shifted stress in our corpus's word families.

As a more specific source of information, figure 2.f itemizes the seventy-four endings that shift strong stress. If statistics show that a **big majority** (about 67%–95%) of words in the category shift stress, the ending is marked by a double tilde ≈ , suggesting majority status: for example, *-al* ≈ . But if **all or virtually all (95%–100%) of the words** that end that way shift stress, the ending is not marked, for example, *-ity*.[1]

Figure 2.f. The seventy-four endings that shift strong stress

ending	a few examples of the shifts
(A) The one ending that shifts strong stress to the pre-antepenult	
-ary ≈	antíque → ántiquary; cónstable → constábulary
(B) The thirty-nine endings that shift strong stress to the antepenult	
-ity	cápable → capabílity; séxual → sexuálity
-iety	váry → varíety; ánxious → anxíety
-al ≈	(but cf. -cial/-tial) pédagogue → pedagógical; techníque → téchnical
-ology	méthod → methodólogy; sócial → sociólogy
-bian	Árab → Arábian; mícrobe → micróbian
-dian	Cánada → Canádian; trágedy → tragédian
-lian	Epíscopal → Episcopálian; réptile → reptílian
-nian	Ámazon → Amazónian; Dárwin → Darwínian
-rian	bárbarous → barbárian; grámmar → grammárian
-ean ≈	Cáesar → Caesárean (*but:* épicure → epicuréan)
-itan ≈	metrópolis → metropólitan; cósmos → cosmopólitan
-icide	ínfant → infánticide; ínsect → insécticide
-ute ≈	dissólve → díssolute; resólve → résolute
-neous/nious	hármony → harmónious; míscellany → miscelláneous
-dious	mélody → melódious; pérfidy → perfídious

Figure 2.f. (*Continued*)

-rious	mýstery → mystérious; lábor → labórious
-lous ≈	rídicule → ridículous; míracle → miráculous
-mous	pséudonym → pseudónymous; ácronym → acrónymous
-nous ≈	vólume → volúminous; mónotone → monótonous
-rous	cárnivore → carnívorous; ómnivore → omnívorous
-tous ≈	círcuit → circúitous; gráteful → gratúitous
-uous	túmult → tumúltuous; ambigúity → ambíguous
-ius	áqua → Aquárius
-ograph	phótograph; chóreograph
-ographer	photógrapher; choreógrapher
-ography	photógraphy; choreógraphy
-ient	nutrítious → nútrient
-ify	sólid → solídify; sýllable → syllábify
-ium	áuditor → auditórium; gýmnast → gymnásium
-cracy	démocrat → demócracy; búreaucrat → bureáucracy
-crat	démocrat; búreaucrat
-ia	xénophobe → xenophóbia; mélancholy → melanchólia
-omy	económical → ecónomy; gástronome → gastrónomy
-pathy	hómeopath → homeópathy; psýchopath → psychópathy
-eria	café → cafetéria
-onia	Cátalan → Catalónia; Ámazon → Amazónia
-ica	hármony → harmónica; mélody → melódica
-ometer	spéed → speedómeter; kílo → kilómeter
-ular	párticle → partícular; mólecule → molécular

(C) **The twenty endings that shift strong stress to the penult**

-tion (-cion/-gion/-nion/-(s)sion/-xion)   abbréviate → abbreviátion; abólish → abolítion

-lion (where 'i' is semiconsonant /j/)   médal → medállion

-ic(s)	ácid → acídic; ácrobat → acrobátic
-cial/-tial	bénefit → benefícial; próvince → províncial
-cian/-tian	mágic → magícian; díet → dietítian
-gian	Nórway → Norwégian
-sian	Cáucasus → Caucásian; Páris → Parísian
-cious/-tious	júdge → judícious; óffice → offícious
-aceous	cúrve → curváceous; hérb → herbáceous
-geous/-gious	óutrage → outrágeous; lítigate → litígious
-sis ≈ /-tis ≈	ánalyze → análysis; appéndix → appendicítis
-nda	ágent → agénda; própagate → propagánda
-(s)sive	ímpulse → impúlsive; prógress → progréssive
-ctive	ínstinct → instínctive; próspect → prospéctive

(*continued*)

Figure 2.f. (*Continued*)

-ata	érror → erráta; sónnet → sonáta
-ella	cínder → Cinderélla
-ina	ballét → ballerína; cóncert → concertína
-o ≈	cóncert → concérto; móderate → moderáto
-C + um	ádd → addéndum; mémory → memorándum
-cent ≈	phósphorous → phosphoréscent; púbis → pubéscent

(D) **The fourteen endings that shift strong stress to the ult**

-ade	lémon → lemonáde; árc → arcáde
-ain	dóminant → domáin; máintenance → maintáin
-aire	dóctrine → doctrináire; légion → legionnáire
-ane ≈	húman → humáne; úrban → urbáne
-ee/-é	phótograph → photographée; exámine → examinée
-een	hállow → Hallowéen
-eer	éngine → engінéer; prívate → privatéer
-ese/-eze	jóurnal → journalése; Chína → Chinése
-esse	fíne → finésse; lárge → largésse
-eur	líquor → liquéur; réstaurant → restaurantéur
-ique	ántiquate → antíque; téchnical → techníque
-oon	fést(ival) → festóon; spít → spittóon
-sque	pícture → picturésque; státue → statuésque
-ette ≈	nóvel → novelétte; kítchen → kitchenétte

In addition, changes in grammatical category—typically from verb (ult stress) to noun or adjective (pen or ant stress)—cause strong stress to shift in the eighty-two word pairs we have listed earlier (§2.2.2), such as, for example, the verb *implánt* versus the noun *ímplant*. The corpus contains just seventy-nine instances of stress shift brought about by compounding (e.g., *hím* + *sélf* = *himsélf*), a complicated phenomenon that is discussed in a later section (§2.11.2). That leaves only 198 exceptional or eccentric stress shifts which cannot be explained by suffixation, changes in grammatical category, or compounding.

The list of ***non*shifter endings**—just thirty-six—is less than half as long as the list of seventy-four shifter endings. However, nearly all the nonshifters are frequently used and highly productive, from the several dozen instances of *-phile, -proof,* and *-sphere* to the more than 3,000 instances of *-ness* to the almost innumerable uses of *-es, -ed,* and *-ing*. (That nonshifters are frequent and productive is not surprising, because we now know that in most English lexical families, stress does **not** shift from place to place.) The nonshifters *-es, -ed,* and *-ing* are grammatical morphemes used to pluralize, indicate possession, or mark a verb for person, number, and/or tense; thus *wísh: wíshes, wíshed, wíshing; transmít: transmíts, transmítted, transmítting*. Other nonshifters serve a variety of purposes as figure 2.g will show.[2] (Note that some nonshifter endings carry weak stress, which we mark.)

Figure 2.g. The thirty-six endings that do not shift strong stress

ending	a few examples
-able	agréeable, appróachable, unwórkable, compánionable
-ant	ascéndant, dóminant, inhábitant, assístant
-ate	rústicate, rádiate, apprópriate, miscálculate
-cy	líteracy, extrávagancy, óccupancy, accóuntancy
-er	ófficer, lícencer, annóuncer, suspénder, núllifier
-ed	públished, mátted, máted, obsérved, fítted, kíssed
-es	wíshes, físhes, sláshes, séizes, snéezes, pásses
-ess	stéwardess, príncess, góddess, archdúchess, drúidess
-ful	revéngeful, púrposeful, méaningful, disdáinful
-ing	sínging, brínging, tálking, wálking, shóuting, béing
-ine	médicine, pórcine, tomátidine, émeraldine, giráffine
-ish	wómanish, curmúdgeonish, impóverish, dílettantish
-ism	fanáticìsm, wítticìsm, tríbalìsm, impérialìsm
-ist	phármicist, geólogist, commércialist, impóssibilist
-ite	metábolìte, pórcellanìte, jéffersonìte, bipártìte
-ize	anthólogize, spécialìze, féderalìze, legítimìze
-less	féatureless, regárdless, vibrátionless, válueless
-like	unstátesmanlìke, géntlemanlìke, ládylìke, chíldlìke
-ly	assémbly, presúmedly, entírely, héavenly, ínstantly
-man/-woman	políceman, cóuncilwoman, nóblewoman, néwspaperman
-ment	disármament, améndment, annóuncement, enslávement
-ness	coldblóodedness, cháritableness, méddlesomeness
-phile	Ánglophìle, Germánophìle, bíbliophìle, Hispánophìle
-phobe	Ánglophòbe, Germánophòbe, bíbliophòbe, Hispánophòbe
-proof	fírepròof, búrglarpròof, shówerpròof, wáterpròof
-ship	stéwardship, acquáintanceship, wórkmanship, kínship
-some	frólicsome, méddlesome, unwhólesome, quárrelsome
-sphere	bíosphère, thérmosphère, magnétosphère, zóosphère
-tor	índicator, consólidator, návigator, artículator
-tory	prédatory, comméndatory, invéstigatory, exclámatory
-ward(s)	wíndward, dównward, straightfórward, héavenwards
-wise	léngthwìse, counterclóckwìse, córnerwìse, ánywìse
-y	flab → flábby, múd → múddy, dándruff → dándruffy

Exercise 2.3

Describe the role of the ending in each of the following words: is it a **shifter ending,** or is it a **nonshifter ending**? To do so, (1) give the base word that each item comes from, indicating (2) where its strong stress falls and (3) to which syllable the ending has shifted the stress. Example: *anxíety*. This item's base is *ánxious*. Adding the ending *-ity* shifts the strong stress to the antepenult—in this instance to *anxíety*'s syllable *xí*. The 02-pen word *ánxious* is now the 04-ant word *anxíety*.

1. abolition	8. applying	15. broadcaster
2. academic	9. objector	16. tiresome
3. acclimatization	10. architectural	17. irritating
4. alphabetic	11. astronomical	18. adornment
5. analytic	12. auctioneer	19. Jewish
6. animated	13. authenticate	20. catastrophic
7. antagonize	14. bestiality	

2.6 The shiftless, stress-free life of the prefix. Roughly 90 percent of all the corpus words that begin with a prefix do not stress it, and most prefixes do not shift stress within a word. The typical English prefix, then, behaves like *un-*, as in these examples: *unármed, unaváilable, unblóck, unbecóming, uncléan, undevéloped.*

The English language has sixty-one prefixes, ranging from the highly productive and frequently used (such as *dis-, ex-, in-, re-,* and *un-*) all the way down to those that are of more limited currency such as *circum-, geo-, psycho-,* and *radio-*. Although the typical prefix behaves like *un-*, it is nonetheless the case that about ten atypical prefixes—including some that are not especially productive or widely used—take strong stress in many instances; the words they begin are therefore left-headed. See figure 2.h for a list of all sixty-one prefixes. The ten that are sometimes or even frequently stressed are followed by comments revealing the extent to which they are. (Prefixes not followed by parenthetical explanations are either never stressed except for purposes of contrast and emphasis—thus *immóral* and *amóral* in the following exchange: "Are you saying that Jane is immóral?" "Jane isn't just ímmoral, she's completely ámoral!"—or else are stressed on a very few lexical items only.)

Exercise 2.4

Identify the word's prefix, if any. Then tell whether it is stressed or not stressed.

1. absent	10. beyond	19. conceive
2. ablutions	11. bilingual	20. conference
3. accident	12. bifocals	21. dedicate
4. accept	13. circumcision	22. dedication
5. addiction	14. circumstances	23. desiccated
6. addict	15. coefficient	24. descend
7. ascertain	16. cohort	25. disability
8. counterterrorism	17. commemoration	26. dissident
9. before	18. commitment	27. downward
		28. downtown

Figure 2.h. The sixty-one prefixes (mostly nonshifting and nonstressed)

ab- (sometimes stressed—*ábdicate, ábject, áblative*—vs. the usual *abbréviate, abdúct, abhórrent*)

ac-

ad-

anti- (not strong-stressed in most of the ca. 700 members of this category; exceptions include *ántidote, ántifreeze, ántigen, ántihero, ántimatter, ántimony, ántiserum,* etc.)

as-

be-

bi-

circum- (half are stressed: *circumcise, circumflex, circumscribe* vs. *circumnávigate, circumvént*)

co-

com-

con-

counter- (half are stressed: *cóunterargument, cóunterbalance, cóunterblast, cóunterblow,* etc.)

de-

des-

dis-

down- (two-thirds are stressed: *dównfall, dównpour, dówntime* vs. *downstáirs, downwind*)

em-

en-

ex-

for-

fore- (60% are stressed: *fórecast, fórefathers, fórehead* vs. *foregó, foretéll, forewárn*)

geo-

grand- (nearly all in this small category are stressed: *grándparent, grándson, grándstand*)

homo-

hyper-

hypo-

il-

in-

inter-

intra-

ir-

macro-

mal-

meta-

micro-

(*continued*)

Figure 2.h. (*Continued*)

mid-

mis-

mono-

multi-

non-

ob-

off-

out- (two-thirds are stressed: *óutback, óutbreak* vs. *outbíd, outdístance, outlást,* which are
     verbs)

over- (one-third are stressed: *óverboard, óvercast, óvercoat* vs. *overánxious,*
     overcónfident)

per-

post-

pre-

pro-

psycho-

radio-

re-

self-

semi-

sub-

super-

tele- (almost all are stressed: *télecast, télegram, télephone*)

trans-

ultra-

under-

up-

vice-

2.7 Applying strong-stress rules to bisyllabic words. Let us now apply the rules
we have learned to the largest single component of our 25,108-word dictionary corpus:
words of two syllables. You recall that 9,858 words (about 40%) of our corpus are bisyllabic. You also recall that because 8,045 or around 82 percent of all bisyllabic words are
strong-stressed on the penult, it is fairly easy to guess where strong stress on a bisyllabic
word will fall. However, a not insignificant 1,808 or about 18 percent of all bisyllabic words
are ult-stressed. Thus to see whether it is easy or tough to predict which words are strong-
stressed on the ult, let us look at both the ult-stressed bisyllabics and the pen-stressed bisyllabics from the standpoint of the three main factors that affect strong-stress position (§2.2):
part of speech, syllable structure, and affixation.

First there is the effect of **part of speech**—in particular whether a word is a verb or not. Although 67 percent (1,213) of ult-stressed bisyllabics are verbs, only about 17 percent (1,399) of pen-stressed bisyllabics are verbs. However, the pen-stressed total (1,399) is larger than the ult-stressed total (1,213). So this information brings us to a not-very-helpful conclusion: although most ult-stressed bisyllabics are verbs, verbs are somewhat more likely to be pen-stressed than they are to be ult-stressed. Part of speech, then, is suggestive but not definitive as a predictor of ult stress.

As for **syllable structure** (closed vs. open last syllable), an overwhelming 93.38 percent (1,693/1,813) of all ult-stressed bisyllabics end in closed syllables: *debár, debáse, debáte, debáuch, debríef, debúg.* But 83.48 percent (6,716/8,045) of all **pen**-stressed bisyllabics also end in closed syllables, and while 83.48 percent is somewhat smaller than 93.38 percent, it is still a large percentage—and the 6,716 pen-stressed total is much larger than the 1,693 ult-stressed total. Thus the syllable-structure statistics have forced us to reach another unhelpful conclusion: ult-stressed bisyllabics are very likely to end in closed syllables, but words ending in closed syllables are as likely to be pen-stressed as they are ult-stressed. In reality, **most** English words end in closed syllables rather than open, regardless of how many syllables they contain. So since closed syllable structure is the norm in word final position, closed syllabicity is not very helpful in predicting ult stress.

The effects of **affixation** depend on particular suffixes and prefixes. As we recall from figure 2.e, the **endings** -*ic(s)* and -*tion* helpfully predict that stress will fall on the pen; also useful in predicting pen stress are C(onsonant) + *um*, -*cious/tious*, and -*cial/-tial*. Those that predict ult stress are -*ee/-é*, -*oon* and -*ain*, -*ade* and -*(e)tte*. Nevertheless, these ten endings' predictive weight is minimal, as only 340 bisyllabic words actually have them (along with the less-used endings such as -*lion*, -*cian/-tian*, et al.), and those words constitute just 3.45 percent of the 9,858 bisyllabic total.

Of the **prefixes** that bisyllabic words begin with, eight (*a-*, *be-*, *com-*, *for-*, *in-*, *per-*, *pre-*, and *sub-*) show no preference—roughly half are unstressed. But a clear preference for null stress typifies the remaining six (*con-*, *de-*, *ex-*, *im-*, *re-*, and *un-*), and this fact lets us classify them as nonshifters or nonstrong-stress-takers. And in bisyllabic words bearing these prefixes, if no stress falls on the prefix, then stress will fall on the ult, as these examples show: *concéal, concéde, conclúde; debáse, debríef, debúg; exchánge, excláim, exháust; impáir, impéde, impúre; reáct, reárm, rebúild; unármed, unblóck, uncléan.* Nonetheless, although slightly more than twice the number of bisyllabic word stresses can be predicted from their prefixes as from their suffixes, the total number of words involved is still not large enough to be more than just moderately helpful.

So what's the solution? There **is** one thing that lets us know where strong stress will likely fall on bisyllabic words: establishing a correlation between a word's part of speech and the language family that English took it from—in this case Latin and the Romance family (the modern languages descended from Latin, that is, French, Spanish, Portuguese, Italian, Rumanian, Catalan, etc.). About 90 percent of all 02-ult verbs were borrowed by English from Latin or Romance (especially French)—*colléct, collíde, combíne, commánd, comménce, commend*, and so on—whereas just 25 percent of all 02-pen verbs were. We conclude, then, that **Romance-origin bisyllabic verbs are quite likely to be strong-stressed on the ult**. The sole problem is that only if you know one or more Romance languages will you be able to tell which bisyllabic English verbs are ult-stressed and which are not. In effect, then, and setting aside the matter of Romance origin, what matters most in predicting bisyllabic stress are the percentages we started out with: about 82 percent of all bisyllabics are strong-stressed on the penult, and about 18 percent on the ult. So a good rule of thumb is: just assume that a bisyllabic word is penultimately stressed unless proven otherwise.

Exercise 2.5

Here are twenty-five bisyllabic words. Tell which ones are strong-stressed on the ult and which on the pen. Then try to explain ult strong stress or pen strong stress in each instance. (In some cases, causality is multiple, that is, there's more than one explanation for why the word is ult- or pen-stressed. In other cases, and as we now know, the only possible explanation will be "82 percent of all bisyllabics are stressed on the pen.")

1. elapse	10. germane	19. obese
2. elite	11. ghoulish	20. lampoon
3. empty	12. goatee	21. largesse
4. envy	13. greenness	22. lavish
5. except	14. handy	23. maintain
6. fabric	15. harmless	24. Marxist
7. faintly	16. incite	25. nation
8. fatigue	17. infest	
9. flaky	18. knifing	

2.8 Applying strong-stress rules to trisyllabic words. What is noteworthy about trisyllabic words' strong stress position is **the great degree to which it is determined by prefixes**. In general terms, 3,978 or 60 percent of all trisyllabics are strong-stressed on the ant because they obey the "shift-to-the-left" rule we've talked about before. However, certain non-strong-stressable prefixes—and most of them are non-strong-stressable (figure 2.h)—prevent stress from moving to the ant. Instead, strong stress on words so prefixed will usually stay on the pen; this is true of slightly more than one-third of all trisyllabic words. There are only 423 **ult**-stressed trisyllabics (6.38% of the total), but most are also prevented by non-strong-stressable prefixes from moving stress to the ant. Many of them strong-stress the ult and not the pen because they are Romance-origin verbs ending in closed syllables, for example, *acquiésce, apprehénd, coexíst, commandéer, comprehénd, contradíct, convalésce, disabúse*. More important though are their prefixes: 52.96 percent of all ult-stressed trisyllabics begin with one of these strong-stress rejecters: *dis-, inter-, over-, re-, un-*, and *under-*. Examples: *disallów, disposséss, intercépt, interspérse, overáct, overlóok, reconstrúct, reuníte, unawáre, unprepáred, undergó, undersóld*.

Trisyllabics beginning with the prefixes *ab-, ac-, ad-, as-, be-, com-, con-, de(s)-, dis-, em-, en-, ex-, for-, im-, in-, ob-, per-, pre-, pro-, re-, sub-, trans-, un-*, and *up-* will usually not strong-stress them. (About 57% of pen-stressed trisyllabics begin with one of these prefixes.) And although no more than 37 percent of the total number of words beginning with *ab-*, *ac-*, *ad-*, *as-*, *be-*, and so on are pen-stressed trisyllabics, other factors such as part of speech—few are verbs—combine to place these words' strong stresses on the pen and not the ult.

In sum, 3,978 or 60 percent of all trisyllabics are strong-stressed on the ant—*ádequate*, *álgebra*, *ápplicant*, *áudible*, *bárricade*, *bígamous*, *búngalow*, *cárnivore*, *cértify*, and so on—but a significant 40 percent "remain behind" in the great shift to the left. Knowing that many of these pen- or ult-stressed trisyllabics contain stress-rejecting prefixes will help us understand why they're stressed where they are.

Exercise 2.6

(A) Here are twenty-five trisyllabic words. Pretend you are an instructor whose students have asked you to explain to them where each word is stressed, and why it is stressed there. (Remember: in some cases the explanation will be multiple because causality is multiple.)

1. youthfulness	10. venomous	19. thunderous
2. wonderful	11. vagrancy	20. terrific
3. wickedness	12. uppity	21. technical
4. volunteer	13. unswerving	22. Taiwanese
5. volcanic	14. unseeded	23. retire
6. vocalist	15. unfriendly	24. restriction
7. Viennese	16. underpaid	25. remoteness
8. vibration	17. tremulous	
9. vertical	18. transfusion	

(B) Two-way dictation: without looking at the textbook, you and a partner each prepare a list of fifteen trisyllabic words marked for strong stress, and then read them out loud for each to write down. Once you have done so, compare your lists and make all necessary corrections for stress.

2.9 Strong-stressing words of four, five, and more syllables. Just 4,896 (19.50%) of all corpus words contain four, five, or more syllables, and the clear majority of them (3,406) are four-syllabled. Equally important is that only 1,172 of corpus entries strong-stress the pre (1,094), the qui (76), or the sixth (2) syllable from the end, thus confirming once more that strong stress moves only so far leftward.

In a language like English that prefers short words, it is no surprise that one reason why words of four, five, or more syllables ("four-plus words") get so long is because lots of affixes are attached to them. Take the five-syllable ant-stressed *insincérity*. If we analyze its MORPHEMES or 'minimal units of meaning' (7.5), we discover that *sincer(e)* is the root, *in-* is the prefix, and *-ity* the suffix. No wonder *insincérity* has five syllables! It's also no surprise that stress on most four-plus words is best understood in terms of their belonging to a particular word family. See, for example, the four-syllable words *accusátion, accúsative,* and *accúsingly.* The word family they belong to is:

04-pen	accusátion
02-ult	accúse
02-ult	accúsed
03-pen	accúser
03-pen	accúsing
04-ant	accúsingly
04-ant	accúsative

The base word is clearly *accúse,* to whose stress pattern *accúsed, accúser, accúsing, accúsingly,* and *accúsative* conform, as all stress the 'u'. Only *accusátion* deviates, and for the obvious reason that its suffix is the shifter *-tion,* which, as we know, always shifts a word's stress to the penult.

It is no accident that about 80 percent of all four-plus words carry affixes. Here are some examples: *inhábitant (inhabit + -ant), inhalátion (inhale + -(a)tion), inhéritance (inherit + -ance), inofénsive (in- + offens(e) + -ive), insánity (in- + san(e) + -ity), insubstántial (in- + substan(ce) + -ial), insúfferable (in- + suffer + -able).* So when you do not know where strong stress falls on a four-plus word, determine the word's base, and once you have done that, try to figure out whether the derived form's strong stress falls on the same vowel as the base's or on a different one. (Here are two examples: in *inhalátion,* the base word is *inhále,* and if it weren't for the suffix *-tion* we could assume that the stress would remain on *hál-,* thus: **inhálation.* In *insánity,* on the other hand, adding the suffix *-ity* to the root *insáne* does not alter the position of the stress because all *-ity* words are stressed on the antepenult.)

Exercise 2.7

Tell which of these four-plus words are strong-stressed on the ult, the pen, the ant, the pre, the qui, or the sex. Then explain stress position in each case. (In some cases there are multiple explanations.)

1. adversity	11. awakening	21. deliriously
2. affirmation	12. barbarity	22. diabolical
3. allowable	13. cannibalize	23. dispassionately
4. alternating	14. categorical	24. elasticity
5. amputation	15. agoraphobic	25. eroticism
6. analytic	16. antiquarian	26. spiritualism
7. appealingly	17. asphyxiation	27. indistinguishable
8. arterial	18. cannibalism	28. macroeconomics
9. atheism	19. conjunctivitis	29. internationalism
10. avaricious	20. conspicuously	30. counterrevolutionary

2.10 Weak stress: Placing the strong, locating the weak. We have already learned that each individual word has one and only one strong stress, and although we've also learned that determining strong stress's location is not always easy, we now have a good idea as to where strong stress goes. Such, alas, is less the case with weak stress.

For one thing, weak stress is variable: sometimes it appears and sometimes not. In a word such as *gráduàte*, it is fixed: the last syllable is always louder than the second one (compare the noun *gráduate*) but less prominent than the first, although this pattern is reversed in the suffixed form *gràduátion*. But in *window*, a weak stress often appears on the final syllable in a relatively slow, careful pronunciation, but it may disappear in a fast, more casual style (the /o/ may then become a schwa). As illustrated here, one factor in this variation is REGISTER (§1.4) or relative tempo, formality, and carefulness of speech. Another factor affecting the presence of weak stress is one's native dialect: regardless of register, Americans typically have a weak stress on the suffixes *-ary* and *-ory* (*prímàry, sécretàry, láboratòry*), whereas Britons do not (*prímary, sécretary, labóratory*).

2.11 Weak stress on bisyllabic words. As we study weak stress patterns, one principle to keep in mind (1.4) is that English stress "skips a syllable": not null stress but present stress is likely to follow a null stress. Chapter 1 also made it clear that the most-used English metrical patterns are the skip-a-syllable trochaic ($'\_'\_$ etc.) and iambic ($\_'\_'$ etc.). And one of the paramount principles of metricalism is that in a bounded language such as English, trochaic and iambic feet are "bound" to predominate. Sections 2.11.1–2.13.5 give details about weak stress in bisyllabic, trisyllabic, and four-plus words.

2.11.1 Bisyllabics that strong-stress the ult. In medium-register speech, bisyllabics that strong-stress the ult may weak-stress the pen if the pen syllable is closed or if its nucleus is a tense vowel (/i e o u/) or a diphthong (/ai au oi/). Otherwise the pen will be null-stressed. Pay attention to the following contrasts and to the transcriptions that follow them (the periods demarcate syllables):

the pen is weak-stressed	the pen is null-stressed
1. abduct /æ̀b.dʌ́kt/	abet /ə.bɛ́t/
abscond /æ̀b.skɑ́nd/	abuse /ə.bjúz/

In the preceding examples the pen syllable is weak-stressed when closed—*abduct, abscond*—but null-stressed when open: *abet, abuse*.

2. bisect /bài.sɛ́kt/	bizárre /bə.zɑ́r/

In these two examples the pen of *bisect* is weak-stressed because the vowel of the prefix *bi-* is pronounced as the diphthong /ài/, whereas the penult of *bizarre* is null-stressed because its *bi-* is **not** the diphthong-bearing prefix /bài/ but merely an inseparable nonprefix part of the word's base.

3. emboss /ɛ̀m.bɔ́s/   enóugh/ə.nʌ́f/

The first word's pen is weak-stressed because its syllable is closed, whereas the second word's pen syllable is open and therefore null-stressed. (Note that in high-register speech the 'e' of *enóugh* can be pronounced as the tense vowel /i/, though typically without weak stress: /i.nʌ́f/.)

The closed syllable/weak stress equivalency is reasonably evident among bisyllabic words beginning with vowels: *abórt, àbstáin, enáct, èndéar, ináne, ìmpéde, upón, ùplíft*. However, we must note again that **register** plays a role in determining whether weak stress or null will appear. Thus medium- and high-register *àbstáin* will become *abstáin* (/əb.stén/) in low-register speech, and the *enáct* /ənǽkt/of medium- and low-register speech may become *ènáct* (/ɛ̀nǽkt/) in high-register speech. It's also true that a complicated interaction between register and vowel quality determines whether weak stress will fall on a first syllable whose vowel may be tense, like *begrúdge* and *belíttle*, which are /bəgrʌ́dʒ/ and /bəlítəl/ in rapid-tempo speech but may be /bigrʌ́dʒ/ and /bilítəl/ in slower, more deliberate speech.[3] The same choice occurs in words that start with open-syllabled *de-*. Also recall what was said in a previous section (§2.6) about which prefixes carry strong stress and which do not.

2.11.2 Bisyllabics that strong-stress the pen. About 85 percent of all English words end in closed syllables, as does an equal percentage of pen-strong-stressed bisyllabics. With the latter there is a conflict between two rules: (1) closed syllables attract weak stress, and (2) weak stress skips a syllable and so should not follow a strong stress. The degree to which pen-strong-stressed bisyllabics weak-stress their ults is a function of **register** and **compounding**. Even low-register bisyllabic compounds will weak-stress ults: *áir-lìne, álmòst, állspìce, Ámtràk, ármpìt, báckstròke, bárebàck, báthròbe, bédpàn, bláckmàil*, and so on. And bisyllabics whose ult contains a tense vowel or a diphthong might weak-stress it in high-register: *ábbèy, áutò, báyòu, bíngò, blúejày*. Thus the percentage of pen-strong-stressed bisyllabics that **weak-stress their ult** can rise to as high as 75 percent. By contrast, here are some pen-strong-stressed bisyllabics that **null-stress their ults**, especially in low-register speech: *ábbot, ábsence, álbum, áltar, ánthem, ápple, áttic, áwful, bácon*.

Exercise 2.8

The following bisyllabic words have already been marked for strong stress. Your job is to determine whether the non-strong-stressed syllable carries **weak** stress or not, or whether it carries weak stress in certain registers only. (Hint: does it always have a schwa?) After deciding to weak-stress a syllable, explain your decision.

1. abóve	9. cascáde	17. decáy
2. arcáde	10. compláin	18. depráved
3. behínd	11. bágel	19. bétter
4. álbum	12. bállpoint	20. bíjou

5. ámply	13. bárber	21. bíshop
6. abóut	14. confórm	22. discúss
7. áshtray	15. báseless	23. divért
8. biséct	16. básement	24. bóbby

2.12 Weak-stressing trisyllabic words. The **skip-a-syllable rule**, first mentioned in chapter 1 and discussed again in this chapter (§2.11), is given full play in trisyllabic words that are strong-stressed on either the ult or the ant (though for obvious reasons not on the pen). As a consequence of this rule, a present stress is more likely to be followed by a null stress than by another present stress. Thus an 03-ant (ant-strong-stressed trisyllabic) is likely to manifest a ′ _ ‵ pattern and an ult-strong-stressed trisyllabic a ‵ _ ′ pattern. (Here, as elsewhere, _ represents null stress.)

Let's put the skip-a-syllable rule to the test, first with **03-ant** words (ant-strong-stressed trisyllabics). Allowing as always for register variability, we can say that about 75 percent of all 03-ants follow a ′ _ ‵ pattern: *ábdicàte, ábsolùte, ácclimàte, áccolàde, ácetòne, ácronỳm, áctivàte,* and so on. But the remaining 25 percent do not; instead, no weak stress appears on the ult, so the pattern is ′ _ _ (*ábdomen, ábstinence, áccident, áccurate, áctivist, áctual,* etc.). One good reason why *ácclimàte* weak-stresses the ult, while *áccurate* does not is that *ácclimàte* is a verb, whereas *áccurate* is an adjective.[4] On the other hand, **all** members of the admittedly smaller category of **03-ult** words follow the skip-a-syllable rule, producing ‵ _ ′ stress patterns: *àbsentée, àcquiésce, àpprehénd, àuctionéer, còexíst, còmprehénd, dèbonáir, dìagnóse, dìsagrée.* In some cases the ant syllable's weak stress is very potent, giving the false impression that a particular word has two strong stresses. This is prompted by the well-known tendency of English to stress the ant.

A trickier category, **03-pen** words either do or do not weak-stress ults or pens according to factors we've already examined: syllabicity, affixation, and register.

Exercise 2.9

(A) The following trisyllabic words are already marked for strong stress. Your job is to determine whether the non-strong-stressed syllables carry **weak** stress or not, or whether they carry weak stress in certain registers only. (Hint: does it always have a schwa?) After deciding to weak-stress a syllable, explain your decision.

1. attaché	9. admónish	17. áppetite
2. bassinét	10. diagnóse	18. appéarance
3. cavalíer	11. disconnéct	19. attríbute
4. ágency	12. dominéer	20. impolíte
5. ágonize	13. agréement	21. misdiréct
6. álcohol	14. albíno	22. báckbiting
7. acérbic	15. ambítion	23. blásphemy
8. acquíttal	16. ánnotate	24. belábo(u)r

(B) The following place names are stressed on the ult in their languages of origin. When you pronounce them in English, on which ones do you move the strong stress to an earlier syllable? Your stress relocations may not be uniform within each group, but what general difference emerges between the way you treat the first group and the way you treat the second? Explain, using what you have learned in this chapter.

Group 1: Panamá, Bogotá, Istanbúl, Trinidád, Uruguáy, Yucatán, Volgográd, Montreál, Afghanistán, Pakistán, Ecuadór, El Salvadór, Bangladésh, Cameróon

Group 2: Beijíng, Brazíl, Perú, Haití, Madríd, Berlín, Beirút, Irán, Dakár, Japán, Taiwán, Versáilles, Kuwáit, Baghdád, Quebéc, Tibét, Shanghái, Sudán, Algíers

2.13 Weak-stressing "four-plus" words. The skip-a-syllable rule is variously applied to four-plus words; many have it, but not all. In order to assign weak stress, it will prove helpful to analyze the nearly 5,000 four-plus words of our corpus on the basis of which syllable they strong-stress—the ult, the pen, the ant, and beyond.[5]

2.13.1 Ult stress patterns. The small **04-ult** and even smaller **05-ult** categories prefer a ` _ _ ' or a ` ` _ ' pattern (with a closed syllable or register-determined second weak stress); thirty-one of the thirty-nine entries follow these two patterns, among them *chàriotéer, ìnòpportúne, mìsùnderstánd, òverachíeve, Sènegalése,* and *sùperimpóse.* The remaining eight have patterned thus— _ ` _ ' —in part because most lack a word-initial closed syllable. Some examples: *apèritíf, commìssionáire, elèctionéer.*

2.13.2 Pen stress patterns. On the other hand, **all** 954 entries in the large **04-pen** category are stressed as follows: ` _ ' _ or else ` ` ` _. Once again, considerations of (closed) syllable status and register determine the presence of a second weak stress, as the following examples show:[6]

* No second weak stress (` _ ' _): *àbolítion, àbsolútion, àcclamátion, àdmirátion, àdmonítion*
* Second weak stress possible (` ` ` _): *àdàptátion, àffèctátion, cóndènsátion*

Other 04-pen entries are stressed like those belonging to the 40 percent of the 04-pen category that consists of nouns ending in *-tion* (also *-sion/-xion/-cian*): *ùltrasónic, ùnàmbítious, ùnassísted, ùnassúming, vìtriólic, whàtsoéver, àcclamátion, còmprehénsion.*

In the 05-pen, 06-pen, and 07-pen categories, the 04-pen ` _ ' _ skip-a-syllable pattern spreads leftward according to the number of syllables in the word; thus ` _ ' _ in *àgitátion* (04-pen), _ ` _ ' _ in *assàssinátion* (05-pen), ` _ ` _ ' _ in *mìsintèrpretátion* (06-pen), and so forth. However, if the word is a compound or an expanded base whose first element preserves a prior stress pattern, or if the word's first syllable is closed, then you will typically find an alternative pattern, that is, a word-initial weak stress plus two null stresses: *àgoraphóbic* (` _ _ ' _), *àmplificátion, àuthorizátion, càrcinogénic, chàracterístic, clàrificátion, còunterprodúctive.* It is also the case, here as elsewhere, that the diphthongs /ai oi au/ and the four tense vowel sounds /i e o u/ do not reduce to schwa even though they lack weak stress. This is particularly true when they occur before a vowel or at the end of a prefix. In these examples, nonreducing tense vowels and diphthongs are underlined: *àntibiótic, àntidepréssant, dècòmposítion, deprèciátion, detèrminátion.*

These constraints produce some extremely unusual stress patterns in 06- and 07-pen words. Take, for example, *dècimalizátion, nàtionalizátion,* and *ràtionalizátion,* whose shared stress pattern is ` _ _ _ ´ _, and *Amèricanizátion,* with _ ` _ _ _ ´ _. What these words share are **three** consecutive null stresses. (Earlier we noted that only a few words contain three consecutive nulls. These four are among them.) To do away with the three consecutive nulls, some speakers—the British, in particular— retain the verb's weak-stressed /ài/ (of *-ize/-ise*) rather than changing it to schwa: *dècimalìzátion, nàtionalìzátion, ràtionalìzátion.* Other nouns ending in *-ization* sporadically retain /ài/ even though they lack the three successive nulls; thus *nòrmalìzátion, fràternìzátion.*

Exercise 2.10

(A) The following four-plus pen words have already been marked for strong stress. Your job is to determine whether the non-strong-stressed syllables carry **weak** stress or not, or whether they carry weak stress in certain registers only. (Once again, check for schwas that are register-proof.) After deciding to weak-stress a syllable, explain your decision.

1. overexpósure	11. demarcátion	21. carcinogénic
2. examinátion	12. diabétic	22. ecclesiástic
3. opportunístic	13. epidérmis	23. gratificátion
4. superinténdent	14. Európean	24. naturalizátion
5. misrepresénted	15. explorátion	25. decentralizátion
6. altercátion	16. incandéscent	26. insubordinátion
7. apopléctic	17. inofténsive	27. misappropriátion
8. avarícious	18. mediócre	28. telecommunicátions
9. condensátion	19. agglomerátion	
10. controvérsial	20. anticipátion	

(B) Two-way dictation: Without looking at the textbook, you and your partner each write a separate list of fifteen four-plus words, which you will mark for strong and weak stress. Each then reads his/her list to the other, who in turn will mark the dictated words for stress. Next, the two of you compare the several lists, checking for accuracy in stress-marking.

2.13.3 Ant(epenultimate) stress patterns. Closed syllable status also affects the location of weak stress in ant words. In items strong-stressed on the ant, most though not all closed syllables carry weak stress. The syllable just to the right of the strong stress is almost always null-stressed—*corróbo̲ràte* (null underlined)—so the word-final syllable of *corróboràte* is the one affected by alternating stress and closed syllable status.

While about two-thirds of all words strong-stressed on the ant begin with open syllables, the rest do not. The following contrasts thus prove instructive; all example words are 04-ants. (Those followed by "(∅)" may null-stress the first syllable in lower registers.)

First syllable open, thus null	First syllable closed, thus weak
abándonment	àbnórmally
abbréviàte[7]	àbsúrdity (∅)
acádemy	àccéleràte (∅)
adáptable	àdmínister (∅)
alácrity	Àlbánia
amícably (more often *ámicably*)	àmphétamìne
banálity	bàctéria
capácity	càptívity

Some prefixes forming closed syllables resist weak stress: *com-* (*compárison, complácency, compúlsory*), *con-* (*condítional, consécutìve, convívial*), *per-* (*percéptibly, perpétuàte, persónifỳ*). However, many other prefixes forming closed syllables **do** carry weak stress, at least in higher registers: *dìscóvery, dìscrépancy, dìsgrácefully; èxcéedingly, èxclúsively, èxtérminàte; ìmpássively, ìmpérsonàte, ìmprísonment, ìncíneràte, ìncórporàte, ìndécency; sùbcónsciously, sùbcóntinent, sùbmíssiveness; trànsférable, trànspárency; ùnbéarable, ùncértainty, ùnclássified.* These examples have been taken from the 04-ant category's 1,676 entries; a look at the smaller 05-ant category reveals that the longer the word, the more likely its prefix will be stressed—even when that prefix is not a closed syllable. This is no surprise, given English's preference for trochaic/iambic metricality, in which stress skips a syllable. Thus an 05-ant word, especially in high register, is almost destined to conform to this stress pattern: ` _ ′ _ `. Some 05-ants conform perfectly: *àphrodísiàc, cìrcumnávigàte, còmpartméntalìze, dìfferéntiàte.* As was true of 04-ants, closed syllables and tense vowels impose eccentric patterns on a significant number of 05-ants. On the other hand, words ending in suffixes such as *-al, -ant, -ia(n),* and *-ous* **never** take any sort of present stress, even in the highest registers: *àboríginal, àcrimónious, àllegórical, Àmeríndian, ànatómical, ànoréxia, àntipérspirant, àrchitéctural, àstronómical.*

Six- and seven-syllable ants behave like 04-/05-ants: the skip-a-syllable weak/null alternation spreads leftward, producing _ ` _ ′ _ ` in most six- and ` _ ` _ ′ _ ` in most seven-syllable words, though again, subject to considerations of syllable status and register. Here are some 06-ants that conform to expectations: *accèptabílity, accèssibílity, accòuntabílity, adàptabílity, avàilabílty, compàtibílity, desìrabílity, dìssìmilárity.* The following 06-ants, though, do **not** conform to the pattern: *ànthropológical, authòritárian, còèducátional, conspìratórial, dìsciplinárian, ègàlitárian.* Almost all the words in the small 07-ant category end in *-y*, and most conform to the expected patterns: *cònfidèntiálity, ìnaccèssibílity, nòn-denòminátional, phòtoòpportúnity, sùperficiálity, ùnenthùsiástically.*

Exercise 2.11

The following four-plus ant words have already been marked for strong stress. Your job is to determine whether the non-strong-stressed syllables carry **weak** stress or not, or whether they carry weak stress in certain registers only. After deciding to weak-stress a syllable, explain your decision.

1. antágonize	9. basílica	17. diálysis
2. protágonist	10. barbítuate	18. aliméntary
3. accéssible	11. concéivable	19. biochémistry
4. acclímatize	12. concéivably	20. susceptibílity
5. acídity	13. amálgamate	21. differéntiate
6. advénturer	14. defíantly	22. choreógraphy
7. affíliate	15. demónstrative	23. extramárital
8. Albánian	16. kleptócracy	24. evolútionary

2.13.4 Pre(antepenultimate) stress patterns. Just over 67.5 percent of all pre words are **four-syllabled** and are stressed on the initial syllable. The stress pattern then is primarily skip-a-syllable (′ _ ` _ ) but it can also be ′ _ _ `, ′ ` _ `, ′ _ `, ′ ` `, ′ ` _ _, or even ′ ` ` `, depending, as usual, on syllable status and register. Examples of the main ′ _ ` _ stress pattern include *ádvertìser, ágitàtor, ágribùsiness, ágricùlture, ácupùncture, álligàtor,* and *álternàtor.* But there are some mouthfuls that show no weak stress at all: *pósthumously, vúlnerable, ámicable, ápplicable, fórmidable, tólerable.*[8]

  Five-syllable pre's pattern are like four-syllable pre's, with the significant difference that an 05-pre's word-initial syllable is either weak-stressed when closed or null-stressed when open. Again, skip-a-syllable patterns predominate, though there is no lack of the other patterns that typify 04-pre's. Here are some 05-pre skip-a-syllables: *accéleràtor, accómodàting, accúmulàtor, adjúdicàtor, ascéticìsm, authóritàtive, demóralìzing, emáncipàted, emúlsifìer, idéalìsm.* As in other categories, certain prefixes—especially if closed syllables—take weak stress in high registers but not in low: *dèpérsonalìze, dìscríminàting, èxpánsionìsm, èxtraórdinàry, ìncórrigible, ìnvéstigàtor, prècáutionàry, prèméditàted, ùnáppetìzing, ùpróariously.* The small-to-tiny **06-pre, 07-pre, and 08-pre** categories only differ from their 04-pre/05-pre siblings in that leftward growth adds null and weak stresses where expected. Thus all 06-pre's begin with a weak stressed syllable (*còunteréspionàge, èducátionally, èxisténtialìsm, ìnstitútionalìze, ìntermédiàry, òverpópulàted, sàdomásochìsm, ùncoórdinàted*). The three 07-pre/08-pre entries show much weak-stressing, especially in the higher registers: *pòlyùnsáturàted, ùncèremóniously, còunterrèvolútionàry.* Such long words may give the impression of having **two** strong stresses: *pólyùnsáturàted, cóunterrèvolútionàry*; however, the prefix stress is only as strong as the root stress when the prefix is "peak-"stressed for contrastive purposes as explained in chapter 3 ("He's not a revo**lu**tionary, he's a **counter**revolutionary!").

Exercise 2.12

The following four-plus pre words have already been marked for strong stress. Your job is to determine whether the non-strong-stressed syllables carry **weak** stress or not, or whether they carry weak stress in certain registers only. After deciding to weak-stress a syllable, explain your decision.

1. áctuary	9. ánybody	17. Jánuary
2. ágitated	10. cálculator	18. léniency
3. árguable	11. cánnibalize	19. márriageable
4. álienate	12. éscalator	20. accúmulator
5. ámiably	13. cáutionary	21. admínistrator
6. ádversary	14. célibacy	22. bellígerently
7. áppetizer	15. cháritable	23. indústrialist
8. átheism	16. dífficulty	24. dispássionately

2.13.5 Qui stress patterns. By definition, all seventy-six qui-stressed words have at least five syllables and so are "very long," and while about 75 percent of them run to just five syllables, fifteen have six, and a tiny handful have seven or even eight syllables. All 05-qui's are stressed word initially and thus give rise to the same complicated weak/null alternations that 04-pre words do: we find our old friend the skip-a-syllable (′ _ ` _ `) in words such as *áircondìtionìng, háberdàshery, írritàtingly,* and *mícrosùrgery* alongside the deviant ′ _ _ ` _ (as in *cánnibalìsm, cápitalìsm*), ′ _ ` ` _ (*álcohòlìsm*), and others. And here too, considerations of syllabicity loom large in determining what gets weak-stressed and what gets null-stressed. Words belonging to the 06-qui group will only weak-stress their initial syllable if it is closed (*èxcrúciatingly, ìmpérialìsm*) or if it is tense-voweled and pronounced in high register (*rèpúblicanìsm, rètáliatòry*). Nonetheless, even very long words such as 07-qui's *indivídualìsm, interdísciplinàry,* and *vègetárianìsm* and 08-qui's *totàlitárianìsm* basically conform to the ever-important skip-a-syllable principle.

Exercise 2.13

The following four-plus qui words have already been marked for strong stress. Your job is to determine whether the non-strong-stressed syllables carry **weak** stress or not, or whether they carry weak stress in certain registers only. After deciding to weak-stress a syllable, explain your decision.

1. ágonizingly	5. mícrocomputer	9. colónialism
2. dísciplinary	6. quálitatively	10. inálienable

3. gérrymandering   7. régulatory   11. unrécognizable

4. lésbianism   8. télecommuting   12. internátionalism

2.14 Vowel reduction: The price we pay for shifting stress. We have just examined many examples of words each containing at least one null stress. As noted in chapter 1 (§1.4), English vowels that are null-stressed tend to be pronounced as schwa—the mid-central lax vowel represented by the symbol /ə/[9] (see figure 1.d). There are exceptions to this trend: the tense vowels /i e o u/ and the full diphthongs /ai au oi/ generally do not become /ə/ when they precede another vowel (*various*) or come at the end of a word (*vary*), even if totally null-stressed. One way we proved that a word has a schwa was by examining pairs of closely related items in which stress shifts from one syllable to another so that a full vowel alternates with a schwa. When full vowels become schwas, the full vowel has been REDUCED to schwa—VOWEL REDUCTION has occurred.

Chapter 4 will examine how vowel reduction complicates English orthography, not only for writers trying to spell, but also for readers trying to figure out how a word should be pronounced. Chapters 5 and 7 will detail the phonological aspects of vowel reduction. The present chapter, which examines the placement of strong and weak stress, has established this rule for predicting reduction: locate the presence of stresses elsewhere in the word. Let us now review—this time using phonetic symbols—specific examples of vowel reduction, the better, once again, to understand the process.

What appears in figure 2.i is a brief list of word pairs in which one or more full vowels or diphthongs turn into schwas, and all because of a shift in stress. For example, in the first syllable of the pair *àbdóminal/ábdomen*, the strong-stressed /æ/ of *ábdomen* remains /æ/ in *àbdóminal*, for though it's now a weak-stressed /æ/, the weak stress is enough to prevent reduction. In the pair's next syllable, however, the /á/ sound of the underlined syllable

Figure 2.i. Vowel reduction

The vowels involved are underlined.

Full vowel	*Vowel is full when stressed*	*Vowel reduces to schwa when unstressed*
/i/	hòmogéneous /hòmədʒíniəs/	homógenize /həmádʒənàiz/
/ɪ/	oríginal /ərídʒənəl/	órigin /ɔ́rədʒən/ or /árədʒən/
/e/	áble /ébəl/	abílity /əbíləti/
/ɛ/	rebéllion /rəbéljən/	rébel /rɛ́bəl/
/æ/	acádemy /əkǽdəmi/	àcadémic /ækədémək/
/ɑ/	abólish /əbɑ́ləʃ/	àbolítion /æbəlíʃən/
/ɔ/	áuthor /ɔ́θər/	authòritárian /əθɔ̀rətérriən /
/o/	convóke /kənvók/	cònvocátion /kànvəkéʃən/
/ʌ/	confrónt /kənfrʌ́nt/	cònfrontátion /kànfrəntéʃən/
/u/	compúte /kəmpjút/	còmputátion /kàmpjətéʃən/
/ai/	admíre /ədmáir/ or /ædmáir/	àdmirátion /ædməréʃən/

àbdóminal gets reduced to the schwa sound /ə/ of *ábdomen*, for the *do* syllable lacks all stress, strong or weak.

How vowel reduction complicates both encoding and decoding is easy to see by comparing the two components of any of the pairs in figure 2.i. In *admíre/àdmirátion*, for example, one **hears** two different vowel sounds, /ái/ and /ə/—but these are spelled alike; in similar fashion one **sees** a single vowel GRAPHEME ('letter of the alphabet'), the 'i,' which is pronounced one way in the first word and another way in the second. Even greater complications arise when there is a schwa not shown by any grapheme (as in the common suffix *-ism* /ɪzəm/) or a grapheme that is not pronounced at all, as when the schwa reduces so much that it actually drops out. As noted in chapters 5–7, this dropping occurs primarily in medial positions before the consonants /l r m n/:

carefully → *"caref'lly"*
temperature → *"temp'rature"*
aspirin → *"asp'rin"*
softener → *"soft'ner"*

Schwa-dropping is just one more indication that English is the sort of language that constantly strives to turn long words into shorter ones, reducing a five-syllable word to four syllables, a four-syllable word to three, a three-syllable word to two, and a two-syllable word to one when possible.

Exercise 2.14

(A) Do three things here: (1) mark all strong stresses; (2) identify which item is probably the base word; and (3) point to changes in vowel quality that took place because of shifts in strong stress.

   1. general, generality, generalization, generalize, generally
   2. drama, dramatic, dramatically, dramatics, dramatist, dramatization, dramatize
   3. ecological, ecologically, ecologist, ecology, ecosystem
   4. fraternal, fraternity, fraternization, fraternize, fratricide
   5. infinite, infinitely, infinitesimal, infinitive, infinity

(B) Write several words that are related to each of the following. The words you write must contain a schwa and must entail a shift in stress. Here is an example of how to proceed:

   Example: *drama*—dramátic, dramátically, dramatícity, dramatizátion

   1. brútal   4. póssible   7. frágile
   2. revére   5. rápid
   3. jánitor   6. bómb

(C) In the following words, circle each null-stressed vowel letter whose pronunciation is reduced to total disappearance. Note: in some words, no vowel is reduced to total disappearance.

1. laboratory	6. artistically	11. brutally
2. alphabetically	7. astronomically	12. categorically
3. annually	8. authentically	13. commercially
4. artificially	9. bashfully	14. restaurant
5. chocolate	10. blissfully	15. politicization

2.15 Teaching the topics of chapter 2 to students of ESOL. The two techniques—DRUMSTICKS and WHISTLING—that chapter 1 recommended for teaching metrical patterns to ESOL students will help teach the stress patterns of individual words; see §1.6 for details. Dalton and Seidlhofer (1994, chap. 8) give a critical overview of other ways to promote recognition and application of English stress patterns, but in our experience the following four techniques are especially effective to teach the stress patterns of single words: (1) STRESS EQUIVOCATION, (2) DRAG STRIP, (3) BACKWARDS BUILDUP, and (4) FLOODING. Let's examine each of them in turn.

(1) STRESS EQUIVOCATION (i.e., "stresSÍNG the inCÓRrect sylLÁBle"): Take any multisyllabic word and pronounce it to your students in as many different ways as the word has syllables. So if the word has two syllables, you pronounce it two different ways, if three syllables then three different ways, and so on. Next you ask your students: "Which was the correct pronunciation—the one that stressed the first syllable or the one that stressed the second (or, in longer words, the third, the fourth, and so forth)?" Repeat the several pronunciations as many times as necessary. Here is an example of how to proceed: "Look at the next word on your handout/the board/the screen (etc.). In theory there are three ways to stress it: *cóndition, condítion,* and *condition.* Which was the correct way?" Among students whose command of English is quite limited, you won't be able to rely entirely on their intuition to let them determine which of the several stress patterns is correct; instead, you yourself will have to model the word's correct pronunciation before you present its incorrect versions. Here is an example of how to proceed when teaching students whose English is limited: "Our next word is *condition—condítion, condítion, condítion.* How did I just pronounce it: as syllable-one-stressed *cóndition,* as syllable-two-stressed *condítion,* or as syllable-three-stressed *condition?*" Remember that when using STRESS EQUIVOCATION to change the position of the stress you will also be changing the way the word's vowels are pronounced. For example, the pen syllable's 'i' will be a schwa when **cóndition* is stressed (incorrectly) on the ant, but a high front lax vowel /ɪ/ when it is correctly stressed on the pen.

(2) DRAG STRIP. One way to make sure that your students fully hear which syllable is stressed is for you to draaaaaaaaaaag oooooooooout its stressed vowel sound(s) and then have your students do the same. This requires a considerable amount of exaggeration. Let's use just one example, the 05-pen *considerátion.* Say the word like this: "con.siiiiii.de.raaaaaaaaaaaaaaaa.tion," making sure that you drag out both stressed syllables

but in proportion to their degree of stress. Have them repeat it that same way. Then point out the weak and strong stresses.

(3) BACKWARDS BUILDUP means pronouncing a word from the back to the front ("right to left") rather than normally, which is from the front ("left") to the back ("right"). Before you build up a word backwards, determine its metric feet and use that knowledge to produce the backwards buildup. Here is how to proceed: *sùbstitútion*—"tútion," "sùbsti." It is not easy to get students to pronounce things backwards, but once they are used to doing so they will gain a greater understanding of the relationship between strong-stressed syllables and weak-stressed syllables. There follows one more example of the BACKWARDS BUILDUP technique: *càpabílity*—"bílity," "càpa."

(4) In FLOODING, students are bombarded with examples of words that illustrate a particular point and conform to a specific pattern. The purpose of FLOODING is twofold: to make students aware of how many words there are that conform to the pattern being presented, and to imprint that pattern on students' memory and give them a maximum amount of practice with it. Any substantial list of words conforming to any given pattern will illustrate flooding—for example, the "03-ant" file in the Corpus on the CD. (The more than sixty files in that Corpus, explained in the appendix, make it very easy for you to quickly locate a large number of words that exemplify all sorts of phenomena.) Several things can be done in the classroom with such a "flooded" list: individual students can read from it out loud, instructors can base an extensive dictation on the list's words, or groups of students can read from the list together, as in a chorus. Students can even pick out 03-ant words that rhyme with each other—for example, *activate, aggravate, allocate, alternate, amputate, animate, arbitrate, automate, candidate, captivate, castigate*, and also *absently, actively, aimlessly, basically, beautifully, blatantly, blissfully, callously, carefully, carelessly, cautiously, cheerfully*—and then write sentences or poems containing them. Or you can write a nonsense verse of your own that is full of items conforming to the specified pattern, such as "Jéremy cállously dénigrates éverything / Éagerly ínjuring móribund prísoners / Sávagely slándering lécherous lándowners / Hátefully chástising pótbellied óutpatients." Then have your students recite the verse that they or you have written, rapidly chanting the rhymes. (Tell them to start their recitation slowly and then work up to a more rapid rate.)

NOTES

1. What we present in figure 2.f. are useful pedagogical generalizations about related words, not a rigorous morphological analysis. We therefore use the term ENDING in the simple sense of 'how a word ends,' not necessarily a suffix. Some of the endings (e.g., *-tion, -ity, -ese*) are clearly suffixes and will be called that; some (*-bian, -dian, -mous*) contain a portion of the stem with the actual suffixes (*-ian, -ous*); others consist of two suffixes (*-ographer*); still others (*-ant, -ent*) can be considered variants of the same suffix; and a few (e.g., *-meter*) might qualify as stems. In pairs such as *húman/humáne* and *úrban/urbáne*, there may be no real suffix at all. This listing simply reflects the basis of our statistical analysis, which showed that not all "endings" containing the same or comparable suffixes (*-bian* and *-ean*, for instance) cued stress shifts with equal frequency.

Note too that the arrow → in this list is not being used in its common sense of 'becomes' but merely as a way of relating two forms that illustrate the stress shift.

2. Remember that there **are** important exceptions for many endings. Thus although *-ant* is predominantly nonshifting, as in the example of *assíst(ant)* in figure 2.g and also in *resíst(ant), depénd(ent), repél(l)(ant)*, and so on, there are indeed exceptions to that tendency: for example, *sígnify* → *signíficant, protést* → *Prótestant*, etc.

3. In a medium register, many speakers also use a sort of lax /ɪ/ in prefixes such as *be-*: *belittle* /bi-, bɪ-, bə-/. Lower registers also produce differences in consonant pronunciation, for example, the flapping of the /t/ and the syllabification of the /l/ (as we will see in chapter 6), but we are keeping a broad transcription here to focus on stress.

4. Cf. also the contrast between the verbs *móderàte, gráduàte, séparàte, artículàte, dúplicàte, assóciàte, ádvocàte, affíliàte, délegàte, delíberàte, degéneràte, subórdinàte, póstulàte* (all ending in *-/èt/*) and the corresponding adjectives or nouns *móderate, gráduate, séparate, artículate, dúplicate, assóciate, ádvocate, affiliate, délegate, delíberate, degénerate, subórdinate, póstulate* (all ending in *-/ət/*).

5. Sufficient numbers of *pre*'s and *qui*'s exist for us to discuss them. But as only two words—*spíritualism* and *mícroorganism*—are strong-stressed on the sixth-last syllable, we eliminate that category from further analysis. (What is more, the second of these words is alternately strong-stressed on the *pre*.)

6. This second weak stress is weaker than the first, and in theories that recognize numbered degrees of stress (Chomsky and Halle 1968) for primary, secondary, and tertiary, *adaptation* would be shown as **a̋dȁpta̒tȉon**. For a critique of theories such as Chomsky and Halle's that recognize three numbered degrees of stress, see Brazil (1985).

7. In *abbréviàte,* the double 'b' gives the false impression that it closes the initial syllable. In actual pronunciation there's only one /b/ sound.

8. In standard English, *ápplicable, fórmidable,* and *ámicable* have three null stresses after the strong stress and thus no weak-stress alternation. The fact that some speakers feel this pattern is abnormal is shown by their restressing these words as *applícable, formídable,* and *amícable*. In the case of *applícable*, one could argue that there has been influence from the stress pattern of the verb *applý*, but there are no comparable base words to prompt the restressing of the other two adjectives.

9. The zone of articulation of schwa /ə/ is sometimes very close to that of /ɪ/, and some speakers in fact use a type of unstressed /ɪ/ in the final syllable of *aspirin* and certain other examples given here. See §5.5 for more on the reduced vowels and their variation in English.

CHAPTER 3

Intonation—
The Melodic Line

3.1 "Peak" stress for contrast and emphasis. In order to contrast ('contrást') two things, or in order to emphasize a word in a sentence, English often employs a heightened form of stress that we call PEAK STRESS. Peak stress combines three effects to highlight a word: pitch, loudness, and sometimes length. PITCH is the frequency of vibration of the sound-producing instrument—in this case, the human voice; faster (more frequent) vibration is perceived as higher pitch, and slower vibration is heard as a lower pitch. LOUDNESS is the amplitude or forcefulness of vibration and is perceived as volume—from loud to soft, as measured in decibels. Pitch and loudness are not the same thing; in the sentence *Did you say to forgét about it?*: the syllable *-get* is loudest in volume, but *-bout it?* has the highest pitch. LENGTH is the duration of a sound or syllable. Thus a syllable with peak stress is louder and has a markedly higher (sometimes lower) pitch than other syllables that carry main stress in the sentence; a peak-stressed syllable may also be longer. (For more on the acoustics of pitch, volume, and length, see the appendix.)

Throughout the rest of this chapter and beyond, example sentences will *double-underline* peak-stressed words or syllables. (Those with the earphones symbol can be heard on audio track 5, "**Section 3.1**" on the CD.) Here is an example:

☊(1) Ì dón't wànt <u>lémons</u>, Ì wànt <u>óranges</u>.[1]

In sentence (1), *lemons* and *oranges* are both peak-stressed for contrastive purposes: the speaker is contrasting a preference for the one with a rejection of the other. If the two components of sentence (1) were not juxtaposed, the need to use peak-stressing for contrastive purposes would disappear, thus:

(1a) *Hè bóught some lémons* becáuse they were òn sále.

(1b) (Now that you're giving me a choice of fruit for breakfast,) *Ì wànt óranges* (, tàngerínes, grápefrùit, and apples).

Peak-stress placement never breaks the rules for strong-stress; thus the peak-stressed version of these two words is necessarily *lémons* and *óranges*, not **lemóns* and **oránges* or **orangés*.[2] However, it is true that for purposes of contrast, otherwise non-strong-stressed prefixes can become peak-stressed and thus strong-stressed. This is known as STRESS RELOCATION. Here is an example:

🎧(2) Whỳ hé ìsn't respéctful, hé's véry dísrespèctful; ìn fáct, hé's bèen extrémely dìsrespéctful évery síngle tíme wè've mét!

Emphasis, not contrast, is marked by the peak-stressing in sentence (3):

🎧(3) Itálians lóve grándiòse óperas.

Sentence (3) peak-stresses the verb to exaggerate the way that Italians supposedly feel toward grandiose operas. In such a sentence, the verb can also be peak-stressed for **contrastive** purposes, perhaps to contradict something that someone has just said. For example:

🎧(3a) [person 1] Sómeone ónce tóld me that Itálians háte grándiòse óperas.
        [person 2] Whỳ thát's nòt trúe at áll. Itálians lóve grándiòse óperas!

In sentences in which peak stress is used to mark emphasis, peak stress can fall on just about any word, depending, of course, on which information the speaker is trying to call attention to or is presupposing as the topic of the discourse (Brazil 1985, 61). For example, the adjective *grandiose* or the noun *Italians* could be peak-stressed, either to emphasize or to contrast:

🎧(3b) Itálians lóve grándiòse óperas but háte mìnimalístic óperas.

🎧(3c) Itálians lóve grándiòse óperas but Koréans do nót.

In words that are long, one syllable can come across as being more peak-stressed than the rest of the word:

🎧(4) Whỳ thát's jùst fábulous!

🎧(5) Hè's nót a rèvolútionàry, hè's a cóunterrèvolùtionàry.

🎧(6) Shé tóld hím to rèwríte the entíre dìssertátion?

It is also possible for more than one peak stress to appear in a sentence, especially if the sentence contains some highly emotional content, or if the speaker is seeking to emphasize a number of different things at once, or if he/she is highly dramatic or is being sarcastic. In sum, the function of peak stress (whether single or multiple) is to catch the hearer's attention; specific intent and interpretation depend on the context of the extended discourse. Here are some examples:

🎧(7) It is <u>áb</u>solùtely ìmp<u>óss</u>ible for mé to dò <u>ány</u>thìng at <u>áll</u> for èither <u>yóu</u> <u>ór</u> your chíldren.

🎧(8) Júst dróp bỳ <u>ány tíme</u>. The cóffee pòt is <u>ál</u>ways <u>ón</u>, and thère's <u>nóth</u>ing <u>móre</u> that Ì lóve to dó than sìt <u>ríght</u> <u>dówn</u> and hàve a <u>lóoooong</u> gábfest.

🎧(9) Wèll if <u>thát's</u> the wáy you féel, thèn by <u>áll</u> <u>méans</u> go <u>rìght</u> <u>ahéad</u> and dó the jób <u>yóur</u> way.

Section §3.4 will explore further the various uses of peak stress.

Exercise 3.1

(A) Read aloud each one of the following sentences. Exaggerate the double-underlined peak stresses by raising the pitch and/or lengthening the vowel while making the whole syllable louder.

    1. Italians <u>love</u> grandiose operas.
    2. Italians love <u>grandiose</u> operas.
    3. I just can't <u>stand</u> her.
    4. You mean we're going to have to <u>move</u>?
    5. You mean we're going to <u>have</u> to move?
    6. You mean <u>we're</u> going to have to move?
    7. Do you really <u>mean</u> we're going to have to move?
    8. The quick brown fox jumped over the lazy sleeping dog.
    9. The <u>quick</u> brown fox jumped over the lazy sleeping dog.
  10. The quick <u>brown</u> fox jumped over the lazy sleeping dog.
  11. The quick brown <u>fox</u> jumped over the lazy sleeping dog.
  12. The quick brown fox <u>jumped</u> over the lazy sleeping dog.
  13. The quick brown fox jumped <u>over</u> the lazy sleeping dog.
  14. The quick brown fox jumped over the <u>lazy</u> sleeping dog.

(B) Now explain the differences in meaning and context among the six sentences—nos. 9–14—involving the quick brown fox and the lazy sleeping dog. Here's an example of how to proceed: "In number 9 we're talking about the brown fox that is <u>quick</u>, as opposed to some <u>other</u> brown fox that is <u>not</u> so quick." Always use the phrase "as opposed to" in your explanation.

(C) Read aloud the following sentences, all of which have multiple peak stresses. (Doing this will really test your skills as an actor!)

   1. It is <u>ab</u>solutely im<u>poss</u>ible for me to do <u>any</u>thing at <u>all</u> for either <u>you</u> <u>or</u> your children.
   2. Unless <u>some</u>body does <u>some</u>thing for that poor victim, she's going to simply <u>shri</u>vel <u>up</u> and <u>die</u> from shame.

3.2 Some analogies with music. People who can read music already know about such notions as musical scales; treble and bass clefs; whole notes, half notes, quarter notes, and eighth notes; and slow, moderate, and fast tempos. It is not the purpose of this section to present anything that even comes close to the sort of instruction you would get in a music class, but we will survey some basics needed for understanding English intonation.

INTONATION is a series of pitches sung over a whole utterance; intonation is also known as MELODIC LINE. Indeed, the Latin origins of the word *intonation*—"*in + ton[e] + ation*" or 'conversion (of something) into a tone, tune, or melody'—make it clear why that is so. Thus when we speak we are actually singing, especially in the sense that the pitch of our voice goes upward and downward, as it would if we were to sing the notes on a musical scale.

When written out on horizontal lines on a sheet of paper, a MUSICAL SCALE is simply a notational system that represents what the human voice or the musical instrument is doing: going up a step or more (= faster vibrations), going down a note or more (= slower vibrations), staying on the same note for a period of time, and so forth. Figure 3.a is a sample of a musical scale (C major).

The higher the line on which the note is written, the higher its pitch. The scale is divided into multiples of eight notes per series; each eight-note series is known as an OCTAVE, from the Latin word *octāvus*, 'eighth.' The octave in figure 3.a starts out on a note whose name is C. The next-highest-pitched note is named D, then E, then F, then G, then A, then B, and, finally, back to C'—though this second C' is pitched a full octave higher than the first C and vibrates at exactly twice its frequency.

But there is a crucial difference between singing and speaking. In singing, one uses precise absolute pitches (C = 256 vibrations or cycles per second, F = 352, G = 390,

Figure 3.a. A musical scale

C D E F G A B C'

Figure 3.b. A representation of intonation

I díd it

etc.), whereas speech adopts a more restricted, relative scale that varies by speaker (men's voices are generally lower pitched than women's) and by mood (higher pitched when excited). So pitch itself will vary according to one's normal speaking voice and emotional "key." The short phrase *I díd it* may thus be "C-F-B" for one speaker but "F-B-E" for another or even for the *same* speaker when he or she gets excited. What matters in intonation, as opposed to music, is that speakers perceive *relative* highs and lows in each other's voices. That is why we portray intonation in a more approximate fashion, using (as in figure 3.b) lines with no clef so we are not limited to a fixed set of specific pitches:

Exercise 3.2

♠(A) Listen while your instructor—or the voice on the corresponding CD recording—hums or whistles an octave similar to the one shown in figure 3.a. The voice will then descend the scale. Then try to replicate the performance in your own voice range, humming or whistling your way up the scale and then down it, then up again and down again.

♠(B) Now listen while your instructor (or the voice on the CD) whistles or hums a series of noncontiguous notes on the musical scale. (By "noncontiguous" we mean notes such as C, G, E, A, and F that do not represent just one step up or down on the scale but, instead, two, three, four, or more steps up or down.) After this has been done, try to replicate the performance, trying to hum or whistle the same pattern in your voice range.

♠(C) Draw the intonational pattern you hear when listening to your instructor's voice (or the CD) as it reads out loud the following sentences, all of which contain peak stresses.

1. Well what <u>we</u> can't understand is <u>why</u> she even <u>took</u> the test.
2. The only way to get an <u>A</u> in this course is to <u>really</u> study.
3. They never told <u>me</u> about it.
4. I didn't say we needed more <u>peas</u>; I said we needed more <u>peace</u>.
5. <u>John</u> didn't initiate divorce proceedings. It was <u>Marsha</u>.
6. All <u>my</u> friends showed up, so why didn't any of <u>your</u> friends?

7. M<u>a</u>dison is the capital of Wis<u>con</u>sin, whereas St. <u>Paul</u> is the capital of Minne<u>so</u>ta.
8. The <u>quick</u> brown fox—<u>not</u> the <u>slow</u> brown fox—jumped over the lazy sleeping dog.
9. The quick <u>brown</u> fox—<u>not</u> the quick <u>gray</u> fox—jumped over the lazy sleeping dog.
10. The quick brown <u>fox</u>—<u>not</u> the quick brown <u>wolf</u>—jumped over the lazy sleeping dog.

3.3 Stressing compound words and phrases.

A COMPOUND WORD consists of two or more lexical components each of which can stand alone as separate words; thus *córn* and *fíeld* can combine to produce *córnfield* ('a field where corn is grown'), *kíck* and *báck* produce *kíckbàck* ('money that someone "kicks" back to someone as a bribe'), *óut* and *hóuse* give *óuthòuse* ('a smaller house located outside a larger house, often containing a primitive toilet'), and tens of thousands more.[3]

3.3.1 Two-word compounds and phrases.

English strongly favors compounding. The following list gives many of the first fifty compounds from our corpus:

> *áfterbìrth, áfterlìfe, àfternóon, áirbàse, áircondìtioning, áirpórt, ánythìng, ány-where, ápplecàrt, ármchair, áshtray, báckpàck, bàckyárd, bándstànd, bándwàgon, bánkbòok, bármaid, bárstòol, bárnstòrm, básebàll, básketbàll, báthròbe, báthròom, báttlefield, bédbùg, bédpàn, bédròom, bígmòuth, bígtòp, bíllbòard, bíllfòld, bírdbràined, bírdcàge, bírthplàce, bírthràte, bítterswèet, bláckbèrry, bláckbìrd, bóokbìnding, bùcktéeth, búlletpròof*

In terms of stress placement, most of these compounds (forty-five out of fifty) strong-stress the **left** component of the compound: *áfterbìrth, áirbàse, básketbàll*. Indeed, about 90 percent of all compounds written as single words strong-stress the left component. But the remaining 10 percent do not, strong-stressing instead the right-hand component though giving the appearance of strong-stressing both components equally, a circumstance that we will discuss in §3.3.3. In any event, here are five right-strong-stressing compounds from our corpus: *àfternóon, bàckyárd, blàck<u>cúrr</u>ant, bròad-mínded, bùck<u>téeth</u>*. We will now pay a lot of attention to the matter of where compound words' strong stress falls, for it is complicated, all the more so because the concept of **peak stress** enters into the picture as well.

One thing we notice about the fifty compounds listed earlier is that all of them are usually written as single words and that most are nouns or adjectives. However, it is by no means true that every English compound is written as a single word. In fact, the CD's "compound" file contains a list of 5,315 compounds that are written as either **hyphenated words** (*African-American, age-old, all-purpose, Anglo-Saxon, armo(u)r-plated, award-winning, awe-inspiring*) or else as **separate words** (*acid rain, adult education, air bag, air traffic, alarm clock, alley cat, apple sauce, aspen tree*), which constitute noun-noun compounds.[4] As already mentioned, roughly 90 percent of all compounds written as single-word items are left-stressing. However, left-stressing characterizes only about 55 percent of the 5,315 compounds that are hyphenated or separate. So if a compound is written as a single word, it is likely to be pronounced with a left strong stress; but if a compound is hyphenated or two-worded, the likelihood of a left strong stress is just a little more than fifty-fifty.

There's one important difference between left-stressed compounds and right-stressed compounds: in a **right**-stressed compound, the word on the left appears to be **almost** as strongly stressed as the word on the right, whereas in a **left**-stressed compound the left-hand word is **definitely** more strongly stressed than is the right-hand word. Examples of left- and right-stressed compounds follow. Note that of the left-stressed compound's two words, the strong-stressed one appears in boldfaced type, whereas **both** the right-stressing compounds' words appear in boldface, given that both words appear to bear strong stress almost equally.

ନ left-stressing compounds	ନ right-stressing compounds
air bag	**adult education**
air conditioner	**adult literacy**
air force	**apple pie**
air supremacy	**artesian well**
bank account	**automatic pilot**
bank balance	**automatic redial**
bank clerk	**back door**
bank holiday	**back seat**
bank statement	**back yard**

Peak stress has an important role to play in compounds: when one word in one compound is being contrasted with another word in another compound, peak stress comes into play. While the following contrasts—sentences (1) and (2)—involve **left-stressing compounds**, it is their **right-hand** words that are contrasted with each other. Therefore, **peak stress gets moved to the <u>right</u>-hand word in these <u>left</u>-stressing compounds:**

ନ(1) I told you he was a bank <u>clerk,</u> <u>not</u> a bank <u>president</u>.

ନ(2) Just the one air <u>base</u> is under attack, <u>not</u> the whole air <u>force</u>.

As noted, sentences (1) and (2) contain compounds that are normally left-stressed (*bánk clèrk, áirbàse*). Peak stress also plays a role in **right-stressed compounds** such as *bàck dóor* and *àpple píe* when we want to express a contrast. If the right-stressed compound's left-hand word is being contrasted with another, peak stress appears on the left; if the right-stressed compound's right-hand word is being contrasted with another, peak stress appears on the right.

🎧(3) I wanted them to come in the <u>back</u> door, <u>not</u> the <u>front</u> door.

🎧(4) I wanted them to come in the back <u>door</u>, <u>not</u> the back <u>window</u>.

🎧(5) They told me they wanted <u>apple</u> pie, <u>not</u> <u>pumpkin</u> pie.

🎧(6) They told me they wanted apple <u>pie</u>, <u>not</u> apple <u>cider</u>.

However, in normal nonemphatic utterances, a left-stressed compound will only strong-stress its left-most word (***bank** account*, ***bank** balance*, ***bank** clerk*), whereas a right-stressed compound appears to strong-stress both words almost equally (***back door**, **back seat**, **back yard***).

Right-stressed compounds behave like phrases in which an adjective precedes a noun. Indeed, many right-stressed compounds actually began their lives as phrases containing an adjective and a noun that eventually became sufficiently "associated" with each other so as to constitute compounds. Here are several examples of such right-stressed entities whose first word can still be taken for an adjective and whose second word is clearly a noun: ***admissible evidence*** ('evidence that is admissible'), ***automatic pilot*** ('a pilot that is automatic'), ***baked beans*** ('beans that are baked'), ***big business*** ('business that is big'), ***black sheep*** ('a sheep that is black'), and the like. English, of course, is full of adjective-plus-noun phrases that are not (yet) considered compounds: *nice dog, old man, terrible cold, snowy landscape, cheap date, bountiful harvest, diseased animal, sharp pencil, open book, wet nurse, black bird, white house,* and so on. Some adjective-plus-noun phrases not only become right-strong-stressed "compounds"—*admissible evidence, automatic pilot, baked beans*—but even take the next step and turn into **left**-stressed compounds. But when they do so, they often change meanings or else acquire narrower ones, such as the foregoing list's last three examples: *wet nurse, black bird,* and *white house.* So when the context makes it clear that *wet nurse* is an adjective + noun phrase and thus right-stressed, the phrase means 'a nurse who has gotten wet'; but if the context shows *wet nurse* to be a left-stressed compound, it refers to 'a woman hired to suckle another's infant.' (That is a big difference!) The contrast between right-stressed '**wet nurse**' and left-stressed '**wet** nurse' is clarified in the following two high-context sentences:

🎧(7a) Returning from her nursing job at the hospital, Connie got caught in a cloud-burst while waiting for the bus, and by the time the bus finally arrived she was one really **wet nurse**.

🎧(7b) After many incidents like these, Connie got tired of having to work in a hospi-tal, so she changed professions and began to hire herself out to milkless moth-ers as a **wet** nurse.

The difference in structure between '**wet nurse**' and '**wet** nurse' is brought out in fig-ure 3.c, where the components are more tightly bound together in the left-stressed com-

Figure 3.c. Compound versus phrase

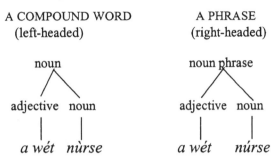

pound than in the more loosely joined words of a right-stressed phrase. (The right-stressed phrase allows further internal expansion: e.g., *a very wet, tired, thoroughly disgruntled third-shift nurse*.)

Contrasts of a similar sort can be made between our list's other two pairs: *bláck bírd* and *bláckbìrd*, *whìte hóuse* and *White Hòuse*. Whereas a *bláck bírd* is any bird that looks black ("The hawk flew into the train tunnel and came out looking like a really black bird"), a *bláckbìrd* constitutes a separate avian species, *Turdus merula*. (Note that *bláck bírd* and *bláckbìrd* are also differentiated by the open space that separates the components of the former but not the latter.) A *whìte hóuse* is any house whose exterior color is white, whereas the *White Hòuse* is the residence and working office of the president of the United States. Compare also *a hót dóg* (canine that's feeling hot) versus *a hótdòg* (sausage on a bun), *a Frénch tèacher* (teacher of that subject, like *biólogy tèacher*) versus *a Frénch téacher* (teacher from France), and many more such pairs.[5]

Is it easy to determine whether a compound is right-headed or left-headed? Do the morphology, the syntax, and/or the semantics of a compound give us useful clues as to whether the strong stress falls rightward or leftward? The answer to both questions is: up to a point. For example, **right**-strong-stress position is predictable in many sets of compounds whose first component is a word that is normally used as an adjective, for example, *double* as in **double agent, double bass, double bill, double Dutch, double-barrel(l)ed, double-breasted, double-clutch**, and so on, on which rightward stress would seem to appear precisely because *double* **is** normally used as an adjective. Other examples of this phenomenon are

- *big*: Big Apple, big bang, big business, big cheese, Big Dipper, big gun, big-headed, big-hearted, big-screen, big-ticket, big wheel (but cf. left-headed **big** shot, **big** time).
- *black*: black box, black cherry, Black Death, black eye, Black Forest, Black hole, black ice, black mark, black market, black poplar, Black Sea, black sheep, black tie, black widow.
- *deep*: deep end, deep(-)freeze, deep freezer, deep fryer, Deep South, deep space, deep-rooted, deep-sea, deep-seated, deep-set.

However, strong-stress position is unpredictable in other such compounds, for example, those involving the normally adjectival *high* as a first element: right-headed **High Church, high command, high fidelity, high finance, high priest,** and so on, but left-headed **high** *jinks,* **high** *jump,* **high** *school,* **high** *spot,* **high** *street,* and others; see also **hot air, hot flush, hot pepper, hot potato, hot spring, hot stuff** on the one hand, but **hot** *dog,* **hot** *flash,* **hot** *line,* **hot** *seat,* and **hot** *spot* on the other. Left-stressing is nonetheless the norm in a majority of compounds that consist of two separate words both of which are nouns, as the following examples will show:

billy club	**blood** bath	**boarding** house
bird dog	**blood** money	**boarding** pass
birth certificate	**blood** pressure	**boarding** school
birth control	**blood** test	**boat** race
birthday card	**blood** vessel	**bobby** pin
birthday party	**blood**-stained	**bobby** socks/sox
birthday suit	**blotting** paper	**body** builder

But there are counterexamples to this rule; thus on the one hand there is the predictably left-stressed **life** *assurance,* **life** *belt,* **life** *buoy,* **life** *cycle,* **life** *insurance,* **life** *jacket, and* **life** *preserver,* but on the other hand **life expectancy, life imprisonment,** and **life sciences** (which is also **life** *sciences*).

However, hyphens can help: the admittedly variable presence of the hyphen does a pretty good job of helping us predict where strong stress will fall. A general rule is that English will right-stress almost all hyphenated compounds consisting of a normally adjectival word plus a noun or another adjective; thus **long-distance, long-haul, long-lasting, long-lost; medium-range, medium-size; middle-class, middle-distance; open-ended, open-eyed, open-heart, open-minded, open-mouthed; red-eyed, red-faced,** and **red-handed.** There are also several large families of (normally) hyphenated words that, although not beginning with adjectives, are right-stressed nonetheless: for example, the "self-" group (**self-addressed, self-appointed, self-assured, self-confessed, self-control,** etc.).

Exercise 3.3

(A) Read aloud the following compounds and adjective-noun phrases. Pay close attention to the placement of boldfaced type and accents. (The purpose of this is to test your ability to contrast left-strong-stressed patterns with right-strong-stressed patterns.)

1. **blind date** = blínd dáte
2. **blind** spot = blínd spòt
3. **blood** money = blóod mòney
4. **blood red** = blóod réd
5. **brown bear** = brówn béar
6. **brown** sauce = brówn sàuce

7. **Christmas** card = Chrístmas càrd
8. **Christmas Eve** = Chrístmas Éve
9. **double-take** = dóuble-táke

10. **double**-talk = dóuble-tàlk
11. **foul-smelling** = fóul-smélling
12. **foul**-up = fóul-ùp

(B) Predict these compounds' stress patterns, that is, right-strong-stressed or left-strong-stressed. Then explain your prediction—to the extent that it is possible to do so. (If you can't predict a compound's stress unless you have a context, write an original sentence with the compound in it.)

1. freedom fighter
2. freight car
3. French horn
4. French-Canadian
5. full employment
6. full-blooded
7. full-length
8. garden apartment
9. apartment garden
10. gift certificate

11. general delivery
12. house dog
13. dog house
14. glove compartment
15. grade crossing
16. great-aunt
17. great-grandmother
18. habit-forming
19. low-grade
20. self-obsessed

3.3.2 Multiple-word compounds and phrases.

So far we have limited our discussion of stresses and compounds to those that run to just two words. We will now analyze compounds that run to three words or more. (English, always the Germanic language, happily produces ever-longer compounds by piling noun upon noun upon noun, though doing so to an extreme degree is considered bad style.) Although four-word compounds are relatively rare in dictionaries (and thus in our corpus), the possibilities of multiple compounding in English are nearly infinite; consider, thus, the following behemoths:

(1) *Milwaukee River Conservation District Budget Committee Report* (i.e., the report from the budget committee of the conservation district for the Milwaukee River)

(2) *Texas state textbook commission study group reorganization proposal* (i.e., a proposal for the reorganization of a study group of the textbook commission for the state of Texas)

(3) *Tri-State Area Harbor Authority Waste Disposal Plan* (i.e., a waste disposal plan drawn up by the harbor authority for the Tri-State area)

To figure out where to put strong stresses and peak stresses in multiple-word compounds such as these, it is often helpful to divide them into constituent units. A CONSTITUENT UNIT is like a small phrase. In a long, multiple-word compound, each of the constituent units can be extracted, forming separate entities in their own right, so we can easily divide into four separate units the compound *Tri-State-Area Harbor Authority Waste Disposal Plan*—and three of these units are compounds themselves: *Tri-State Area, Harbor Authority, Waste Disposal,* and *Plan.* (To prove that this division is correct, let us force the status of "unit" on other, unworkable combinations from the same compound; thus **Authority Waste*, which as a compound makes no sense. And while *Disposal Plan* would be a workable unit in some other context, we are not talking about a *"disposal plan that is waste," but, rather, a "plan for waste disposal.") Figure 3.d shows the full structure of these layered constituents, all functioning as a single noun. Once these compounds are divided into their respective units, we can follow the rules we have already learned and ask these questions: (1) Where does **strong stress** fall on each unit? (2) Which one of the several units will take **peak stress**? Of these questions, let's answer the second one now. On the basis of what we have learned, we can easily figure out where to place strong stress in the two-word compounds *Trí-State Àrea, Hárbor Authòrity,* and *wáste dispòsal.* What we haven't yet learned is where this long noun-noun compound's **peak** stress will fall—why peak stress falls where it does on *Trí-State Àrea / Hárbor Authòrity / Wáste Dispòsal / Plán* (again, peak stress is double-underlined). The answer to the question is relatively simple: peak stress usually falls on the **penultimate unit**, and, within it, on the strong-stressed word. So in multiple compounds, peak stress is typically attracted to the pen(ultimate), whether the pen is a multiple-word unit, a one-word unit, or simply the next-to-the-last word in the compound.

Let's look at the peak-stress patterns of some of the multiple-word compounds from the first half of our corpus. Of these 105 compounds, a clear majority (70—exactly 66.67%) is peak-stressed on the pen, as predicted:

acquired <u>immunodeficiency</u> syndrome
American <u>Automobile</u> Association
American Civil <u>Liberties</u> Union
American <u>Medical</u> Association

Federal <u>Housing</u> Administration
Federal <u>Reserve</u> Board
foot-and-<u>mouth</u> disease
full-length <u>feature</u> film

Figure 3.d. Internal construction of a complex compound

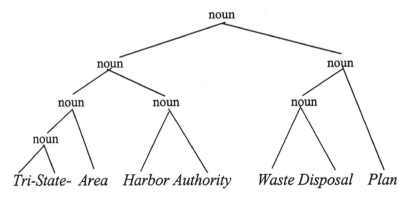

American <u>Stock</u> Exchange
annual <u>percentage</u> rate
automated <u>teller</u> machine
British <u>Broadcasting</u> Corporation
Central <u>Intelligence</u> Agency
Central <u>Standard</u> Time
Civil <u>Aeronautics</u> Board
Civil <u>Aviation</u> Authority
Columbia <u>Broadcasting</u> System
Consumer <u>Price</u> Index
Dutch <u>elm</u> disease
Eastern <u>Standard</u> Time
eight <u>hundred</u> number
Environmental <u>Protection</u> Agency
Equal <u>Rights</u> Amendment
European <u>Currency</u> Unit
European <u>Economic</u> Community
fast <u>forward</u> button
Federal <u>Communications</u> Commission
Federal Deposit <u>Insurance</u> Corporation

golden <u>wedding</u> anniversary
Government <u>Printing</u> Office
Greenwich <u>Mean</u> Time
health <u>maintenance</u> organization
hormone <u>replacement</u> therapy
hot <u>water</u> bottle
human <u>rights</u> violation
human <u>immunodeficiency</u> virus
Individual <u>Retirement</u> Account
intensive <u>care</u> unit
Internal <u>Revenue</u> Service
International Atomic <u>Energy</u> Agency
International <u>Monetary</u> Fund
International Standard <u>Book</u> Number
joint <u>stock</u> company
junior <u>high</u> school
Latin American Free <u>Trade</u> Association
Little Red <u>Riding</u> Hood
long-distance <u>telephone</u> call
low-<u>water</u> mark

Most of these pen-peak-stressed compounds have this in common: their ult and pen units contain nouns, and it is the **nouns** in these units that are peak-stressed—though predictably on the units' pen.

3.3.3 Pitch adjustment in compounds' post-peak words.

Once we have assigned a compound's peak stress, we need to look again at the parts of the compound that do **not** receive peak stress. Let's use *Federal Deposit <u>Insurance</u> Corporation* as an illustration. When pronounced in isolation, each of these four words has a strong stress (and, in one instance, a weak stress): *féderal, depósit, insúrance, còrporátion*. When the four combine, two things happen: peak stress is assigned to <u>*insurance*</u> (for reasons we already know), and the word appearing immediately afterward, *còrporátion*, appears to lose the strong stress it had on the *rá* when pronounced alone. But what really happens to *còrporátion* is that since it appears in post-peak-stressed position, its pitch drops about **three notes lower** than the pitch on the stressed syllable <u>*súr*</u> of peak-stressed *insúrance*. It is also true that post-peak-stressed words such as *còrporátion* are **not pronounced as loudly** as the peak-stressed items preceding them. So if "sung," *Féderal Depósit <u>Insúrance</u> Còrporátion*'s melodic line would be that of figure 3.e.

If **two** or even **more** compounded words appear in post-peak stress position, they too will be "sung" with notes that are lower on the scale and not as loud. Proof of this is, once again, our old friend "Tri-State Area Harbor Authority Waste Disposal Plan" (see the second line of figure 3.e).

Figure 3.e. Melodic lines of long compounds

Féd(e) ral De pó sit In súr ance Còr po rá tion

Trí-Stàte Áre a Hár bor Au thór i ty Wáste Dis pó sal Plán

Of the remaining thirty-five compounds, twenty-eight peak-stress their right-most unit—*First World War, four-wheel drive*—rather than their pen unit. It appears they do so because the pre-ult words are mostly adjectives, not nouns, and many of the adjectives (*four-letter, four-poster, funny-looking, hot-air, knee-length, long-grain*) are hyphenated, whereas several others could be: *dry-goods, fresh-ground, hot-cross, in-vitro, low-tar.* In effect, ult-peak-stressed three- or four-word compounds behave like two-word right-stressed compounds: in both, one mainly finds adjectives and not nouns appearing to the left of the peak-stressed noun. Here is a sample of the ult-stressing compounds:

First World War   in vitro fertilization
four-letter word   International Phonetic Alphabet
four-poster bed   Irish Republican Army
four-wheel drive   knee-length boots
fresh ground coffee   long-range missiles
funny-looking character   low-tar cigarettes
gross national product   low-level language
hot-air balloon   lowest common denominator

The remaining seven multiword compounds are left-stressing entities whose first two words—nouns or nouns plus adjectives that constitute a single unit—are eligible for peak stress. So a "Drug Enforcement | Administration" is an 'administration (agency) for drug enforcement' rather than an *'enforcement administration that drugs.' These seven entries therefore conform to the many left-stressing models already analyzed such as ***birth*** *certificate,* ***boarding*** *school,* and ***life*** *insurance.* Note that four of the seven have hyphens, often a sign that English views them as single units—and indeed, *hot-dog* can be written as *hotdog* and *ice-cream* as *icecream.*

Drug Enforcement Administration
dry goods store
Exchange Rate Mechanism
hot-dog stand

ice-cream parlor
law-enforcement officer
life-support system

Exercise 3.4

(A) Read the following multiple compounds out loud. Pay close attention to strong-stress accent marks as well as double-underlinings marking peak stress. Apply what you have just learned about music. (This exercise tests your ability to interpret multiple compounds orally.)

1. Sócial Secúrity Trúst Fúnd
2. hígh-énergy campáign stýle
3. civílian compláint revíew bóard
4. gránd slám ténnis kíng
5. àntismóking ád blítz
6. éarly retírement sávings accóunts
7. tobácco contról prógram diréctor
8. búrial plót sálesman
9. Nátional Lábor Relàtions Bóard
10. Néw Yórk Stóck Exchánge
11. Nórth Américan Frée Tráde Agréement
12. Nórth Atlántic Tréaty Órganizátion

(B) Predict each of the following compounds' stress patterns, paying special attention to the location of peak stress. Then explain your choice (to the extent that it is possible to do so).

1. Nuclear Regulatory Commission
2. Los Angeles Police Department
3. optical character recognition
4. parent-teacher association
5. personal identification number
6. United States counterterrorism officials
7. conservative watchdog group
8. pressurized water reactor
9. Central Intelligence Agency
10. public service corporation
11. Registered General Nurse
12. Saint Patrick's Day

3.4 Peak stresses and info units. We have just examined peak stress placement in compounds, some of which ran to four words or more. We will now deal with the topic of peak-stress placement in word combinations that will include entire sentences in some instances. These word combinations will be called "information units" or INFO UNITS for short. Each info unit is centered on a word on which a peak stress falls. The more peak stresses a sentence contains, the more info units it has.[6] Here is an example:

🎧(1) They would always come late.

🎧(2) They | would always | come late.

Sentence (1), with only one peak stress, is the typical neutral or unmarked sentence whose sole peak stress falls on a word appearing near or at the sentence's end. As observed by Chafe (1980) and other discourse analysts, information that is new will typically appear in that position. In neutral or unmarked sentences, peak stresses falling on the stressed syllable of the last content word are usually less loud, less long, and less strong than peak stresses appearing earlier in the sentence. Sentence (1), for example, could form part of a longer discourse such as the following:

(3)   I knew when writing the invitations for the party that it simply didn't matter what time we told Jane and Joan the event would start. They would always come <u>late</u>.

Sentence (2), however, clearly contains several peak-stressed words serving to contrast and emphasize, important functions of peak stress that were discussed in §3.1. We could easily imagine sentence (2) appearing in a context such as this one:

(4)   While Frank was well known for his extreme punctuality, Jane and Joan seldom got their act together. He would never arrive any time but early. <u>They</u> would <u>always</u> come <u>late</u>.

When peak stress falls toward the beginning of an info unit, it serves a purpose that is contrastive, emphatic, or in some other way exceptional. Thus <u>they</u> ('Jane and Joan') contrasts with <u>he</u> ('Frank'), <u>always</u> with <u>never</u>, and <u>late</u> with <u>early</u>. As there are three contrasts in sentence (2), so too are there three info units: "<u>They</u> | would <u>always</u> | come <u>late</u>." (The vertical line represents an INFO-UNIT BOUNDARY that indicates the start of a new info unit.)

Punctuation often serves to mark the end of one info unit and the start of another. Here are several examples:

🎧(5a) The department's <u>biggest</u> major | is <u>Linguistics</u>, | <u>right</u>?

🎧(5b) <u>Yes</u>, | and it was started in <u>1965</u>.

🎧(5c) Nowadays it's got a large <u>faculty</u>: | four <u>full</u> professors, | five <u>associates</u>, | three <u>lecturers</u>, | and one <u>endowed</u> <u>chair</u>.

🎧(5d) You can also major in <u>French</u>, | <u>Spanish</u>, | and <u>Swahili</u>.

🎧(5e) <u>That</u> major was inaugurated in 1967, | by popular <u>demand</u>.

As is obvious from sentence (5a), one can separate a subject ("The department's <u>biggest</u> major") from a predicate ("is <u>Linguistics</u>"), provided that the subject contains a peak stress, which it does here to contrast a big major from the smaller majors. However, subjects and predicates are not normally separated, as the pre-comma part of sentence (5e) shows ("<u>That</u> major was inaugurated in 1967"). Here are two more examples of how punctuation can mark the boundaries of info units:

☏(6) His friend <u>Jennifer</u> | and <u>Jessica</u> | got into a terrible <u>fight</u>.

☏(7) His <u>friend</u>, | <u>Jennifer</u>, | and <u>Jessica</u> | got into a terrible <u>fight</u>.

In (6), just two people fought—Jennifer and Jessica—whereas three people did so in (7): Jennifer, Jessica, and some unnamed "friend."

Punctuation marking info-unit boundaries will serve to distinguish a nonrestrictive clause from a restrictive clause,[7] as the following two sentences demonstrate:

☏(8) He was kept awake by the barking of the <u>dogs</u>, | who were in the <u>kennel</u>.

☏(9) He was upset by the barking of the dogs who were in the <u>kennel</u>.

Peak stresses can mark info-unit boundaries without needing punctuation to do so. Let's look at the following sentence, which is ambiguous unless pronounced out loud or else embedded in a longer discourse:

(10) He didn't leave because he was angry.

Sentence (10) can be disambiguated and its two meanings extrapolated by adding peak stresses, thereby establishing info-unit boundaries:

☏(10a) He didn't leave because he was <u>angry</u> (| but because he was <u>sick</u>).

☏(10b) He didn't <u>leave</u> | because he was <u>angry</u> (| and his anger prompted him to <u>stay</u>).

Clearly, the presence or absence of peak stress has a major impact on a sentence's melodic line, a topic we will deal with in §3.5.

One highly useful concept is STRESS RELOCATION. It teaches us that neutral sentences typically present new information at or near the end. So of the following two sentences, only the first (11) is what we expect to hear from someone who bursts into a room with some startling news:

(11) I just saw a man biting a <u>dog</u>!

(12) A man biting a <u>dog</u> | is what I just <u>saw</u>!

Because new information rarely appears in subject position, and since peak stress typically highlights the most important element in an info unit, stress relocation assumes that the role of non-sentence-final peak stress is to emphasize or contradict something that someone said before. Here is a conversation between two people in which peak stress advances leftward as the interlocutors talk:

🎧(13a) I just married a <u>Martian</u>.

🎧(13b) There <u>are</u> no Martians, | so you <u>can't</u> have married one.

🎧(13c) <u>Oh</u> yes there are, | and I'll bet you <u>anything</u> | that you're just <u>dying</u> to meet it.

Peak stresses also come in handy when a selection must be made between two or more possibilities, as the following show:

(14) Do you want to go to Palm <u>Beach</u> | or Palm <u>Springs</u>?

(15) Should we serve <u>caviar</u> | or <u>hot</u> dogs?

(16) Did you ever meet Jack and Geri <u>Foster</u>? — Well, | I met <u>him</u>.

Exercise 3.5

🎧(A) Tell which of the following sentences are likely to be a single info unit and which are likely to contain multiple info units. Then divide the sentences into their respective info units. (Listen carefully to the way these sentences are read on the corresponding recording on the CD.)

1. I've had it up to here with nickels and dimes. What this school needs is at least a billion dollars in federal grants.
2. If you ask me, it couldn't even begin to spend a sum that large.
3. Well, getting that kind of money would most certainly do something to help us out, don't you think?
4. You know, we'd probably just end up wasting more than half of it on needless administration, if you want my opinion.

(B) Each of the following sets contains two or more sentences. Explain how each set's sentences **differ in meaning** from the others in its set. One way to do so is by making the sentence longer, thereby expanding its context. Another way to do so is by coming up with an entire paragraph so that the sentence can be embedded within a context.

1a. Marilyn speaks German <u>too</u>.
1b. Marilyn speaks <u>German</u>, | <u>too</u>.

2a. Paul's chocolate cake is <u>delicious</u>.
2b. Paul's chocolate <u>cake</u> is delicious.
2c. Paul's <u>chocolate</u> cake is delicious.

3a. Sandra's Portuguese is almost <u>native</u>.
3b. Sandra's Portuguese is <u>almost</u> native.

3c. Sandra's <u>Portuguese</u> is almost native.
3d. <u>Sandra's</u> Portuguese is almost native.

(C) On your own, invent a set of two or more sentences in which the difference in meaning between them is the product of where peak stress is placed. Use the sentences of section (B) as models.

3.5 Melodic lines long and short, falling and rising, and so on. We now return to the analogies that we previously made with music. In some languages—Spanish, for example—the melodic line (intonation) is relatively flat, rising or falling in standard pronunciation by no more than one step on the scale. That is quite untrue of English. If in topographical terms the melodic line of Spanish can best be characterized as a flat plateau, the melodic line of English most closely resembles a mountain range, full of peaks and valleys.[8]

3.5.1 Falls and rises, statements and questions. Speaking very generally, the melodic line of English rises on a strong-stressed syllable. English intonation rises two or more notes, but on a null-stressed syllable it falls a note or more. The sentences in figure 3.f—the first metrically iambic, the second trochaic—illustrate that point.

The neutral, unmarked, and by far most frequently used melodic line is the **long fall**. In a long fall, the pitch of the last stressed word drops down several notes, as shown by the arrows in figure 3.f. (If the last word has only one syllable, it bears the brunt of the fall, whereas the long fall on a multisyllable word will be evenly distributed throughout its several post-tonic syllables.) The long fall's **falling melodic line** asserts certainty and finality; because English uses falling pitch to declare things, it is no surprise that falling pitch typifies declarative sentences and also commands.

On the other hand, a **rising melodic line** suggests just the opposite: uncertainty. So it is also no accident that a melodic line whose pitch rises several notes in a **long rise** is

Figure 3.f. Intonation of full sentences

I thínk that Í shall néver <u>sée</u> | a póem lóvely ás a <u>trée</u>.

Stícks and stónes may bréak my <u>bónes;</u> wórds will néver <u>húrt me</u>.

Figure 3.g. Long falls and rises

melodic line type	type of sentence	example of that sentence type
long fall (↘)	declarative statement	(3) Sticks and stones may break my <u>bones</u>.
		(4) I was planning to pay them <u>yesterday</u>.
long fall (↘)	command	(5) Go to the <u>mall</u>.
long fall (↘)	WH-content question	(6) Where are you planning to <u>live</u>?
		(7) When did they leave for <u>work</u>?
long rise (↗)	yes-no question	(8) Will you be going to <u>Greenland</u>?
		(9) Did Gary tell you about his new <u>job</u>?

typically used in **yes-no questions** that request information rather than conveying it. Thus it's a bit of a surprise that the other main interrogative device, the **WH-content question**, employs the same **long fall** that a declarative sentence uses as its melodic line. (Here is the difference between the two types of questions: a WH-content question—so named because it typically begins with a *wh*-word such as *who, what, where, when, why, which, whose,* or *how*—can never be answered by "yes" or "no," whereas a yes-no question usually **is** answered with a "yes" or a "no.") Figure 3.g sums up and exemplifies these two melodic lines (symbolized by arrows) and the types of sentences that employ them.

As these unmarked example sentences show, peak stress falls where we expect it will: at or near the end. So these sentences' peak stresses nicely coincide with their rises (in yes-no questions) or falls (in declarative statements or WH-content questions). **But if these same sentences express surprise and shock or request repetition and clarification, peak stress will shift leftward.** Let's show how this process works in the following questions:

⌒(1a) Where are you planning to <u>live</u> ↘?

⌒(1b) <u>Where</u> are you planning to live ↗?

To express surprise or shock, sentence (1b) has a **rising** intonation, starting high (or scooping up to high) on the peak-stressed word and then moving even higher right up to the end, and it might form part of a longer discourse unit like the following:

⌒(2) JOE: Where are you planning to <u>live</u>?
SANDY: I'm planning to live in a <u>cave</u>.
JOE: <u>Where</u> are you planning to live?

Obviously, Joe would not answer Sandy's declarative statement "I'm planning to live in a <u>cave</u>" by saying, "Where are you planning to <u>live</u>?" Doing so would make no sense; given that Sandy has already informed him about where she plans to live, she is likely to respond to such an inappropriate question by saying, "I already <u>told</u> you!"

🎧(3a) When did they leave for <u>work</u> ↘?

🎧(3b) <u>When</u> did they leave for work ↗?

The same rising melodic line that applied to (1b) applies to (3b), which would also form part of a longer discourse unit in which surprise or shock was expressed:

(4) PERRY: Mom and dad left for work at 3 A.M.
TERRY: <u>When</u> did they leave for work?

Not shock but a request for repetition and/or clarification born out of frustration is what characterizes the variant forms of questions (5) and (6):

(5) BETTY: Will you be going to <u>Greenland</u>?
FREDDY: Well you see my dad said that he wasn't sure about the itinerary the travel agent had prepared, and my mom was worried about all the reports she'd heard in the news, and then my aunt said that her boss's cousin's boyfriend had told her that . . .
BETTY: Well <u>will</u> you be going to Greenland, | or <u>not</u>?

(6) SAM: Did Gary tell you about his new <u>job</u>?
PAM: Well you see everyone was so excited that they were all talking at once and then Karen came in, and we all wanted to hear about her neighbor's accident, and then the phone rang and it was Pat, who just had to talk to Tish because . . .
SAM: Well <u>did</u> Gary tell you about his new job | or <u>what</u>?

If repeated, the *wh*-word can mean one thing with rising intonation and another thing with falling, as examples (7–10) will demonstrate:

🎧(7) BARRY: I'm going to Florida next month.
LARRY: Where ↗? (rising = Larry didn't hear right)
BARRY: Florida.

🎧(8) BARRY: I'm going to Florida next month.
LARRY: Where ↘? (falling = Larry wants more info)
BARRY: Miami Beach.

(9) JESSICA: I tried to call you last night.
BARBARA: When ↗? (rising = Barbara didn't hear right)
JESSICA: Last night.

(10) JESSICA: I tried to call you last night.
BARBARA: When ↘? (falling = Barbara wants more info)
JESSICA: Around eleven.

Not long falls (or rises) but **short falls** and **short rises** are typical of shorter utterances, many of them running to just one word or even one syllable. A **short fall** response, a one-note drop, which often functions as an answer to a question, comes across as being especially abrupt. That is because the voice of someone uttering a short fall stops quickly, as in a "Yes," a "No," a "Really," or an "Uh-huh" that was said by a person too busy to be bothered. In similar fashion, a **short rise** is a one-note-rise question functioning as a dismissal, a question uttered by someone not terribly interested in something: "Oh?" "Yes?" "Yeah?" On the other hand, the same set of one-worders articulated with **long falls or long rises** would show greater interest and/or greater warmth.

3.5.2 Fall-rise and rise-fall. Different from both long falls/rises and short falls/rises are the melodic lines known as **fall-rise** and **rise-fall**, which differ considerably from each other in terms of the uses to which each is put and the connotations that each suggests. Thus the **fall-rise** line (∨) expresses what could be termed "reserved and cautious agreement," which orthography often tries to replicate by repeating one or more letters in a word followed by a question mark, thus: "Yeeeesss?" "Oooohhhhh?" "Aaaannnddd?" On the other hand, the **rise-fall** line (∧) goes in just the opposition direction, expressing enthusiasm, dynamism, passion, even gush. Orthographic conventions expressing rise-fall intonation often make use of boldface or uppercase type as well as grapheme repetition (also suggesting lengthening), as in "Why that's **juuuust faaaa**bulous!" As figure 3.h shows, a two-peak-stress utterance like that will require a full clef's worth of notes to depict.

3.5.3 Some other melodies. Various long/short fall/rise combinations characterize other language functions also. The intonation patterns of **greetings** vary in part according to their formality; thus the highly colloquial "Yo!" and the slightly less informal "Hi" (or "Hey!") are both falls from high onsets, whereas the neutral "Hello" lends itself to a wide variety of intonation patterns, ranging from the interrogative long rise that many people use when they answer the telephone ("Hellooooo ↗?") to a neutral short-fall "Hello ∨" that is said by strangers who have just been introduced. The melodic lines of **farewells** are equally complicated, all the more so because there are so many ways of saying goodbye, from the word *goodbye* itself through derived phrases such as "Bye," "Bye bye," or "Bye now." (*Goodbye* is itself derived, for it is a short form of "God be with you.") In sum,

Figure 3.h. A two-peak utterance with a rise-fall-rise

*Why that's **juuuust** | **faaaabulous!***

goodbye ranges from short-rise-then-extended-long-fall "Goodbyyyyyyyyye ⤳ " (which you'd say—or yell—out a car window while driving off) through the demonstrably huffy "Good ↘ bye ↘!" (two sequential short falls) that you'd say to someone you were mad at.

Exercise 3.6

🎧(A) Does the utterance "No(,) he isn't" differ in both **melodic line(s)** and **meaning** in the following two contexts? If so, explain how.

    1. "Is the Pope a Presbyterian?" "No, he isn't."
    2. "The Pope is a Presbyterian." "No he isn't."

🎧(B) Using the arrows that were presented in §3.5.3, describe the melodic lines of the following sentences in terms of peak stresses, info units, long falls, long rises, short falls, short rises, fall-rises, and rise-falls. (Numbers and blank spaces divide the blocks of sentences into little "stories.")

    1a. What do you do for a <u>living</u>?
    1b. Are you a <u>plumber</u>?
    1c. When <u>I</u> grow up, | I want to be an <u>electrician</u>.
    1d. <u>However,</u> | I don't think I have the patience to learn a <u>trade</u>.

    2a. Where do you plan on going to <u>college</u>?
    2b. I'd thought about Lower Junkyard County <u>Reform</u> School.
    2c. <u>Where</u> do you plan on going to college?

    3a. JO: I'd like to spend next Christmas skiing in the <u>Alps</u>.
    3b. MO: <u>Oh</u>? And where are you going to get the <u>money</u>?
    3c. FLO: Well <u>IIII</u> think that that's the most <u>wooonn</u>derful idea you've <u>eever</u> <u>had</u>! Can I come <u>along</u>?

(C) Take the word *no* and pronounce it as shown in figure 3.i. Then label each melodic line correctly (as long fall, long rise, short fall, short rise, fall-rise, or rise-fall).

Figure 3.i. Ways of saying *No*

(D) Some observers (e.g., Dalton and Seidlhofer 1994, 53) stress the idea that intonation reflects the ways in which two speakers are negotiating their conversation from moment to moment. Examine the examples in sections (A) and (B) of this exercise: in what kinds of interactions could you envision such negotiation taking place? Explain your conclusions.

(E) Take the word *hello* and try to determine how many different intonation patterns you would use it with. (Or, as a dictation, transcribe your instructor's patterns.) What social circumstances might prompt the use of each melodic line?

3.6 Melodic lines and compound melodies. Many other intonational patterns combine the basic melodies we have just examined in order to form more complex patterns. In the following sections we look at several important ones: enumeration, selection questions, tags, and complex sentences.

3.6.1 Enumeration. When we **enumerate,** or list items in a series—numbers, people, places, things, ideas, and so on—we generally employ a melodic line that applies a short rise to each item but the last, on which a long fall appears. As is the case with other intonational particulars, speakers of other languages often use a different pattern here. Examples follow, using arrows instead of staves:

(1) I want tea ↗, milk ↗, cheese ↗, ham ↗, eggs ↗, bread ↗, and butter ↘.

(2) . . . six ↗, seven ↗, eight ↗, nine ↗, ten ↗, eleven ↗, twelve ↘.

3.6.2 Selection questions. SELECTION QUESTIONS (also called choice questions) present two or more alternatives, each of whose info units carries a long rise except the last one, which carries a long fall. Note the arrows in the example in (1):

(1) Do you think we should live in Oak Forest ↗, Oak Lawn ↗, Oak Park ↗, or Oak Cliff ↘?

Selection questions can often be quite long, as some of the following show:

(2) Should I buy the blue car, the white car, the green one, the black one, or the yellow one?
(3) Are you going to major in Arabic, Chinese, French, German, Hindi-Urdu, Italian, Portuguese, Russian, or Spanish?
(4) Is Sara at Harvard or Princeton?

When there is just a two-choice selection, the options are *usually but not always* separated by commas. So in print, sentence (4) can have two meanings, as the following discourse units reveal:

(4a) S<small>TEVE</small>: Carol, is Sara at Harvard or Princeton? (= selection between just these two)
C<small>AROL</small>: Harvard.

(4b) S<small>TEVE</small>: Carol, is Sara at Harvard or Princeton? (= yes/no, i.e., 'at some Ivy League school?')
C<small>AROL</small>: No, she decided she wanted a big state school instead, so she chose Virginia.

Therefore, anyone reading sentence (4) out loud is forced to make an interpretation: either two peak stresses and their two respective info units, each with its own melodic line (as in 4a/c), or else just one peak stress and thus just one info unit and only one sentence-final long rise (as in 4b/d):

☊(4c) Is Sara at <u>Harvard</u> ↗ | or <u>Princeton</u> ↘? (long rise | long fall)

☊(4d) Is Sara at Harvard or <u>Princeton</u> ↗? (one long rise only)

3.6.3 Tags. T<small>AGS</small> are add-ons that typically appear at the end of the sentence and are set off in writing by commas and in speech by an optional break. They may also appear at the beginning of a sentence or may be inserted in the middle at a phrase break. Tags' intonation is easy to understand if the tag is a comment or a vocative, but harder to get a handle on if the tag is a question.

T<small>AG</small> C<small>OMMENTS</small> generally indicate a speaker's attitude toward the sentence with a melodic line that tends to be low-pitched (relative to what precedes the comma) and "flat" (→), that is, neither rising nor falling, although rise-falls can be used to imply doubtfulness. Here are examples, using arrows instead of musical staves. (Tag comments are in italics.)

☊(1) Just go out and buy yourself an Alfa <u>Romeo</u> ↘, *if you'd like* → (or ∨↗).

☊(2) There's absolutely <u>nothing</u> wrong with me ↘, *in fact* →.

☊(3) I simply can't <u>agree</u> ↘, *unfortunately* →.

☊(4) <u>What</u> ↘, *for example* →?

☊(5) We aim to <u>please</u> ↘. <u>You</u> | aim <u>too</u> ↘, | *please* →.

Similar tag comments take one type of melodic line when appearing in sentence-initial position and another type when appearing in sentence-final position. We thus note the fate of the commonplace discourse marker *actually* ('here's another thought on the subject') in the following:

☊(6a) <u>Actually</u> ↗ (or ∨↗), I think you're right ↘! (short rise or fall-rise)

☊(6b) I think you're <u>right</u>, actually →. ("flat" melodic line)

The words *yes* (*yeah*) and *no* (*nope*) can also serve as initial tags on a sentence, and may have either an emphatic fall of their own or else a slow rise into the rest of the sentence.

(7) Are you interested in switching your phone service? —No ↘, I'm not ↘. (*or* No ↗, I'm not ↘.)

A VOCATIVE is a person's name—plus, sometimes, title—that you use when speaking directly to him or her. TAG VOCATIVES similarly assume a low-pitched "flat" melodic line, unless, of course, their speaker is trying to sound very polite or highly enthusiastic or trying to get the person's attention. Compare the following examples, in which the tag vocative appears in italics:

🎧(8a) Good <u>afternoon</u> ↘, *Professor Fidgit* →. (flat vocative line)

🎧(8b) Good <u>afternoooon</u> ↘, *Professor Fidgit* ↗! (rising vocative line)

Note the important contrast between a vocative and an APPOSITIVE (which just renames the immediately antecedent noun and then carries on that information unit):

🎧(9a): This is my sister ↘, Connie ↗. (= vocative: You are Connie; I introduce my sister to you)

🎧(9b): This is my sister(,) Connie ↘. (= appositive: my sister's name is Connie)

TAG QUESTIONS, a difficult construction in English syntax,[9] bear **long falls** if the speaker is simply seeking to confirm a statement he or she has just made, but **long rises** if the purpose of the tag question is genuinely interrogative. Note the following four examples:

🎧(10a) It's about to <u>rain</u> ↘, isn't it ↘? (long fall on the tag—speaker is pretty sure it will)

🎧(10b) It's about to <u>rain</u> ↘, isn't it ↗? (long rise on the tag—speaker truly doesn't know what the weather will be and seeks an answer)

🎧(11a) It isn't about to <u>rain</u> ↘, is it ↘? (long fall—speaker is sure that rain isn't coming)

🎧(11b) It isn't about to <u>rain</u> ↘, is it ↗? (long rise—speaker is not sure about the rain)

A fifth type of tag with two affirmative clauses is useful to convey sarcasm, scorn, and disbelief:

🎧(12) So you've done your homework ↘, have you ↗? (long rise)

3.6.4 Complex sentences. Another class of compound intonation patterns identifies the internal clauses of complex sentences. For example, longer ADVERBIAL CLAUSES (beginning with *when, before, although, if, while, so, because*, etc.) have a normal falling intonation at the end of the sentence. If such clauses are long, they may be set off by a preceding short fall as well, but when moved to the beginning their intonation tends to become a fall-rise, as if to show that they have been dislocated and the main point is still to follow. Note the following example (the clause is italicized):

🎧(1a) A funny thing happened (↓) *while I was going to the forum* ↘.

🎧(1b) *While I was going to the forum* ↗, a funny thing happened ↘.

A PARENTHETICAL EXPRESSION interjects a relatively minor thought into the main clause, as when citing a reference. Generally the speaker sets off a parenthetical expression with a DOWNSTEP, a drop to a lower musical key, and then returns to the main idea with a corresponding UPSTEP, as in the following examples:

🎧(2a) The <u>real</u> problem ↗, → *according to the government* ↗, is the <u>deficit</u>.

🎧(2b) "So ↘," → *said the big bad wolf* ↗, "and what else are you taking to Grandma's house?"

Exercise 3.7

(A) Tell what melodic lines the following sentences carry. Indicate which sentences are ambiguous when written in conventional orthography, what their ambiguity consists of, and how the sentences' several spoken versions succeed in getting rid of that ambiguity. (Use arrows to mark intonation.)

1. I'd like you to meet my brother, George.
2. Who sent me that e-mail? Cathy?
3. Who sent me that e-mail, Cathy?
4. What did you say, and whom did you say it to?
5. Do you want coffee or tea?
6. To be perfectly frank, I simply have no idea what you're trying to say!
7. I simply have no idea what you're trying to say, to be perfectly frank.
8. "Were you aware that he's published 294 articles?" — "294?"
9. "I'm going to get an 'A' in this course, aren't I?" said the confident young man.
10. "I'm going to get an 'A' in this course, aren't I?" said Percival, nervously.
11. However, you're likely to get a second chance.
12. You're likely to get a second chance, however.
13. The subway stops at 59th, 66th, 72nd, 79th, and 86th.
14. Why don't you ask Alice?
15. Why don't you ask, Alice?
16. The administrative assistant said, "The CEO was late."

17. "The administrative assistant," said the CEO, "was late."
18. They were going to bring ice, cream, and coffee.
19. They were going to bring ice cream and coffee.
20. Hi, Jack!
21. This is a hijack!
22. Hi, Jean!
23. He's lacking in personal hygiene.

(B) Two-way dictation. Your partner will dictate several tag-bearing sentences to you. Write them down, and then dictate some sentences of your own to him/her. Each of you should then use arrows to indicate intonation. After doing so, compare results.

3.7 Approaches to intonation. There have been numerous approaches to the analysis and representation of intonation, and for further reading we will survey them briefly. Some scholars have focused on complete patterns, depicting each dip and rise. Bolinger (1978), for example, pioneered the use of **contoured text** to produce a detailed representation; diagram (1) in figure 3.j shows how he depicted the intonation of the proverb *Necessity is the mother of invention*. This technique is visually effective, although it was easier to produce on old-style typewriters than on present-day word-processors. Other linguists (Ladd 1986) have extracted the intonation from the words as a peaking and dipping line over the sentence, as in diagram (2), or drawing it as a more rectilinear shape through the words themselves (Fries 1945), as in diagram (3).

Figure 3.j. Some ways of representing intonation

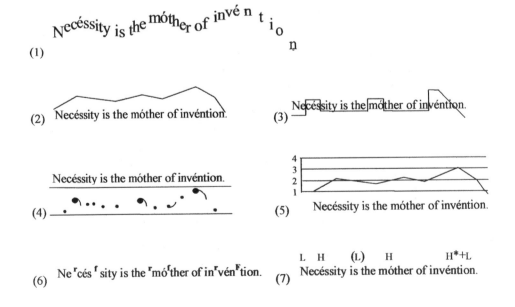

Linguists in the British tradition (e.g., Cruttenden 1986) have favored a different approach: intonation is broken down into pitches on each syllable in an INTERLINEAR TONETIC diagram, as shown in diagram (4). Two horizontal lines define the normal speaking range, and left-to-right dots depict each syllable's level, with heavier dots for stressed ones and small arcs extending from them to show falls and rises. Given their appearance, interlinear tonetic diagrams have also been called "tadpole notation" (Clark and Yallop 1995, 353).

The advantage of contoured text, lines, and tadpoles is their precise indication of the pitch on each syllable. But this attention to detail also has a drawback: such representations yield a different analysis for every sentence depending on its number of syllables and location of stresses, making it difficult to bring out overall patterns.

Other linguists have preferred to analyze intonation into key parts, just as we analyze the blur of sound heard in the word *lean* into three segments: consonant + vowel + consonant. For these key parts, musical notes naturally suggest themselves, and some linguists (e.g., Viëtor 1894) have indeed adopted standard musical notation. But because the familiar five-line staff of music is associated with *absolute* pitch, it is less suitable for a melody that varies according to the speaker's voice range and mood. Many American linguists have therefore adjusted the staff so that it is independent of absolute pitch, as we did in this chapter, but usually with four lines and just four basic pitches. In diagram (5) of figure 3.j, the numeral **1** means a relatively low pitch, **2** a mid pitch, **3** a higher pitch, and **4** an especially high pitch for an emphatic accent. Like others who have adopted this approach, Gleason (1967) and Dalbor (1989) then analyze the melody into its component pitches, adding a vertical down-arrow to indicate the final fall. This permits a simpler, generalized notation for most declarative sentences:

1 2 . . . 3↓/

The **1** is assigned to initial null-stressed syllables (if present), the **3** to the phrasal peak, and remaining syllables receive the mid pitch, **2**. If the final contour (or TERMINAL), ↓, is changed to ↑ (/**1 2 . . . 3**↑/), this statement becomes a yes/no question: *Necessity is the mother of invention?*

Kreidler (1989) likewise analyzes an intonation into component parts, but as a sequence of small rises and falls (**r, f**) versus longer ones (**R, F**), as shown in diagram (6). In this chapter, we have substituted slanted arrows (↓↗ ↘↗ ↘) for these falls and rises. Brazil (1985) and Coulthard (1985), who also adopt these arrows, interpret the falls as indicating an overall "proclaiming" function, in contrast with the merely "referring" function that rises have; other pitches result from successive jumps up or down into different "keys" according to how the discourse is progressing. In autosegmental phonology, on the other hand, intonations are described on a separate level or tier of representation as a sequence of **H**(ighs) and **L**(ows). An asterisk conventionally marks the peak (Beckman and Pierrehumbert 1986) in this approach, as illustrated by (7) in figure 3.j.

The disadvantage of approaches that render melodic lines' contours as numbers or letters is that some detail gets lost: "/1 2 . . . 3↓/" or "L H H H*+L" is obviously more abstract than curves or even tadpoles. But what one loses in detail, one gains in generalizations about overall patterns that can then be compared with other languages for similarities and differences. As Dalbor (1989) noted, the normal Spanish declarative pattern is /1 2 . . . 2↓/ with a final fall (like English) but with the highest pitch reaching **2**, not **3** as in English. The English-like /1 2 . . . 3↓/ is reserved in Spanish for emphasis, which English expresses as /1 2 . . . 4↓/. But no matter what the approach, intonation remains difficult to analyze, and while this chapter has presented the major patterns of English intonation, much work remains to be done.

3.8 Teaching the topics of chapter 3 to students of ESOL.
For advanced ESOL students who have become more sensitive to meaning in discourse and who are therefore able to understand its nuances, various ways to present intonation and manipulate it for different effects have been proposed; see Dalton and Seidlhofer (1994, chap. 7) for a critical review of these. In this section, however, the more fundamental challenge that many teachers face at lower levels—how to develop awareness of English intonation in the first place—will be focused on.

Have you ever played a tonette? It's an inexpensive flutelike plastic-bodied wind instrument that elementary schoolchildren often learn before tackling more sophisticated ones because tonettes are so easy to play—just put your fingers atop its holes and then blow. The tonette is the ideal low-tech medium to use when first presenting the concept of pitch to students. The instrument's pitch range is just one octave, but that's enough to get your students started. What's more, tonettes behave just like flutes, clarinets, horns, or other members of the wind family: the harder your students blow, the louder the sounds they produce will be; in addition, the longer they blow, the longer will be the "vowel" sound that they produce. Lacking tonettes or another musical instrument, the voice itself will serve the purpose, for as you can quickly show your students, it is easy to make the vocal apparatus go up or down in pitch (indeed, some peoples' voices can rise or fall two octaves or more); the vocal apparatus can also readily produce sounds that vary in loudness as well as vowels that can be extended beyond the normal length. In sum, there are lots of ways to present the concepts of pitch, loudness, and length, whether by musical instrument or with our own vocal cords.

Presenting the concept of *peak stress* will require that you lose some inhibitions. Practice, at home, really lengthening vowels, raising pitch, and speaking loudly before you try your new-found skills on your students in class. Many will be shocked at first— and perhaps embarrassed. When producing a peak stress that's really salient, you run the risk of violating the classroom "space" between teachers and students as well as some cultures' preferences for lower, flatter speaking pitch. So warn them that you are merely seeking to reproduce the sort of speech that is typical of conversation. And make sure that your students immediately start to produce peak stresses right after you have shown them how, for otherwise they will quickly become victims of their embarrassment at "misbehaving" and will be less and less willing to act out in ways that the production of peak-stressed syllables demands. One good way to forestall embarrassment is for you and your class to undertake all peak-stress activities together, as a group (or choir, or chorus) before calling on individual students to do so.

As for presenting in class the various melodic lines of English, it is once again the case that exaggeration—at least initially—is the price that one must pay for getting one's students to hear and appreciate the difference between long falls and long rises, short falls and short rises, rise-falls, fall-rises, and the like. When presenting intonation, emphasize the great extent to which intonation is precisely that—tone. Singing a sample sentence will initially (and once again intentionally) violate the sacred classroom space, but if singing is needed to get a point of intonation across, then sing! Even if you have the world's worst singing voice (as does, for example, the first author of this textbook), that too can be turned to a pedagogical advantage, for when students laugh at a creaky voice, they are breaking the ice that has stood as a barrier to appreciating the various melodic lines of English.

NOTES

1. Other books mark peak stress in other ways, including CAPITALS, **boldface**, or *italics* on the word or syllable, or (especially in the International Phonics Association, IPA) double vertical accents, $^{||}$, before it: ÓRANGES, **óranges**, *óranges*, $^{||}$óranges.
2. Remember that an asterisk, or "star," before a form indicates that it is incorrect or impossible.
3. A **noun-noun compound** is not the same thing as a **noun phrase**, which consists of a noun and one or more adjectives. In a noun-noun compound, the first noun does not allow adjectives to modify it and it alone, whereas the noun in a noun phrase **does** allow that. Two examples prove the point: *airbase*, a noun-noun compound, allows one or more adjectives to modify the noun-noun compound as a whole (thus *a large strategic fortified airbase*), yet it is not possible for adjectives to modify the "air" part of *airbase* alone—hence the ungrammatical *a fresh airbase*, an incorrect attempt to represent the equally nonsensical *'a base for fresh air.' (One goes to the mountains, the countryside, or the seashore for fresh air, not to a base.) On the other hand, *air* alone—as the noun of a noun phrase—can indeed be modified by one or more adjectives (*the warm humid air*), as can the noun *base* in its own noun-noun compound (*an important army base*).
4. To determine whether an English compound is written as a single word, as a hyphenated word, or as two or more separate words, students should consult a reliable dictionary recommended by their instructors. That's because the writing of English compounds is not always logical or even consistent. In general terms, it is possible to say that compounds begin their lives as separate words (*apple cart*, 'a cart for transporting apples'), but once they are accepted as a unit and are viewed as belonging together in permanent association, writers may decide that the words should be more closely linked through hyphenation (*apple-cart*); later, the hyphen may disappear and the two words may merge into one (*applecart*). However, by no means all writers of English agree on what is single-worded, what is hyphenated,

and what is two-worded. For these reasons as well as others we will examine, compiling exact statistics about two-word versus hyphenated versus one-word compounds is not recommended, and we do not attempt it here. One language in which the rules for noun-noun compounding are far easier is German, which shares its brother-language's fondness for compounds (and then some), but essentially writes all noun-noun compounds as single words. Here are four of them, all beginning with the same prefix: *Abfertigungsstelle* 'dispatch office'; *Absatzmöglichkeit* 'sales opportunity'; *Abstellvorrichtung* 'stopping mechanism'; *Abstimmungsgebiet* 'plebiscite region.' (If English functioned like German, *outspeakingsregion* and not 'plebiscite region' is how we'd translate the last of these items.)

5. The same stress difference appears in the combination "verb + particle" used as a verb phrase versus its derived compound noun: *to màke úp* ('a test or one's face') versus *a máke-ùp; to rùn awáy* versus *a rúnawày; to prìnt óut* versus *a prínt-òut; to lòg ón* versus *a lógòn, to tùrn óver* versus *a túrnòver, to shùt dówn* versus *the shútdòwn*, and so on.

6. There exists a strong analogy between the metric foot (see chapter 1) and the info unit. Just as each metric foot is constructed around one strong-stressed syllable, so too is each info unit constructed around one peak-stressed word.

7. A restrictive relative clause restricts the reference of its antecedent noun. Thus in sentence (9), the relative clause *who were in the kennel* restricts the reference of *dogs*: only those dogs that were in the kennel were actually barking, which implies that some other dogs elsewhere were **not** barking. On the other hand, a nonrestrictive clause (8) implies that all the dogs we care to mention were barking and that their being in the kennel was an ancillary circumstance.

8. The peaks and valleys are not entirely uniform across all speakers, though. English speakers vary somewhat, both individually and regionally (e.g. British vs. American). What we focus on in this chapter are the major patterns that predominate, especially in the United States.

9. Tags are syntactically difficult because speakers must perform several operations at once. Thus if the pre-tag statement is positive, the tag must be negative (usually with contraction), and vice versa: "You're sick, aren't you?" versus "You're not sick, are you?"; the person, number, tense, and modality of the pre-tag statement's verb must all be copied into the tag ("*They have* worked there for fifty years, *have*n't *they*?"); if the statement lacks an auxiliary verb, a form of *do* must be added to the tag ("They work very hard, *don't* they?"); and as the foregoing examples show, subject/verb inversion must occur. Indeed, tag questions may be **the** most difficult constructions in the English language!

Wrap-Up Exercises

(A) In the following sentence pairs, version (a) uses its sentence-final name as a vocative, whereas in version (b) the final name appears in apposition to the noun, whether as the same person or as the object of the verb. Read each pair aloud and then mark each one's overall intonation pattern.

1a. Where's your daughter, Gloria?   1b. Where's your daughter Gloria?

2a. I don't much like your friend, Pat.   2b. I don't much like your friend Pat.

3a. I'd like to introduce you to my uncle, Mike.

3b. I'd like to introduce you to my uncle Mike.

4a. Have you met my lawyer, Mr. Jones?

4b. Have you met my lawyer Mr. Jones?

5a. This may hurt, Mr. Reeves.

5b. This may hurt Mr. Reeves.

6a. Don't you remember, Mrs. Cohen?

6b. Don't you remember Mrs. Cohen?

7a. Have you seen my dog, Schnappsie?

7b. Have you seen my dog Schnappsie?

(B) Say each sentence in two ways: (a) as a neutral statement or command ($\searrow$) and then (b), without changing word order, as a question ($\nearrow$).

1. It's going to rain.
2. The lock's broken.
3. You're sure of that.
4. So that's Mount Mitchell.
5. Empty the dishwasher.
6. She left the living room light on all night.
7. Eat up all the food on that plate.

(C) Pronounce each tag question in two ways: (a) to show that you think the statement is probably true (tag = $\searrow$) and (b) to show that you are not certain about the statement (tag = $\nearrow$).

1. You don't believe them, do you?
2. It's not going to rain, is it?
3. Mark wasn't finished, was he?
4. You couldn't control your class, could you?
5. She succeeded in pulling the wool over your eyes, didn't she?
6. That's a horse of a different color, isn't it?
7. Oh, so you've wrecked the car again, have you?

(D) Summarize the functions of intonation on the basis of this chapter's examples and descriptions of their effects. Distinguish three types: *grammatical functions* (e.g., sentence structure), *discourse functions* (e.g., information delivery in context), and *emotional functions* (e.g., affect and attitude). Given these meanings of intonation, summarize the ways in which learner errors affect communication with other speakers.

CHAPTER 4

From Orthography to Pronunciation

4.1 Even *English* spelling can be reduced to rules. The PHONOLOGY of a language is its sound system, including suprasegmentals; the ORTHOGRAPHY of a language is its writing system. The two are distinct components with separate units and rules, as we will see. Not all languages have a writing system, and even when they do, it is quite possible to learn and speak the language proficiently without recourse to its orthography. For these reasons, many linguists (e.g., Kreidler 1989) exclude orthography from an analysis of English phonology. The situation is different in the classroom, however: learners of English need (and want) to read and write, and much of what they learn is filtered through the written version of the language. Therefore we devote this chapter to an examination of the sort of phonological/orthographic links that will be useful to the teacher.[1]

This doggerel will illustrate what everyone using *PEASBA* knows all too well: that certain well-chosen examples of English spelling can climb to the very heights of orthographic absurdity.

"Dearest Creature in Creation"

Dearest creature in creation,
Fancy English pronunciation.
I will teach you in this verse
Words like *corpse, corps, horse,* and worse.
I will keep you, Suzy, busy,
Make your head with heat grow dizzy.
Tear in eye, your dress will tear.

So shall I? Oh hear my prayer.
Just compare *heart, beard,* and *heard,*
Dies and *diet, lord* and *word,*
Sword and *sward, retain* and *Britain.*
(Mind the latter, how it's written.)
Now I surely will not plague you
With such words as *plaque* and *ague.*
But be careful how you speak:
Say *break* and *steak,* but *bleak* and *streak;*
Billet does not rhyme with *ballet,*
Bouquet, wallet, mallet, chalet.
Blood and *flood* are not like *food,*
Nor is *mould* like *should* and *would.*
Viscous, viscount, load and *broad,*
Toward to *forward* to *reward.*
And your pronunciation's OK
When you rightly say *croquet,*
Rounded, wounded, grieve, and *sieve,*
Friend and *fiend, alive* and *live.*

Dr. Gerald Nolst Trenité ("Charivarius") (1870–1946)

And so on and so forth, through eighty-four more lines over nine more stanzas. Orthographic humor has long been an English-language staple, as is vividly shown by these visual jokes:

- "We must polish the Polish furniture."
- "He could lead if he'd just get the lead out of his pants."
- "That farm can really produce produce."
- "The soldier decided to desert in the desert."
- "When shot at, the dove dove into the bushes."
- "The bandage was wound around the wound."
- "The crew had a row about how to row the boat."
- "They were too close to the door to close it."
- "A buck does funny things when does are present."
- "They sent in a sewer to stitch up the sewer line."
- "To help plant corn, the farmer taught his sow to sow."
- "After a number of shots, my jaw got number."

Ever since English became an important vehicle of culture in the sixteenth century and an internationally used language in the seventeenth, many well-meaning scholars have attempted to reform its spelling in hopes of doing away with—or at least diminishing—the many inconsistencies. These inconsistencies are mainly due to three factors:

(1) The way many English vowels were **pronounced** underwent radical changes (known as The Great Vowel Shift; see §7.7.1) in late medieval and early modern times, whereas the way these vowels were **spelled** has hardly changed at all; therefore English spelling is archaic.

(2) English spelling has been complicated by the variety of **dissimilar orthographic conventions**—Celtic, Norwegian, Danish, French, Latin, Greek, and so on—in its borrowed vocabulary. Since the eleventh century, English speakers have chosen—both consciously and unconsciously—to adopt, wholesale, tens of thousands of foreign words without changing their spelling significantly if at all. English thus imports not just words but also the diverse orthographic conventions they represent.

(3) The limited alphabet that English ended up with has restricted its spelling of vowel sounds to just two possibilities: GRAPHEMES[2] (i.e., individual letters) and DIGRAPHS (two contiguous letters representing a single sound). This means that English attempts to represent some fourteen stressed vowel sounds by using just five graphemes (*i, e, a, o, u*) in various combinations; it has foregone the option, used in other languages, of adding new letters or diacritics (*ä, ë, ö, â, ê, ô, à, è, ò, á, é, ó, ø, æ*, etc.). The language has likewise never recognized word stress in its orthography even though this is an important feature of pronunciation as we saw in preceding chapters.

Couldn't something be done about this? Unfortunately, all attempts to systematically reform the spelling of English have failed in the past and will continue to fail in the future for two reasons.

For one thing, only languages that do not already have a large body of printed materials—books, journals, encyclopedias, dictionaries, magazines, newspapers, signs, webpages, and databases—can succeed in making substantive changes to their orthographies (as did Rumanian, in 1864, when it abandoned a Cyrillic alphabet for a Roman one). If English ever achieved a system of perfect orthographic fit and managed to impose that new system on the entire worldwide community of its native and nonnative speakers, the words being written on this page and in a trillion other places would become unintelligible to the new system's users within a generation, and all alphabetically retrieved data would become inaccessible. Let us pretend that English adopted what we will call the Teschner and Whitley Orthographic Reform (TWOR) in which these commonsensical grapheme/digraph-to-phoneme correspondences are uniformly established for vowels: /i/ = 'ii', /ɪ/ = 'i', /e/ = 'ee', /ɛ/ = 'e', /æ/ = 'ae', /ɑ/ = 'a', /ɔ/ = 'o', /o/ = 'oo', /ʊ/ = 'u', /u/ = 'uu', /ʌ/ = 'oe', /ə/ = 'ü', /oi/ = 'oi', /ai/ = 'ai', and /au/ = 'au'. Although some pre-TWOR spellings would be similar or even identical to their new TWOR equivalents, most other pre-TWOR spellings would confuse the users of TWOR to the point of rendering them totally unintelligible, as figure 4.a shows.

For another thing, languages spoken in more than one area tend to develop regional variants or DIALECTS, which are sufficiently different that they turn any attempt at

Figure 4.a. The Teschner and Whitley Orthographic Reform Chart

pre-TWOR spelling	TWOR spelling	pre-TWOR spelling	TWOR spelling
seed/cede	**siid**	book	**buk**
meat/meet/mete	**miit**	look	**luk**
him/hymn	**him**	Luke	**luuk**
through/threw	**thru**	loud	**laud**
knew/new/gnu	**nuu**	laud	**lod**
way/weigh	**wee**	but	**boet**
we/wee	**wii**	nothing	**noething**
bet	**bet**	might/mite	**mait**
bat	**baet**	bit	**bit**
goddess	**gadüs**	bite/byte/bight	**bait**
not	**nat**	bait	**beet**
gnat	**naet**	beat/beet	**biit**

spelling reform into a political battle over whose norms—country X's? region Y's? continent Z's?—should be adopted in the new orthography. For many decades, this very problem dogged the best efforts of Brazil and Portugal to reach widely accepted agreement on some relatively minor changes in the spelling of Portuguese, a language whose orthographic fit was not all that bad to begin with. In the case of English, multiple and not-altogether happy compromises would have to be made, especially concerning the spelling of vowels; thus how would we end up writing words such as *can't*, which is /kænt/ in American English but /kɑnt/ in British, or *laboratory*, which is pronounced /lǽbrətɔ̀ri/ in American but /ləbɔ́rətri/ in British?

One goal of spelling reform might be **perfect fit** ('one-on-one correspondence') between writing and pronunciation. As already pointed out, the units of writing are GRAPHEMES, and the units of pronunciation are PHONEMES, shown by symbols enclosed by diagonals, for example, /w/ for the sound spelled 'u' in *quit*. Perfect fit, then, means that each individual phoneme would correspond to just one grapheme, and each individual grapheme would correspond to just one phoneme. The /w/ = 'u' correspondence is obviously imperfect because /w/ is also spelled with the letter 'w' as in *wit*. On the other hand, the correspondence /v/ = 'v' shows a much better fit because the grapheme 'v' represents the phoneme /v/ nearly everywhere,[3] and the reverse is also true because almost all words containing the phoneme /v/ spell it with the grapheme 'v.' Other English phonemes enjoying a pretty good fit are /h/ and /p/. Phoneme /h/ is almost always represented by grapheme 'h' (*hat, hate, help, heaven, him, hit*) and vice versa—grapheme 'h' is usually pronounced as phoneme /h/—whereas phoneme /p/ = 'p' and 'p' = /p/ most of the time.

The problem with units such as 'p' and 'h' is that they don't always function as single graphemes. Instead, 'p' and especially 'h' are often part of a digraph. English is full of digraphs, as illustrated in figure 4.b.

As figure 4.b shows, the digraph 'th' represents two different phonemes, /θ/ or /ð/, depending on the word. Thus English uses /θ/ in *ether* but /ð/ in *either*. This digraph's

Figure 4.b. Digraphs representing vowel phonemes and consonant phonemes

digraph	phoneme	examples
'ng'	/ŋ/	bring, thing, wrong, wrongful, ringing
'ph'	/f/	philosophy, phosphate, Philip, emphasize
'th'	/θ/; /ð/	think, thin, zither; they, there, neither
'sh'	/ʃ/	she, shall, shove, fish, wishful, fresh
'ch'	/tʃ/	chill, choose, check, such, much, gulch
'tch'	/tʃ/	watch, match, catcher, witch, switch
'ee'	/i/	need, feed, sneeze, freeze, sleek
'oo'	/u/	choose, noodle, snooze, tooth, zoo
'ay'	/e/	play, say, pray, clay, may, Wayne
'pp'	/p/	stopping, dropping, shopping, wrapping

fit is therefore perfect in one direction: when moving from phoneme to digraph; however it is not perfect in the other direction—when moving from digraph to phoneme—given the fact that digraph 'th' represents two different phonemes, /θ/ and /ð/, as figure 4.c illustrates.

In the rest of this chapter we do all we can to explain the most important rules of English orthography, hopefully making a complex system simpler. ESOL students differ in the ways that they learn the spelling of English: some hear words spoken before seeing them printed and somehow associate the spoken and written forms, others spend much time checking a dictionary until a word's spelling becomes routine, whereas a third group seeks to master the sort of spelling rules that we set forth here to infer pronunciation more readily. The goal of this chapter is to search for better rules, because not all ESOL materials make the correspondences clear. We subscribe to the principle, known as PHONICS, that, despite its many problems, English spelling is based on general rules with explanatory power and that once informed by these rules, students can learn to read and spell proficiently. Phonics therefore differs from the LOOK-SAY APPROACH which, when applied to spelling, says that each word should be viewed (recognized and processed) as a whole instead of being broken down into its grapheme-phoneme correspondences, whose essence a reader must recognize and then process as a unit. The notion of linguistics-based rules of orthographic analysis is foreign to the look-say approach, but constitutes the very heart of phonics, which nonetheless cannot be properly taught without

Figure 4.c. Digraph 'th' and the two phonemes it represents

the sort of information we provide here. (For additional sources of useful information on English orthography, see Dickerson 1975, 1977, 1978, 1985, 1990; and Dickerson and Finney 1978.)

Exercise 4.1

Divide each of the following words into their respective graphemes and digraphs. (Here is an example of how to proceed: *choosing* 'ch' is a digraph, 'oo' is a digraph, 's' is a grapheme, 'i' is a grapheme, 'ng' is a digraph.)

1. porch	6. supper	11. buzzer
2. think	7. singing	12. navy
3. neither	8. engineer	13. pal
4. adorn	9. frank	14. Paul
5. phrase	10. regardless	15. road

4.2 Consonants: The (somewhat) easy part. It is easier to spell most English consonants than most English vowels. That is not just because consonant phoneme/grapheme relationships show fewer inconsistencies than vowels do; it is also because there are fewer ways to spell most consonant phonemes than there are to spell most vowel phonemes.

English has twenty-four or twenty-five consonant phonemes.[4] Chapter 6 describes their pronunciation in detail. Here we only give the phonemic symbols that the International Phonetic Alphabet (IPA) uses to represent the consonant phonemes, the graphemes/digraphs that English spells these phonemes with, and several examples of words containing them. The most common grapheme(s)/digraph(s) appear in boldfaced type and the somewhat less common appear in regular type, whereas those between parentheses represent that phoneme in just a few words. When appropriate, our discussion of phoneme-grapheme relationships is complemented by figure 4.d's information, based in part on Dewey (1970). For brevity, we adopt certain conventions that will be explained more fully in chapter 5: the formulation "/__ e/i/y" means 'when before the letters *e, i, y*'; **C** = any consonant and **V** = any vowel (so "**ti** + V" means '*ti* plus vowel'); and the symbol **#** means 'word boundary' (so "the#" means 'the sequence -*the* at the end of a word' and **#u** means 'the letter *u* at the beginning of a word').

Eleven of these twenty-five phoneme/grapheme correspondences are reasonably simple and easy to master, for in all eleven the grapheme simply doubles under certain circumstances (and in four of the eleven, a few eccentric digraphs also appear). So it is easy to spell /b d f g l m n p r t v/. The only major concern is to remember—in the case of seven of them (/b d l p r t v/)—when to reduplicate and when not to, that is, when to write 'b' or 'bb,' 'd' or 'dd,' and so on. And in the case of the remaining four (/f g m n/), the only problem is whether to use the single grapheme, its double, or else a digraph such as 'ph,' 'gh,' 'gu,' 'mb,' 'mn,' 'gn,' or 'kn.'

Figure 4.d. Consonants—Phonemes to graphemes/digraphs

phoneme	graphemes/digraphs	examples
/b/	**b**	beat, bit, rob, grab, habit, neighbor, about
	bb	robbing, grabbing, robbed, grabbed
/k/	**c**	climb, cat, cost, cut, crawl, corner, color
	k	kill, kitchen, keep, oak, cook, cooked, cooking
	ch	archaic, chlorine, chlorophyll, choir
	ck	stick, trick, tricked, tricking, tricky
	q	quit, quite, quiet, quaint, quail
	(que)	plaque
/tʃ/	**ch**	choose, chill, church, which, much, touch
	tch	watch, watched, watching, witch, bitch, snitch
	(t)	nature, Christian
/d/	**d**	deal, dull, mad, dial, hide, older, sadist
	dd	hidden, madder, sadder, bladder, odd
/f/	**f**	fat, faint, feel, fork, awful, defeat, scarf
	ff	staff, cliff, stiff, off, miffed
	ph	philosophy, phonetics, phosphate, emphasis
	(gh)	tough, cough, enough
/g/	**g**	go, get, gum, sag, game, gargle, big, hag
	gg	sagged, sagging, struggle, snuggle
	gu	guess, guard, guilt, plague, rogue
/h/	**h**	hat, him, heaven, horrible, ahem, unhinged
	(wh)	who, whole, whore, whose
/dʒ/	**g**	gentle, generous, rage, raged, raging, giant
	j	joke, just, join, journal, enjoy, cajole
	dg	badge, budget, midget, pudgy
/l/	**l**	lake, lame, leak, link, like, welcome, mail
	ll	well, tell, spell, bell, still, kill, mill
	le	able, cradle, table, stable (= /əl/)
/m/	**m**	matter, meat, mine, middle, marry, mother
	mm	common, communicate, hammer, slumming
	mb	climb, climbing, thumb, thumbing, dumb
	mn	autumn, column, condemn, damn, hymn, solemn

(continued)

Figure 4.d. (*Continued*)

phoneme	graphemes/digraphs	examples
/n/	**n** nn (gn) (kn)	neighbor, negative, nice, nobody, none, nut winner, dinner, innovate, inn, innate gnaw, gnu knob, know
/ŋ/	**ng** n	wrong, bring, thing, string, ringing, wrongful ink, mink, think, wrinkle, adjunct, anxious
/p/	**p** pp	pick, paint, complete, incompetent, nip, zap nipping, zapping, shopped, dropped
/r/	**r** rr (rh) (wr)	run, roar, bare, very, hairy, Mary, corner merry, marry, Larry, carry, horrible, torrid rheumatism, rhomboid wrack, wring, wrong
/s/	**s** **ss** **c / __ e/i/y** sc / __ e/i z (ps)	skill, save, same, sell, case, base, mistrust mess, guess, loss, missing, kissing cereal, cent, civil, rice, violence, mercy scene, science, scent, scintillate ersatz, glitz, kibbutz, klutz, pretzel psychology, psychiatrist, psychic
/ʃ/	**sh** **ti + V** ci + V ssi + o ch (s) (ss)	she, shall, shove, bash, bashing, welsh nation, station, diminution, relation, negotiate appreciate, sufficient admission, compassion, discussion, emission chic, chiffon, chartreuse, touché insurance, sugar, sure fissure, pressure, tissue
/z/	**s** **z** (ss)	raise, please, trees, bugs, judges, easy, as amaze, zinc, zip, realize, zebra, finalize dessert, dissolve, po<u>ss</u>ess, scissors
/ʒ/	**s** **si + V** ge (z)	treasure, pleasure, measure, leisure allusion, amnesia, Asia, aversion, Caucasian rouge, garage, ménage, barrage seizure

(*continued*)

Figure 4.d. (*Continued*)

phoneme	graphemes/digraphs	examples
/t/	**t**	tell, tall, hit, knit, later, statistics
	tt	little, hitting, knitted, knitting, butter
	(th)	Thomas, thyme
/θ/	**th**	bath, think, thin, thistle, thaw, with, wrath
/ð/	**th**	they, them, their, there, that, this, bother
	the#	bathe, breathe, lathe, loathe, tithe, writhe
/v/	**v**	van, vain, very, virtue, crave, craving, vote
	(vv)	navvy, savvy, skivvy
	(f)	of, hereof, whereof
/w/	**w**	wash, Welsh, weld, wither, wonder, wild
	wh	what, where, which, white, while
/ks/	**x**	affix, ambidextrous, anxiety, extract, Xerox
/j/	**u** / #__, C__	use, utilize, Ute; abuse, cute, fuel, huge
	y	yell, yesterday, yolk, youth; canyon
	i	billiard, billion, brilliant, million, onion

Consonant REDUPLICATION, or doubling, is a regular convention of English orthography for preserving the phonemic value of a grapheme. Many vowel graphemes have a different value when placed before a consonant that is followed by a so-called silent *e*. This 'e' signals a preceding tense vowel or diphthong rather than a lax vowel. Thus *cap* is /kæp/ but *cape* is /kep/; similarly, *snip* /snɪp/ but *snipe* /snaip/, *cut* /kʌt/ but *cute* /kjut/, and so on. The 'e' drops before a suffix beginning with another vowel grapheme, so when the verb endings *-ing* and *-ed* are added to *hope* /hop/, the spellings are *hoping, hoped*. But now consider the verb *hop* /hɑp/: how can these endings be added without confusing this verb's forms with the differently pronounced forms of *hope*? The English solution is to double the consonant letter after a stressed lax vowel or /ɑ æ/: *hopped, hopping*. The following list sums all this up:

verb base form	expanded forms	process employed
hop	*hopping*	consonant reduplication
hop	*hopped*	consonant reduplication
hope	*hoping*	'i' (once the 'e' has been dropped)
hope	*hoped*	'e' retention

The vast importance of the word-final 'e' in English orthography will be further commented upon in §4.3, where vowels are discussed. For the moment let's just add a few details to our study of the reduplications affecting /b d f g l m n p r t v/. One such detail involves what we will call "those **annoying Latin prefixes**," nicely illustrated by the word *abbreviate* and its reduplicated 'bb,' which is unnecessary from the standpoint of the rules of English orthography.

How did this 'bb' come about? The answer lies in Latin itself: the Latin verb *abbreviare* consists of the prefix *ad-* ('to') plus the root *brev-* ('brief') and the infinitive ending *-iare*. Through a process known as ASSIMILATION, the 'd' of *ad-* changed to the 'b' of *brev-* when attached to it: *ad-* + *brev-* = *ab-brev*, and each /b/ was pronounced separately. English, ever respectful of the spelling of Latin, simply kept the doubled consonant when it borrowed the word and turned it into *abbreviate*, even though English pronounces only one /b/ there. Examples of this Latin doubling abound: *addiction, additive, immense, connect, correct, corrupt.* Another unnecessary complication arises from the respect that Latin, in turn, showed for the orthographic norms of **Greek**: for example, Latin retained its digraph 'ph' for a Greek letter that came to be pronounced like Latin 'f,' and English retained this quirk in its own borrowings of Latinized Greek: *alphabet, amorphous, amphetamine, amphibian, aphrodisiac, phalanx, physics,* and so on.

Another complication stems from English's insistence on applying to all members of a family the graphemes that are pronounced one way in some words but another way in others, for example, the 'mb' as /m/ + /b/ in *bombard, bombardment,* and *bombastic* but as /m/ only in *bomb, bomber, bombing,* and *bombshell.* (This is because English doesn't allow the consonant combination /mb/ in syllable-final position, but in the case of *bombard,* etc., the /m/ ends one syllable and the /b/ begins the next.) Similar strictures apply to some words containing 'gn' = /n/ alone or else /g/ + /n/: *assign* versus *assignation, design* versus *designate*; see also 'mn' = /m/ or else /m/ + /n/ as in *autumn* versus *autumnal, hymn* versus *hymnal,* and so on. Still another complication stems from English's lengthy love affair with **French**: the use of *gu* and *qu* to represent phonemes /g/ and /k/, primarily when appearing before 'i' or 'e'—thus *grotesque, guide, plague, vague.* A final complication arises from English's reliance on doubled consonant graphemes to show vowel differences: thus the *gg* of *baggage, braggart,* and *faggot* is its way of showing that the 'a' is /æ/, not /e/ or /ə/.

The remaining fourteen phoneme/grapheme correspondences can be divided into two groups: (1) these seven—/tʃ h ŋ θ ð w j/—which are fairly easy to spell, and (2) these seven—/k/, /s z ʃ ʒ dʒ/, and /ks/—which are not so easy to spell. Let's talk about the fairly easy ones first.

4.2.1 The fairly easy equivalencies: Phonemes /tʃ h ŋ θ ð w j/.

Phoneme /tʃ/: This phoneme is spelled in two main ways: 'ch' and 'tch.' Combination 'tch' only appears in word-final position—*batch, blotch, catch*—or, if word-medially, in expansions of those words: *catching, catchword, catchy.* There are only a few exceptions to this rule, such as *ki<u>tch</u>en* and *sa<u>tch</u>el*; in twenty *-ion* words /tʃ/ is spelled

-tion (*sugges̲t̲i̲o̲n̲, question*). On the other hand, digraph 'ch' appears word-initially, word-medially, and word-finally: *child, chore, achieve, anchovy, approach, arch,* and so on. About 82 percent of all words with phoneme /tʃ/ represent it with the digraph 'ch.' Alas, not every 'ch' represents phoneme /tʃ/, as is shown by a significant number of Greek-origin words where 'ch' = /k/: *alchemist, anachronism, anarchist, archangel, architecture, archive, Christ.*

Phoneme /h/: This phoneme is represented by just one grapheme, 'h', as in *he, him, help, horrible, history, hominy,* and *hear.* Yet the reverse is not always true, as these two problem areas attest: (1) the muteness of 'h,' mostly at the beginning of these five families' words: *herb, herbal(ist); homage; honest, honestly, honesty; hono(u)r, hono(u)rable; hour, hourglass, hourly*; and (2) the already-commented-upon (4.2) and highly frequent use of 'h' as part of digraphs such as '(t)ch,' 'ph,' 'gh,' 'sh,' and 'th,' in which, of course, 'h' is not pronounced as a separate sound.

Phoneme /ŋ/: This phoneme is spelled by the digraph 'ng,' by grapheme 'n' before 'k' or 'x,' or by 'n' before 'c' = /k/. But while 'ng' indeed spells phoneme /ŋ/ in the high-frequency morpheme *-ing* (*betting, crying, singing*) and in hundreds of typically mono-syllabic words such as *thing, bring, cling, spring,* and *sing,* 'ng' does not always function as a digraph. Thus 'n' and 'g' in *anger, angle, angora, anguish, angular,* and *bingo* represent a cluster containing the separate phonemes /ŋ/ and /g/: /ǽŋgər/, /ǽŋgəl/, /æŋgórə/, /ǽŋgri/, and so on. And the 'g' followed by 'e' or 'i' in *angel, engine, arrange, binge, congested,* and so on represents a different phoneme, /dʒ/, whereas the 'n' itself is no longer /ŋ/ but /n/. It is also true that while 'n' represents /ŋ/ in most 'nk' combinations (or in 'nc' where 'c' = /k/)—*puncture, adjunct, avuncular, bronchial*—it does not always do so, especially in compounds or prefixes, as the following show: *humankind, innkeeper, painkiller, unkind.* In sum, in almost nine out of ten words containing digraph 'ng,' 'ng' is pronounced /ŋ/, but nondigraphic 'ng' appears in exceptions that must be learned—and some of the exceptional words are very common.

Phonemes /θ/ and /ð/: As noted in §4.2, digraph 'th' represents two different phonemes, /θ/ and /ð/. So its fit is perfect in one direction, because you always know that phonemes /θ/ and /ð/ will be spelled with 'th'; however, fit is **not** perfect in the other direction, because 'th' represents two different phonemes, /θ/ and /ð/. About 65 percent of all 'th' digraphs are pronounced /ð/ and the rest /θ/. One rule is that 'th' is /ð/ when followed by 'er' or 'ing': *together, other, bathing, bother, breather, brother, clothing, dither, either, father, feather, further, gather, loathing, mother.* (There are two *-er* exceptions, *ether* and *panther*; *-ing* exceptions are the word *thing* and its derivatives *anything, plaything,* and so on.) It is also true that 'th' is /ð/ in words ending in 'the': *bathe, breathe, clothe, sheathe, soothe, teethe.* Note that removing these words' 'e' changes /ð/ to /θ/: *bath, breath, cloth, sheath, sooth, teeth.* Also note the following, mostly DEICTICS ('words that point to something') where 'th' is word-initial and renders /ð/: *the, their, theirs, them, then, thence, there, these, they, though, those, thus.* In general, then, 'th' = /ð/ predominates, though there are plenty of 'th' = /θ/ exceptions.

The phoneme /w/ versus the combination /hw/: Some English speakers distinguish between /w/ (*witch*) and /hw/ (*which*), whereas most do not (§6.10). For those who distinguish between /w/ and /hw/, orthographic fit is nearly perfect, because almost all /w/ phonemes are spelled with the grapheme 'w' and all /hw/ phonemes are spelled with the digraph 'wh.' It is only in dialects that have dropped the /h/ in /hw/ and **fail** to distinguish between /w/ and /hw/ that the spelling problems arise. What follows is an attempt to predict where 'wh' will occur; in all other environments the learner can assume that /w/ = 'w.'[5]

Digraph 'wh' is mainly a word-initial phenomenon: of our 130 Corpus entries containing 'wh,' 80 percent begin with it. However, 'wh' is **/h/** and never /hw/ in twenty-one of those entries whose post-'wh' vowel is /u/ or /o/: *who* and *whole* and their derivatives *whoever, whom, whose, wholesale,* and so on. And in certain compound words, 'wh' does not function as a digraph and thus is never /hw/: *cowherd, cowhide, knowhow, rawhide, sawhorse.* So here is what remains: (1) thirty-five word-initial 'wh' words in which 'wh' **is** pronounced as /hw/ by those who do so—for example, *whack, whale, what, wheat, wheel, wheeze, when, where, whet, whether, which, while, whim, whimper, whine, whisky, whisper, whistle, white, whiz, why,* and so on—and (2) eighteen 'wh' words and their derivatives, whose word-medial 'wh' is pronounced /hw/ by those who do so: *where (anywhere, elsewhere, everywhere,* etc.), *nowhere, somewhere, awhile, wheat, wheel, overwhelm, somewhat,* and so on.

Phoneme /j/: When we think of consonant /j/ (pronounced 'yuh' but in linguistics known as 'yod' /jod/) and how to spell it, we think of the grapheme 'y,' for it is true that just about all words beginning with 'y' pronounce it as /j/. But in reality the main problem is remembering **not** to write 'y' in most of the words containing /j/ immediately followed by /u/. English has sixty families of 'u' words whose 'u' is pronounced /ju/. Here are some of the more common ones: *-buse- (abuse, abusive), -cum- (accumulate), -cuse- (accuse), -muse- (amuse), commun- (communicate, community, commuter), compute (computer), -fuse (confuse), cube (cubicle), cure (curiosity, curious), eu- (Europe), fume (fumigate), funeral, fury/furor/furious, huge, human (humane, humanity), humid (humidity), humility, humo(u)r, municipal/municipality, munitions, mural, music (musician), mute, mutant (mutilate), mutual, puberty, pure, ubiquitous, Uganda, Ukraine, unanimous, unicorn,* all words with the prefix *uni- (uniform, uniformity, unify, unification, union, unionize, unique, universe, unit,* and so on), *unite, utopia, Uranus (uranium), ureter (urethra, urine), Uruguay, use (usage, usual), usurp, Utah, uterus, utilize (utilitarian),* and abbreviations pronounced with the name of the grapheme (*UNESCO, UNICEF*). But note that the 'u' = /ju/ equivalency is a minority phenomenon, for at least 75 percent of all 'u' graphemes do not give /ju/ but /ʊ/ (*put, full*) or /ʌ/ (*gut, much*), and of the remaining 25 percent in which 'u' = /u/, many /u/s are not preceded by yods, at least in some dialects: *absolutely, adjudicate, allude, aluminum, assume, astute* (see §6.9). To complicate matters, the number of words containing yods that really **are** represented by 'y' barely reaches 100; most **begin** with 'y'—*yacht, yard, yarn, yawn, year, yeast, yell, yellow, yes, yesterday, yew, yield, yodel, yoga, yoke, yolk, you, young, your,* *youth, yuppie*—but in a few the 'y' is medial (*canyon, bayou, lanyard*). And more importantly, the main use of 'y' is to represent not the yod /j/, but the vowels /i/, /ɪ/, or /ai/, as in, respectively, *happy, typical, type.* This last function, however, is mainly limited to word-final or preconsonant positions; before a vowel letter, 'y' is generally /j/. In sum, the 'y' = /j/ equivalency is as limited and partial as is its reverse, /j/ = 'y.' So to spell /j/ and pronounce 'u,' it is helpful to become familiar with the series of words we have presented.

Exercise 4.2

(A) Write five words that contain each of the following consonant phonemes. Do not use the examples in figure 4.a.

1. /b/	5. /w/	9. /g/
2. /r/	6. /θ/	10. /tʃ/
3. /ŋ/	7. /m/	11. /j/
4. /d/	8. /k/	12. /ð/

(B) Pronounce each of the following words and then tell whether the word really exists. (Not all of them are "real" words.)

1. rob	7. spit	13. not	19. nut
2. robe	8. spite	14. note	20. nute
3. cab	9. mad	15. fatted	21. pet
4. cabe	10. made	16. fated	22. Pete
5. slopping	11. yips	17. vot	23. Sam
6. sloping	12. yipes	18. vote	24. same

(C) On each line, underline the symbols representing the consonant phonemes that the word contains when you pronounce it. (Here's how to proceed: *chill:* /t̲ʃ̲/, /ʃ/, /m/, /l̲/.)

    1. match /b/, /m/, /t/, /k/, /tʃ/
    2. Smith /θ/, /m/, /s/, /ʃ/, /t/
    3. loathe /ð/, /θ/, /l/, /h/
    4. cube /dʒ/, /tʃ/, /j/, /k/, /b/
    5. nowhere /r/, /n/, /hw/, /w/
    6. young /n/, /g/, /ŋ/, /w/, /j/
    7. helpful /h/, /b/, /l/, /f/, /j/, /p/, /l/
    8. honorific /h/, /k/, /tʃ/, /r/, /n/, /j/, /f/
    9. wife /f/, /j/, /hw/, /w/
   10. architect /tʃ/, /k/, /k/, /t/, /d/, /t/, /r/

11. philosophy /f/, /p/, /l/, /s/, /f/, /j/
12. vague /g/, /w/, /j/, /v/
13. whether /w/, /t/, /h/, /hw/, /ð/, /θ/, /r/
14. Unitarian /n/, /j/, /t/, /w/, /ks/, /r/

4.2.2 The tough equivalencies: Phonemes /k s z ʃ ʒ dʒ/. To understand why phonemes /k/ and /s z ʃ ʒ dʒ / are tough to spell, let's anticipate chapter 6 by speaking briefly of a category of consonant sounds known as "sibilants." A SIBILANT makes a hissing sound like a snake; indeed, people imitate snakes by saying the sound /s/. The other sibilants are /z ʃ ʒ tʃ dʒ/. These six sibilants form pairs according to whether they are VOICED ('accompanied by the vibrations of the larynx's vocal cords') or VOICELESS ('**not** accompanied by the vibrations of the vocal cords'). Figure 4.e gives the pairs that the six sibilants form. (Don't worry about the other technical terms that are about to appear. You will learn their meanings in chapter 6.)

We have already examined /tʃ/, one of the easy sounds to spell, for it is usually spelled either 'ch' or 'tch.' The other five sibilants and /k/ are harder to spell, as shown in these correspondences.

/k/	c	climb, cat, cost, cut, crawl, corner, color
	k	kill, kitchen, keep, oak, cook, cooked, cooking
	ch	archaic, chlorine, chlorophyll, choir
	ck	stick, trick, tricked, tricking, tricky
	q	quit, quite, quiet, quaint, quail
	(qu)	plaque
/dʒ/	**g**	gentle, religion, rage, raged, raging, giant
	j	joke, just, join, journal, enjoy, cajole
	dg	badge, budget, midget, pudgy
	(dj)	hadj
/s/	**s**	skill, save, same, sell, case, base, mistrust
	ss	mess, guess, loss, missing, kissing
	c / __ e/i/y	cereal, cent, civil, rice, violence, mercy
	sc / __ e/i/y	scene, science, scent, scintillate, scythe
	z	ersatz, glitz, kibbutz, klutz, pretzel
	(#ps)	psychology, psychiatrist, psychic

Figure 4.e. The six sibilant phonemes of English

	Alveolar fricative	Alveopalatal fricative	Alveopalatal affricate
Voiceless	/s/	/ʃ/	/tʃ/
Voiced	/z/	/ʒ/	/dʒ/

/ʃ/	**sh**	she, shall, shove, bash, welsh, fashion
	ti + V	nation, station, diminution, relation, negotiate
	ci + V	appreciate, sufficient, suspicion
	s(s)i + o	admission, compassion, extension, propulsion
	ch	chic, chiffon, chartreuse, touché
	(s)	insurance, sugar, sure
	(ss)	fissure, pressure, tissue
/z/	**s**	raise, please, trees, bugs, judges, easy, as
	z	amaze, zinc, zip, realize, zebra, finalize
	(ss)	dessert, dissolve, po<u>ss</u>ess, scissors
/ʒ/	**s**	treasure, pleasure, measure, leisure
	V + **si** + V	illusion, television, decision, amnesia, occasion
	r + **si** +V	version, submersion, excursion
	ge	rouge, garage, ménage, barrage
	(z)	seizure

Since /k/ is not a sibilant, why is /k/ discussed here with the sibilants? Indeed, why **is** /k/ a tough-to-spell phoneme? To answer that, let's look at the history of the word *concentration*. It is one of the thousands of words that English took from Latin or French. In Latin, *concentrationem* was formed from the root word *centrum,* 'center,' to which the prefix *con-* and the suffix *—ation(em)* were added, thus: *con-* + *centr(um)* + *ationem.* The pronunciation, in Classical Latin, was /kon**ken**tratjónem/: all grapheme 'c's were /k/. The reason English assigned the 'c' to its /s/ phoneme is because in French—a language that profoundly influenced English—all 'c's preceding /e/ or /i/ had changed to /s/, so the tradition of Latin /k/ → French /s/ and therefore English /s/ was well established. In addition, the /tjon/ (minus its ending *-em*) became /sjón/ and later /ʃon/, via a process known as palatalization. Finally, English vowel reduction rules kicked in, and the vowel of /ʃon/ became /ʃən/. In thousands of words like *concentration*, **consonants' *sounds* changed but consonants' *spellings* did not.** That simple fact is at the heart of why it is tough to spell sibilants.

Let us now relate graphemes/digraphs to phonemes. We note that 'c' represents /k/ but also /s/ and /ʃ/. When does 'c'—alone or in combination—equal /k/? /s/? /ʃ/? Here are some answers:

(1) 'c'= /s/ before 'e'/'i'/'y': *cereal, celebrate, civil, civic, cynical, mercy* (provided the 'i' is pronounced as a vowel, which it is **not** in *artificial;* see (3)).

(2) 'sc' = /s/ before 'e'/'i'/'y': *scene, science, descend, scintillate, scythe*

(3) 'c' = /ʃ/ before 'i' in *-cion, -cial, -cian,* and so on: *coer<u>ci</u>on, suspi<u>ci</u>on, artifi-<u>ci</u>al, benefi<u>ci</u>al, magi<u>ci</u>an, politi<u>ci</u>an.* (Note that this 'i' is **not** pronounced as vowel /i/, but merely combines with 'c' as a digraph that renders the /ʃ/ sound.)

(4) 'c' = /k/ elsewhere (in all other environments; i.e., before 'a,' 'o,' and 'u,' before consonants, at ends of words, etc.): *cat, cost, cut, climb, crawl, magic.* In Dewey's (1970) lists, most 'c' graphemes render /k/ (about 73.50%) or /s/ (about 26%). Only 0.5 percent of grapheme 'c's spell /ʃ/.

Having established the rules equating grapheme 'c' with phonemes /k/, /s/, or /ʃ/, let us now work in the opposite direction, equating phoneme /k/ with graphemes 'c,' 'k,' or 'qu':

Although nonsilent 'k' equals /k/ in all environments—*keep, kennel, kill, kitchen, alike, ask* (cf. silent 'k' in *know, knock*)—the reverse is not true, for /k/ is often represented by 'ck' (and, in a limited way, 'q'). Yet despite this potential for confusion, the following seven rules are useful:

(1) /k/ **at the beginning of words** is either 'k' or 'c'—*kennel, kill, kept, kiss, cat, cost, cut, climb, crawl, creep.* Digraph 'ck' never appears in word-initial position. Although 'k' can appear word-initially before all six vowel graphemes— *kale, keen, kick, kook, Kurd, Kyle*—it mostly appears before 'e' and 'i': *keep, kettle, key, kick, kid, king.*

(2) /k/ is often 'ck' at the **end of words**: *attack, back, rack, struck.* The general rule is this: when 'k' alone appears word-finally, it is usually preceded by another consonant: *talk, bank, bark, flask.* When that consonant is 'c,' the two form a digraph that always follows a vowel: *back, brick, deck, shock.*[6] If 'k' in word-final position is preceded by a vowel, that vowel is shown by a digraph: *break, oak, cheek, book, hawk.* (Exceptions are imports: *kulak, Bolshevik, springbok, dybbuk.*)

(3) /k/ is spelled 'ke' (the 'e' is silent) **at the end of** about 500 words, many containing the highly productive suffix -*like*: *childlike, ghostlike, sportsmanlike, warlike.* When /k/ = 'ke,' the preceding vowel sound is represented by a single grapheme, not a digraph: *bake, choke, eke, pike, rebuke, snake.* (Cf. *book, Greek, sneak, boat, boot,* etc.)

(4) 'k' = Ø ('null,' unpronounced) in forty-five words ranging from *knack* and *knave* to *know* and *knuckle.* Word-initial 'k' is always null when followed by 'n.'

(5) Phoneme /k/ joins /l/ or /r/ to produce the consonant combinations /kl/ and /kr/ syllable-initially: /klæʃ/, /kle/, /krʌntʃ/, /kraud/. The /k/ in these combinations is almost always represented by 'c,' not 'k': *clash, clay, crunch, crowd, climb, clumsy, crude, crawl.* The exceptions are imports: *klaxon, klutz, kringle, Sanskrit, Ukraine.* Grapheme 'k' does precede 'l' in several dozen words ending in -'(c)kle' (*ankle, buckle, cackle, chuckle, crackle, freckle*).

(6) Phoneme /k/ is represented by the 'q' in 'qu'; in turn, all 'q's render /k/. What makes 'qu' tough is whether to pronounce or leave silent its 'u.' A general rule is that when *que* is word-final it is only /k/, with 'u' and 'e' mute: *antique, baroque, boutique, burlesque, clique, critique* (cf. *communique* /kəmjùnəké/). In all other positions, *que* is typically /kw/: *quench, quell, queer, aqueduct, banquet, conquest, delinquent, adequate, acquaint, acquiesce, quiet, quota, quotient.*

(7) /k/ = 'ch' in about ninety items, mostly of Greek origin: *ache, alchemy, anachronism, archaic, architecture, archive, chaos, character, charisma, chasm, chemistry, choir, cholesterol, Christianity, chrome, chronic.*

Exercise 4.3

(A) Look at the underlined consonant graphemes/digraphs and then write down the phoneme that each represents. Here is how to proceed: *scientism* /s/, /t/, /z/

1. quiet
2. celebrate
3. cellophane
4. scientific
5. gigantic
6. hydrochloride
7. brick
8. nudge
9. praise
10. proficiency
11. possessions
12. civilize
13. nationalism
14. gauge
15. suspicion

(B) Write five words that contain each of the following consonant phonemes. Do not use examples from the chart in figure 4.d.

1. /dʒ/
2. /ʒ/
3. /k/
4. /s/
5. /z/
6. /ʃ/

(C) Your ESOL students have asked why the underlined consonant(s) are pronounced the way they are. Use the rules from the previous sections to explain their pronunciations.

1. knave = Ø
2. chaos = /k/
3. trickle = /k/
4. superficial = /ʃ/
5. suspicion = /s/, /ʃ/
6. commercialize = /k/, /ʃ/
7. suspicion = /ʃ/
8. relic = /k/
9. queer = /k/
10. crawl = /k/

4.2.3 Grapheme 'i' and the consonants that precede it. We have already seen that when 'c' appears before 'i,' the result is pronounced /ʃ/ in words such as *suspicion, artificial, beneficial,* and *beautician.* In these words the 'i' is **not** pronounced as vowel /i/; its sole function is to combine with 'c' to make the /ʃ/ sound. This happens frequently in English where, in combinations such as *ci + o/a, (s)si + o/a, ti + o/a,* and *xi + o/a,* the 'i' "affects" the preceding consonant in what is called PALATALIZATION. We examine palatalization more closely in chapters 6 and 7. For now we merely note that the upper part of the roof of the mouth is called the **palate** and that when certain consonant sounds are followed by the palate-pronounced /j/ spelled 'i,' they become **palatalized**. Here are six examples; the pertinent consonants appear in boldface in both the base word (which lacks palatalization) and in the derived word, which shows palatalization:

base word   derived word showing palatalization

(1) create /kriét/   creation /kriéʃən/

The 't' = /t/ of *create* becomes the 't' = /ʃ/ of *creation*.

(2) race /res/   racial /réʃəl/

The 'c' = /s/ of *race* becomes the 'c' = /ʃ/ of *racial*.

(3) discuss /dəskʌs/   discussion /dəskʌʃən/

The 'ss' = /s/ of *discuss* becomes the 'ss' = /ʃ/ of *discussion*.

(4) press /prɛs/   pressure /préʃər/

The 's' = /s/ of *press* becomes the 's' = /ʃ/ of *pressure*.

(5) circumcise /sɔ́rkəmsàiz/   circumcision /sɔ̀rkəmsíʒən/

The 's' = /z/ of *circumcise* becomes the 's' = /ʒ/ of *circumcision*.

(6) sex /sɛks/   sexual /sɛ́kʃuəl/

The 'x' = /ks/ of *sex* becomes the 'x' = /kʃ/ of *sexual*.

Examples (4) and (6) are especially interesting because neither is spelled with the 'i.' So how did palatalization occur? The answer lies in what we learned about yod /j/ in §4.2.1: when 'u' is pronounced /ju/, the yod is present even though no separate letter spells it. (Thus words such as *cute* and *fuel* are pronounced /kjut/ and /fjúəl/ even though they're never spelled *kiute*, *fiuel*.) The yod doesn't even have to be present in modern English; thus the yod that was present long ago in the now-out-of-date pronunciations of *pressure* as /présjur/ and *sexual* as /sɛ́ksjuəl/ served to palatalize the preceding consonant—the /s/—and then eventually dropped out.

In combinations such as *ci, si, ssi, ti,* and *xi,* followed by *o/a* in which palatalization occurs, the only remaining question is whether the 'i' is pronounced (as vowel /i/ or yod /j/), or whether its sole purpose is to palatalize the consonant and then die. In most instances it dies. Though the 'i' has left behind a palatalized consonant, that 'i' has ceased to function as an orthographic representative of a vowel or consonant sound of its own.

It is possible to list, as the following shows, words in which 'i' tends to be pronounced as /i/ or /j/ after palatalizing a consonant and in which the 'i' may even yield two pronunciations (shown with the number 2), but the student must ultimately learn these as he/she hears them from other speakers. Pre-yod or pre-vowel consonants boldfaced and underlined are pronounced as palatalized /ʃ/ or /ʒ/. When a word has two or more 'i's, it is the underlined 'i' that is pronounced as /i/ or /j/.

graphemes	words whose 'i's are pronounced as /i/ or /j/
cia	appreciate, appreciation, associate [as verb], beneficiary (2), depreciate, depreciation, excruciating, judiciary (2), officiate, superficiality
cio	sociologist, sociology
(s)sia	anesthesiology (cf. *anesthesia* [2]), Asiatic, ecclesiastic, enthusiastic, euthanasia (2)
(s)sio	anesthesiologist, physiognomy, physiological, physiology
tia	confidentiality, differentiate, impartiality, ingratiate, ingratiating, initiate, initiation, negotiate, negotiation, negotiator, partiality, penitentiary, propitiate, satiate, substantiate, tertiary (2), uninitiated, unsubstantiated, vitiate

Exercise 4.4

(A) Tell whether (a) the underlined 'i' is pronounced as **vowel /i/ or yod /j/** or (b) the underlined 'i' just palatalizes the preceding consonant (and isn't pronounced as /i/ or /j/) or (c) both happen.

1. abomination
2. disassociate
3. officiated
4. anesthesiology
5. racialism
6. concussion

(B) Write /ʃ/ beside all graphemes representing it; write /ʒ/ beside all graphemes representing it.

1. confidential 2. substantial 3. Asian 4. Haitian 5. elimination
6. assurance 7. collision

4.2.4 When is 's(s)' /s/ and when is it /z/, /ʃ/, or even /ʒ/? Before reading what follows, review figure 4.e to refresh your memory about the phonemes /s/, /ʃ/, /z/, and /ʒ/ and how they are spelled.

The main concern of this section is to figure out which phoneme is represented by which of the various sibilant-spelling graphemes: 's,' 'ss,' or 'z.' As you see from figure 4.e, 's' can represent /s/, /z/, and /ʒ/, so 's' has the poorest fit of any English consonant grapheme. On the other hand, a full 94.6 percent of 'z's render /z/ (Dewey 1970), so this grapheme seldom represents other sounds.

Before tackling 's,' let's deal with the easier equivalencies.

'z': If grapheme 'z' enjoyed perfect fit with phoneme /z/ (whose pronunciation is always voiced, i.e., accompanied by the vocal cords' vibrations), then all 'z's would equal /z/ and vice versa. As we know, nineteen of every twenty 'z's do render /z/—everything from *lazy* and *crazy* to *zeal* and *zoo*. It is also useful to know that the reduplicated 'zz' almost always renders /z/: *blizzard, buzz, dizzy, drizzle, embezzle, fizz, frazzle, frizzy, fuzz*. The exceptions include 'zi' for /ʒ/ in *glazier* and a few loanwords in which 'z' = /s/ (*klutz, pretzel, kibbutz*, etc.) or /ts/ (*schizophrenia, pizza*).

'ss': This reduplication **usually** renders /s/ (93% of the 'ss' words in Dewey 1970), as in *abscess, access, across, mess, messy, obsess(ed)*; see also the multitude of words that end in -*le̲s̲s̲* and -*ne̲s̲s̲* (*ageless, heedless, meaningless; blindness, kindness, usefulness*). Palatalization explains 'ss' = /ʃ/ in several dozen words such as *admission, assure, commission, compassion, confession*, and *pressure*. In a handful of words, 'ss' even renders /z/: *bra̲s̲s̲iere, de̲s̲s̲ert, di̲s̲s̲olve, po̲s̲s̲ess, po̲s̲s̲ession, sci̲s̲s̲ors*.

'c' and 'sc': We've already learned (4.2.2) that /s/ can be represented by 'c' (/__ e/i/y: *cereal, celebrate, civic, civil, rice, mercy*) and by 'sc' (/__ e/i/y: *scene, science, scent, scintillate*).

'ci,' '(s)si,' or 'ti' with vowel; 'ge' or 'gy': We recall that palatalization produces /ʃ/ in *ci, ssi*, or *ti* + V (*appreciate, sufficient, admission, nation, negotiate, relation*). We also recall that palatalization produces phoneme /ʒ/ in *si* + V (*allusion, amnesia, Asia, aversion, Caucasian*). Phoneme /ʒ/ also appears in V + 'ge,' primarily in word-final position (*barrage, espionage, garage, ménage, mirage, rouge*), although in the overwhelming majority of the more than a thousand words ending in 'ge' or 'gy,' V + 'ge' renders /dʒ/, for example, *bandage, cabbage, courage, garbage, language, message*, and the numerous words in -*logy* (*biology, psychology, sociology*, etc.). It is also the case that in word- or syllable-initial position, 90 percent of all 'ge' words have 'ge' as /dʒ/: *gelatin, gem, gender, gene, general(ity)* (but see 'g' = /g/ in *gear, geese, geezer, geld, get, geyser*). Note that 'gi' is much less likely than 'ge' to spell phoneme /dʒ/, for just half the smaller body of words containing 'gi' will render it as /dʒ/—*giant, gibber(ish), gibe, gigantic, gin, ginger*—whereas the other half will render 'gi' as /g/: *gibbon, giddy, gift(ed), gig, giggle, give, gimp*.

4.2.5 Grapheme 's' and /s/, /z/, and /ʒ/.

We now come to grapheme 's' itself. We already know that 's' renders, profusely, the three phonemes /s/, /z/, and /ʒ/. Let's figure out which, when, and how.

's' = /ʒ/: We start with the most marked or atypical of the 's' relationships, 's' = /ʒ/. We have learned that 's' renders /ʒ/ before a 'u' that represents or used to represent /ju/. This is a regular generalization for V + -*sure*, such as *closure, composure, exposure, leisure(ly), measure, pleasure*, and *treasure*. When not postvocalic, -*sure* tends to have /ʃ/: *censure, fissure, pressure*, and *sure* itself.

's' = /z/: A healthy minority—39 percent, or 1,902, of the 4,906 words with grapheme 's' in Dewey (1970)—pronounce that 's' as /z/. Let's identify those words by observing how the /z/-rendering 's' behaves in certain environments.

's' = /z/ in word-final position: Word-final 's' is mostly /s/, not /z/, so the "marked" equivalency in that position is 's' = /z/. Therefore once we learn where 's' equals /z/, we can say by process of elimination that 's' equals /s/ in all other word-final environments.

The grapheme 's' spells the frequent ending *-(e)s*; this ending represents three different morphemes: plural (*horses*), possession (*the horse's hoof*), and the third-person-singular present tense (*he horses around a lot*). All three morphemes change systematically according to the kind of phoneme they follow: /əz/ after sibilants (*horses, rushes, judges*), /s/ after the voiceless sounds /p f t θ k/ (*cats, puts*), and /z/ after all other phonemes, including vowels (*cubs, throws*). This variation is described at length in chapter 7, but this chapter's orthographic generalization is this: whenever final 's' represents an "ending," it follows separate rules based on English grammar, and this takes precedence over generalizations such as those in the following discussion.

English has a large number of words that end in an /s/ that does **not** serve to pluralize, indicate possession, or represent the third-person-singular present tense. Among them are *chaos, cosmos, rhinoceros, thermos, bus, crocus, discus, focus,* and *syllabus* as well as thousands of words ending in /əs/ = *-ous*: *carnivorous, conscious, delicious, extraneous, gregarious, miscellaneous, posthumous, ridiculous, studious.* On the other hand, in a relatively small group of high-frequency native monosyllables, 's' is /z/: *as, his, has, is, was* (and their contractions *isn't, wasn't,* etc.). In addition, the word-final 's' of a number of Greek-origin words such as *caries, herpes, isosceles,* and *rabies* is rendered /z/ even though this 's' usually doesn't represent morpheme /z/. Then there are the Greco-Latin nouns ending in *-sis* that form their plurals by changing an already-present /s/ to /z/, thus *thesis* → *theses* (/θísəs/ → /θísìz/, also *emphasis* → *emphases* (/ɛmfəsəs/ → /ɛmfəsìz/).

's' = /z/ in intervocalic and word-medial position: For this correspondence, there are two rules that admit no exceptions: **'s' = /z/ in all nouns ending in *-ism*** (from *atheism* to *Zionism*), and **'s' = /z/ in all words ending in *-ese*** (*Chinese, Japanese, Portuguese,* etc.) Otherwise, **'s' = /z/** is unpredictable. While about 75 percent of all words containing the 's' in intervocalic and word-medial positions use that 's' to represent /z/ (*rose, phase, ease,* etc.), some 25 percent do not (e.g., *caboose, cease, chase, concise, crease, erase, goose*). And as it has proven impossible to come up with rules that tell us where intervocalic and word-medial 's' is /z/, we simply list them in the CD in an alphabetical list of the 462 Corpus words whose intervocalic and mid-word 's' = /z/, underlined in words containing more than one 's.' (Excluded are derived participles, gerunds, and *-ly* adverbs, i.e., *eased, easing, easily.*) **If an intervocalic or word-medial 's' does *not* appear in the CD's list, one assumes that its 's' = /s/ and not /z/.**

's' = /s/ in word-initial position: This rule admits almost no exceptions and is very simple: when grapheme 's' begins a word, it is pronounced /s/. More than 2,800 words from *safe, same,* and *save* through *swear, swell,* and *switch* exemplify this rule. The two common exceptions are *sugar* /ʃúgər/ and *sure* /ʃʊr/. Also appearing word-initially, digraph 'sh' is always pronounced /ʃ/ in that position.

Exercise 4.5

(A) Here, words are written out and then transcribed. Fill in the blanks with the correct sibilant-sound symbol (/s z ʃ ʒ/) to complete the transcription.

1. sure /_ʊr/
2. pass /pæ_/
3. splashes /splǽ_ə_/
4. precious /prέ_ə_/
5. nose /no_/
6. desertion /də_ɔ́r_ən/
7. sparse /spár_/

8. frivolous /frívələ_/
9. residency /rέ_ədən_i/
10. please /pli_/
11. cease /si_/
12. communism /kámjənì_əm/
13. commission /kəmí_ən/
14. sophism /sáfì_əm/

15. misery /mí_əri/
16. measles /mí_əl_/
17. the Ritz /ðə.rít_/
18. muzzle /mʌ_əl/
19. raisin /rέ_ən/
20. poise /pói_/
21. hasn't /hǽ_ənt/

(B) In the blank space to the left, write the phoneme corresponding to the graphemes/ digraphs that usually represent it. Then write five example words in the space to the right.

phonemes: /s z ʃ ʒ/

phoneme	graphemes/digraphs	examples
_____	'z'	_____
_____	'ss'	_____
_____	'sc' / __ e/i/y	_____
_____	'sh'	_____
_____	'si' + V	_____
_____	's' / V__V	_____

(C) Using the explanations from 4.2.2–4.2.5, tell why the underlined consonant(s) are pronounced the way they are.

1. puzzle = /z/
2. klutz = /s/
3. success = /s/
4. commerce = /s/
5. fission = /ʃ/

6. bison = /s/
7. prison = /z/
8. Japanese = /z/
9. wise = /z/
10. loose = /s/

11. runs = /z/
12. chases = /z/
13. stops = /s/
14. marvelous = /s/
15. herpes = /z/

4.2.6 Grapheme 'x' and the five things it renders. We say "things," rather than "sounds or combinations of sounds," because grapheme 'x' actually renders all of the following (the most important numbers are boldfaced):

(1) /z/: the single sound /z/, as in *anxiety, xenophobia, xenophobic, Xerox*, *xylo-phone*

(2) **/ks/**: the combination /ks/, as in *affix, ambidextrous, annex, anorexic*

(3) /kʃ/: the combination /kʃ/, as in *anxious, complexion, crucifixion, sexual* (and its many derivatives), *obnoxious, reflexion* (more often *reflection* in the U.S.)

(4) /gz/: the combination /gz/, as in *auxiliary, coexist, exacerbate, exact*

(5) /gʒ/: the combination /gʒ/, as in *luxury* /lʌgʒəri/ (also /lʌkʃəri/), *luxuriant, luxuriate, luxuriously*.

Of these five possibilities, numbers (2) /ks/ and (4) /gz/ together account for 80 percent (40% each) of the 'x' corpus. Possibilities (1), (3), and (5) are limited to the words listed. Let's now determine which conditions produce /ks/ and which /gz/.

A useful general rule is that 'x' represents /gz/ when 'x' (especially in the prefix *ex-*) appears before a strong- or weak-stressed vowel. Here are more examples of 'x' = /gz/: *exággerate, exám, exàmination, exécutive, exécutor, exémplary, exémplify, exémpt(ion)*. Grapheme 'x' is /ks/ elsewhere: *anthrax, apex, appendix, approximate, asphyxiate, axiom, axis, axle, wax, box, climax*.

Exercise 4.6

Write the number and the sound(s) of the explanation of how 'x' is pronounced in these words:

number; its sounds	'x' word	number; its sounds	'x' word
_____	exertion	_____	exacerbate
_____	toxic	_____	xenophilia
_____	pansexual	_____	dexterity
_____	luxuriously	_____	Mexico
_____	extravagant	_____	exactly

4.3. Vowels: Which are easy and which are tough to spell. As noted earlier (§4.1), one limitation of English orthography is that, unlike other languages, it has not adopted new letters or diacritics (accents, tildes, slashes, and macrons) to show other vowel differences. Thus English depends solely on graphemes or digraphs to represent its eleven simple vowel sounds (/i ɪ e ɛ æ ɑ ɔ o ʊ u ʌ/), its three full diphthong sounds[7] (/oi ai au/), and the /ər/ combination. That's a lot of sounds to be represented by graphemes or digraphs alone!

The English alphabet contains just five vowel graphemes—'a,' 'e,' 'i,' 'o,' and 'u,' to which one must add 'y' (because in some environments it behaves like a vowel), and also 'w,' which combines with 'a e o' to produce digraphs. With such combinations, English might employ forty-two possible digraphs ranging from 'aa' to 'yy.' By adding these digraphs to the total number of vocalic graphemes we get forty-eight possible ways to spell the stressed English vowel sounds as well as unstressed /ə/. Of the forty-eight theoretical possibilities, twenty-seven of the digraphs and all six graphemes—thirty-three out of forty-eight, or 68.75 percent—are actually used to spell the vowel

Figure 4.f. Graphemes and digraphs that English uses to spell vowel sounds

i	e	a	o	u	y
ia	ea	aa	oa	ua	ya
ie	ee	ae	oe	ue	ye
ii	ei	ai	oi	ui	yi
io	eo	ao	oo	uo	yo
iu	eu	au	ou	uu	yu
iy	ey	ay	oy	uy	yy
iw	ew	aw	ow	uw	yw

sounds of English. This is shown by the table in figure 4.f, in which all graphemes/digraphs actually representing individual vowel sounds appear in boldfaced type. (Lightfaced ones are either used to represent two or more contiguous and different vowel phonemes, e.g., *cha*_os_ + /kéɑ̀s/, *continu*_uu_*m* /kəntínjuəm/, or are never used to represent anything, e.g., *yy.)

In addition, a very small number of individual vowel sounds can be represented by the following five TRIGRAPHS, or three-letter combinations: *aye, eau, eye, ieu (lieutenant),* and *owe.*

The English vowel system is analyzed in full in chapter 5. The following table (figure 4.g), which first appeared as figure 1.d, remains a preview of that system. The limited information the following table provides will help us clarify the relationship between the way the vowels are spelled (with vowel graphemes and digraphs) and the way the vowels are pronounced (vowel phonemes).

When dealing with vowels and their orthography, the nature of the relationship between English phonemes and their spellings depends to a large extent on whether the phoneme is tense—/i e o u/—or lax: /ɪ ɛ ʌ ɔ ʊ/. Briefly put, **most lax vowels are fairly easy to spell, whereas all tense vowels are frankly difficult to spell.** Let's put this new information in context by looking at the table in figure 4.h, which relates phonemes to

Figure 4.g. English vowel phonemes

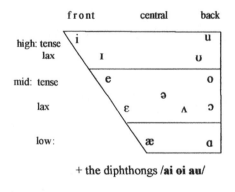

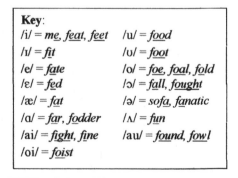

+ the diphthongs /**ai oi au**/

Key:
/i/ = *me, feat, feet*   /u/ = *food*
/ɪ/ = *fit*   /ʊ/ = *foot*
/e/ = *fate*   /o/ = *foe, foal, fold*
/ɛ/ = *fed*   /ɔ/ = *fall, fought*
/æ/ = *fat*   /ə/ = *sofa, fanatic*
/ɑ/ = *far, fodder*   /ʌ/ = *fun*
/ai/ = *fight, fine*   /au/ = *found, fowl*
/oi/ = *foist*

Figure 4.h. Vowels—Phonemes to graphemes/digraphs

The symbol appearing at the beginning of each vowel phoneme's section is the one this textbook uses. Graphemes/digraphs appearing in boldface ('**ee**,' '**ea**') are the ones most frequently used to represent the particular phoneme. Other combinations are less frequently used to do so, while those in parentheses only represent a handful of items.

phonemes	grapheme(s)/digraphs	example words
/i/	**ea**	please, lease, meal, grease, sea, flea, leap, heat, speak
	ee	need, feed, greed, sneeze, feel, freeze, bee, see, flee, sleek
	y	happy, sloppy, piggy, lazy, crazy, windy, cranky, marry
	e	region, exterior, cereal, me, he, be
	e-e	plebe, eke, here, Chinese, theme, scheme
	ei	receive, deceive, conceive, perceive, seize, leisure, weird
	ey	alley, donkey, hockey, key, money, monkey, journey
	i-e	machine, ravine, valise, elite, routine, sardine, police
	ie	niece, piece, shriek, thief, chief, brief, grief, siege, fiend
	(eo	people)
/ɪ/	**i**	bit, fit, miss, kiss, crib, snip, him, sin, tin, slim, think
	(e	English)
	(ee	been)
	(ei	counterf<u>ei</u>t)
	(u	b<u>u</u>siness)
	(y	gym, hymn)
/e/	**a-e**	gate, hate, grave, save, late, date, fate, rate, plane
	ai	wait, bait, straight, pain, gain, main, train, plain, praise
	ay	play, say, lay, pray, Wayne, gay, hay, clay, may, gray
	ei	weigh, neighbor, sleigh, freight, inveigh, eight, deign, vein
	a	nation, razor, situation
	ea	yea, great, steak, break
	ey	they, grey, fey, hey
	(ae	reggae, sundae, (a)egis)
/ɛ/	**e**	bet, get, hell, bell, let, set, red, fled, men, gentle, step
	ea	head, bread, threat, sweat, dead, homestead, spread, deaf
	(a	any, many)
	(ae	aerial, aerobatics, aerodynamic)
	(ai	said)
	(ei	heifer)
	(ie	friend)

(continued)

Figure 4.h. (*Continued*)

phonemes	grapheme(s)/digraphs	example words
/æ/	**a**	bat, cat, mat, pat, rat, sat, vat, back, track, lack, mack
	(ai	plaid)
	(au	laugh)
/ɑ/	**a**	father, are, bar, art, wasp, want, Slav, star, palm, waffle
	o	top, mop, slop, job, knob, knock, block, lock, modern, fodder
	(aa	Afrikaans)
	(ea	heart)
/ɔ/	**au**	fraught, fraud, pause, applause, haunt, fault, haul, launch
	aw	paw, thaw, jaw, draw, hawk, awful, dawn, lawn, yarn, crawl
	o	off, boss, toss, floss, soft, lost, crossed, honk, golf, cost
	a	talk, walk, stalk, small, stall, bald, fall
	ou	ought, bought, cough, trough, thought
	(oa	broad)
/o/	**o**	no, go, so, don't, pro, fro, ocean, motion
	o-e	rope, slope, robe, vote, code, cope, mope
	oa	soap, boat, goat, bloat, toad, road, loaf, coach, roach
	ow	know, show, mow, low, snow, glow, grow, flow, crow, bowl
	oe	foe, doe, woe, goes, throes
	ou	dough, mould, soul
	(au	mauve, gauche)
	(eau	beau, nouveau)
	(ew	sew)
	(owe	owe)
/ʊ/	**oo**	foot, soot, good, stood, book, took, look, cook, wool, croof
	u	put, push, bush, full, pull, bull, cushion, pussy, bushel
	(o	wolf, woman)
	(ou	could, should)
/u/	**oo**	goo, zoo, coop, loop, troop, tooth, goof, proof, groove, booth
	u-e	attitude, brute, flute, dude, nude, rude, crude, truce, spruce
	ew	chew, Jewish, brew, drew, crew, screw, shrewd
	o	do, who, move, lose, prove, whose, womb
	ou	through, soup, group, you, youth, douche, coupon
	u	ablution, absolution, adjudicate, aluminum, truth
	ue	blue, ensue, flue, true, clue, glue, duel, rueful
	ui	suit, fruit, sluice, bruise
	(eu	sleuth, leukemia, neurosis)

(continued)

Figure 4.h. (*Continued*)

phonemes	grapheme(s)/digraphs	example words
	(ieu	lieutenant)
	(oe	shoe)
	(uu	vacuum)
	(wo	two)
/ʌ/	**o**	love, glove, come, from, done, ton, tongue, monk, shove
	ou	young, tough, rough, cousin, couple, double, trouble
	u	cup, puppy, tub, rub, cut, nut, stud, duck, rug, puff, plus
	(oo	flood, blood)
	(a	was)
/oi/	**oi**	voice, noise, coin, join, void, groin, oil, boil, moist, point
	oy	boy, toy, joy, joyful, ahoy, soy
	(uoy	buoyancy, buoyant)
/ai/	**i**	fight, sigh, tight, sight, might, pint, bind, mind, kind, find
	i-e	pipe, ripe, stripe, site, bribe, tribe, bite, mite, rite, kite
	y	by, shy, my, why, try, cry, fly, spy, sky, sly, type, nylon
	ei	height, eiderdown, feisty, heist, kaleidoscope, seismic
	ie	tie, die, pie, vie
	(aye	aye)
	(eye	eye)
	(ia	diamond, diaper)
	(ui	guise)
	(uy	guy, buy)
	(ye	rye, dye)
/au/	**ow**	plow, cow, vow, how, chow, brow, browse, brown, down, town
	ou	bough, out, doubt, shout, trout, scout, cloud, south, mouth

graphemes/digraphs.[8] Note that some digraphs in this table are DISCONTINUOUS, separated by an intervening consonant: thus a representation such as 'i-e' means grapheme 'i' with an 'e' after the following consonant (as in *mach*__in__*e*, but not *machination*).

4.3.1 Vowels that are fairly easy to spell. Seven of the vowel phonemes are fairly easy to spell. They are (1) the two **low vowels** /æ ɑ/, (2) three of the **lax vowels** /ɪ ɛ ʊ/, and (3) two of the **diphthongs** /oi au/ (but not the third, /ai/).

/æ/ is nearly always spelled 'a' (*bat, cat, back, track*); indeed, 98 percent of Dewey's (1970) /æ/'s are spelled that way.

/ɑ/ is more complicated but still spellable, primarily (78.5%) as the 'o' of *top, job,* and *block* in American English (but not British, see §5.6.1), but also (21%) as the 'a' of *spa, yacht, father,* and *scar.* There are no reliable rules for when to use which spelling.

/ɪ/ is spelled 'i' almost without exception: *him, crib, mink, fit, bit, knit.* Words in which /ɪ/ is rendered otherwise are rare or isolated, though one of the great ironies of English orthography is that the word *English* itself—/íŋglɪʃ/—is one of them.

/ɛ/ is spelled 'e' in more than 90 percent of all cases (Dewey 1970); examples are *get, spell,* and *went.* About 5 percent of all /ɛ/ words use the digraph 'ea'; for example, *bread, meadow, heaven.*

/ʊ/ prefers the digraph 'oo,' especially before consonants such as 'k' (*book, look, crook*), but also uses 'u' profusely, especially before 'l' or 'sh' (*full, bull, push*).

/oi/ is a learner's dream, for it is almost always represented by 'oy' at the end of words or syllables (*joy, alloy, loyal, soy*) and by 'oi' medially and before consonants (*boil, voice, noise, join, moist*).

/au/ is more complicated, for it is represented—according to Dewey (1970)—in 78 percent of all cases by 'ou' and in 22 percent by 'ow.' However, the two show a pattern: 'ou' almost never represents /au/ in word-final position, whereas 'ow' often represents /au/ there (*how, now, brown, cow, plow, vow*).

Exercise 4.7

(A) List the seven vowel phonemes that are easy to spell.

(B) Write at least three words that use the indicated grapheme/digraph to spell the particular phoneme.

grapheme/digraph	phoneme	example words
'a'	/æ/	_____
'a'	/ɑ/	_____
'o'	/ɑ/	_____
'i'	/ɪ/	_____
'e'	/ɛ/	_____
'ea'	/ɛ/	_____
'oo'	/ʊ/	_____

'u'	/ʊ/	_____
'oi'	/oi/	_____
'oy'	/oi/	_____

4.3.2 Vowels that are tough to spell. The orthographic representations of the remaining seven vowels—/i e o u ʌ ɔ ai/ are frankly problematic. Yet even most of them can be reduced to useful sets of descriptive rules. The seven tough vowels are best analyzed by dividing them into clusters: (1) the four tense vowels /i e o u/, (2) diphthong /ai/, and (3) the two mid lax vowels /ʌ ɔ/.

4.3.2.1. The four tense vowels /i e o u/. /i/: *Bea, bee, be; feel, field, veal; see* and *sea*—one feels oneself to **be** at sea when spelling phoneme /i/. However, with the exception of the second segment of digraph 'ea,' the orthography of /i/ is limited to the "front-vowel" graphemes/digraphs 'ee,' 'y,' 'e,' 'ei,' 'i,' and 'ie.' Other useful generalizations are the following:

- Grapheme 'y' typically represents /i/ when unstressed at the end of a word (including a compounded one): *happy, marry, Mary, merry, sleepy, jellybean.*
- Grapheme 'i' only represents /i/ when followed by a consonant (often 'n') plus a silent 'e': *machine, police, elite, ravine, sardine.* Annoyingly though, this same sequence more often renders the diphthong /ai/, as in *time, ride, side, pine, crime.* See §4.3.2.2 for more on /ai/.
- The famous elementary-school rule "'i' before 'e' except after 'c'" is largely true, as these words illustrate: *niece, piece, shriek, thief,* but *receive, deceive, conceive, perceive.*
- If word-final 'e' is pronounced, it will render /i/: *adobe, be, he, me, she.* However, bear in mind that the overwhelming majority of word-final 'e's are **not** pronounced: *probe, peace, lace, service, dance, distance, experience, trade, homage.* In a 581-page inverse English dictionary (Lehnert 1971), words ending in mute 'e' occupy a full 20 percent of the volume, so it is no wonder that 'e' is the most frequent grapheme in the English language.
- Without exception, all 'ee' digraphs render /i/. This is one of the best examples of digraph/phoneme fit in English.

/e/: In Dewey (1970), nearly 70 percent of all words containing /e/ use 'a' to spell it, either as 'a' + consonant + (mute) 'e'—*gate, hate, grave, plane*—or else as 'a' alone in words such as *nation, situation,* and *razor.* Yet large numbers of words represent /e/ with digraphs 'ai,' 'ay,' and 'ei' as well, and quite a few do so with 'ea' and 'ey.' But as was true of /i/, phoneme /e/'s spellings reveal a pattern: /e/ is largely represented by 'a' alone or else 'a' or 'e' in combination with 'i' or 'y.' Additional information about /e/ and how it is spelled involves three exclusive representations:

- Digraph 'ay' represents /e/ exclusively. (Thus all 'ay's will be pronounced /e/.)
- The 'a' of the discontinuous grapheme combination 'a' + C + 'e' represents /e/ exclusively. Thus although the 'a' of words such as *bar, scar* and *hat, fat* is respectively /A/ and /ë/, the 'a' of *bare, scare,*[9] *hate,* and *fate* can only be /e/.
- The 'ei' that renders /e/ in *weigh, neighbor, freight, vein, veil,* and so on exceeds the 'ei' that renders /i ɪ ɛ/ by a 4:1 ratio. What's more, 'ei' representing /i/ largely occurs "after 'c,'" which it never does when representing /e/.

/o/: The good news about /o/'s orthographic representations is that all the significant ones—'o,' 'o-e,' 'oa,' 'ow,' 'oe,' 'ou'—involve grapheme 'o.' The bad news is that there are so many of them. However, just two—'o' itself and 'o-e' (the discontinuous 'o' plus C(onsonant) plus 'e')—account for 79 percent of all representations in Dewey (1970). More good news derives from the fact that digraph 'oa' represents /o/ almost exclusively (though only 6% of Dewey's /o/ words spell it as 'oa'). Here are some other useful bits of information about /o/ and how it is spelled:

- The 'o' of the discontinuous 'o' + C + 'e' represents /o/ exclusively; thus *cope, mope, robe, slope* (as opposed to *cop, mop, rob, slop,* where 'o' = /ɑ/)
- Almost all 'o's appearing as graphemes in word-final position are pronounced /o/: *limbo, gumbo, tobacco, video, go, bingo, cargo, radio, buffalo, cello, tempo, tomato, potato, ghetto.* (But compare the frequent *do, into, to, two,* where 'o' = /u/. Also note that in word-final position the digraph 'oo' is always /u/, not /o/: *too, moo, goo, taboo, igloo.*)

/u/: We can state categorically that /u/ is the toughest English vowel phoneme to spell. Consider these facts:

- None of the spellings of /u/ in Dewey (1970) achieves majority status. The most frequent is digraph 'oo,' which represents just 27.33 percent of all instances of /u/. Next comes 'u,' but at only a bit more than half that (14.91%). Both represent other vowel phonemes as well.
- Seven of the eight major orthographic representations of /u/ involve "back" graphemes or digraphs—'oo,' 'u-e,' 'o,' 'ou,' 'u,' 'ue,' 'ui'—yet only five of them involve 'u' itself. The eighth representation, 'ew,' is orthographically "back" thanks solely to the presence of 'w.'
- Not even digraph 'ue' (*blue, gruesome, rueful, flue, construe,* etc.) represents /u/ exclusively. One problem is that 'ue' is often pronounced bisyllabically, as in *cruet, duet, fluent, suet.* Then too, the 'u' of some 'ue' combinations is pronounced with yod (/j/) + /u/, as in *fuel* /fjúəl/, *hue, imbue, revue.*

The only good /u/ news is that the discontinuous 'u' + 'e' **does** represent /u/ exclusively, though only about 8 percent of Dewey's /u/ corpus uses 'u-e' to represent /u/. As is true of the other three discontinuities ('a-e,' 'i-e,' 'o-e'), students will need to learn that the "silent 'e'" is a device that English uses to change the pronunciation of graphemes in words such as *dud, Jud,* and *crud* (/dʌd/ /dʒʌd/ /krʌd/) into that of words such as *dude, Jude,* and *crude* (/dud/ /dʒud/ /krud/).

4.3.2.2. Diphthong /ai/. Much of /ai/'s news is good: 73 percent of all /ai/ items in Dewey (1970) spell /ai/ with grapheme 'i,' whether alone—*bind, fight, find, kind, might, mind, sight*—or else discontinuously followed by mute 'e': *bite, kite, pipe, ripe, site, stripe.* (We can easily predict which phoneme—/ɪ/—would appear in words like those without the mute 'e': *bit, kit, pip, rip, sit, strip.*) When stressed /ai/ appears at the end of monosyllabic words it is represented by 'y' (thus *by, cry, dry, fly, my, sky, sly*) and not by 'i' or 'i-e.' But there's bad news too: word-final 'y' more often represents either the second part of digraphs 'ay' or 'ey,' which render other phonemes (/e/ and /i/ in particular), or else unstressed word-final grapheme 'y,' which renders phoneme /i/: *happy, lazy, ready, tricky, needy, sloppy.* Also unfortunate is the use of both 'ei' and 'ie' to represent /ai/: *eiderdown, feisty, height, kaleidoscope,* but also *applied, denied, die, lie,* and *tie.* And of course not all instances of 'ie' = /ai/ are monosyllabic: *diet* /dái.ət/, *quiet* /kwái.ət/ (cf. *quite* /kwait/).

One of the most regular rules of English orthography involves word-final 'y,' whether stressed or unstressed, whether /ai/ or /i/: when a verb whose final letter is 'y' adds -*ed* (past or past participle form), the 'y' changes to 'i.' Thus: *apply* → *applied, bury* → *buried, carry* → *carried, cry* → *cried, deny* → *denied, multiply* → *multiplied, parry* → *parried, satisfy* → *satisfied, try* → *tried.* The same rule applies before -*es,* whether on verbs or nouns: *baby* → *babies, try* → *tries.*

4.3.2.3. The mid lax vowels /ɔ/ and /ʌ/. Exactly half of all words containing /ɔ/ are spelled with 'o,' and many words spell /ɔ/ with 'a' (24%) or with these three digraphs: 'au' (9%), 'aw' (8%), or 'ou' (2%). The bad news is that 'o' is one of the most overworked graphemes in English, representing seven different phonemes: /ɔ u ʌ ɑ ʊ ɪ/. But there is good news too: 'au' and 'aw' represent /ɔ/ exclusively in dialects having that vowel sound, which most do. (Others substitute /ɑ/, §5.6.1). So every time you see 'au' or 'aw,' you will know it is pronounced /ɔ/: *applause, fault, fraud, haul, launch, pause,* and *awful, crawl, dawn, draw, hawk, jaw.* Also good to know is that 'au' never appears in word-final position; if we wish to represent /ɔ/ there, we write it 'aw.' All examples of 'ou' = /ɔ/ appear in 'ough,' thus: *bought, cough, thought.* Then too, 'au' is sometimes followed by the mute 'gh,' a digraph representing a consonant that modern English has lost: *caught, daughter, distraught, haughty.* And when 'a' equals /ɔ/, it often does so before 'l' whether the 'l' is pronounced or mute: *bald, call, fall, talk, balk, stalk.*

About 73 percent of all instances of phoneme /ʌ/ spell it with 'u'; thus *buff, cup, cut, duck, plus, puff, rub, tub, up.* Yet 'u' also represents /ʊ/ and /u/; indeed, many words in which 'u' now renders /ʌ/ were formerly pronounced /ʊ/. The next most common way to spell /ʌ/ is with the digraph 'ou'; 14 percent of all /ʌ/ words do so: *couple, cousin,*

Figure 4.i. Vowel graphemes and the phonemes they represent

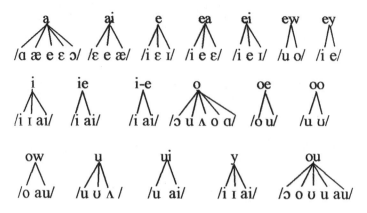

rough, trouble, young. And nearly 13 percent of all /ʌ/'s are represented by 'o': *come, done, honey, monk, ton, love.*[10] The problem with knowing how to spell /ʌ/ is that all these phonemes compete for the same available spellings. Grapheme 'o' predominates before 'm' and 'n,' as does digraph 'ou' in multisyllabic words, but not to the point where any useful pedagogical trend can be spotted.

4.3.3 Vowel phonemes and graphemes: An encapsulated review.

The eighteen trees in figure 4.i serve two purposes: they sum up what has just been learned about vowel phonemes and how they are spelled (see figure 4.h), and they provide a global vision of the problems that students encounter when spelling English vowels. Each tree's "top" is a particular grapheme/digraph; the roots then move downward to list the phonemes that the grapheme or digraph represents. (Minor figure 4.h equivalencies appearing only in parentheses are not included here.)

Here is an alphabetical list of the nine main graphemes/digraphs that represent just one phoneme:

grapheme/digraph	phoneme	grapheme/digraph	phoneme
a-e	/e/	ee	/i/
au	/ɔ/	oa	/o/
aw	/ɔ/	oi	/oi/
ay	/e/	oy	/oi/
		ue	/u/

Exercise 4.8

(A) Write out the four tense-vowel phonemes and then list the main ways that English spells each one.

(B) On the left, write the tense vowel (/i e o u/) that each word uses.

phoneme	word	phoneme	word	phoneme	word
_____	brief	_____	seed	_____	team
_____	load	_____	note	_____	believe
_____	pain	_____	rude	_____	late
_____	news	_____	moon	_____	scope
_____	goof	_____	very	_____	uncouth

(C) Without looking back to §4.3.2.2, write as many words as you can that illustrate the diphthong /ai/. Use at least three different spellings of it. Now list all the graphemes/digraphs representing diphthong /ai/, and then indicate what if anything they have in common.

(D) Write the vowel (/ɑ ɔ ʌ/) that each of these words uses, or else transcribe each word in full.

phoneme	word	phoneme	word	phoneme	word
_____	cause	_____	awning	_____	halt
_____	tough	_____	among	_____	caught
_____	done	_____	gun	_____	fuzzy
_____	lost	_____	mud	_____	enough
_____	law	_____	cop	_____	false

(E) Without looking back, tell which phoneme each of these graphemes/digraphs usually represents:

grapheme/digraph	phoneme	grapheme/digraph	phoneme
a-e	_____	ey	_____
aw	_____	oi	_____
ay	_____	oy	_____
ee	_____	oo	_____

4.4. Vowel reduction redux. In the remaining sections we turn to schwa. It is perhaps the hardest sound to spell because /ə/ is what other vowels often reduce to when unstressed, yet schwa is spelled with the same graphemes and digraphs as those other vowels.

4.4.1. General guidelines for spelling the schwa.

As pointed out earlier (§1.4), when English vowels are unstressed, they tend to reduce to the schwa sound "uh" (/ə/). This creates spelling problems, particularly among the nearly 55 percent of all English words that are French, Latin, or Greek in origin. Although many reduction problems involve grapheme 'a'—Dewey (1970) says that a third of all schwas are spelled with 'a'—all the graphemes and many of the digraphs are implicated too. Nor is the problem limited to any given word part or syllable type, for reduction-caused spelling troubles appear at the beginning, in the middle, and at the end of thousands of words, and in syllables that end in consonants as well as in vowels.

In a textbook such as this we can only provide a general idea as to the nature of the problem. The extent of the trouble that schwa creates can be appreciated by discussing pairs of similar words in which one spells schwa one way and the other does so another way. Take, for example, the pair *accèptabílity/accèssibílity*. (We underline all schwas discussed.) The first word spells /ə/ with an 'a,' whereas the second does so with an 'i.' Remembering such spellings can be a real memory-taxer, and the average student finds it no help to learn that two words in Latin—one pronounced with an /a/ and the other with an /i/—are the source of the problem; to the English speaker, both underlined vowels are /ə/. Or take as another example the French-and-thus-Latin-origin pairs *benévolence/irrélevance—benévolent/irrélevant*, illustrative of the large number of unstressed *-ence/-ance* or *-ent/-ant* contrasts that complicate spellers' lives. Then there's *gállery/dispénsary* (many words exemplify the *-ery/-ary* difference), *indéfinite/subórdinate* (the same is true of unstressed *-ite/-ate*), *acknówledge/advántage, nórmative/cógnitive, ágitate/végetate, fréshen/fáshion, állegory/álligator, álphabet/élephant, catatónic/categóric, clássicist/Méthodist*—and the list goes on and on. Most telling is the fact that for several dozen words the spelling of schwa is unresolved, so that there are competing spellings: *adviser/advisor, ambiance/ambience, ascendant/ascendent, artefact/artifact, conjurer/conjuror, dependant/dependent, enquire/inquire, gabardine/gaberdine, hiccough/hiccup, imposter/impostor, jailer/jailor, manikin/mannequin, pajamas/pyjamas, retractable/retractible, scalawag/scallywag, scepter/sceptre, sepulcher/sepulchre, smidge(o)n/smidgin, twerp/twirp*.

In sum, schwa's orthography is a major problem. Although some spellings can be predicted from other members of the word families that we examined in chapter 2 (thus *astrónomer/astronómical, attríbutable/áttribute, authéntic/authentícity*), others cannot and therefore must be memorized.

4.4.2 How to spell unstressed final /ər/.

An unstressed final /ər/ is likely to be spelled 'er,' as in *amplifier, broker, chopper, leather, officer, order, outsider, reader, remember, slobber, smuggler*, and *tiger*. Indeed, 74 percent, or about 7,900, of all word-final /ər/'s are spelled 'er.' The second-most common spelling of final /ər/ is 'or,' as in *anchor, bachelor, chancellor, colo(u)r, detector, liquor, mediator, prosecutor, reactor,* and *sculptor*; 16 percent (about 1,700) of all word-final /ər/ words use 'or.' The spelling 'ar' accounts for 10 percent, or about 1,100 words, among them *altar, beggar, burglar, calendar, cellar, cellular, collar, cougar, dollar,* and *grammar.* Only a handful of items spell word-final /ər/ with 'ir'/'ur': *elixir, tapir; murmur, sulfur.* As with /ə/, sometimes multiple spellings arise: *liter/litre, humor/humour.*[11]

4.4.3 The three ways to spell stressed /ər/. The combination 'ar' is never used to spell /ər/ when strong- or weak-stressed, and only a few words spell stressed /ər/ with 'o(u)r': for example, *courteous, flourish, journey, nourish, word, work, world, worm, worry, worse, worship, worst, worth.* As was true of word-final unstressed /ər/, the most common spelling is 'er' (or less often 'ear'/'eur'), which 183 or 48.54 percent of our 377 /ər/ entries employ. (See the CD's Corpus files for a complete list.)

   The second-most widely used spelling of schwa + /r/ (135 entries or almost 36%) is 'ur.' (See the CD's Corpus files for a complete list of these and subsequent spellings.) In third place is 'ir' (fifty-nine entries, 15.65%). Unfortunately, an analysis of these 377 entries produces no helpful synchronic rules about when to spell /ər/ as 'er,' 'ir,' or 'ur,' so once again, memorization is necessary—though knowledge of which groups predominate is useful.

Exercise 4.9

(A) Test your knowledge of English orthography by filling in the following blanks with the correct grapheme or digraph that's needed to spell the schwa sound. (Strong stresses have been marked.)

1. reliabíl__ty	7. áver__ge	13. tréas__n
2. incómpet__nce	8. knówl__dge	14. shárp__n
3. elemént__ry	9. décor__tive	15. cómm__nist
4. bák__ry	10. séns__tive	16. sóci__list
5. cónsul__te	11. ác__tate	
6. défin__te	12. debíl__tate	

(B) Continue filling in the following blanks with the correct grapheme or digraph that's needed to spell schwa when followed by 'r.'

1. c__rve	5. c__rcumstance	9. conv__rgence
2. prosecut__r	6. muscul__r	10. c__rry
3. glandul__r	7. sculpt__r	11. spectacul__r
4. cons__rvative	8. c__rculation	12. aff__rmation

(C) Look at the examples of how English spells unstressed word-final /ər/ (§4.4.3). Although purely orthographic rules for when to use 'er,' 'or,' and 'ar' are elusive, what grammatical and semantic generalizations can you extract from those examples?

4.5 Teaching the topics of chapter 4 to students of ESOL. Experience has taught us that the technique known as flooding, already described in §2.15, is a good way to present English orthography to students of ESOL. For orthographic purposes, flooding moves in two directions: students should be shown a sizeable list of words that exemplify the graphemes/digraphs that are used to spell a particular phoneme, and then another list of all the words that exemplify the phonemes that a particular grapheme/digraph can represent. Although our CD's Corpus files do not include the latter, they do include an important component of the former: fifteen lists that present all the words that spell each of the fourteen strong-stressed-vowel phonemes and /ər/. Here's an example of how one of the Corpus files starts out: "Strong-stressed phoneme /e/ can be spelled with 'a,' 'ai,' 'ay,' 'ea,' 'ei,' or 'ey.' The following words exemplify each of those graphemes or digraphs. We'll start with a list of those words that spell /e/ as 'a.'" Teachers of ESOL will find these lists to be rich sources of lexical items, which can be extracted from the Corpus file and then used to create "flooding" activities.

Let's take one such list as an example: the 1,610 Corpus words whose strong-stressed vowel is /ʌ/. As we know from §4.3.2.3, /ʌ/ for the most part is spelled three ways in English, primarily with grapheme 'u' (just over 72%) but also with 'o' and with digraph 'ou' (and, rarely, 'oo,' 'au,' or 'a'). To set up a flooding exercise, one would first extract from the corpus some of the 1,162 /ʌ/ = 'u' words—items such as *abduct, abrupt, abundant, adjust, adult, begun, bluff, blunt, blush, brush, bubble, bucket, buddy, budget,* and hundreds more. Next comes the /ʌ/ = 'o' list (*accompany, among, become, color, come, comfort, company, cover, discover, does, cone, dove,* etc.) and then the /ʌ/ = 'ou' list (items such as *country, couple, cousin, double, enough, rough, southern, tongue, touch, young*); if wanted, an 'oo' list would be limited to *blood, flood* and their derivatives (*bloodshed, bloodstain, bloodthirsty, floodgate, flooding, floodlight,* etc.). Lists should avoid the sort of words that only advanced students would know or even want to know, such as *amok, aplomb, asunder, august, avuncular, befuddle, begrudge, blunderbuss,* and so on.

As was true when flooding was employed to instruct ESOL students in single-word stress patterns (chapter 2), flooding techniques are surprisingly flexible. Orthographic flooding at its simplest means presenting students with a list of like-sounded/-spelled words (/ʌ/ = 'u'), reading it out loud with them, checking for comprehension by using the words in contexts, basing a dictation on the wordlist, and so forth. More artful ways to employ flooding include teacher- or student-composed doggerel verse or nonsense prose ("But the bug on the rug had a buffalo buddy who brushed him off the bus as it bumped along the budding bluff"; "The butler busted the chubby butter-tummied bumpkin who clung to the button as he clutched the conductor"). Some of these creations might approach Carolyn Graham's (1978) jazz chants in sophistication and playfulness. Students of all ages love nonsense verse and prose. Orthographic flooding exercises provide plenty of opportunity for that sort of thing, and all the more happily because students of ESOL acquire new lexical items as they are learning this chapter's spelling patterns.

NOTES

1. Given our goal of relating English pronunciation to spelling, we necessarily view as a separate issue the teaching of the alphabet in the first place. In many ESOL situations, teachers can assume that their students are already accustomed to reading and writing with the Roman alphabet because their native languages use it too (Latin Americans and most Europeans and Africans) or because they have learned it in addition to their native scripts (many South and East Asians). These students can therefore take for granted consonant versus vowel values, the usual variants (upper/lowercase, cursive, etc.), alphabetical order in lists, and keyboard layouts for word processing and other computer applications. Nevertheless, some classes may contain beginners who are unfamiliar with the Roman alphabet (or indeed with any writing system at all), and they will need to start from scratch.

2. GRAPHEMES are units of a writing system—letters of the alphabet in the case of English, but also punctuation marks and symbols such as &, %, @, and numerals. When a grapheme has more than one shape, the variants are called ALLOGRAPHS. Thus *R r* and *ʀ* count as allographs of the same grapheme, as do *L l* and *ℓ*. In this chapter we will focus less on properties of the graphemes themselves than on how they render phonemes (units of pronunciation). Symbols for phonemes appear between slashes: /e/ (= a vowel *sound*), whereas symbols being discussed as graphemes are placed between single quotes. Other works may refer to graphemes with italics or enclose them in angled brackets: 'e', *e*, <e> (= the *letter* 'e').

3. Only four corpus words violate the perfection of this fit: /v/ = 'vv' (*návvy, sávvy, skívvy*) and /v/ = 'f' (*of* along with its derivatives *hereof, thereof, whereof*), plus—in British English—*ph* in *nephew* /névju/. The corpus contains thousands of examples of 'v' = /v/ and /v/ = 'v.' Indeed, 'v' is the closest English ever comes to showing perfect orthographic fit.

4. This discrepancy stems from the fact that two units are understood as BISEGMENTAL (i.e., combinations of two phonemes). The first, /hw/, is a variable depending on both region and register. Many English speakers consistently use /hw/ for 'wh' in the 104 Corpus words that begin with 'wh' such as *whack, whale, wheel, wheeze, whim, white,* and *whiz* along with the pronominal relatives/interrogatives *what, when, where, which,* and *why* (but not *who[m]*). And while 'wh' is rendered /hw/ in the slow tempo and careful registers of many other speakers, they just use /w/ in other registers. The second combination of phonemes is the one that is spelled by grapheme 'x.' We will represent it as /ks/, a necessary compromise given that four of its five pronunciations—/ks/, /kʃ/, /gz/, /gʒ/—involve /k/ or /g/ followed by /s/ or /z/ in the indicated sequence. Only the fifth pronunciation, /z/, is not bisegmental.

5. Exceptions to this rule involve the 'u' = /w/ of 'qu' when followed by another vowel that doesn't appear in word-final position: *acquaint, acquiesce, acquire, acquisition, acquit, adequate, antiquated, antiquity* (but not *antique* /æntík/), *aqua, aquarium, aqueduct, banquet, bequeath, bequest, colloquial, conquest, consequence, delinquent, disqualify, disquiet, earthquake, eloquence, enquire/inquire, equal,* and several score more.

6. The digraph *ck* also functions as the reduplicated version of *c* = /k/: *picnic, picnicking.*

7. A DIPHTHONG is a complex vowel of two parts, for example, the /ai/ of *nice* = "ah-ee". See chapter 5 for more information.

8. See chapter 5 for discussions of variant pronunciations of certain vowels (e.g., *laugh* = American /læf/, British /lɑf/) and alternative analyses of English vowels.

9. The sound rendered by the 'a' of words such as *rare* and *scare* is not quite the same /e/ as the sound of 'a' in *rate* and *skate*. This stems from what is known as "'r' coloring," whereby /r/ neutralizes the preceding tense or lax vowel and produces something that is neither. See chapter 6 for more information on this.

10. As earlier forms of English used the same symbol—'u'—for both (modern) 'u' and (modern) 'v', the /ʌ/ in a word like *love* was spelled *o . . . e* (*loue*) to avoid a confusing form like *luu*.

11. There are differences between American and British standards in the spelling of unstressed final /ər/ in certain words, primarily due to changes introduced by Noah Webster: (mainly) British *theatre, metre, litre, centre, honour, colour, labour;* (mainly) American *theater, meter, liter, center, honor, color, labor.* Because final /ər/ is pronounced /ə/ in standard British and similar dialects unless a vowel follows (§6.4.1), the spelling of schwa is complicated even more.

Wrap-Up Exercises

(A) Do you speak or have you ever studied languages such as French, Latin, or Greek from which English has borrowed so heavily, or languages such as Italian, Portuguese, or Spanish whose words are mostly derived from Latin and thus resemble their English cognates orthographically? To what extent does your knowledge of these languages help you to spell English? Why is that so?

(B) Relating Graphemes/Digraphs and Phonemes

  1. The following words contain the digraph 'oo.' In some, 'oo' = /u/, whereas in others, 'oo' = /ʊ/. On a sheet of paper, sort them out by writing all the /u/ words in one column and the /ʊ/ words in another.

> *book, boom, booth, brood, cook, food, foot, goo, good, hood, look, loom, loop, mood, poop, room, scoop, shook, soot, soothsayer, stood, took, troop, wool, zoo*

2. The following words contain the digraph 'u.' In some, 'u' = /u/, in others, 'u' = /ʊ/, whereas in others 'u' = /ʌ/. On a sheet of paper, sort them out by writing all the /u/ words in one column, the /ʊ/ words in another, and the /ʌ/ words in another.

> *altitude, attitude, bluster, Bruce, bullet, bush, crude, fluffy, fluster, flute, guppy, gut, intrude, longitude, luster, magnitude, mustard, nude, prude, pus, push, rush, Russell, slut, solitude*

3. The following words contain the digraph 'ea.' In some, 'ea' = /i/, in others 'ea' = /e/, and in others 'ea' = /ɛ/. On a sheet of paper, sort them out by writing all the /i/ words in one column, the /e/ words in another. and the /ɛ/ words in another.

> *appeal, bead, beaten, bread, break, breast, deafen, flea, greaseball, great, head, heaven, knead, lease, leave, meager, measure, please, pleasure, ready, sleaze, spread, steak, threatening, treasure*

4. The following words contain the grapheme 'a.' In some words, 'a' = /æ/, in some 'a' = /ɑ/, in some 'a' = /e/, in others 'a' = /ɛ/, and in still others 'a' = /ɔ/. On a sheet of paper, sort them out writing all the /æ/ words in one column, the /ɑ/ words in another, and so on.

> *able, any, artistic, car, chalk, clap, determination, far, fat, gigantic, spa, lack, maple, map, mall, mantle, rage, calm, partner, relation, situation, snack, stalk, star, table, tall, trance, wrap, father*

5. The following words contain the digraph 'ou.' In some, 'ou' = /u/, in others /ʊ/, /o/, /ɔ/, /ʌ/, or /au/. On a sheet of paper, sort them out by writing all the /u/ words in one column, the /ʊ/ words in another, and so on.

> *acoustic, aloud, although, announce, boudoir, bought, boulder, boulevard, bouquet, brought, cloud, compound, cougar, coughing, could, country, couple, found, group, hour, mould, sought, soul, through, trough*

6. The following words contain the grapheme 'i.' In some, 'i' = /i/, in others 'i' = /ɪ/, and in others 'i' = /ai/. On a sheet of paper, sort them out by writing all the

/i/ words in one column, the /ɪ/ words in the second column. and the /ai/ words in a third column.

> *beneficial, bliss, pint, hint, boutique, chlorine, cuisine, delight, find, fright, grind, grit, hit, livid, mind, miss, night, oblique, police, sister, slight, slit, tight, twister, unfit, unique, wrist, ski*

7. The following words contain the digraph 'ss.' In some, 'ss' = /s/, in others 'ss' = /ʃ/. and in others 'ss' = /z/. On a sheet of paper, sort them out by writing all the /s/ words in one column, the /ʃ/ words in the second column. and the /z/ words in a third column.

> *accessory, addressing, aggression, assault, assure, bassinet, blessing, blossom, bossy, brassiere, colossal, commissioner, confess, depressant, dessert, assert, dissolve, fissure, glossy, guessing, issue, possess, pressure, scissors, stress, tissue*

8. These words contain the grapheme 'g,' In some, 'g' = /g/, whereas in others, 'g' = /dʒ/. On a sheet of paper, sort them out by writing the /g/ words in one column and the /dʒ/ words in the other column.

> *gear, geese, gene, general, generous, genocide, begin, genuine, vague, age, geology, gesture, get, geyser, giant, gibbon, giddy, gift, gigantic, giggle, gilt, gin, ginger, gipsy, girdle, girl, give, gyp*

(C) Silent graphemes/digraphs. Circle all the graphemes or digraphs that are not pronounced in the following words. (In some words, **all** graphemes/digraphs are pronounced.)

1. night	5. thumb	9. honesty	13. ptarmigan
2. debt	6. sign	10. though	14. gneiss
3. knee	7. signatory	11. drought	15. walk
4. psychology	8. marriage	12. knowledge	16. incognito

CHAPTER 5

Vowels

5.1 Vowels, broadly and narrowly. A vowel is a sound with full resonance (you can sing it) that occurs as the peak of a syllable. Ordinarily, there are as many syllables as there are vowel sounds, so that *banana* /bənǽnə/ has three syllables and *email* /ímèl/ has two. Orthography matters little for determining syllables: *leaves* /livz/ has three vowel *graphemes,* but only one vowel *phoneme* and therefore just one syllable.

We represent vowels and other speech sounds in either of two ways. A BROAD TRAN-SCRIPTION, enclosed in diagonals / /, shows a phoneme's essential characteristics as a unit in the system, omitting details that do not matter in defining its contrasts with other phonemes in the language. A NARROW TRANSCRIPTION is used to show those minor details where relevant and is enclosed in square brackets, [ ]. Individual sounds or whole words and phrases can be transcribed in either way, depending on the focus.

For example, English /u/ is like French or German /u/ in contrasting with /o/ and /i/ (*loon, loan, lean*), and in its basic pronunciation: a high back rounded vowel (explained in the following discussion). But on closer examination, its articulation is more forward in the mouth than the well-backed French and German /u/. This detail is shown as [u̟] or [u˱] in narrow transcription (the International Phonetic Alphabet's (IPA) subscript plus and the raised wedge both mean 'advanced, less back'), but because it does not make a difference in distinguishing the words of English, the vowel is shown simply as /u/ in a broad transcription.

As a second example, consider *leaves* and *leans,* which have the same vowel phoneme, /i/, contrasting with /o/ in *loaves* and *loans.* But there is a slight difference in each pair: the vowel has a nasal resonance or "twang" when it precedes the nasal con-sonant /n/. You can verify this difference by prolonging the vowels (and delaying the final consonants) in *leaves, leans* and in *loaves, loans* and comparing their sound. The nasality is shown in a narrow transcription by a tilde over the vowel: [lĩnz lõnz]. But because this feature is nondistinctive (by itself, it never differentiates one English word from another), we factor it out of a phonemic representation.

Put another way, English assigns nasalized [ĩ] and oral (nonnasalized) [i] to a COM-PLEMENTARY DISTRIBUTION——one in one position or environment (before nasals) and one in another (elsewhere)—and treats them as variants or ALLOPHONES of the same phoneme, /i/. By the same token, [õ] and [o] are allophones of /o/. Ordinarily, we are not sensitive to allophonic differences as we are to the phonemic distinctions that distinguish the words of our language. In fact, the test for phonemic distinctions is the presence of a MINIMAL PAIR, two words that are identical except for two sounds in contrast, for example, /mit/ *meet* versus /mot/ *moat*. This minimal pair shows that /i/ and /o/ stand in CONTRASTIVE DISTRIBUTION, occurring in the same positions and there contrasting words; but there are no minimal pairs for the purely allophonic difference between [õ] and [o]. Other languages differ in this regard: French contrasts nasal and oral vowels as distinct phonemes, as in the minimal pair [bo] 'beautiful' versus [bõ] 'good.' Thus, in French, nasality would definitely be included in a broad or phonemic representation: /bo/, /bõ/.

5.2 How to make vowels: Tongue and lip position. In all languages, speakers make different vowel sounds by using their voice and altering its resonance in their mouth by changing the position of their tongue and lips. The principle is similar to how a trombonist gets different sounds by moving the slide in a tube. The tongue, though, does not move in and out, but up and down and forward and back. You could see that movement if the mouth were split down the middle on a plane perpendicular to the body, a SAGITTAL VIEW commonly used in linguistics—although determined not by splitting the head but by painting the tongue with a substance that shows up on an X-ray from the side. Figure 5.a shows a sagittal view of the tongue positions for the four vowels /i/ (as in *heat*), /æ/ (as in *hat*), /ɑ/ (as in *hot*), and /u/ (as in *hoot*).

Only a centimeter's difference or so in tongue position suffices to create a different resonance and therefore a different vowel sound. But before continuing, verify these tongue positions in your own articulation. Say /i/—/u/, /i/—/u/, and so on in rapid succession. You should feel your tongue jump forward a little for /i/, and back for /u/. You can feel a second difference in your lips, and it is visible in a mirror: the lips are spread, as in a smile, for /i/ but protrude for /u/, an effect called LIP-ROUNDING, or simply ROUNDING. We therefore describe /i/ as an "unrounded (or spread) front vowel" and /u/ as a "rounded back vowel."

Now proceed to the other two vowels, again saying in rapid succession /æ/—/ɑ/, /æ/—/ɑ/, and so on. You should again feel a front-back difference, although these two are closer than /i/ and /u/ are. The lips are unrounded for both /æ/ and /ɑ/. Now do the same for the pair /i/—/æ/: you should feel the tongue rising high in the mouth for /i/ and

Figure 5.a. Sagittal view of tongue and lip positions for /i æ ɑ u/

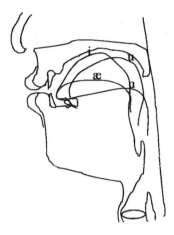

dropping for /æ/. (Because the jaw ordinarily moves with the tongue, you can place your hand on the underside of your jaw to feel this difference.) Thus the tongue is in a HIGH front position for /i/ and a LOW front position for /æ/; or as it is also described, the mouth is more CLOSE for /i/ and more OPEN for /æ/. Finally, repeat the test for /u/—/ɑ/: again, you should feel a high-low (or close-open) difference.

So far, then, we can define these vowels as follows:

/i/: high front unrounded   /u/: high back rounded

/æ/: low front unrounded   /ɑ/: low back unrounded

(For the acoustic side of English vowel description, see the appendix.)

5.3 Other vowels, other languages. As shown in figure 5.a, these four vowels define a roughly trapezoidal "vowel space" within which the tongue moves to produce different vowels. Other vowels are intermediate between these: for example, in the /e/ of *say* the tongue is fronted, between /i/ and /æ/, and therefore neither high nor low, but MID. The schwa /ə/ of the unstressed syllables of *about* and *circus* is also mid in tongue height, but neither front nor back: the tongue in this case is in the center of vowel space, and for that reason, /ə/ is MID CENTRAL. For English speakers, that is the tongue's rest position, which is why we say "/ə/" (*uh*) when we turn on the voice to speak but hesitate before proceeding to specific vowel and consonant articulations. Other languages have different hesitation vowels—Spanish speakers hesitate with front /e/, whereas French speakers use a rounded version of that—which suggests a different default position of the characteristic articulation of these languages. At least for English, that

Figure 5.b. More English vowels

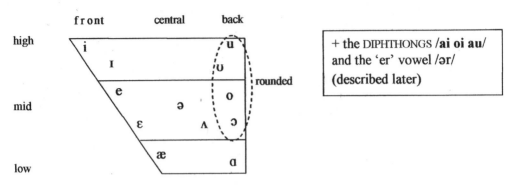

default position is /ə/, other vowels being made by moving the tongue up, down, forward, or back from that position.

Other English vowels fit onto the trapezoid as shown in figure 5.b (see also §1.4). But before proceeding to a fuller description of them, we should note that people from other language backgrounds use this same "vowel space" but make different distinctions within it. Obviously, one's tongue does not lock into preset positions; the high-low and front-back dimensions are continuous, so that instead of the five front vowels English speakers commonly produce (*meet/mit/mate/met/mat*), it is normal in other languages to make as few as two height distinctions or as many as seven.

It would be interesting to determine how many different vowels the human ear can discern. But under normal circumstances—when speaker and listener are focused on each other's meaning (while multitasking other concerns) in fast, connected speech against background noise—it would be impractical to listen for 100 possible vowel choices in each syllable. That is why language makes communication more economical: it restricts the number of *sounds* we must listen for to a limited number of *phonemes*. In a stressed syllable such as /b__d/ (as in *bead, bid, bed, bad, bud*) we can hear quite a variety of vowel sounds among English speakers, but we only listen for the differences that we know to be typical of some fifteen potential vowel phonemes. This is hardly a record number, because some languages have more, but it is still at the upper end of the scale.

The most common vowel system, found in Greek, Spanish, Swahili, and many more, sets up only five phonemes within the vowel space, as shown in figure 5.c. Speakers of such languages will have trouble with distinctions like *cat* versus *cot* because their sole low vowel, /a/, is central, midway between English /æ/ and /ɑ/. They may also have problems in hearing and making the difference between *heat* and *hit* or *Luke* and *look*, because they are accustomed to only two high vowels, /i/ and /u/, whereas English distinguishes four. It is therefore useful for the teacher to have a clear idea of how English vowels are articulated.

Figure 5.c. A typical five-vowel system

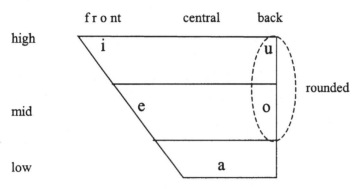

Note on symbols

The IPA distinguishes the symbols script *A* 'ɑ' and printed *A* 'a': /ɑ/ is a low back vowel, and /a/ is one that is central or more front. We observe that distinction here but point out that some linguists use the two symbols interchangeably. For a full chart of the IPA, see the appendix.

In discussing vowels, we ordinarily refer to them by their sound, for example, "the *ah* vowel" for /ɑ/. Do not use English letter names, because "ay" will be misconstrued as the vowel /e/, not /ɑ/. Some symbols do have names, though: 'æ' = *ash*, 'ə'= *schwa*, 'ɔ' = *broken o*, 'ɛ' = *epsilon*.

5.4 Stressed vowels. One more preliminary to consider is the impact of stress. In languages such as English, German, and Russian, stress has a strong effect on vowel quality, which is why we began this book with accentual patterns. In English, stress has three main effects on vowels:

Lengthening: Unstressed vowels are shortened, whereas stressed ones tend to be lengthened, especially before voiced consonants (/b d g v z l r m n/) and in the word-final position. The /i/ of *bead* or *bee* can be up to twice as long as the /i/ of *beat* or the unstressed /i/ ending *silly*: same vowel, different duration. This lengthening is shown in the IPA by [ː]: *beat* [bit], *bead* [biːd], *bee* [biː].

Variation: Because of their constant stretching and squeezing in a crowded vowel field, the stressed vowels of English "wobble" a lot, showing unsteady tongue positions, numerous variants, and ongoing shifts in articulation (§5.4.2, 5.6–5.6.4). These wobbles are unthinkable in a language like Spanish or Japanese with five precise vowels that have been stable for centuries and show little variation in different dialects or registers.

Reduction: Unstressed vowels tend to REDUCE in volume (loudness), in length (even to the point of disappearance), and in the number of distinctions made. Unstressed vowels usually (but not always) reduce to schwa (§2.14). Put in terms of the *speaker,* this means that he/she generally lapses into the default tongue position whenever there is null stress; put in terms of the *listener,* it means that he/she must listen for some fifteen vowel distinctions in stressed syllables but can often ignore the quality of the vowel in unstressed ones. Spanish, on the other hand, does not really have a simpler system because even though there are just five vowels, speakers and hearers observe a potential five-way contrast in *every* syllable, stressed or unstressed.

Exercise 5.1

(A) Compare figures 5.a and 5.b, and for each English vowel phoneme that is absent from the common five-vowel system, illustrate with an English word containing it.

(B) Say the following word sets, listening to the indicated vowel's length. In which words is the vowel longer? Shorter? Is it possible to rank them in terms of increasing length? Which factors seem strongest in lengthening a vowel? In what way are the lengthened variants just allophonic?

   1. vowel /e/: *cáke, Káy, cáve, cáve-ìn, chaótic*
   2. vowel /ɪ/: *dízzy, díd, díp, discúss, díscus, díd it to her*
   3. vowel /i/: *sléaze, sléep, sléepy, sléepily, Lée*

(C) Prepare a list of five descriptions of English vowels based on the diagram in figure 5.c, then read your list to a class partner, who after each description responds by pronouncing the vowel you describe. For example: "tense mid back rounded vowel" = "/o/".

5.4.1 Low /ɑ/ and /æ/. Although mid-central schwa may be the default position for English, /ɑ/ can be called the center of gravity in the system. It is the lowest and most sonorous, fullest-sounding vowel. For most speakers, it is backish, which is why we symbolize the phoneme as /ɑ/. But /ɑ/ is more central or front, [a], in northern England and in a U.S. tier extending from New England through upstate New York into the Great Lakes area. The difference is audible but nonsignificant, and given this dialect variation, speakers of languages that have only /a/ as their low vowel may use it in English. On the other hand, this strategy gives them less articulatory and auditory room to play with in distinguishing it from /æ/, the other low vowel of English.

   The vowel /æ/ is fully fronted and not quite as low as /ɑ/. It is less common in the world's languages than [ɑ] or [a], so many learners confuse /æ/ and /ɑ/ (*cat, cot; band, bond; battle, bottle*) using [a] for both. On hearing /æ/, they may perceive it as sounding between [a] and [ɛ]—which it is. That is one way to learn it: by striving for an intermediate tongue position between [a] and [ɛ]. The following instructions may also be helpful:

- For [ɑ]: pull your tongue back; the tip should be away from the lower teeth and the mouth should be more open.
- For [æ]: push the tip of your tongue firmly against the inner surfaces of the lower teeth while pressing the whole body of the tongue forward.

Exercise 5.2

🎧 (A) Say the following minimal pairs involving /æ/ and /ɑ/ and compare your pronunciation with the corresponding recording on the CD.

pad, pod	rat, rot	map, mop	racket, rocket
black, block	cam, calm	knack, knock	fallow, follow
valley, volley	axe, ox	battle, bottle	adapt, adopt

(B) Why may phrases like the following give trouble to many learners of English?

an odd ad	a botched batch	not the gnat
a bland blond	the packet in your pocket	the cat on the cot

(C) Circle words with low vowels in the following sentence and identify each one as /ɑ/ or /æ/ with the appropriate phonemic symbol.

1. Pat got a plaid skirt with a solid top.
2. Kathy dropped her mom's plaque.
3. Don's heart attack was not planned in advance.

5.4.2 Mid and high vowels: Tense /i e o u/ versus lax /ɪ ɛ ʊ ɔ/. Most languages contrast mid /e/ versus /o/ with high /i/ versus /u/; some (e.g., French) add a subdistinction between /e/ and /ɛ/ and between /o/ and /ɔ/. But relatively few (e.g., German and English) make a subdistinction at both heights, mid and high, by also differentiating /i/ versus /ɪ/ and /u/ versus /ʊ/. It is therefore common for nonnatives to confuse pairs like *bait* and *bet* (/e/ vs. /ɛ/), *boat* and *bought* (/o/ vs. /ɔ/), and especially *beat* and *bit* (/i/ vs. /ɪ/) and *Luke* and *look* (/u/ vs. /ʊ/).

These subdistinctions are generally described as TENSE versus LAX, and we retain those terms here. But this difference tends to be reinforced by a second one, DIPHTHONGIZATION, so it is useful to examine the two sets of vowels in more detail.

- TENSENESS: For /i e o u/, the musculature of the tongue and lips is tenser, more taut, whereas for /ɪ ɛ ɔ ʊ/ it is looser, more relaxed. Most native speakers can feel the

Figure 5.d. Tense versus lax positions for high vowels

Solid lines = tense
dotted lines = lax

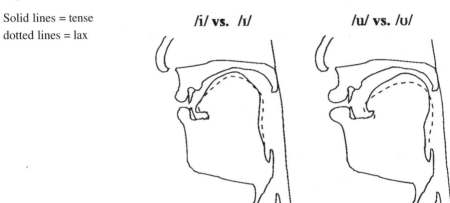

difference as they alternate between *heat* and *hit*, *bead* and *bid*, *suit* and *soot*, *raid* and *red*, and so on. Articulatorily, the effect of tensing is to bunch the body of the tongue up a little higher in the mouth, while relaxing it lets the tongue sink inward, lower and closer to the center of the mouth, as illustrated in figure 5.d for the high vowel pairs /i/ versus /ɪ/ and /u/ versus /ʊ/.

• DIPHTHONGIZATION: For /i e o u/, tenseness is reinforced by a tendency to DIPH-THONGIZE the articulation slightly, so that the tongue glides upward a bit. For the high vowels /i/ and /u/, this means gliding up a little higher toward the /j/ of *yes* and the /w/ of *wet*; thus /i/ is phonetically [ij] and /u/ is [uw]. (If you look in the mirror as you say /u/ as in *who,* you will probably see your lips reach a typical [w] position at the end of the diphthong.) For the mid vowels /e/ and /o/, diphthongization means gliding toward [i] and [u] respectively: → [ei ou]. The lax vowels /ɪ ɛ ɔ ʊ/, on the other hand, tend to be MONOPHTHONGS, steady-state vowels, in most varieties of the language. (See §5.6.2.)

Tense-vowel diphthongization is a definite tendency in English, so much so that it often causes a recognizable accent when English speakers speak other languages. Thus an English speaker may render Japanese /sore/ 'that' as "[sóu.rei]," and Spanish /puso/ 'he/she put' as [púw.sou]. However, tense vowels do not always diphthongize. Many varieties of the language show little or no diphthongization, especially in /i/; the degree of upgliding is seldom as distinctive as it is for the true diphthongs /ai oi au/ (§5.4.3 fol-lowing); and even in those speakers who do diphthongize all four tense vowels, the up-gliding is variable—more when the vowel is lengthened under strong stress, less or none when it is shortened and weakly stressed. Thus *ode* or *owed* is likely to be [oud], whereas *odometer* may have an undiphthongized [od]-.

The English tense/lax distinction is NEUTRALIZED or canceled out in one position: before /r/. Thus in a context like /b__r/ (*beer*), there is no difference between /i/ and /ɪ/. General usage favors lax /ɪ/ or something in between, and the difference (if you attempt it) is ignored. The same is true for /e/ and /ɛ/ in *there, hair,* for /u/ and /ʊ/ in *poor, lure,* and for /o/ and /ɔ/ in *north, more.* Some speakers (see figure 5.e) do retain a few contrasts such as /o/ in *mourning* versus /ɔ/ in *morning,* but for most, these are now HOMOPHONES (or HOMONYMS), words that are pronounced alike.

For learners unaccustomed to tense/lax distinctions, the pairs /i ɪ/, /e ɛ/, /o ɔ/, and /u ʊ/ tend to be the biggest challenge in mastering the stressed vowel system of English.[1] Three typical situations are the following.

1. Learners' languages may contrast diphthongs and monophthongs, [ei] versus [e] and [ou] versus [o], and substituting these for the contrasts in *bait/bet* and *boat/bought* seems to work, at least for the contrasts in mid vowels. But such students still need to learn to open up their vowels more for *bet* and *bought* so that natives do not misunderstand "[bet]" and "[bot]" as *bait* and *boat.* The real challenge is for learners to make a difference in relative muscle tautness in mid and high vowels when the vowels in their native languages may be uniformly tense or relatively lax.

2. Other learners speak languages that do use tense/lax vowels, but as allophones of the same phoneme, for example, tense vowels in open syllables but lax ones in closed (checked) ones. They therefore tend to use the same vowel, [ɛ], in pairs such as *taste* and *test* (both of which are closed by two consonants). Yet, although most English lax vowels do appear only in closed syllables, the tense ones occur in both open and closed syllables: /mi/ *me*, /mit/ *meet*, /go/ *go*, /got/ *goat*, and so on.

3. Many other learners are accustomed to languages that contrast long and short vowels (i.e., the *same* vowels, but different in duration), so they may perceive English as behaving the same way. In many of their schools they have been incorrectly taught that the vowel of *ship, sit, mitt, lip* is [i], whereas that of *sheep, seat, meet, leap* is long [iː], i.e., the same vowel but doubled in duration. Experience with native speakers will quickly teach them that in neither North America nor the British Isles is "[fit fiːt]" likely to be understood as *fit feet,* but as the same word, *feet,* oddly repeated: "feet! <u>feet</u>!" Length in English depends on stress and surrounding consonants (§5.4); it is not, by itself, employed to contrast vowel phonemes as it is in many other languages. Knowledgeable teachers can help learners identify the ways in which these vowel pairs actually differ and can diagnose precisely the problems each learner is having with them.

Exercise 5.3

🎧(A) Pronounce the following minimal pairs for /i e o u/ versus /ɪ ɛ ɔ ʊ/, and listen to the corresponding CD recording. Listen for the degree of diphthongization of the tense vowels.

1. for /i/ versus /ɪ/: reach, rich   feel, fill   green, grin   sleep, slip
   jeep, gyp   sneaker, snicker feast, fist   leaks, licks
   sleek, slick   gene, gin   leave, live (verb) treacle, trickle

2. for /e/ versus /ɛ/: rake, wreck   sale, sell   hail, hell   trade, tread
   bacon, beckon   sakes, sex   chaste, chest   later, letter
   flame, phlegm   date, debt   braid, bread   baste, best

3. for /o/ versus /ɔ/: low, law   choke, chalk drone, drawn foal, fall
   node, gnawed   toast, tossed coat, caught   flowed, flawed

4. for /u/ versus /ʊ/: cooed, could   pool, pull   kook, cook shooed, should
   stewed,[2] stood wooed, wood fool, full

(B) Why might phrases such as the following give trouble to many learners of English?

a taste test	Look, Luke!	to choke on chalk
pitch me a peach	Lowe's law	each itch
a cheap chip	it needs less lace	a wet wait
sit in a seat	soot on my suit	a hole in the hall

(C) Identify each underlined vowel with the appropriate phonemic symbol.

1. You need steady heat for great bread.
2. Move over and give me room.
3. They said she paid people to do it.
4. I saw him put eight pieces of gold on the table.

(D) Make up five sentences that show tense/lax contrasts, for example, *Get me some beans/bins*. Both words should fit and seem plausible in the context.

(E) Although we noted a tendency to neutralize certain distinctions before /r/, some speakers do retain them. Figure 5.e's tables show historical contrasts with the original vowel in parentheses. Determine the extent to which you, yourself, say the same or different vowels in each column.

Figure 5.e. Historic vowels before /r/

Set 1

(/o/)	hoarse	cored	adore	wore	boarder	borne	four, force	mourning
(/ɔ/)	horse	cord	adorn	war	border	born	for(ty)	morning
(/ɑ/)		card	a darn		barter	barn	farce	Marner

Set 2

(/e/)	Mary	fairy	baring	hairy	a parent	vary	Carey	area
(/ɛ/)	merry	ferry	berry	herring		very	Kerry	error
(/æ/)	marry		Barry	Harry	apparent		carry	arrow

5.4.3 Full diphthongs: /ai oi au/. If the diphthongization of the tense vowels in *key, Kay, Coe,* and *coo* is rather slight and variable, it is much more distinctive for those in *Kyle, coil,* and *cowl,* which is why we represent these phonemically as true diphthongs, /ai oi au/. For /ai/, the tongue starts in a low position, generally that of central [a], which lies between /æ/ and /ɑ/. Then it glides up toward the palate, as shown in figure 5.f. You can feel this movement by placing your hand on your jaw as you say words such as *height* and (for most speakers) *hide.*

Another way to show diphthongization is as a movement of the tongue across the trapezoid representing vowel space, as in figure 5.g. Here we add the other two diphthongs:

- /au/, which likewise begins at [a], or just a bit to the front of it (closer to [æ]) for some speakers, but glides up toward the position of [w] with progressive lip rounding
- /oi/, which begins near [o] (or for some speakers, closer to [ɔ]) and glides forward, with the tongue rising a little toward the palate and the lips progressively spreading.

Figure 5.f. Tongue movement in /ai/

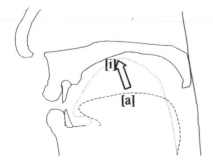

Figure 5.g. Three English diphthongs

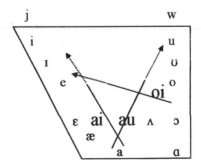

The exact endpoint of these three gliding movements is very indefinite: some dialects glide higher than others, and even the same speaker may glide higher from one utterance to the next of the same word. What seems to matter is simply the **perception of changing vowel resonance**. In that respect, diphthongs are rather like vectors: they have a (relatively) fixed starting point, and move off in a certain direction without a definite endpoint.

For learners, these three diphthongs seldom cause problems except (in some cases) before the liquids /r/ and /l/. Most learners' languages have these diphthongs or similar ones, or else two-vowel sequences (e.g., [a-i], [o-i], [a-u]) that they can adapt to English pronunciation. If the way they render diphthongs sounds accented, it is often because their native diphthongs reach a much higher position than the more indefinite upglides that native English speakers are accustomed to.

Note on symbols

There are two ways to transcribe diphthongs, both of them permitted in the IPA. One is to show the direction of the gliding, toward palatal [j] or labiovelar [w]: **[aj oj aw]**. The advantage of vowel + glide is that it distinguishes true diphthongs from vowel sequences in separate syllables, as in the words *payee* and *snowy*. The other way is to use vowel + vowel, **[ai oi au]**, or [aɪ ɔɪ aʊ] when the endpoint seems closer to a lax vowel. The second vowel is optionally marked with a subscript arc (meaning 'nonsyllabic') or raised to indicate that it is not a full vowel by itself: **[ai̯ oi̯ au̯], [aⁱ oⁱ aᵘ]**. We use vowel + vowel in this book, but vowel + glide in the case of /i/ /u/ → [ij uw] because for a high vowel the only higher position to glide up to is a glide. (The representations [ii] and [uu] imply double or GEMINATE vowels, not diphthongs.) Hence for the diphthong in *like*, you may see [ai aɪ aj ai̯ aⁱ], with no real difference intended.

Exercise 5.4

⌒(A) Pronounce the following minimal pairs or triplets for /ai au oi/ and listen to the corresponding CD recording. You might also want to study the diagrams in figures 5.f–g and try to determine your own typical beginning and endpoint for each gliding.

alloy, ally	points, pints, pounce	foul, file, foil
aisle, oil, owl	soy, sigh, sow (pig)	buy, bough, boy
tile, toil, towel	loud, Lloyd, lied	loiter, lighter

(B) Why might phrases such as the following give trouble to some ESOL students?

I'll oil it.	nine nouns	trout is trite
The crowd cried.	a round rind	How high?

(C) Identify each underlined vowel with the appropriate phonemic symbol.

1. It's hard to relax outside because the Browns have a noisy lawnmower.
2. I know now why the power went out. Lightning hit a wire down the street.
3. Don't pour so much soy sauce on the rice. It makes it too salty to eat.

5.4.4. Uh, er . . . : The lax vowels /ʌ/ and /ər/. The stressed vowel system of English includes two other lax mid vowels, both of them high frequency. Vowel /ʌ/, as in *up, love, tough,* and *blood,* is misleadingly called 'short *U.*' It is usually defined as a lax mid back unrounded vowel, which would make it the unrounded counterpart of /ɔ/. It often has that back position before /l/ (see §6.4.1), as in *bulk, dull,* and *bulge,* but otherwise it tends to be pronounced in a more forward position, almost central. For many Americans, it verges on schwa, which is shorter and more muffled-sounding, but has a similar TIMBRE or acoustic quality. Indeed, because the two never contrast in English (/ʌ/ is stressed and /ə/ is unstressed except in /ər/), some linguists treat them as allophones of the same phoneme. Try saying words such as *oven, onion, above,* and *abut* that have both vowels to determine how much difference you make in your own speech.

For most Americans and Canadians, /ər/ is the "er" vowel in *heard, fur = fir, her, stir, word,* and both syllables of *murder* or *learner.* Although it is generally analyzed as /ə/ + /r/, it is not really two distinct sounds; for most speakers, the tongue takes the mid-central position of /ə/ with the tip already curled up for the retroflex /r/ (§6.4.1), so that the two fuse into one sound. To emphasize the unitary nature of that vowel in a narrower transcription, the IPA provides a special schwa symbol with a right hook on the side (meaning 'retroflexed, rhotic'): [ɚ].

On the other hand, in so-called *r*-less dialects[3] such as British RP (Received Pronunciation), [ɚ] evolved into a mid-central vowel that lacks American and Canadian retroflexion but is still more constricted (tenser) than a regular schwa, at least when stressed. Some linguists also regard this tenser schwa as longer than regular schwa, although it is difficult to separate its length from the normal stretching of stressed vowels in the language. The IPA symbol for this RP "er" vowel is a reversed epsilon (or small 3): [ɜ]. Hence, *murder* /mə́rdər/ is pronounced [mɜ́də] instead of [mə́ɚdɚ]. In addition, both [ɜ]-users and [ɚ]-users often round their lips slightly, and although this rounding seems nondistinctive (and is seldom commented on or shown in transcription), it does contribute to the acoustic impression of the sound.

Note on symbols

You may sometimes see stressed [ɚ] transcribed as 'ʌr,' 'ɜr,' or 'ɜ·,' although these have little justification in standard IPA usage.[4] In this book, we use the broad transcription /ər/ for the vowel phoneme, switching to the symbols 'ɚ' and 'ɜ' only when a narrower transcription of the vowel's precise quality seems pertinent.

Modern /ər/ (either pronunciation) comes from several sources in the earlier language as shown by its spellings: *heard* (originally /hɛrd/), *fur* (originally /fʌr/), *sir* (originally /sɪr/), *word* (originally /wɔrd/). This fusion of lax vowel + /r/ continues today on both sides of the Atlantic in /ʊr/ after palatals or alveopalatals, /j ʃ ʒ tʃ dʒ/. Thus, although many continue saying *your, Europe, cure, sure, jury* as /jʊr jʊ́rəp kjʊr ʃʊr dʒʊ́ri/, others have changed to /jər jə́rəp kjər ʃər dʒə́ri/.

To learners of English, the vowels /ʌ/ and /ər/ present two special problems. First, for those who come from linguistic backgrounds that do not use the mid-central area for stressed vowels (e.g., French, German, Russian), or for any vowels (Spanish, Italian, Japanese, Swahili), mastering one new phoneme between fully front and fully back can be a major challenge, let alone mastering two (or three, counting /ə/ in unstressed syllables). Learners' usual strategy is to substitute [a], [e], or [ɔ], whatever vowel from their native system sounds closest, and this can cause considerable confusion to English speakers trying to hear the difference between *cut* and *curt* and between these and *Kate, cot* and *caught*.

Second, /ʌ/ and /ər/ vary in articulation, but remain distinct in numerous pairs such as *cut-curt, bud-bird, ton-turn, cuddle-curdle, thud-third*, and so on. That variation, though, makes it hard to settle on a single model. We offer the following strategies for approximating a typical American pronunciation until students can fine-tune their articulation with more exposure and practice.

- For /ʌ/: begin with a low vowel, back [ɑ] if possible or at least an [a] that is not too fronted. Close your mouth about halfway, but leave it a little more open than you would for [ə]—at about the height of English [ɛ]. There should be no lip rounding at all.
- For /ər/ as [ɚ]: begin with [ə], and learn to say it with the tip of your tongue curled up a bit (practice with a mirror), rounding your lips slightly. Do *not*, however, let your tongue slide forward into a front position. From another point of view, [ɚ] is simply a syllabic (vowel) version of the usual North American /r/ (see §6.4.1), so learners who have mastered the latter as a consonant can try to relax it and lengthen it a bit for a more vowel-like sound.

Exercise 5.5

🎧(A) Pronounce the following minimal pairs and listen to the corresponding CD recording. Note any cases where your pronunciation differs from those that you hear.

1. /ʌ/ and /ər/: shut, shirt   bud, bird   luck, lurk   stud, stirred
                   stun, stern   huddle, hurdle cuddle, curdle   thud, third

2. /ʌ/ and /ɑ/:   snub, snob   fund, fond   won (one), wan   muck, mock
                   nuzzle, nozzle   stuck, stock   suds, sods   dull, doll
                   come, calm   bum, balm   crutch, crotch   rump, romp

3. /ʌ/ and /æ/:   uncle, ankle   stub, stab   rum, ram   sudden, sadden
                   come, cam   funny, fanny   crush, crash   butter, batter

4. /ər/ and /ɑr/: burly, barley   curd, card   spur, spar   purse, parse
                   yearn, yarn   shirk, shark   curl, Carl   hurt, heart

(B) Why might phrases such as the following give trouble to many learners of English?

the girl's gull   hurl the hull   the first fuss
tough turf   a curt cut   the bun burned

(C) Identify each underlined vowel with the appropriate phonemic symbol.

1. My cousin wandered around at the church bazaar wondering what to purchase.
2. One of the worst problems is learning to manage your money.
3. Some cultures believe that a large flood covered the whole earth.

(D) The sound /ʌ/ can be a special challenge because it is a relatively rare vowel in other languages. The following substitutions can be heard. In each case, give another pair of words (other than the examples shown earlier!) that may be confused if pronounced this way, and explain how you would help each learner acquire a better rendition of this phoneme.

1. Speaker A: /ʌ/ → [ɛ]   3. Speaker C: /ʌ/ → [ɔ]
2. Speaker B: /ʌ/ → [a]   4. Speaker D: /ʌ/ → [ʊ]

(E) Pair work dictation: Prepare a list of five English monosyllables exemplifying difficult contrasts between vowels' spellings and sounds (e.g., striped /straɪpt/). Dictate the list to your partner for phonemic transcription, and then confirm your results.

Figure 5.h. Reduction and vowel alternations with schwa

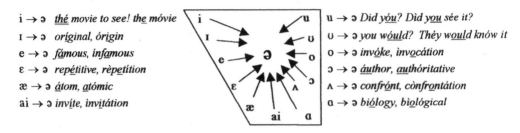

i → ə *thé movie to see! the móvie*

ɪ → ə *original, órigin*

e → ə *fámous, infamous*

ɛ → ə *repétitive, rèpetition*

æ → ə *átom, atómic*

ai → ə *invíte, invitátion*

u → ə *Did yóu? Dìd you sée it?*

ʊ → ə *you wóuld? Théy would knów it*

o → ə *invóke, invocátion*

ɔ → ə *áuthor, authóritative*

ʌ → ə *confrónt, cònfrontátion*

ɑ → ə *biólogy, bìológical*

5.5. Unstressed vowels: The schwa zone.

When vowels are unstressed in English, they tend to reduce to /ə/, with the tongue returning to its mid-central rest position, as illustrated in figure 5.h. Yet there are several notable exceptions to this process:

- Unstressed tense vowels /i e o u/ show resistance to reduction in final position. Final /e/ (*yesterday, Monday, karate*) may reduce to /i/ but never to /ə/; but final /o/ (*tomato, window*) does reduce to /ə/ in faster tempos and casual registers. High /i u/ (*silly, tissue*) do not reduce at all in final position: note the full /i/ at the end of *beauty*, protected from the reduction that it does undergo in *beautiful*.
- Prevocalic vowels—such as the /i/ in *various*, the /e/ in *chaotic*, or the /o/ in *poetic*—do not reduce. This is why unstressed *the* stays /ði/ before a vowel (*the apple*) instead of reducing to /ðə/ as in other positions.
- The vowel of unstressed -*ing* (= lax /ɪ/ for most speakers, tense /i/ for others) does not reduce, unless the following /ŋ/ changes to /n/: *nothing, speaking* (cf. reduction in *nothin', workin'*).
- Reduction is avoided in the initial syllables of certain words felt to be "fancy" in some way. Thus, for one of the authors of this book, the initial syllables of *astronomy* and *pastrami* have /ə/ as expected, but those of *gastronomy* and *mascara* receive a weak stress and keep their /æ/. Similarly, words such as *hypotenuse, archaic, magnanimous, amorphous, clairvoyant,* and *oviparous* are likely to have full vowels and weak stress in their initial syllables.

Even so, reduction is certainly a strong tendency in English, and for learners it can be difficult to learn to alternate, as native speakers do, between full vowels and a relaxed mid-central vowel according to stress as in figure 5.h. This is one of many reasons why both the description and the acquisition of English phonology must begin with mastery of stress patterns.

Given the relaxation of the tongue for schwa, its articulation is imprecise and the IPA defines it as a general area of vowel space rather than a point. As noted earlier, it is similar to /ʌ/ but less open, less back, more relaxed, more muffled-sounding. Between voiceless consonants, as in the first syllable of *potato*, it may devoice to [ə̥] (the IPA's under-ring means 'voiceless') and sound as if it has dropped out. At times the reduced vowel may actually be high central rather than mid central, in which case it sounds like a centralized /ɪ/, one that is not as far forward as the /ɪ/ of *pick*. If desired, this higher variant between /ɪ/ and /ə/ can be shown in narrow transcription as [ɨ] (a barred small capital *I*).

Some speakers (e.g., in RP) contrast this lax high [ɪ] or [ɨ] with a more open [ə] in the unstressed syllables of *roses* versus *Rosa's* and use it in the final syllables of words such as *aspirin, women, humid*, and *English*. But if there is a contrast between unstressed /ɪ/ and /ə/, it has a low FUNCTIONAL LOAD or role in distinguishing words: few minimal pairs depend on that difference. For that reason, other speakers, especially in North America and Australia, tend to use [ɨ] and [ə] as freely varying unstressed central vowels that are not felt to be different. You should verify your own pronunciation in such cases; but for most English speakers, contrasts in reduced vowels seem marginal or rare, so we generally transcribe them as just /ə/. Note, however, that for most North Americans, /ə/ does contrast with unstressed /ər/ = [ɚ]: *panda, pander*.

Because schwa is a short, weak vowel, it sometimes drops out, especially in a medial syllable between a stressed and unstressed one. *Séparate* (adjective), *véteran, végetable, témperature, próbably, ínteresting*, and *tráveler* vary today between retention and loss of the posttonic (poststress) vowel: /sɛ́p(ə)rət/, /vɛ́t(ə)rən/, /vɛ́dʒ(ə)təbəl/, /tɛ́mp(ə)rətʃər/, /prɑ́b(ə)bli/, and so on. In *restaurant, family, laboratory, every, evening, favorite*, and *business*, on the other hand, the loss of the second syllable's /ə/ is quite general, and only historians of the language know that *curtsey* and *fancy* were originally two-syllable versions of *courtesy* and *fantasy*.

Exercise 5.6

🎧(A) Pronounce the following minimal pairs for unstressed /ə/ and /ər/ and listen to the corresponding CD recording. (In *r*-less dialects, they may have the same vowel.)

media, meteor	panda, pander	parka, Parker	manna, manner
pita, Peter	feta, fetter	chatted, chattered	seizes, Caesar's
pledges, pledgers	data, dater	coda, coder	

(B) Pronounce the following pairs and determine whether you have a difference ([ɨ] or [ɪ] vs. [ə]) in the unstressed syllables.

roses, Rosa's	caret, carrot	careless, callous	arid, Herod
kindness, heinous	pallet, ballot	Lisa's, leases, leasers	taxes, Texas

(C) Identify each underlined vowel's pronunciation with the appropriate phonemic symbol.

1. Better late than never.
2. The early bird gets the worm.
3. Practice makes perfect.

(D) Pair work: follow the two-way dictation technique (as in Exercise 5.5:E), but this time, use two- and three-syllable words (with varied stress patterns) containing reduced vowels.

5.6 Shifting vowels make the dialect. The English consonant system is fairly stable and uniform. The vowel system, on the other hand, has shifted in drastic ways during the history of the language and the changes continue today, especially in local dialects. At least at first, it is useful for learners to get used to one basic native model in order to avoid confusion. Yet they will come into contact with speakers who proudly use their own local accents, and it is very possible that you know some speakers who differ in certain ways from the model we have described. We therefore offer the following outline of some of the main vowel variants in contemporary English.

5.6.1 Low back problems. There is notable variation in the vowels corresponding to /ɑ/ and /ɔ/ in the model we have described in this chapter, but the dialect differences make more sense if you keep in mind three historical developments:

1. *R*-less dialects (in Britain, Australia, New Zealand, and some parts of the eastern U.S.) merged /ɑr/ with /ɑ/ and /ɔr/ with /ɔ/, so that *spar spa, bar bah, farther father, source sauce,* and *fort fought* are homophones.
2. However, most of these *r*-less dialects retained an earlier low back *rounded* vowel, symbolized [ɒ], in so-called short *O* words—*pot, cod, body, rock*—and also in words such as *water* (because of the rounding effect of the /w/-). Most *r*-ful North Americans and Irish, on the other hand, unrounded this [ɒ] to [ɑ]. We have adopted the latter norm in this book, with *pot, cod, body, rock,* and so on having the same vowel as *father, far, spa*.
3. More recently, much of Canada and a strip of the central United States from Pittsburgh to California have unrounded /ɔ/ to /ɑ/ (except before /r/), merging them into one phoneme. Thus, for most English speakers, the following remain minimal pairs with different vowels, but some North Americans pronounce them the same: *caught cot, walk wok, taught tot, caller collar, dawn Don, naughty knotty, sawed sod, bawdy body*.

Together, these three developments have created a complex situation summed up in figures 5.i–j. Examine these figures to determine how you, yourself, render these variables.

Exercise 5.7

🎧Pronounce the following minimal pairs in which /ɑ/ contrasts with /ɔ/ and determine whether you observe the distinctions you hear on the CD recording of this exercise. Then listen to other speakers in your class to see if their usage is like yours.

knotty, naughty	pond, pawned	sod, sawed	hock, hawk
tot, taught	cot, caught	collar, caller	fond, fawned
body, bawdy	wok, walk	Otto, auto	bobble, bauble

5.6.2 Vowel breaking. The lengthening of stressed vowels (§5.4) has caused even the lax vowels to diphthongize in some dialects, notably in the American South and Midwest. These diphthongs, however, have *centering* glides, which glide into the mid-central schwa zone. The effect is most audible for front /ɪ/ and /ɛ/, and with especially heavy stress the beginning may tense to [i] and [e]. Thus, depending on the degree of stress and lengthening, one can hear *hid* = [hɪd ~ hɪəd ~ hiəd], *head* = [hɛd ~ hɛəd ~ heiəd]. (The tilde, ~, means 'varying with.') Linguists call this process VOWEL BREAK-ING, although it is popularly known as "drawling."

But these are not the only vowel breakings. In parts of the United States, /æ/ and /ɔ/ have taken on a tenser articulation causing them to diphthongize. The results vary. In the South, strongly stressed /æ/ becomes a complex diphthong, or perhaps triphthong,

Figure 5.i. Distribution of /ɑ ɔ ɒ/ in the U.S. and British Isles

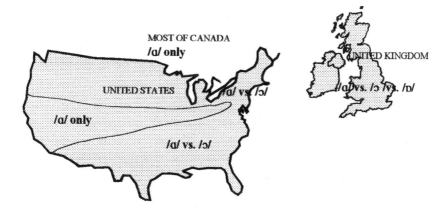

Figure 5.j. English dialect differences regarding /ɑ/ and /ɔ/

	U.S. north and south	U.S. Pittsburgh to California, and many Canadians	Std. British and Australian
father, spa, bra, calm	/ɑ/	/ɑ/	/ɑ/
far, spar, cart, darn	/ɑ(r)/	/ɑr/	/ɑ/
cot, hot, don	/ɑ/	/ɑ/	/ɒ/
caught, haughty, dawn	/ɔ/	/ɑ/	/ɔ/
court, horde	/ɔr/	/ɔr/	/ɔ/

that can be shown as [æiə]; whereas tensed /ɔ/ takes on the same upglide as /o/, → [ɔu],
remaining distinct from it in its more open beginning. Thus many Southerners say *I cán,
it's the láw* as [à kǽiən, ìts ðə lɔ́u].

Meanwhile, in the North as part of what has been called the "Northern Cities Shift"
(Labov 1972), tensing has caused /æ/ to start higher in the mouth and then glide down.
The heavier the stress, the greater this downgliding, yielding variable diphthongs in a
word such as *bad*: [bɛæd ~ beæd ~ bɪæd ~ bɪəd]. The process is especially prominent
before nasals, and for some speakers *candles* may sound very much like *kindles*. In the
Northeast, /ɔ/ also tends to join in, so that in the same example of *I cán, it's the láw*,
many say [ài kǽæn, ìts ðə lɔ́ɔ]. Although the Northern Cities Shift of /æ/ and /ɔ/ seems
to have attracted less attention than the Southern drawl, it is very noticeable to speakers from other areas because of its strikingly "flattened" acoustic effect.

A different diphthongization is heard in the /ər/ vowel in some *r*-less dialects that use
[ɜ] (§5.4.4) and especially its rounded version, symbolized [ɞ]. When before consonants, this vowel glides up slightly toward [i], so that *bird* becomes [bɞid]. This pronunciation is often associated with "Brooklynese," although it is not limited to New
York City. It reminds other speakers of their /oi/ as in *Boyd*, which nevertheless starts
as a back vowel, not a central one.

5.6.3 Diphthongs on the move. In terms of overall English phonology, as we
noted earlier, the diphthongization of the tense vowels /i e o u/ → [ij ei ou uw] is relatively slight, and quite a few dialects—for example, the Upper Midwest in the United
States—tend to have pure vowels (monophthongs) with no gliding. In certain other
dialects, though, back /o/ and /u/ are not only diphthongized, but start with a more central tongue position: /o u/ → [ou uw] → [ɵu, ʉw] (the barred *o* and barred *u* are IPA
symbols for central rounded vowels). These central beginnings may even be unrounded:
thus, many younger Americans have [ɨw] for [ʉw] as in *two* ([ɨ] is similarly a centralized [i]), and in RP diphthongized /o/ begins as mid-central schwa, [əu]. For that reason,
/o/ is often shown as [əu] in British dictionaries and pedagogical materials: *go* = "gəu."

A current trend in diphthongized /i e o u/ is to increase the gliding by beginning at a
lower, more open position. In parts of the American South, for example, /e/ glides up
from a more open position: *rate* = [rɛit ~ ræit ~ rait]. This tendency has progressed
further in Cockney and Australian dialects, where /i e o u/ → [ʌi æi ɔu ʌu]. Despite
jokes about "Austrilians" with a spelling that suggests merger of /e/ with /ai/, the diphthong representing /e/ remains distinct from the one representing /ai/, which compen-
sates by starting further back in the mouth: [ɑi] or [ɒi].

5.6.4 Smoothed diphthongs. On the other hand, the gliding of /ai oi au/ has *weakened* in some dialects, notably among many American Southerners and African Americans. When before /l/, /oi/ only moves halfway across the vowel space: *oil* = [oəl]
instead of [oil]. Likewise, although /ai/ remains a diphthong in educated Southern usage
when before a voiceless consonant (*nice, white, rice*), it is simplified before voiced ones

(*nine, hide, rise, mile*) or in word-final position (*why, sigh, I*); in these latter environments the vowel remains at [a], with little or no upgliding. Despite jokes about Southerners' "Ah" for the pronoun *I*, this central [a] for /ai/ remains distinct from both front /æ/ and back /ɑ/: *sad* ≠ *side* ≠ *sod*. And that seems to be a generalization for most local changes: vowels migrate but somehow they usually remain distinct from each other.

In Britain and Australia, there has also been a weakening of the diphthongs that resulted when *r*-dropping left behind a schwa. The vowels of *hear, there,* and *fire* are [ɪə ɛə aiə] in standard speech, but in popular speech a process called "smoothing" simplifies them to just a longish [ɪ ɛ a]. On the other hand, in Canada, parts of the United States, and Scotland, /ai/ and /au/ are smoothed when before a voiceless consonant (e.g., /p t k f s/): in that position, they begin higher in the mouth, with mid [ə], so that the gliding is much shorter then. *Nice eyes* therefore shows distinct allophones of /ai/, [nəis aiz], as does *out loud* for /au/, [əut laud].

5.6.5 Lexical incidence: "You say *tomayto* and I say *tomahto* . . ." One last type of variation results when speakers share the same vowel system but disagree on which vowel to assign to a particular word. For example, in the weak-stressed first syllable of *èconómics*, speakers use the /i/ of *heed* or the /ɛ/ of *head* with no difference in meaning. The fact that everyone otherwise agrees on the contrast between /i/ and /ɛ/ in *heed/head, seat/set, lease/less,* and so on shows that we are not dealing here with differences in the system of phonemes or their rules for pronunciation. Instead, speakers only show a minor difference in the distribution of shared units in their vocabulary, that is, a difference in LEXICAL INCIDENCE. Put another way, this word and its derivative *èconómical* have two competing pronunciations in the language and speakers choose whichever one they like, or even go back and forth between the two, often without being aware of it.

However, they *do* tend to be aware of lexical incidence when it corresponds to a regional or social preference, whether in single words or whole classes of them.[5] Three examples:

- American Southern dialects use /ɪ/ instead of /ɛ/ before nasals (/m n ŋ/): *pen = pin, hem = him.*
- Where most Americans retain the original /æ/ before the voiceless fricatives /f θ s/ (*half, path, fast*) or the three clusters /ns nt nd/ (*dance, aunt, can't, demand*), Britons and Australians switched to /ɑ/ in these words.
- Where most Britons retain the pronunciation /ɪ/ for final unstressed *-y* (*pity, party, calamity*), North Americans have tensed it to /i/. Thus the first group uses the same vowel in the two syllables of *city*; the second group has the same vowels in the syllables of *easy*.

But in other instances—as in the case of *economics*—the two pronunciations with different vowels coexist in the same areas and are used interchangeably. In this case the two pronunciation variants are said to be in FREE VARIATION.

To illustrate, in the following we show several other words that have alternate pronunciations in free variation, again using the tilde as the conventional linguistic symbol for 'varying with.'

tom<u>a</u>to: /e/ ~ /ɑ/	r<u>ou</u>te: /u/ ~ /au/	coop, roof: /u/ ~ /ʊ/	ant<u>i</u>-, sem<u>i</u>-: /i/ ~ /ai/
wh<u>a</u>t: /ɑ/ ~ /ʌ/	<u>e</u>nvelope: /ɛ/ ~ /ɑ/	(n)<u>ei</u>ther: /i/ ~ /ai/	f<u>o</u>reign, f<u>o</u>rest: /ɔ/ ~ /ɑ/
Appal<u>a</u>chian: /e/ ~ /æ/	fut<u>i</u>le: /ə/ ~ /ai/	Nev<u>a</u>da: /ɑ/ ~ /æ/	l<u>ei</u>sure, l<u>e</u>ver: /i/ ~ /ɛ/
pr<u>o</u>cess, pr<u>o</u>gress: /ɑ/ ~ /o/	s<u>y</u>rup: /ər/ ~ /ɪr/	<u>au</u>nt: /æ/ ~ /ɑ/	ag<u>ai</u>n: /e/ ~ /ɛ/ ~ /ɪ/

These differences are conspicuous to native speakers, who may argue about which vowel is "correct." As we have seen, though, they are trivial in terms of the shared phonemic system. In fact, given an overall communal vocabulary (lexicon) of close to a million words shared by an estimated 400,000,000 native speakers of English who get little support from their joint writing system (chapter 4), it is amazing that we disagree so seldom about our vowels.

Exercise 5.8

🎧(A) Study the list of free variants in §5.6.5 and listen to them on the corresponding CD recording. In each case, determine which is your usual pronunciation (or do you have another variant?), and cite a minimal pair that shows that the two vowels otherwise contrast. Do you know of other cases of free variation? Are there dialectal or stylistic links that you are aware of?

(B) To what extent might free variation or differences in the lexical incidence of vowels cause problems for nonnative students?

(C) For each dialect variant mentioned in §5.6–5.6.5, determine your **own** usage and transcribe it in a narrow phonetic representation. Why should teachers and scholars be aware of their own usage and also of the extent to which it is representative of the language as a whole? Should people (teachers in particular) alter their native dialects? Justify your answer.

(D) Pair work: use the two-way dictation technique (as in Exercise 5.5:E), but this time, alongside the broad or phonemic transcription of your partner's words, add a narrow one showing any special vowel qualities (e.g., dialect variants such as those described in preceding sections) that you perceive in his/her speech.

5.7 Rules and regularities. Our survey of English vowels and their variants may leave the impression that anything can happen, and does. But language is a rule-governed system, and even rather striking changes in pronunciation tend to conform to regular processes that can be stated as PHONOLOGICAL RULES—not "rules" in the sense of the prescriptions for how one *should* speak, but operations that speakers of a language apply in the way they *do* speak, even though they may be unaware of them.

Phonological rules are generally expressed with the format "**X → Y**," using an arrow for 'becomes.' This represents an UNCONDITIONED CHANGE, one with no limitations: all **X**s change to **Y**s in all positions without exception. Most rules, though, are CONDITIONED, occurring just in a specific environment or under specific conditions. That environment is expressed by a slash for 'when,' and a blank to show where the change occurs relative to neighboring sounds that trigger the rule. For example, if **X** only changes to **Y** when it comes before **A**, then we write:

$$X \rightarrow Y / \_\_\_A$$

Other environments are expressed as shown in figure 5.k.[6] (Note that 'syllable-final' position for a consonant is also indicated by referring directly to a syllable's coda position; see §6.1.)

When the rule just changes a property or FEATURE of the sound, we name that feature in square brackets. Most features are binary, that is, either/or, specified as "+" when present and "-" when the opposite is true.

$$X \rightarrow [\pm \text{ feature}] / \_\_\_\_A$$

For example, regardless of degrees of lip constriction, rounding tends to be binary in phonemic contrasts: a given vowel acts as if it is either rounded, [+round], or not, [-round]. The feature specifications recognized for English vowels are shown in figure 5.l.[7] Other specifications such as [±long] or [±nasal] may be introduced by conditioned phonological rules. Stress likewise tends to be binary in its effect on vowels, which is why we use the feature [+stress] *under* the blank in the box (figure 5.k) to mean 'when this specification is present in the vowel.'

Two other distinctions in phonological rules are the following:

- GENERAL/LOCAL: general rules apply in (virtually) all native varieties of the language; local ones are limited to certain regions or social groups.
- CATEGORICAL/VARIABLE: categorical rules apply (virtually) 100 percent of the time, subject to factors specified in the conditioning. Variable rules apply in varying degrees, more in certain registers, speech styles, and/or social strata than in others.

Figure 5.k. Ways of specifying where rules apply

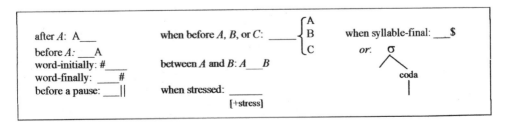

Figure 5.l. Feature specifications of English vowels and glides

	/i/	/ɪ/	/e/	/ɛ/	/æ/	/ɑ/	/ʌ/	/ə/	/ɔ/	/o/	/ʊ/	/u/	/j/	/w/
[syllabic]	+	+	+	+	+	+	+	+	+	+	+	+	-	-
[high]	+	+	-	-	-	-	-	-	-	-	+	+	+	+
[low]	-	-	-	-	+	+	-	-	-	-	-	-	-	-
[tense]	+	-	+	-	-	-	-	-	-	+	-	+	-	-
[back]	-	-	-	-	-	+	+	-	+	+	+	+	-	+
[round]	-	-	-	-	-	-	-	-	+	+	+	+	-	+
[reduced]	-	-	-	-	-	-	-	+	-	-	-	-	-	-

Let's get more specific now as we use rules to review key processes studied in this chapter and to prepare for the rules of chapter 6. The following is an unconditioned change but local because, as we have seen, a different rule applies in *r*-less dialects:

Schwa-*r* Merger: ər → ɚ

The next one is also unconditioned and local, but variable—more in some styles than others: /æ/ and /ɔ/ become [+tense] and then diphthongize:

Northern Cities Shift: æ → eæ, ɔ → oɔ

The next rule formulates the American Southern change in *pen, hem* → [pɪn, hɪm], which is likewise local but categorical and conditioned, in this case by the presence of a following nasal, which we can indicate either with the feature [+nasal] or by the symbol **N**:

Southern Pre-nasal Raising: ɛ → [+high] / ___[+nasal] (or: / ___N)

Another process we saw was Vowel Lengthening, which occurs when the vowel appears before a voiced consonant or word-finally—*if* it is stressed. This rule is general in English and fairly categorical, but its conditioning is obviously complex. As we did when representing **N** = nasals, we use a capital letter for a class of sounds, so **V** = vowels here in the rule shown in figure 5.m. Alternatively, the condition "[+stress]" could be shown by an accent mark on the **V**: V́.

On the other hand, when *unstressed*, English vowels tend to become schwa—a general rule but variable (more in rapid, casual registers than careful, deliberate ones) and subject to several conditions, as we have seen (§5.5). In such a case, we might formulate just the general tendency and describe restrictions separately, as shown by an ellipsis (. . .) here:

V̆ → [+reduced] . . .

Figure 5.m. One way to show vowel lengthening

$$V \rightarrow [+\text{long}] / \underset{[+\text{stress}]}{\underline{}} \begin{cases} [+\text{consonant}, +\text{voiced}] \\ \\ \# \end{cases}$$

The breve over the **V** is a common way of indicating "unstressed" or "null stressed" (the opposite of an accent mark); the feature [-stress] could of course be used too.

You will note that all these rules either **fuse two sounds into one** (e.g., Schwa-*r* Merger) or **change one sound into another** (one of its allophones) by altering its features, often as an assimilation to the environment. These are the usual processes that speakers apply to the phonemes of their language, but there are others, and we briefly note below three other effects of phonological rules:

- **delete** phonemes or phones.
- **insert** phonemes or phones (= EPENTHESIS)
- **permute** phonemes or phones (= METATHESIS)

Formats: $\mathbf{X \rightarrow \emptyset \, / \, A\underline{}B}$
$\emptyset \rightarrow X \, / \, A\underline{}B$
$XY \rightarrow YX \, / \, A\underline{}B$

Exercise 5.9

(A) Express the following processes as phonological rules, using the formats illustrated earlier in this chapter. Given the information in this chapter (or other information that occurs to you), indicate whether each one seems to be *conditioned* or *unconditioned, general* or *local,* and *categorical* or *variable.* If your results differ from those of your classmates, discuss your different observations.

Example: 0. Stressed vowels are lengthened when word-final: One answer: "V́ → [+long] (or V:) / ___#. Conditioned, general, categorical."

1. Tense high and mid vowels become diphthongs when stressed.
2. /r/ drops when before a consonant or when at the end of a word.
3. /ai/ and /au/ raise to [əi] [əu] when before /p t k s f θ . . . /

5.8 Other analyses of English vowels. Especially when reading other treatments of the English vowel system or when consulting dictionaries, you may encounter different symbols. In figure 5.n we summarize for reference five main analyses (omitting vowels such as /ɒ/ not generally used in the United States.).

Webster's, the traditional system of American dictionaries, is based on the pronunciation of Middle English (1200–1400), when *bite* and *bit* really did have roughly the same vowel [i], long (ī = [i:]) versus short (ĭ). Although reference works in other countries

Figure 5.n. Five analyses of the English vowel system

	Webster's	Fries-Pike	Trager-Smith	Jones	Gimson-Wells
heed, beat, she	ē	i	iy	iː, ii	iː
hit, bit, myth	ĭ	ɪ	i	i	ɪ
bait, face, say, they	ā	e	ey	ei	ei
bet, said, head	ĕ	ɛ	e	e	ɛ
bat, sad	ă	æ	æ	a	æ
father, spa, U.S. *cot*	ä, ŏ	ɑ	a	aː, aa	ɑː
thought, law, caught	ô	ɔ	ɔh	oː, ɔɔ	ɔː
boat, go, know	ō	o	ow	ou	əʊ
book, soot, wood	o͝o	ʊ	u	u	ʊ
boot, suit, do	o͞o	u	uw	uː, uu	uː
butt, sun = *son, cud*	ŭ	ʌ	ə	ʌ	ʌ
circu̱s, of, data̱	ə	ə	ə	ə	ə
fir = *fur, work, her*	ûr	ər, ɝ, ɽ	ər	ɚː, əə	ɜː
bite, night, my, eye	ī	ai , aj	ay	ai	aɪ
voice, boy, coin	oi	oi, ɔj	ɔy	oi	ɔɪ
bout, sound, cow	ou	au, aw	aw	au	aʊ

adopted a rational and international IPA-based system, Webster's jumble of diacritics has had such tenacity in the United States that most Americans can only describe their vowels /ai/ and /ɪ/ in *bite* versus *bit* as "long *I*" and "short *I*," as indeed they were—700 years ago. This antique way of showing pronunciation is especially hard on ESOL students when they use American dictionaries; it is like the need to master pounds, inches, and Fahrenheit for the only country in the world that has not adapted to the international metric system.[8]

The **Fries-Pike** analysis (Fries 1945; Pike 1947; Kenyon and Knott 1953) forms the basis of the one that is adopted in this book. It seems the best overall way to represent the vowel system, and it is also the usual system of introductory linguistics books, for example, Fromkin and Rodman (1998) and O'Grady, Dobrovolsky, and Aronoff (1997). Differences are mainly in how to show diphthongs and the /ər/ vowel, but there is consensus on the units themselves.

The **Trager-Smith** analysis (Trager and Smith 1951) is based on three assumptions: (1) that the key difference between tense and lax vowels is diphthongization, shown by **y** and **w**, (2) that [ʌ] is an allophone of /ə/, and (3) that diphthongized [ɔə] (§5.6.2) is phonemically "ɔh." Thus *beat* and *bait* are treated as diphthongs /biyt beyt/, whereas *bit* and *bet* supposedly have the same vowels without a glide, /bit bet/. This system was popular in the United States during the mid-twentieth century and although it is still found in some ESOL materials, its use has declined.

The analysis of **Jones** (1950) was equally influential in the United Kingdom. It likewise assumes that the vowels of (e.g.) *bait* and *boat* are phonemically diphthongs, but also that the vowels others treat as /i u ɑ ɔ ɜ/ are phonemically *long,* /iː uː aː oː əː/—or as Lass (1984) and Kreidler (1989) reinterpreted them, double (/ii uu/, etc.). Thus the difference between *beat* and *bit* (etc.) is not in their *sound* (quality) but in their *duration* (quantity). This analysis was adopted in British pedagogical and reference materials and has misled learners into thinking that *bit* is pronounced like *beat,* only shorter. In reality, for speakers of English on both sides of the Atlantic as well as in the Antipodes, lengthening varies (§5.4) according to stress, rhythm, and the following consonant. *Bead* is longer than *beat* because of the voiced /d/; likewise, in a sentential context such as *She beat/bit it,* the difference between the two vowels is clearly in quality, not quantity.

Because of such problems, other British phoneticians have adopted analyses such as that of **Gimson** (1962) and **Wells** (1982), who use different symbols **(i/ɪ)** for phonetically different vowels while keeping the length mark as a compromise—and taking it with a grain of salt.

5.9 Teaching pronunciation: Vowels and consonants. The traditional way to teach pronunciation is repetition: the teacher models the sound (by itself and in words, pairs, and full phrases or sentences), students repeat in imitation, and if they are not successful, the teacher describes the articulation and tries again. But there are alternatives for practice that can be more interesting and motivating (Bowen 1972; Allen and Valette 1977; Dalton and Seidlhofer 1994; Celce-Murcia, Brinton, and Goodwin 1996; Avery and Ehrlich 1992). Most are based on minimal pairs for AURAL or auditory discrimination (hearing) and ORAL discrimination (producing). The following list illustrates some of the most common techniques.

1. The teacher asks, "Which of these words is different from the rest? *bat, bat, bet, bat.*" On their paper, students circle a number: 1, 2, 3, 4.
2. The teacher says, "Tell me if these words are the same or different: *meet, mit.*" Listeners respond "Different." "*Seek, seek.*" "Same" (and so forth).
3. Students see a list of minimal pairs for a target distinction, or pictures representing them, as the following shows for /ɔ/ versus /o/.

ball	bowl
raw	row
called	cold
bought	boat (etc.)

After modeling the words, the teacher goes down the list again, this time randomly choosing just one word in each pair; students circle which ones they hear, and then check their answers. Next, in pairs, students repeat the exercise with each other, so that they not only hear the difference but must make it for their partners to perceive it. As a more challenging variant, minimal triplets such as *cot caught coat* can be substituted. As another variant, the teacher embeds suitable pairs in the same sentence frame, for example, *Get me the bowl/ball.*

4. Small groups are given a list of minimal pairs and instructed to select a certain number of them and compose (and then present) a brief story using them.

5. As a form of Total Physical Response, the teacher uses realia or pictures (on the board or on cards) that illustrate minimal pairs such as *ball* versus *bowl*. He/she then gives students instructions such as "Draw a *bowl*," "Point to the *ball*," or "Give me the *bowl*."

6. In Fluency Squares (Knowles and Sasaki 1980), the teacher projects a diagram that cues a short story based on target distinctions. Thus for /s/ versus /θ/ and /æ/ versus /ʌ/ (p. 9), there are four cells depicting situations that the teacher describes as "*Cassie* takes the *bus* in the morning; she takes a *bath* at night. *Cathy* takes a *bath* in the morning; she takes the *bus* at night." The teacher then poses questions such as "Who takes a bath at night?" and "When does Cathy take the bus?" and students respond. Students then do the same kind of questioning with each other in pairs. This technique contextualizes minimal pairs and also integrates target grammatical structures.

7. In a similar technique, the teacher shows the class a three-generation family tree of names liberally seeded with a target phoneme or contrast (e.g., *Cathy, Seth, Matthew, Beth, Bess,* etc.) and poses questions about them.

8. For recognizing phonemes in different spellings or for distinguishing allophones of them, the teacher may give students written sentences containing the target item(s) and ask them to circle each instance or mark it with a symbol. For an example, see Exercise 5.5:C in this chapter.

9. Celce-Murcia, Brinton, and Goodwin (1996, 122) point out that many English vowels are used alone as exclamations: [ɑ] 'satisfaction,' [ɔ] 'disappointment,' [au] 'pain,' [o] 'comprehension,' [ʌ] 'hesitation,' [ʔʌʔo] 'trouble,' and so on. After learning these meanings, students can be placed in pairs in which one reads a brief situation and the other responds with the appropriate vowel exclamation. For an information-gap activity, the same authors (121) suggest partially filled-in grids in two versions for pair work, as illustrated in figure 5.o, for a focus on words in which /æ/ and /ʌ/ might be confused. In order to complete their grids, students must ask each other questions such as "What word is in box B2?"

Some of these techniques are more appropriate than others, depending on a course's level, goals, and teaching methods; for a practical introduction to these areas, see Omaggio-Hadley (1993), and for games suitable for practicing phonemes with young children, see Lee (1979).

Figure 5.0. A sample information-gap activity

Student "A"	1	2	3	4
A	cap		dust	bug
B			fan	
C		stuck		
D	some		rough	hag

Student "B"	1	2	3	4
A		fun		
B	stack	dub		cat
C	love		ton	rub
D		hang		

NOTES

1. As one ESOL student once confessed, what most motivated her to master the tense/lax distinction was the uncertainty and embarrassment she felt with the pairs /ʃit ʃɪt/ and /pis pɪs/.

2. The word *stewed* is /stud/ for some, but /stjud/ for others (§6.9).

3. The "*r*-less" (or "nonrhotic") dialects are those that lost /r/ at the end of a syllable, as in *car* and *cart*, as explained in §6.4.1. They include most of England, Australia, New Zealand, and, in the United States, the traditional speech of eastern New England, New York City, and the lowland South. Other dialects are called "*r*-ful" (or "rhotic").

4. "*R*-ful" varieties have the same vowel in both syllables of *murder* [mɚ́dɚ], and by the principles of the IPA, it is shown the same way. See Ladefoged's illustration (IPA 1999, 44) using [ɚ] whether stressed or unstressed. Those who prefer 'ɜr,' 'ɝ,' or 'ʌr' for the stressed version apparently assume that a reduced vowel must be unstressed, so that 'ə,' 'ər,' and 'ɚ' must be limited to unstressed syllables. This assumption is contrary to IPA usage, in which [ə ʌ ɜ] are defined as distinct vowels that may be stressed or unstressed. Bulgarian, for instance, has a stressed /ə/ that is neither [ʌ] nor [ɜ]. REDUCTION refers to a neutralization of high-low and front-back contrasts, which has certainly occurred in most unstressed positions in English, but *also* in stressed lax vowels before /r/, as noted in the text. On the other hand, the reason for treating [ɚ] phonologically as /ər/ is that this is how the vowel acts in English: note how it emerges from a sequence such as *uvula* /júvjələ/+ -*r* → *uvular* /júvjələr/ [júvjələɚ] or from the reduction of *for* when unstressed: /for/ reduces to /fər/, which then (exactly as in *fur* or *fir*) is rendered [fɚ].

5. Note that in such variants, as in numerous others we describe in chapter 7, there may be strong local tendencies and preferences, but not homogeneity: it is very rarely the case that *all* English speakers in a given region use variant *X,* whereas all speakers elsewhere do *not.* This is why lists of "British" versus "American" usage can be misleading. Consider, for example, the list offered by Celce-Murcia, Brinton, and Goodwin (1996, 363–70): in virtually every case, the supposedly "British" pronunciation is also heard among many Americans

who have lived their entire lives in the United States, and the supposedly "North American English" variants can also be found in the British Isles.

6. We adopt a simplified rule notation for the sake of students with little formal training in linguistics, but note alternative formalisms elsewhere (metrical §1.2, autosegmental §6.4.2, optimality 7.7.3).

7. The diphthongs /ai oi au/ are generally analyzed as adjacent sets or MATRICES of feature specifications—one being treated as [+syllabic] and the other as [-syllabic]—occupying a single vowel slot in syllable structure (§6.1).

8. It is for this reason that terminology such as "long *I*, short *I*, flat *A*, broad *A*, hard *G*, soft *G*" and so forth have little usefulness in the ESOL classroom; interpreted literally, it is a puzzlement to learners from other countries. (The "short *I*" of *kid* is long in duration, and how can a vowel be "flat," or a consonant "hard"?) Description is not needed when modeling suffices, but when it is needed in the classroom, any labels and symbols will have to be explained, so one might as well adopt or paraphrase accurate terms based on actual articulation.

Wrap-Up Exercises

(A) **Practice with broad transcription.** In each row, identify each word (checking with the answers in the KEY box that follows), then read each row out loud, making sure you are using the indicated vowel and noting its sameness in the set of words despite the spelling. For reverse practice, go to the KEY box, transcribe the words, and check your results with the following list.

/i/: /ʃip/, /wi/, /tri/, /ki/, /kwin/, /hit/, /ðiz/, /livz/, /hʌni/, /síʒər/, /tʃip/, /pípəl/, /rid/

/ɪ/: /ʃɪp/, /trɪk/, /kwɪt/, /wímɪn/, /hɪt/, /ðɪs/, /lɪvz/, /mɪθ/, /sízərz/, /tʃɪp/, /lɪm/, /θɪk/

/e/: /ʃep/, /test/, /det/, /edʒ/, /gedʒ/, /ðe/, /beð/, /kwek/, /fez/, /ek/, /gret/, /strendʒ/

/ɛ/: /sɛd/, /tɛst/, /dɛt/, /dʒɛm/, /ɛdʒ/, /jɛt/, /bɛg/, /θrɛd/, /brɛd/, /tʃɛk/, /ɛ́kstrə/, /pɛr/

/æ/: /sæd/, /kæt/, /næt/, /dæn/, /stæk/, /æd/, /kwæk/, /hǽftə/, /flændʒ/, /æks/, /ǽkʃən/

/a/: /sad/, /kat/, /náti/, /dan/, /stɑk/, /ad/, /far/, /fáðər/, /jat/, /dʒɑt/, /gəráʒ/, /bam/

/ɔ/: /sɔd/, /kɔt/, /nɔ́ti/, /dɔn/, /stɔk/, /ɔd/, /dɔ́tər/, /ɔ́to/, /wɔl/, /brɔt/, /brɔd/, /fɔrt/

/o/: /sod/, /kot/, /dom/, /θrot/, /od/, /groθ/, /do/, /ðoz/, /no/, /hol/, /ʃon/

/u/: /pul/, /hu/, /luk/, /muvd/, /luz/, /ju/, /mud/, /rul/, /tu/, /fju/, /kjut/, /sut/

/ʊ/: /pʊl/, /hʊk/, /lʊk/, /kʊd/, /wʊd/, /wʊ́mən/, /pʊʃt/, /kʊkt/, /bʊ́tʃər/, /sʊt/

/ʌ/: /pʌls/, /ʌp/, /lʌk/, /fʌs/, /kʌd/, /tʌf/, /sʌŋ/, /dʌz/, /tʌŋ/, /ʌ́vən/, /blʌd/, /wʌn/, /ʌ́njən/

/ər/: /pərl/, /lərk/, /fərst/, /kərd/, /tərf/, /túbər/, /mɔ́rdər/, /wərd/, /fər/, /hərd/

/ə/: /əbʌ́v/, /əbáut/, /sófə/, /səpóstə/, /mélədi/, /túbə/, /lébəl/, /bátəm/, /bəháind/, /júnjən/

/ai/: /naif/, /mai/, /sait/, /dai/, /ail/, /sain/, /kwair/, /tráiŋ/, /láiən/, /hait/, /ráitʃəs/

/au/: /braun/, /nau/, /kaunt/, /ʃaut/, /plau/, /draut/, /daut/, /mauθ/, /aur/, /kautʃ/

/oi/: /koin/, /boi/, /dəstrói/, /dʒóintli/, /kánvòi/, /dəvóid/, /oiŋk/, /poizd/.

KEY:

/i/: sheep, we, tree, key, queen, heat, these, leaves, honey, seizure, cheap, people, read = reed

/ɪ/: ship, trick, quit, women, hit, this, lives (*verb*), myth, scissors, chip, limb, thick

/e/: shape, taste, date, age, gauge, they, bathe, quake, phase = faze, ache, great = grate, strange

/ɛ/: said, test, debt, gem, edge, yet, beg, thread, bread, check = cheque = Czech, extra, pear = pare = pair

/æ/: sad, cat, gnat, Dan, stack, ad = add, quack, have to, flange, axe, action

/ɑ/: sod, cot, knotty, Don, stock, odd, far, father, yacht, jot, garage, bomb

/ɔ/: sawed, caught, naughty, dawn, stalk, awed, daughter, auto, wall, brought, broad, fort

/o/: sowed = sewed, coat, dome, throat, owed = ode, growth, dough = doe, those, no = know, hole = whole, shone = shown

/u/: pool, who, Luke, moved, lose = Lou's, you = ewe = yew, mood = mooed, rule, to = two = too, few, cute, suit

/ʊ/: pull, hook, look, foot, could, wood = would, woman, pushed, cooked, butcher, soot

/ʌ/: pulse, up, luck, fuss, cud, tough, sung, does, tongue, oven, blood, one = won, onion

/ər/: pearl, lurk, first, curd, turf, tuber, murder, word, fir = fur, heard = herd

/ə/: above, about, sofa, supposed to, melody, tuba, label, bottom, behind, union

/ai/: knife, my, sight = cite = site, die = dye, I'll = aisle, sign = sine, choir, trying, lion, height, righteous

/au/: brown, now, count, shout, plow, drought, doubt, mouth, our = hour, couch

/oi/: coin, boy, destroy, jointly, convoy, devoid, oink, poised

---

(B) Homographs. HOMOGRAPHS are words that are pronounced differently but spelled the same. For each of the following, transcribe the two pronunciations and explain their meanings.

lead	sow	tear	dove	live	read	desert
re(-)creation	primer	separate	wound	bass	bow	wind

(C) **Word recognition.** In each row, some transcriptions represent real words, whereas others do not. Identify the real ones by writing them in normal orthography; use an X for nonexistent words.

1. /bid bɪd bed bɛd bæd bɑd bɔd bod bʊd bud bʌd baid boid baud bərd/

— — — — — — — — — — — — — — —

2. /din dɪn den dɛn dæn dɑn dɔn don dʊn dun dʌn dain doin daun dərn/

— — — — — — — — — — — — — — —

3. /kit kɪt ket kɛt kæt kɑt kɔt kot kʊt kut kʌt kait koit kaut kərt/

— — — — — — — — — — — — — — —

4. /mis mɪs mes mɛs mæs mɑs mɔs mos mʊs mus mʌs mais mois maus mərs/

— — — — — — — — — — — — — — —

5. /nit nɪt net nɛt næt nɑt nɔt not nʊt nut nʌt nait noit naut nərt/

— — — — — — — — — — — — — — —

6. /pi pɪ pe pɛ pæ pɑ pɔ po pʊ pu pʌ pai poi pau pər/

— — — — — — — — — — — — — — —

(D) **Word play.** How many actual words can you extract from the following list of frames by filling in the blank with each of the fifteen vowels (including /ər/) of English? (See the preceding exercise.) Here is how to proceed: (1) insert each vowel, (2) pronounce the result, then (3) indicate whether the result is a real word or not. Use this example as your guide:

0. /b__t/: Real words: /bit/, /bɪt/, /bet/, /bɛt/, /bæt/, /bɑt/ (it exists!), /bɔt/, /bot/, /but/, /bait/, /baut/. (False words: /bʊt/ and /boit/—and /bərt/ exists but only as a name, *Bert*).
   1. /b__k/   4. /f__t/
   2. /b__l/   5. /f__z/
   3. /b__m/   6. /f__n/

(E) **Pair work: two-way dictation.** Use the dictation technique described in this chapter (Exercise 5.5:E), but give your partner a list of five two-syllable English words to transcribe phonemically according to your dictation, and deliberately *mispronounce* one vowel in each word. For example, for *touchdown*, say "/tʊ́tʃdàun/." Each should identify the errors in the other's dictation.

(F) Rhymes. Mario is a student of English who likes the language and is already writing poetry in it. But he has trouble with the vowels, relying too much on orthography, and he often tries to rhyme words that do not have the same vowel. Correct the following attempted rhymes by writing each pair in a phonemic (broad) transcription to contrast their real vowels.

1. *father, lather:* _____, _____

2. *advice, police:* _____, _____

3. *allow, below:* _____, _____

4. *rage, garage:* _____, _____

5. *soot, boot:* _____, _____

6. *war, scar:* _____, _____

7. *thread, bead:* _____, _____

8. *limb, climb:* _____, _____

9. *love, move:* _____, _____

10. *mouth, vermouth:* _____, _____

11. *roll, doll:* _____, _____

12. *rough, through:* _____, _____

13. *done, shone:* _____, _____

14. *worse, horse:* _____, _____

(G) Stress makes the difference. Each of the following words has two competing stress patterns even in standard English. For each one, show with accent marks the two patterns (dictionaries often show both), and then use phonemic transcriptions to point out the vowel differences.

1. controversy
2. harass
3. advertisement
4. secretary
5. irrefutable
6. Caribbean

(H) Analysis. Your instructor will read the following sentences out loud. Try to guess (if you do not know already) where he/she is from, and determine how his/her way of pronouncing English differs from your own. Use the terms and symbols that you have been studying.

1. I had a real nice time.
2. Go load the bags on the truck.
3. The newer schools usually lose.
4. There ought to be a law against a band being so bad.
5. To repel the attackers, they poured boiling oil on their heads.
6. You can't park your car in the yard.
7. Don't cast pearls before swine.

🎧 (I) **Different kinds of English.** From the CD recording, listen to the pronunciations of the following words and transcribe the vowel of each speaker as narrowly as possible.

	Brooklyn, N.Y.	Concord, N.C.	Green Bay, Wisc.	London, England
1. *fine*	_____	_____	_____	_____
2. *house*	_____	_____	_____	_____
3. *go*	_____	_____	_____	_____
4. *can't*	_____	_____	_____	_____
5. *heard*	_____	_____	_____	_____
6. *shoot*	_____	_____	_____	_____
7. *friend*	_____	_____	_____	_____
8. *lawn*	_____	_____	_____	_____
9. *head*	_____	_____	_____	_____
10. *card*	_____	_____	_____	_____

CHAPTER 6

Consonants

6.1 Consonants and syllable position. Consonants are sounds that are articulated with some kind of oral constriction in the air stream. They range from a complete obstruction such as the /p/ of *pit*, producing brief silence, or a partial obstruction such as the /f/ of *fit*, producing noise, to a briefer movement as in the /w/ of *wit*, that suffices to just "pinch" briefly the surrounding resonance.

Consonants tend to "sound with" (Latin *con-sonāns*) a vowel in forming syllables. Thus, in *baste*, there are three consonants /b . . . st/ that are not pronounced alone but are grouped around one vowel (a vowel *phoneme*); the result is that the word has only one syllable: /best/. (The silent letter *-e* serves a purely orthographic purpose, §4.2.) As we will discover later, it is possible to have a vowel-less syllable, but in all languages, syllables ordinarily consist of V (= a vowel, as in *owe* /o/), or CV (= consonant + vowel, as in *go*), CVC (*tone*), CCVC (*stone*), or CVCC (*won't*), and so on.

Syllables have an internal structure. The vowel is the peak or NUCLEUS, and together with the CODA of consonants following it, forms the RHYME. The rhyme has a psychological reality for speakers; even at an early age before learning to read and write, children can tell that *baste* rhymes with *taste, waist, faced,* and so on, and *stone* with *own, bone, clone, condone* (but not with *one* /wʌn/, whose vowel sound is different). The consonants preceding this rhyme form the ONSET. This internal structure is shown as a tree headed by the Greek letter sigma, σ, which means 'syllable,' as depicted in figure 6.a. As we will see, different phonological rules apply depending on whether the consonant is in the onset, where articulatory energy concentrates on release into the vowel, or in the coda, where the sound trails off after the syllabic peak.

When a word has several syllables (i.e., is POLYSYLLABIC), like *condone*, the structure is often abbreviated by just placing a period (official in the International Phonetic

Figure 6.a. Internal syllable structure

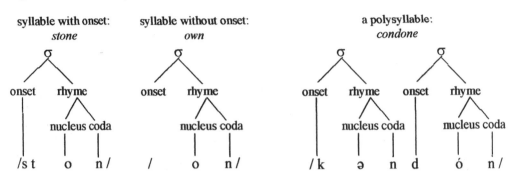

Alphabet [IPA]), hyphen, or dollar sign between the syllables: /kən.dón/, /kən-dón/, /kən$dón/. To be sure, SYLLABICATION, or a word's division into syllables, is clearer in some languages than in others. One English quirk is that intervocalic consonants are sometimes AMBISYLLABIC, fence-straddlers belonging to both syllables (coda of one and onset of the next), as shown in figure 6.b. Thus, in *many*, the nasality of the /n/ carries into both syllables, and the /r/ of *very* or *berry* (despite the spelling, there is only one /r/) may smear into both syllables. Dictionaries arbitrarily decide on *ve.ry* or *ver.y*, but native speakers often feel unsure. The reason is phonotactic (§6.10): in syllabication, a nucleus takes for its onset as many consonants to its left as the language allows to start a word (O'Grady, Dobrovolsky, and Aronoff 1997, 80). Thus in /méni/, the /i/ gets the /n/, /mé.ni/, because /ni/- can start an English word (and *is* a word, *knee*); but that leaves lax /ɛ/—normally a checked vowel in English (§1.3)—"open," that is, unchecked by a consonant. The English solution is to share the /n/.

Figure 6.b. An ambisyllabic consonant

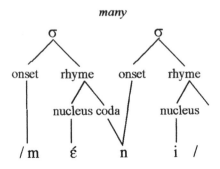

Exercise 6.1

(A) Transcribe the following words phonemically and separate the syllables with a period. (Beware of digraphs and especially doubled consonant *letters* representing single sounds.) Do not consult a dictionary; check your intuitions against those of other students in class. If you sense an ambisyllabic consonant, circle it.

picnic	garbage	umbrella	student
abstraction	rambunctious	penalty	condemned
derelict	recovery	population	impetuous
liquid	failure	hypnotist	anthrax

(B) Now show the internal syllable structure of these monosyllables, using a tree diagram:

camp   stunk   asked   three

(C) One problem with English syllabication is the status of /(ə)r/ and /(ə)l/ after tense vowels, /ər/, or diphthongs. The parenthesized schwa may be present for an additional syllable, or it may *not* be, depending on the individual speaker, the register, and sometimes a merely impressionistic "feel." Thus *fire* may be /faɪr/ or /fáɪ.ər/.

1. Determine whether you pronounce the following pairs as homophones or not:

higher, hire	vile, vial	flower, flour	royal, roil
layer, lair	real, reel	lyre, liar	mayor, mare

2. Now that you are sensitized, determine whether you pronounce the following words as monosyllables or bisyllables:

iron	Carl	squirrel	foyer	stirrer	hour
coil	jewel	power	sewer	towel	vowel

6.2 Types of consonants. We describe and classify consonants according to their voicing, place and manner of articulation, and any additional modifications that are imposed.

6.2.1 Voicing. The LARYNX or "voice box" is the large, topmost cartilage ring of the windpipe (trachea). Its front bulge is what we call the Adam's apple. Look in a mirror, touch your larynx with your fingers, and feel it as you hold out the /f/ sound of *fat*: [ffff . . .]. You will see your upper teeth touching the lower lip, and as the air stream pushes through with noise, you should feel no vibration in your larynx. Now say the whole word *fat* slowly (but do not whisper!): there should be vibration now when you reach the vowel, and the vibration should end with the /t/. That vibration is called VOICE, and it is the product of two muscle folds in the larynx called the VOCAL CORDS (or VOCAL FOLDS) that come together and vibrate for vowels like the /æ/ in *fat*.

Now do the same for the /v/ of *vat*. Notice that your lips and teeth are exactly the same as they were for /f/, but now that you are pronouncing /v/ you can feel your Adam's apple vibrate. The sounds /f/ and /v/ are exactly alike except that /f/ is VOICE-LESS and /v/ is VOICED. If you repeat this experiment for the /s/ of *sip* and the /z/ of *zip*, you will perceive the same difference: /s/ is voiceless, /z/ is voiced, but otherwise they have the same articulation. As a second test for voicing, stop up your ears with your fingertips and again say /f/, /v/, /s/, and /z/ (the *sounds*, not the letter-names: "eff, vee, ess, zee"). What you hear is the sound transmitted through your head bones, and while you hear noise for all four, only /v/ and /z/ have a buzzing of the voice. Many consonants come in such voiceless/voiced pairs, described in terms of the feature [±voice].[1]

The GLOTTIS is the gap between the vocal cords, and voice and voicelessness are sometimes called "states of the glottis." A third state is the GLOTTAL STOP, in which the vocal cords slam completely shut, as when you hold your breath and then release it abruptly. This sound is transcribed as [ʔ], and we will meet it again later (§6.5.1).

6.2.2 Place of articulation.

A consonant's sound depends on where in the mouth it is pronounced. The diagram in figure 6.c indicates the parts of the vocal tract that are relevant for consonant production. (For the acoustic side of consonant description, see the appendix.)

The /p/ of *pin* is made with the two lips together, whereas the /f/ of *fin* is made with the upper teeth against the lower lip. There would be nothing wrong with terms such as "lip sounds" or "lip-teeth" sounds to identify these consonants' place of articulation, but

Figure 6.c. The mouth

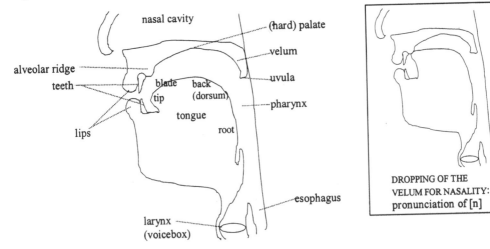

DROPPING OF THE
VELUM FOR NASALITY:
pronunciation of [n]

just as other sciences do (*skull* → "cranium," *backbones* → "vertebrae"), linguistics generally switches to Latin for its technical terms. Thus /p/ is described as "bilabial," that is, 'both-lips.'

In what follows, we review the main places of articulation. Say each consonant example (and observe it in a mirror), using figures 6.c and 6.d to verify where you are making it.

1. LABIAL: pronounced with the lips.
   a. BILABIAL: pronounced with both lips, as in English /p/, /b/, and /m/.
   b. LABIODENTAL: made with the upper teeth against the lower lip, as in English /f/ and /v/.
   c. LABIOVELAR: pronounced with both lips (usually rounded) and, simultaneously, a pulling of the back of the tongue (dorsum) toward the velum, as in English /w/ in *win*.
2. CORONAL: made with the front part of the tongue. When the exact part of the tongue needs to be specified, the modifiers APICAL or *apico-* and LAMINAL or *lamino-* are added to indicate the tip (apex) and blade, respectively.

Figure 6.d. Some places of articulation

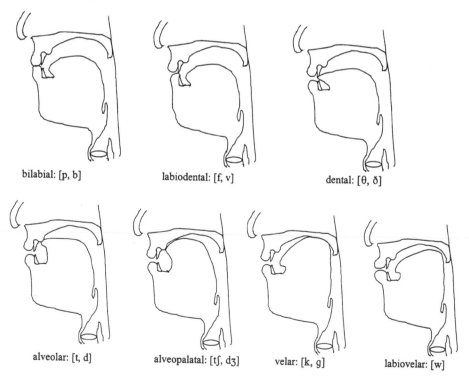

bilabial: [p, b]   labiodental: [f, v]   dental: [θ, ð]

alveolar: [t, d]   alveopalatal: [tʃ, dʒ]   velar: [k, g]   labiovelar: [w]

    a. DENTAL: made with the tongue on the upper teeth, such as the /θ/ of *thin*.

    b. ALVEOLAR: pronounced with the tip and/or blade at or on the alveolar ridge, as in English /t d n s l/.

    c. RETROFLEX: made with the tip curling up and back toward the palate, as in a common type of English /r/.

    d. ALVEOPALATAL (also called postalveolar, or palato-alveolar): pronounced with the tip close to the upper teeth and alveolar ridge and the blade up close to the forward part of the palate, as in English /tʃ/ (*chin*) and /dʒ/ (*gin, Jim*).

3. DORSAL: made with the middle or back of the tongue (dorsum) against the roof of the mouth.

    a. PALATAL: made with the middle of the tongue raised to or near the palate, with the tip pointing down and even tucked behind the lower teeth. (If the tip is *up*, the sound is alveopalatal.) The English /j/ sound spelled *y* as in *yacht* approaches the palate and is thus described as palatal.

    b. VELAR:[2] made with the dorsum raised up to the velum (soft palate). The English /k/ sound beginning *kit, cat,* and *quit* is a voiceless velar stop.

    c. UVULAR: made with the dorsum pulled as far back as possible on the velum, against the uvula (the appendage hanging down in the back that you see in the mirror when you open your mouth wide). English speakers make no use of the uvula, except to gargle (= a uvular trill).

4. LARYNGEAL: made primarily in the larynx, without any specific obstruction in the mouth. The main type in this category is GLOTTAL, produced by narrowing or closing the glottis. The /h/ of *hot* is described as glottal in its place of articulation, and we have already met the glottal stop [ʔ]. The latter can be heard as the popping sound at the beginning of the syllables of *uh-oh*, [ʔʌʔo].

    In FEATURE THEORY (§5.7) consonantal places of articulation are distinguished by four main features: [+anterior] describes sounds made in the front of the mouth (labials, dentals, alveolars), [+coronal] describes sounds that are made with the front of the tongue, [+high] refers to sounds that are made with the tongue high in the mouth, and [+back] refers to sounds made with the dorsum. The table in figure 6.e distinguishes the main places according to their specifications for these four features. Additional features are adopted for subdistinctions when necessary, for example, [+round] for lip rounding

Figure 6.e. Feature specifications for the main places of articulation

	Labials	Dentals, alveolars	Retroflex	Alveopalatals	Palatals	Velars	Uvulars	Glottals
[anterior]	+	+	-	-	-	-	-	-
[coronal]	-	+	+	+	-	-	-	-
[high]	-	-	-	+	+	+	-	-
[back]	-	-	-	-	-	+	+	-

(as with [w]), [+distributed] for broader surface contact (as in [s] as opposed to [θ]), and [+constricted glottis] (for [ʔ] and similar sounds).

6.2.3 Manner of articulation. After determining where a consonant is made and whether it is voiced or voiceless, we identify its MANNER OF ARTICULATION, how it modifies the air stream coming through the mouth from the lungs. Again, there are several types, and since birds of a feather flock together, the members of one type often act as a NATURAL CLASS in phonology.

1. OBSTRUENTS: In an *obstruent*, you form an *obstruction* that produces momentary silence or turbulence in the air stream. Obstruents generally come in [+voice]/[-voice] pairs.
   a. STOP (or PLOSIVE): The articulators block the passage completely and then may release the pressure that has built up behind them. The /t/ of English *tin* is a voiceless stop whose voiced counterpart is /d/ as in *din*. Both are made by pressing the tip of the tongue against the gum ridge (ALVEOLAR RIDGE) just behind the upper front teeth to block the air stream.
   b. FRICATIVE: Unlike stops, which are [-continuant], fricatives are [+continuant] because the articulators constrict the air stream without stopping it. The result is noise called FRICTION or FRICATION, although "turbulence" is more accurate. The /s/ of *sin* and the /ʃ/ of *shin* are fricatives because the front part of the tongue is at the alveolar ridge but allows the air to continue through. The /f/ of *fin* and the /θ/ of *thin* are also fricatives but their turbulence is weaker. For this reason, "hissy" fricatives such as /s/ and /ʃ/ are called SIBILANTS, whereas /f/ and /θ/ are nonsibilant. In feature theory, especially noisy fricatives such as sibilants are described as [+strident].
   c. AFFRICATE: An affricate is a stop that is released as a fricative: instead of pulling away cleanly as in other stops, the articulator lingers in the same place of articulation to create turbulence. The English *ch* of *chin* is an affricate: we form a [t] and then release it as [ʃ]. That is why the IPA uses the compound symbol tʃ for this consonant. Because /tʃ/ contains [ʃ], it is also classified as a sibilant and is therefore [+strident]. But in the way they pattern, affricates are a subtype of stop: /tʃ/ is to /ʃ/ as /t/ is to /s/ ([-continuant] vs. [+continuant]).
2. SONORANTS: In sonorants, the articulator does not block the air stream but modifies its resonance. This group includes nasals, liquids, glides, and also vowels. Unlike obstruents (= [-sonorant]), sonorants are usually voiced and can be sung (i.e., pronounced with varying pitch).
   d. NASAL: In the final sound of *din,* your tongue blocks the voiced air stream at the alveolar ridge as for [d], but the velum drops slightly (see figure 6.c), deflecting the air stream into the nasal passages and yielding nasal resonance (nasality). Thus /n/ and /d/ are identical in articulation except that /n/ is

NASAL (velum down) and /d/ is ORAL (velum up). In terms of features, [n] is [+nasal, + sonorant], whereas [d] is [-nasal, -sonorant].

e. LIQUID: Liquids are *l* and *r* sounds, such as the initial consonants of *lip* and *rip*. They share an acoustic similarity as the voiced air stream passes over or around the tongue's body, reminding poets, at least, of the sound of flowing liquids—which is why poems about babbling brooks abound in *l*s and *r*s. This similarity in oral resonance is captured by the feature combination [+consonantal, +sonorant, -nasal]. But there are various subtypes that differ from one language to the next, and they interact strongly with vowels as we will see later.

f. GLIDE: Glides include the *y*-sound of English *yet*, transcribed as [j], and the [w] of *wet*. For both, the tongue glides into or out of a high position in the mouth, hence the name GLIDE; and because they just approach a place of articulation without making contact, glides are also known as APPROXI-MANTS. Although they often act like consonants, glides are vowel-like, [-consonantal].

6.2.4 Secondary modifications. The previous classification generally suffices to describe the articulation of consonants. English /t/ is a "voiceless (apico-)alveolar stop" (or [+consonantal, -continuant, -sonorant, -voice, +coronal, +anterior]), and these labels can be considered an abbreviated recipe for how to make the sound: with voicing turned off (vocal cords separated, not vibrating), the tongue tip touches the alveolar ridge and blocks the air stream there. At times, though, it is necessary to specify additional mod-ifications that are brought into play. For example, English /t/ at the beginning of a word is ASPIRATED, released with an explosion of breath, whereas /t/ after /s/ is not. (Put your hand in front of your mouth as you contrast the articulation of *tick* and *stick*; you can feel the difference in the air being released.) We will explore this difference more in §6.5.1; for now, just bear in mind that the vocal tract is capable of adding numerous other effects to the basic types that we have described in these sections.

Exercise 6.2

(A) Use the voicing tests to determine whether each of the following sounds is voiced or voiceless:

| [s] | [w] | [k] | [m] | [au] |
| [θ] | [r] | [ʌ] | [æ] | [tʃ] |

(B) The following sounds are not normally used in English, but do occur as consonants in other languages. To practice the terminology of this section and to gain more conscious control over your vocal tract, try to make each sound from the descrip-tion alone.

1. a voiced dental stop
2. a voiceless velar fricative
3. a voiceless bilabial fricative

4. a dental lateral
5. a labiodental nasal
6. a voiceless palatal (not alveopalatal) stop

6.3 English consonant phonemes. For reference, we show the consonant phonemes of English in figure 6.f. Most of these also have variants (allophones, §5.1) that we will take up later. There are a few dialect variations, but in general, the English consonant system is more stable and uniform than the vowel system we described in chapter 5.

How much can this system be taken for granted in a classroom of students from other language backgrounds? There has been a great deal of research comparing the phonological systems of the world,[3] and English turns out to be fairly average in its number of consonants; some languages have fewer, others many more. There are even commonalities, or UNIVERSALS, in the units themselves and in the overall architecture. Thus, most languages distinguish at least three places of articulation for stops on the basis of the features [anterior, coronal, back]; the most frequent fricatives are /s f h/; the [+anterior] /m n/ are the most common nasals; and the two glides /j/ and /w/ are widespread.

Yet there are also major differences in consonantal inventories. English has several units that its speakers take for granted as obvious in their pronunciation, although these turn out to be rare in other languages, and therefore difficult for learners. The fricatives /θ/ (*thin*) and /ð/ (*then*) are high frequency in English but less common elsewhere; voicing contrasts vary in other languages or may not be used at all; even /p b/, despite their visible articulation and quick acquisition by children, are lacking in some languages. Even when languages share the same basic units, their rules for pronouncing them may vary: as we noted earlier, English /t/ is often aspirated, and although some languages (e.g., Hindi) use aspiration to distinguish two different /t/ phonemes, others (e.g., French) make no use of aspiration at all. Likewise, although most languages have some kind of /r/ (or several), the articulations favored by English speakers are unusual, and it is a safe bet that learners from other language backgrounds will have some trouble with English /r/.

Figure 6.f. Table of English consonant phonemes

		bi-labial	labio-dental	dental	alve-olar	retro-flex	alveo-palatal	pala-tal	velar	labio-velar	glottal
stops	[-voice]	p			t		tʃ		k		
	[+voice]	b			d		dʒ		g		
frica-tives	[-voice]		f	θ	s		ʃ				h
	[+voice]		v	ð	z		ʒ				
nasals	[+voice]	m			n				ŋ		
liquids and glides [+voice]					l	r		j		w	

6.4 Consonants that can behave like vowels. Like vowels, liquids and nasals are normally voiced and are characterized by their resonance. They also interact with vowels in several ways.

1. When in the syllable coda (as in *pill, peer, pin*), they often color the preceding vowel, which anticipates their articulation and takes on some of the features of it.
2. In unstressed syllables, the vowel may drop out, and in that case the liquid or nasal acts like a vowel (more precisely, they move into the vacated nucleus) by carrying the syllabic beat.
3. Liquids may even weaken to a vowel-like articulation, a process called VOCALIZATION.

6.4.1 Liquids: /s and rs. Liquids as a class are abbreviated as **L** (like **C** = consonant and **V** = vowel). English uses the feature [±lateral] to distinguish two liquid phonemes, /l/ and /r/, as in *lace/race, clash/crash, hill/here* and numerous other minimal pairs. Some languages, such as Irish, distinguish many more by utilizing other places of articulation and secondary modifications such as voicelessness and friction. Others, like Japanese, have a single liquid phoneme, and because it then has more elbowroom for articulation, it may range indistinctly over several allophones, sounding (to English speakers, at least) sometimes like an /r/, sometimes like an /l/. To Japanese speakers, on the other hand, English *race* and *lace* sound the same because Japanese disregards [±lateral] for contrastive purposes, and learning to distinguish the two can be as formidable a task as it is for English speakers to master the multiple liquids of Irish.

English /l/ is a voiced alveolar lateral: you place the tip (apex) of your tongue on the alveolar ridge as for /d/, but instead of stopping the air, you pull away the edges of the tongue from the gums so that the voiced air stream continues over the sides. (Think of football, where a *lateral* pass is one off to the *side*.) You can verify this lateral articulation by saying a word such as *ill* and holding the final tongue position as you inhale sharply through your mouth: you should feel the sides of your tongue cooled by the rush of air over them.

But secondary modifications yield two kinds of /l/, both of them apicoalveolar yet different in what the rest of the tongue does (see figure 6.g). In a CLEAR /l/, the body of the tongue is rather high in the mouth, close to the position for the /ɪ/ of *hit*. This kind of /l/, sometimes shown in narrow transcription as [l̠], is normal in French, Spanish, Italian, and German. In a DARK /l/, on the other hand, the middle of the tongue is sunken while the dorsum is pulled back close to the velum. This backing, or VELARIZATION, is shown by a tilde through the symbol: [ɫ]. Although the difference between clear ([-back]) and dark ([+back]) /l/ may seem subtle, acoustically it is striking: [l̠] has a light /j/-like resonance, whereas [ɫ] has the quality of /w/ or /u/.

In their lateral preferences, English speakers sort into three groups. Some (Welsh, Highland Scots, Irish) use only clear /l/. Others (many speakers in England and some in

North America) have clear /l/ initially and before front vowels (*leak, silly*) but otherwise dark /l/, especially in a coda (*pool, all, milk, elbow*). Still others (Lowland Scots, Australians, New Zealanders, many North Americans) generalize dark /l/. Check your own articulation(s) of /l/: you may have two allophones depending on position, or the same one in all positions. But in comparison with other languages, English definitely tends toward velarization of its /l/, and this articulation affects preceding vowels: for example, the /ɪ/ of *pill* tends to be further back (less fronted) than in *pitch*.

In casual speech, English speakers often relax their articulation of [ɫ] before a consonant (*milk*) or word-finally (*mill*), failing to make apical contact at the alveolar ridge. The /l/ thereby loses its [+consonantal] specification, becoming vowel-like:

/l/ → [-consonantal, -lateral] / _____(C)$

By this process of DELATERALIZATION, all that remains is a residual [w]- or [u]-like sound. Cockney English is well-known for this development, as in *ball* [bɔu], *milk* [mɪuk], *full* [fʊu], *sell* [sɛu], *pal* [pæu]. Yet far from London—from Australia to Atlanta and New York— pronunciations such as [sɛu] for *sell* are more common than is usually realized.

Nonlateral liquids are *r*-sounds, or RHOTICS (Greek for '*r*-sounds'). The rhotics of other languages tend to be the more vigorous trilled or flapped type of Spanish, Italian, Arabic, and Russian. Older English also used a trilled /r/, but in most modern varieties it has weakened to an approximant in which the tongue just approaches the zone behind the alveolar ridge without making contact. The resulting sound is vowel-like, and to reinforce it, many speakers round their lips, especially at the beginning of a word or before a stressed vowel as in *rich* or *arrest*. This secondary modification of [+round] is shown in a narrow transcription by a raised *w*: [rʷ].

Yet the place of articulation of English /r/ varies (figure 6.g). For many Britons, the apex approaches the alveolar ridge; for most Americans and Canadians, it curls up a little further back in a retroflex position; and for some Midwestern Americans, the whole

Figure 6.g. Articulations of English liquids

Types of English /l/   Types of English /r/ (all shown rounded)

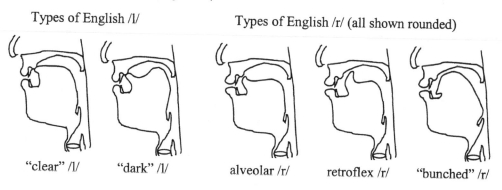

"clear" /l/   "dark" /l/   alveolar /r/   retroflex /r/   "bunched" /r/

front of the tongue bunches up toward the same zone, often with nasality. The acoustic result of the three is similar, and many speakers are unaware of which articulation they use. You should verify your tongue position in a mirror as you say a word such as *rich* or *rob,* noting also the degree of rounding.

Note on symbols

The articulations of English /r/ can be distinguished in a narrow transcription with special IPA symbols: [ɹ] (turned *r*) for the alveolar approximant, [ɻ] (turned *r* with a tail) for the retroflex one, [ɹ̺] (with an under-box meaning 'laminal') for the bunched one—or with rounding shown too, [ɹʷ ɻʷ ɹ̺ʷ]. But because of the acoustic similarity, linguists often use 'ɹ' for all three as a general approximant type, or just '/r/' if dealing solely with English. Linguists of other languages likewise use plain '/r/' for a broad or phonemic transcription of rhotics in their languages, switching to a more precise symbol to pinpoint differences: for example, apicoalveolar trill [r̄] or flap [ɾ] in Russian, Italian, and Spanish, uvular trill [ʀ] in German, uvular fricative [ʁ] in French.

In some areas, the vocalization of /r/ went a step further by a change known as R-DROPPING:

r → Ø / ___(C)\$

that is, /r/ becomes zero (silent) when in a syllable coda, as in *car, cartoon,* and *cart.* This process began in the London area in the eighteenth century, spread to eastern seaboard areas of the United States, and then to Australia and New Zealand. The map in figure 6.h shows the distribution of *R*-dropping as of the mid-twentieth century. No other consonant change has had such an impact on dialect alignment. Variation continues today on both sides of the Atlantic, but the cultivated norm in England is *r*-lessness, whereas that of Ireland and North America is *r*-fulness.

Like /l/, English /r/ affects preceding vowels. As noted in §5.4.2, /r/ neutralizes certain vowel distinctions (those who still distinguish *mourn/morn* or *merry/Mary/marry* are in the minority today), and it often blends with the vowel. In *r*-ful dialects, this blending takes the form of a smear of "r-coloring" (retroflexion) in a word such as *here* as the apex starts rising for /r/ in mid-vowel, whereas in *r*-less dialects, it appears in a schwa off-glide left behind when the apex stopped approaching the alveolar ridge. Thus, in British Received Pronunciation (RP), front and high vowels that used to be followed by /r/ are now center-gliding diphthongs, as in *here* [hɪə], *there* [ðɛə], *poor* [pʊə], whereas with other vowels not even that much remains: *star* [stɑ], *third* [θɜd], *four* [fɔ].

Figure 6.h. Syllable-final *r* in English (*car, cart*)

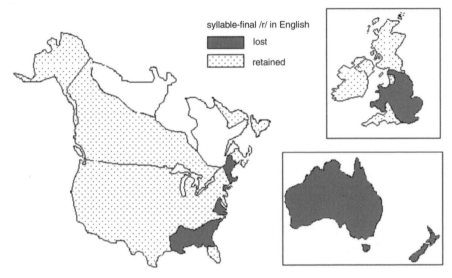

Yet even in "*r*-less" dialects, the /r/ remained before a vowel as in *ray, tray,* and *array,* and this condition includes (in standard varieties) a word-final /r/ followed by a vowel-initial word grammatically joined with it. Thus *four* is [fɔ] in *four* (by itself), *fourteen,* and *four chapters,* but [fɔr]- in *four o'clock* and *four eggs.* Likewise, *mother* is [mʌðə], but [mʌðər]- in *my mother is.* This now-you-hear-it-now-you-don't final /r/ is called "Linking *r.*" Some *r*-less speakers, though, also insert it where it historically does not belong, as in *law-r and order,* and it is then called "Intrusive *r.*"

Especially difficult for some learners is learning to combine the two liquids as [ɹɫ], or in the case of /ər/, as [ɚɫ]. The /rl/ combination is frequent in *r*-ful dialects (*curl, girl, snarl, world, early, rarely,* etc.) and may require special practice for both hearing and speaking.

Exercise 6.3

🎧(A) While listening to the corresponding recording on the CD, say the following minimal pairs.

late, rate	loom, room	climb, crime	lack, rack
leaf, reef	cloud, crowd	glue, grew	splay, spray
flock, frock	belly, berry	wily, wiry	allay, array
dale, dare	owl, our	scowl, scour	file, fire

(B) It is natural for adjacent consonants to assimilate to each other in one or more features. Say the following words, paying attention to the indicated consonants, and determine whether you assimilate them or not. (IPA symbols for the additional phones are supplied in order to facilitate discussion.) If you sense a change in articulation, try to formulate a rule for it.

1. The /l/ of *health, filth*: does it stay alveolar, or does it become dental ([l̪]) with the /θ/?
2. The /r/ and /l/ of *pray, clue, trip, strike, flit, three, shrimp*: do they stay voiced (compare *bray, glue, drip*), or do they become voiceless ([r̥], [l̥])?
3. The /t/, /d/, /l/, and /n/ of *heart, hard, snarl*, and *barn*: does the tongue touch the alveolar ridge, or does it stay curled back in the /r/ position to make these sounds (yielding retroflex [ʈ], [ɖ], [ɭ], [ɳ])?

6.4.2 Nasals. Nasals are symbolized collectively as **N**, like **L** for liquids. English has three of them as phonemes: bilabial /m/, alveolar /n/, and velar /ŋ/, as in *dumb, done, dung* or *Kim, kin, king*. The three are pronounced exactly like the corresponding voiced stops /b d g/ except that the velum is down, permitting the air stream to pass into the nasal chamber for nasal resonance. That is why, when you have a cold and your velum is swollen shut, nasals sound like oral stops: *good morning* /gʊd mɔ́rnɪŋ/ → [gʊd bɔ́rdɪg], or [+nasal] → [-nasal].

The phonemes /m/ and /n/ seldom give trouble in language learning, but /ŋ/ may, because many languages lack it. Some do have it as an allophone of /n/ before velars, so learners may add a [g] or [gə] to differentiate it from /n/: *song* /sɔŋ/ → [sɔ́ŋgə]. Historically, in fact, English /ŋ/ came from earlier /ng/, which is why it is still spelled that way—and also why it cannot occur word-initially in a language that still does not allow words to begin with /NC/-. Note, however, that 'ng' does not always spell /ŋ/: in *anger* it spells /ŋg/, and in *angel*, /ndʒ/ (§4.2.1).

Although the three nasals have been more stable than the two liquids, they also affect vowels. With a nasal in the coda, a vowel assimilates to it by NASALIZING (which means that the velum drops ahead of time while the vowel is still being articulated):

V → [+nasal] / _____ N

This nasality is transcribed with a tilde over the vowel: *bomb* [bãm], *soon* [sũn], *dung* [dʌ̃ŋ]. Say these words slowly and listen for the vowel's nasality in comparison with the unnasalized counterparts in *Bob* [bɑb], *soup* [sup], *dug* [dʌg].

Alternatively, an assimilation such as nasalization is interpreted as resulting from the spread of a feature to adjacent sounds or syllables. This is the approach of AUTOSEGMENTAL PHONOLOGY (Goldsmith 1976), which recognizes features as behaving autonomously on a separate level or "tier" from the segments (consonants and vowels) that they specify. In this case, as depicted in figure 6.i, the vowel loses its separate specification of [-nasal] (as shown by the double strike-out lines) and reassociates to the value of [nasal] in its neighbor to the right.

Figure 6.i. An autosegmental representation of vowel nasalization

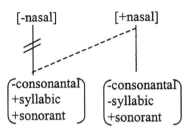

By this rule, every English vowel phoneme has at least two allophones (§5.1), oral and nasalized, depending on its environment. Yet, unlike certain other rules, nasalization need not be taught; it is so widespread that many students do the same thing in their native languages too, and even if they do not, the lack of vowel nasality in *bomb, soon, dung,* and so on is likely to go unnoticed. This may change, though: many current English speakers can be heard dropping nasal consonants from the coda, in which case the vowel nasality becomes the sole distinguishing feature between *band* [bæ̃(n)d] and *bad* [bæd] or *stomp* [stɑ̃(m)p] and *stop* [stɑp].

Exercise 6.4

(A) Again, in relaxed speech, adjacent consonants commonly assimilate to each other in one or more ways. Say the following words, paying attention to the indicated consonants, and determine whether you assimilate them or not. (IPA symbols are again supplied for the additional phones in order to facilitate discussion.) If you sense a change in articulation, try to formulate a rule for it.

  1. The /n/ of *tenth, month*: does it stay alveolar, or does it become dental ([n̪]) like the /θ/?
  2. The /m/ or /n/ of *emphasis, confident, symphony, envy, camphor, comfort*: is the nasal articulated as a bilabial, as an alveolar, or as a labiodental ([ɱ])?
  3. The /n/ of *congress, concrete, concur, income, conquest*: does it stay alveolar, or does it assimilate (as [ŋ]) to the following velar /k/ or /g/?

(B) Many languages have a phonological rule that globally assimilates a nasal to the place of articulation of a following consonant; the two are then said to be HOMOR-GANIC. In English, this is obviously not the case: *creamed* /krimd/. List ten other English words with nonhomorganic /NC/ clusters—five with final clusters and five with medial ones.

(C) Pair work: two-way dictation. Prepare a list of five English monosyllabic words in phonemic transcription using a variety of consonants; include some with consonant clusters and challenging sound/spelling differences (e.g., *sphinx* /sfɪŋks/). In pairs, each dictates his/her list to the other for transcription, and then confirms the results.

6.4.3 Goin' s'llabic. We have noted (§5.4) that unstressed vowels in English tend to shorten and reduce to /ə/. But /ə/ is a weak vowel, and in faster registers it often drops out when a nasal or liquid follows. Thus in a fairly slow, deliberate speaking style or in singing, words such as the following may be pronounced with a schwa in the unstressed syllable:

/əl/: *sizzle* /sízəl/ (also *label, able, nickel, pickle, tassel, total, travel, channel, special*)
/əm/: *fathom* /fǽðəm/ (*bottom, bosom, prism, capitalism, chasm*)
/ən/: *sudden* /sʌ́dən/ (*cotton, mountain, fasten, kitchen, vision, solution, dozen, doesn't*)

But in faster speech, the following rule of SCHWA-DROP applies:

$$ə → Ø /C\_\_\_ \{L, N\} \text{ (i.e., /C\_\_ [+consonantal, +sonorant])}$$

and the schwa-less liquid or nasal then inherits the syllabic beat, becoming [+syllabic] like a vowel. This syllabicity is shown in a narrow transcription by a vertical tick under the symbol: [sízl̩] (or [sízɫ̩]), [fǽðm̩], [sʌ́dn̩]. Pronounce these to yourself, paying attention to your tongue's movement: in *sizzle*, you should feel your tongue contact the alveolar ridge for the /z/ and remain there for the /l/, without pulling away to form a vowel between them.

Schwa-drop is not limited to final syllables: *syllabic* /səlǽbɪk/ → [sl̩ǽbɪk], *Sinatra* /sənátrə/ → [sn̩átrə], *cologne* /kəlón/ → [kl̩ón]; compare with [-syllabic] /l/ and /n/ in *slab, snot,* and *clone.* It also applies across word boundaries, as in the frequent reduction of *and* → [n̩] (*trucks 'n cars*), or initially as in the [m̩ ḷ n̩] of *impossible, allowed,* and *annoying* when after a consonant (*It's ___*). Many speakers have minimal pairs (at least in some registers) for medial nonsyllabic/syllabic /n/ and /l/: *ordnance* 'ammunition' versus *ordinance* 'law,' *lightning* 'electric charge' versus *lightening* 'relieving (a load),' *finely* 'in a fine way' versus *finally* 'at last.'

To be sure, the process is not straightforward; as noted long ago by Chao (1934), the type of consonant preceding the schwa affects its retention. For example, /əl/ freely schwa-drops after nasals (*channel, camel*), but /ən/ and /əm/ do *not* do so after liquids (*fallen, alum, harem, apron*) or after other nasals (*common, Barnum*) or /sC/ (*aspen*). Moreover, when the syllabic sonorant is followed by an unstressed vowel, its loss of syllabicity is variable: *traveling* and *traveler* have either three syllables, /trǽvəlɪŋ trǽvələr/ (pronounced with [l̩]), or two, /trǽvlɪŋ trǽvlər/.

The third nasal, /ŋ/, does not join its fellow nasals in this rule because it can follow unstressed /ɪ/ (*nothing, reading*) but not /ə/. However, in casual styles /ŋ/ variably changes to [n] throughout the English-speaking world by a rule popularly called "G-dropping":

ŋ → n / V̆___# (where V̆ = unstressed vowel)

at which point the /ɪ/ is free to reduce to /ə/ and then drop as usual: *nothin'* [nʌθn̩], *readin'* [rídn̩]. Neither change occurs in *thing* or *ding,* however, because their /ɪ/ is stressed.

With the other liquid, /r/, the /ə/ does not drop, but fuses with it (§5.4.4): /ər/ → [ɚ]. There are pairs of words that contrast the two, at least in slower registers: *parade* with [pɚ]- versus *prayed* with [pr]-, likewise *derive≠ drive, terrain≠ train, corrode ≠ crowed, Hungary≠ hungry.* But [ɚ] could also be considered a syllabic /r/, [r̩], because the vowel is essentially a longer version of the approximant. That is the relationship suggested by words such as *angr-y* [ǽŋgri], which has a stem-final /r/ that becomes syllabic when no vowel follows, as in *anger* [ǽŋgɚ] (see §7.7.2).

To what extent is the nonnative learner prepared for syllabic liquids and nasals? These do exist in some languages (e.g., Czech and German), but not in most, so many learners have problems with them. Even if they have learned to reduce most unstressed vowels to /ə/, they may not then drop /ə/ in favor of a syllabic liquid or nasal, and many misperceive, or simply do not hear, the latter sounds as pronounced by English speakers.[4] Because the rules are complex, it seems best to focus on listening rather than active production so that learners can perceive these unstressed syllables within the typical rhythm of the language. Ironically, the fact that teachers often adopt a more careful register when speaking to ESOL students only deprives the latter of the chance to get used to processes that have been characteristic of English for centuries.

Exercise 6.4

(A) Say these words in a normal conversational style. How many syllables does each have for you?

traveler	spasm	simple	simpler
mirror	fatten	fattening	troublesome

(B) Use narrow phonetic representations to show the different ways that English speakers may pronounce the underlined parts of the following words:

auct<u>ion</u>eer	w<u>orking</u> peop<u>le</u>	Anch<u>or</u>age	mack<u>erel</u>
orig<u>inal</u>	burge<u>oning</u>	se<u>lection</u>	iron<u>ing</u>

6.5 Stops. English has two series of stops (including affricates): voiceless /p t tʃ k/ and their voiced counterparts /b d dʒ g/. Stops /p/ and /b/ are bilabial, made by pressing the lips together. Stops /t/ and /d/ are alveolar, with the tongue tip contacting the alveolar ridge and the edges of the tongue sealing off the airflow at the gums (unlike lateral /l/). Affricates /tʃ/ and /dʒ/ are alveopalatal, with the tip touching the alveolar ridge while the blade behind it is raised close to the forward part of the palate for /ʃ/. Stops /k/ and /g/ are velar, made by pressing the dorsum against the velum. These places of articulation seldom give trouble except in two cases:

- In many languages, /t/ and /d/ are dental ([t̪ d̪] in a narrow transcription) instead of alveolar, requiring an adjustment in articulation to avoid possible confusion with English /θ ð/.
- In some languages, /t/ and /d/ become alveopalatals [tʃ] and [dʒ] before high front vowels, where English requires a distinction (*tease/cheese, dear/jeer*).

Sometimes stops give problems because of the way that English juxtaposes them. When one word's final consonant comes up against the initial consonant of the next, English speakers tend to leave the first one unreleased (shown as [C˥] in the IPA) or, if the two are identical, to merge them into one long one: *red car* [rɛd˥kʰɑr], *black car* [blækːʰɑr]. Speakers of many other languages are used to releasing the first consonant with what sounds to English speakers like a confusingly inserted schwa: [rɛdəkʰɑr], [blækəkʰɑr].

The few learners whose native languages lack voicing contrasts may need to feel their larynx so they perceive the difference in voicing, learn to control it, and then apply [±voice] to pairs such as *pay/bay, tie/die, char/jar, come/gum*. But most learners speak languages in which voicing contrasts are present, and thus can differentiate such pairs in ways that English speakers understand. However, not all learners may understand the contrasts that native English speakers produce. The problem is that although it is convenient to state the distinction between /p t tʃ k/ and /b d dʒ g/ as one of [±voice]—voicing off or voicing on—English speakers alter the basis of that contrast depending on syllable and word position, as the following section makes clear.

6.5.1 Stops and VOT. Let's consider initial position first. Place your fingers on your larynx as you slowly say *bill*. You should sense that voicing does not begin as soon as you close your lips for /b/, but a bit later, before you release it and begin the vowel. In other words, the voicing is delayed. But there is no danger of confusing /b/ with /p/ because English reinforces the voicelessness of /p/ with ASPIRATION. Once again, place the fingers of one hand on your larynx and the fingers of your other hand in front of your mouth as you say *pill*. You should feel no voicing until well after you release the /p/ with aspiration (a puff of air). That aspiration is also due to a delay in voicing, one that lasts some fifty milliseconds into the vowel so that unused air up rushes through the wide-open glottis before the vocal cords come together to start vibrating for the vowel (see figure 6.j). The voiceless stop acquires the feature [+aspirated] (or in some analyses, [+spread glottis]) by the following rule:

[-continuant, -voice] → [+aspirated] / $____

Figure 6.j. Voice onset time (VOT) in voiceless and voiced stops

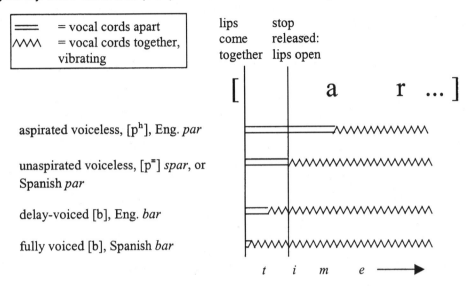

whereby '$__' (syllable-initial position) includes 'word-initially' (*pill, till, chill, kill*) and 'medially before a stressed vowel' (*appéar, détòur, achíeve, recórd*). The aspirated allophones are shown in a narrow transcription with a raised *h*: [pʰ tʰ tʃʰ kʰ]. In other positions, especially after /s/ (*spill, still, skill*), voiceless stops are unaspirated, an effect that is optionally shown with a raised equals sign: [p⁼ t⁼ tʃ⁼ k⁼].[5] Because of the effect of the word boundary, English speakers may contrast aspirated and unaspirated stops in the following pairs: *peace talks / pea stalks, race pits /Ray spits, tea chat / teach at, that's tough / that stuff, loose keys / Lou skis.*

The key difference between English *pill* and *bill* (and *till* and *dill*, etc.) is therefore not just the presence or absence of voicing but also VOICE ONSET TIME, or VOT. Other languages often lack such delays, favoring a "clean" release of the stop; and to show the difference we compare the timing of /p b/ in English (similar in German) with that of Spanish (similar in other Romance languages such as French and Italian).

To speakers of Romance languages, an English speaker's *bar* resembles their *par*, whereas the aspiration in *par* may be ignored as wasted air rather than a reinforcement of voicelessness.

In medial position (*trouble, adore, ledger, digger*), the voiced obstruents of English—/b d dʒ g/ and also /v ð z ʒ/—are fully voiced from beginning to end. But in final position (*rib, rid, ridge, rig*) they are half-devoiced again, in a mirror-image of what happens in initial position: they begin as voiced but then the voicing turns off about half-way through their duration. In compensation, the preceding vowel lengthens before voiced consonants: compare *rib, rid, ridge, rig, rev, sheathe, fleas* with *rip, writ, rich,*

Rick, ref, sheath, fleece. This length is shown in a narrow transcription with [ː]: *rib* [rɪːb]. Meanwhile, the voiceless obstruents do their part to maintain the distinction in final position by being reinforced with a glottal stop:

$$\emptyset \rightarrow ? \ / \ \underline{\quad} \ [\text{-continuant, -voice}] \ \$$$

This process, PREGLOTTALIZATION, can be observed in the word *rip* [rɪʔp] (cf. *rib* [rɪːb]). It is not as regular as aspiration but it is nonetheless a strong tendency in the modern language. The voicing of a preceding vowel is cut off abruptly as the vocal cords slam shut, inserting a glottal stop before /p t tʃ k/ at the end of a syllable—especially when the stop is unreleased before another consonant (*ca<u>p</u>ture, A<u>t</u>kins, a<u>c</u>tion, a<u>c</u>ne*) or at the end of an utterance (*Jum<u>p</u>! Si<u>t</u>! Du<u>ck</u>!*).

In some contexts, English /t/ is so preglottalized that alveolar contact drops out and the glottal stop is interpreted as representing the /t/ as its allophone. This process has been called GLOTTALING (Wells 1982). In North American English, glottaling of /t/ is common before nasals (including syllabic ones after schwa-drop), before nonsyllabic /l/, and before stops that begin a second word. Thus, *cotton* [kʰɑ́ʔn̩], *satin* [sǽʔn̩], *atmosphere* [ǽʔməsfìr], *atlas* [ǽʔləs], and *what kind?* [(h)wʌʔ kʰáind]. In urban British dialects, glottaling is extended to intervocalic /t/: *butter* [bʌ́ʔə]. The reason that glottaling does not apply in this intervocalic environment in North American English is that a different rule comes into play, flapping (§6.5.2).

Must learners of English master the intricacies of VOT, preglottalizing, and glottaling for active production? Not necessarily—or at least not right away, as long as learners' own voicing contrasts are clear to listeners. But it *is* important to be able to comprehend native pronunciation based on these rules. To someone unaccustomed to lengthening, aspiration, and glottal stops, these effects are not signals of the distinction between /p t tʃ k/ and /b d dʒ g/ but inaudible details with no significance—that is, noise.

Exercise 6.5

🎧(A) Pronounce the following contrasts in voicing, listening to the CD recording of them:

crab, grab	choke, joke	trip, drip	plead, bleed
muck, mug	rack, rag	heart, hard	fat, fad
colt, cold	flocking, flogging	flap, flab	rich, ridge
lunch, lunge	scents, sends	leak, league	rabbit, rabid

(B) Pronounce the following contrasts between alveolar and alveopalatal stops:

tier, cheer	deep, jeep	aiding, ageing	deans, jeans
teak, cheek	dip, gyp	din, gin	bunting, bunching

(C) The following words contain the phonemes /p t k/. In some words, these phonemes' allophones are unaspirated ([p⁼ t⁼ k⁼]), while in others they are aspirated ([pʰ tʰ kʰ]). Copy each word; then, over each grapheme representing /p t k/, write the symbol for the appropriate allophone:

pit, spit, spine, pine, transparent, plate, splat, trip, strip, skill, kill, lick, stop, top, not, snot, flip, kick, pop, tot, access, quick, account, destroy, apparent, aptitude, publicly

6.5.2 Stops that flap.

Despite the rules that reinforce the contrast of /t/ and /d/ and compensate for voicing delays, there is one environment in which their contrast is wiped out or NEUTRALIZED: between vowels when the second vowel is unstressed, and especially when the first one is stressed.[6] When this happens, both /t/ and /d/ weaken to an alveolar FLAP in which the tip fails to hold a firm stop and instead just flips up and hits the alveolar ridge. In the IPA, this flap is shown as [ɾ] (a turned small capital *J*), although some linguists prefer a small capital *D*: *city* [síɾi] ([síDi]). The rule can be stated as follows:

$$\text{alveolar stop} \rightarrow [ɾ] \ / \ V(r, n) \ \_\_\_ \ \verb|V̆|$$

In terms of features, a relatively tense stop, [-continuant, -sonorant, +coronal, +anterior, ±voice], becomes [-tense].

As formulated, this FLAPPING rule not only applies to words such as *city, data,* and *lady,* but also when there is a preceding /r/ or /n/ as in *party, winter,* and *wanted.* (But in the case of /n/, flapping is limited to /t/; the /d/ of /nd/, as in *sandy,* is normally *not* flapped.) Pronounce the preceding examples to yourself at a normal rate of speaking: note that there is no real build-up of pressure as in a real stop, but just a weak banging against the alveolar ridge. Flapping also applies to forms such as *total* or *rattle* in -/əl/ while their /t/ is still intervocalic (i.e., before schwa-drop applies): → [tʰóɾl̩]. But in the case of -/ən/, as in *beaten,* glottaling takes precedence and "bleeds" (as it is technically called) flapping of its chance to apply: we say [bíʔ(t)n̩], never *[bíɾn̩].

Flapping is widespread in North American and Australian English, and although RP has traditionally retained full stops in this position (*data* = [détə], not [déɾə]), flapping has been making inroads in the United Kingdom too (Wells 1982, 250). To the learner of English, flaps can pose problems in comprehension because [ɾ] in most other languages represents the phoneme /r/, not /t/ or /d/. Thus an English speaker's [béɾi] may be misinterpreted as *berry* instead of *Betty.*

Flapping creates several other complications for the listener:

- Numerous homophones: *latter = ladder, hearty = hardy, atom = Adam, metal = medal.*

- Changes in form: the /t/ of *commit* is pronounced [t] or, by preglottalization, [ʔt], but in *commitment* it becomes [ʔ] by glottaling, whereas in *committed* it becomes [ɾ] by flapping.
- Variations according to stress: as we saw earlier, stress dominates English phonology, and due to rules such as flapping that depend on it, words such as *átom* and *métal* have a flap, whereas the derived *atómic* and *metállic* have a full [tʰ], strongly articulated with aspiration.

Consider how all these processes work together: all native speakers make a distinction between *wait* and *wade, bleat* and *bleed,* but the addition of suffixes such as *-ing* and *-ed* neutralizes these words because the stop becomes intervocalic: *"The lamb is* [blíɾɪŋ]*"* and *"Grandma* [wéɾəd]*"* can therefore be ambiguous. For that reason, in higher registers (for example, in a newscast) some native "flappers" self-correct and use careful stops [t] (or even [tʰ]) and [d] to make sure they are understood. Once they shift back to normal speech, though, flapping resumes.

Exercise 6.6

(A) Pronounce the following contrasts. Why might they give problems to some learners?

spotting, sparring	patty, parry	fighting, firing	Betty, bury
heady, hairy	hiding, hiring	cuddle, curl	pedal (petal), peril

(B) Flapping
   1. Say the following words in a normal register, paying attention to the underlined /t/.

agitate, agitated	appetite	observatory	seventeen
started	attitude	detail	button

   2. Repeat the experiment for these words; English speakers (even flappers) vary for these.

   Plato   potato   veto   NATO   motto   auto   pinto (beans)   ditto

   In which words is the /t/ flapped for you? Do you see an explanation?

(C) The following words contain phoneme /t/ in medial or final position, where it can appear as the following allophones: plain [t] (= unaspirated [t⁼]), aspirated [tʰ], flapped [ɾ], or glottalized [ʔt]. Copy the words; then, above each grapheme representing /t/, write the allophone that it is pronounced with.

ditto, hearty, attack, matter, actor, atone, best, tot, atrocious, city, contain, continent, phonetics, phonetician, rot, rotten, rotting, fat, fatter, fatten, remit, remitted, remittance

(D) Let's make /t/'s glottaling, aspiration, and flapping rules more precise, using as test cases the pronunciation of the suffix -*ton* (a reduced form of *town*) in place names. The following are real places in the United States, Canada, or the United Kingdom. Say each one in a normal register, then indicate your pronunciation of each /t/ of -*ton* with the appropriate symbol ([t^h], [t$^=$], [ʔ] or [ʔt], [ɾ]).

Washington	Binghamton	Fredericton	Edmonton	Southampton
Barton	Trenton	Middleton	Brighton	Scranton
Stockton	Stratton	Newton	Dayton	Princeton
Wheaton	Lexington	Hamilton	Charleston	Germanton

Study your results and look for patterns and conditions that favor one allophone over the other.

6.6 All those sibilants. If you can hear any consonants in whispered speech, they will be the fricatives /s z ʃ ʒ/. This is because these fricatives are "hissy" or SIBILANT (Latin for 'hissy'), with a high acoustic frequency described as [+strident]. The hiss comes from a special articulation involving a grooved tongue surface. For the alveolar ([+anterior, + coronal]) /s/ and its voiced counterpart /z/, the jaw is raised so that the teeth are close together, and the blade of the tongue is placed near the alveolar ridge while forming a narrow channel or groove down its upper surface. The air is forced along this groove at high velocity like water through a hose, and is squirted by the tip at the inner surfaces of the teeth. The eddies of air rushing around behind the teeth are what we hear as a hiss. You can verify this grooving as follows: pronounce [s], keep your tongue in that position, and reverse the airflow by sucking air in sharply. You should feel a cooling effect down the middle of your tongue, the channel that is open in this articulation; but you will also note that the sibilance disappears when you reverse the airflow rather than directing it at your teeth. (If you are missing teeth, your sibilants may not sound right.)

For /ʃ/ and its voiced counterpart /ʒ/, the articulation is similar, but the tongue is domed up higher in the mouth so that the blade forms its groove against a broader area just behind the alveolar ridge—hence the term "alveopalatal" (or, in features, [-anterior, +coronal, +high]). From this more retracted position, the grooved tongue squirts the air stream down over the tip toward the *lower* teeth. Because the air stream for /ʃ/ or /ʒ/ swirls around in a larger area between teeth and tongue than for /s/, some of its force is lost, so what is produced is a lower-frequency turbulence or "friction"—a "hush" rather than a "hiss." The affricates /tʃ/ and /dʒ/ are sibilants because they are released as /ʃ/ and /ʒ/. But because they are also stops, they undergo the same rules (aspiration, glottaling, partial devoicing) as other stops, and this is one reason that *why choose?* (with [tʃ^h]) differs from *white shoes* (where the two sounds appear in separate syllables).

English speakers are (unconsciously) sensitive to sibilants, because it is precisely the nouns that end in sibilants that insert a vowel /ə/ (or /ɪ/) before the plural ending *-(e)s*, usually pronounced /z/ (as explained further in chapter 7). Thus *cub, rag, key,* and *ring* add /z/ for their plurals, but *bush, bus, maze, garage, ditch,* and *ridge* add /əz/.

Note on symbols

For alveopalatals, the IPA uses ʃ ʒ for the fricatives and the compound symbols tʃ dʒ for the affricates. A clarifying tie bar, t͡ʃ, is optionally added to show that the stop and fricative are pronounced together. Some linguists, though, prefer symbols with a Czech hachek (*háček*) for these four phones, š ž č ǰ. These dual sets of symbols have coexisted for almost two centuries.

The phonemic contrasts among these six English sibilants (*seat/sheet, batch/badge,* etc.) are frequent and need to be articulated in a way that listeners can recognize. Fortunately, /s/ and /z/ are widespread in the world's languages, and the other four sibilants are far from rare. But sometimes they do not sound exactly right because learners are used to a different articulation, and for sibilants, even a slight change in tongue placement alters the hiss. The chart in figure 6.k summarizes common substitutions heard among learners, along with the symbols for these substitutions. (We assume there is no real physical problem such as missing teeth, enlarged tongue, or cleft palate.) All these articulations are normal consonants elsewhere, and you would have to master them if you were studying languages that use them.

Exercise 6.7

🎧(A) Pronounce the following contrasts, listening also to the corresponding CD recording.

1. For /s/ versus /z/

sip, zip	niece, knees	rice, rise	bus, buzz
ass, as	mace, maze	lacy, lazy	price, prize
precedent, president	facing, phasing	fleece, fleas	racer, razor

2. For /s/ versus /ʃ/

sin, shin	sign, shine	mass, mash	sifter, shifter
fasten, fashion	seek, sheik	seen, sheen	seep, sheep

Figure 6.k. Articulatory problems with /s/ and /z/

Acoustic impression	Possible problem
1. a lisp or [θ]-like quality	If light sibilance is mixed with [θ], then the sound may be [s̪] (voiced: [z̪]), a dental sibilant. The tongue tip is too close to the upper teeth and needs to be pulled away from them, leaving just the blade near the alveolar ridge.
2. [s] with a [ʃ]-like quality (or [z] with a [ʒ]-like quality); apparent confusion of the two	If the sibilance is hollow-sounding, it may be apical /s/ = [s̺] (voiced: [z̺]): only the tip is being pointed at the alveolar ridge, and more of the blade should be used. If it has a [j]-like quality, then it is palatalized, [sʲ] (voiced: [zʲ]), with the body of the tongue raised too close to the palate; the tongue needs to be flatter. If it sounds like a cross between [s] and [ʃ] or [z] and [ʒ] with a hint of [j], then it may be prepalatal [ɕ], [ʑ], requiring a flatter tongue shape.
3. a "slurpy" friction	[ɬ] or voiced [ɮ], lateral fricatives: the air is flowing over the sides of the tongue. The edges of the blade need to be raised to the gums to seal off this flow and to direct the air stream along a grooved tongue surface.
4. r-like quality that is not true sibilance	[ɹ̝], a nonsibilant apical alveolar fricative. The blade should be used, not the tip alone, and the tongue needs to be grooved.
5. good [s] and [ʃ], but [z] and [ʒ] merge with them or begin with a stop: [dz], [dʒ]	Some languages (a) do not have voiced fricatives (so voiceless ones are substituted), or (b) begin them with stops, that is, turn them into affricates. The solution is to become more aware of voicing contrasts (in the first case) and continuous fricatives without stop onsets (in the second case).

3. For /ʃ/ versus /ʒ/

Aleutian, allusion   pressure, treasure   fishin', fission   vicious, vision
mesher, measure   Asher, azure   leash, liege

4. For /z/ versus /ʒ/

ruse, rouge   brazen, brazier   lose, luge   (door-)closer, closure

5. For /ʒ/ versus /dʒ/

version, virgin   pleasure, pledger   lesion, legion   aphasia, aphagia

6. For /ʃ/ versus /tʃ/

shin, chin   marsh, march   sheet, cheat   washes, watches
sheep, cheap   mashed, matched   crushes, crutches swishing, switching
ship, chip   fish, Fitch   cashing, catching Welsh, Welch

7. For /z/ versus /dz/ versus /dʒ/

size, sides   buzz, buds, budge   phase, fades   as, adds
AIDS, age   Ed's, edge   heads, hedge   frizz, fridge

(B) Take the nonsense words *bleeg, hoob, smon, critch, plass,* and *dudge.* Assign them any meaning you like—but how would you pronounce their plurals? Why?

(C) Pair work: follow the two-way dictation technique (as in Exercise 6.4:C), but this time use nonsense (made-up) words that are still English-like, for example, /blæʃ/. In pairs, each dictates his/her list to the other for transcription, and then confirms the results.

6.7 Slits up front. Four other English fricatives are labiodental /f/ with its voiced counterpart /v/, and dental /θ/ with its voiced counterpart /ð/. Pronounce and hold the initial consonants of *fin, vend, thin,* and *then;* then contrast their sound with that of /s/ in *sin* and /ʃ/ in *shin.* You should note that /f/ and /θ/ have a similar noise, as do /v/ and /ð/, and that all four are considerably less noisy than /s ʃ z ʒ/. That is because the labiodental and dental fricatives are nonsibilant: you simply blow the air stream through a transverse slit between the upper teeth and lower lip for /f/ and /v/, and between tongue and teeth for /θ/ and /ð/, with no grooving of the tongue surface. This makes for less turbulence, that is, weaker stridency. Acoustically, the dental friction is similar to labiodental, so the one is sometimes misheard as the other; some dialects even merge them, as in /bə́rfdè/ for *birthday.* Although nonstandard, this substitution already occurred long ago for another slit fricative that English used to have: *rough* and *enough* formerly ended in the voiceless velar fricative [x] (German *ch* as in *Bach,* Spanish *j* as in *jota*), but [f] replaced it.

For labiodentals /f/ and /v/, the upper teeth contact the thrust-in lower lip. (Doing it the other way around, lower teeth on upper lip, is possible but not normal in any known language.) The dentals /θ/ and /ð/ are articulated in either of two ways:

• As apicals (apicodentals): the tip touches the lower edges of the upper teeth.
• As laminals (laminodentals): the blade (just behind the tip) is what makes contact with the teeth, so that the tip protrudes between the teeth—an articulation also called INTERDENTAL.

Some speakers favor one, others the other, and still others go back and forth depending on relative forcefulness of articulation; acoustically, there is little difference. There is a third articulation, though, that uses dental *stops* [t̪ d̪] for these fricatives, as in Ireland and parts of New York City. Although this substitution may preserve contrasts with alveolar /t d/ (*tin* [tʰɪn] vs. *thin* [t̪ʰɪn]), it tends to be stigmatized in other areas.

Consonants /f/ and /v/ seldom pose problems in language learning, because the two are fairly widespread in the languages of the world and their articulation is visible. The usual problem is when learners come from languages in which labial fricatives are *bilabial* ([ɸ], [β]) instead of labiodental ([f], [v]), and they may need to focus more on using the teeth instead of the upper lip. The sounds /θ/ and /ð/ tend to cause more problems, though, because despite their high frequency in English (try to say many sentences without using *the, this,* or *that*), they are uncommon in the rest of the world. Learners often substitute the following sounds for /θ/ and /ð/:

- [s] and [z], as the closest fricatives. For [θ] and [ð], contact must be dental, not alveolar, and with a slit, not a groove.
- [t] and [d], especially when they are dental in the other language. In this case, for [θ] and [ð] students must learn to let the air stream continue through a slit instead of stopping it.

Exercise 6.8

⌒(A) Pronounce the following subminimal pairs, listening also to the corresponding CD recording.

1. For /f/ versus /v/

   | fat, vat | proof, prove | half, have | safe, save |
   | shuffle, shovel | infest, invest | fuse, views | belief, believe |

2. For /f/ versus /θ/

   | fin, thin | roof, Ruth | free, three | sheaf, sheath |
   | oaf, oath | deaf, death | fret, threat | fought, thought |

3. For /v/ versus /ð/

   | vat, that | van, than | river, wither | leather, lever |
   | sliver, slither | clove, clothe | veil, they'll | live (adj.), lithe |

4. For /d/ versus /ð/

   | dare, there | side, scythe | fodder, father | ladder, lather |
   | dine, thine | udder, other | load, loathe | sued, soothe |

5. For /t/ versus /θ/

   | tin, thin | tree, three | trill, thrill | trash, thrash |
   | mat, math | boat, both | tent, tenth | Burt, birth |

6. For /θ/ versus /ð/

   | thigh, thy | breath, breathe | thin, then | ether, either |
   | mouth, mouth (verb) | cloth, clothe | teeth, teethe | loath, loathe |

7. For /θ/ versus /s/

   | theme, seem | thimble, symbol | thighs, size | tenth, tense |
   | thumb, sum (some) | thicker, sicker | truth, truce | worth, worse |

8. For /ð/ versus /z/

lathe, lays	lithe, lies	tithe, ties	writhe, rise
soothe, sues	bathe, bays	clothing, closing	seethed, seized

9. For /b/ versus /v/

berry, very	best, vest	buy, vie	cab, calve
curb, curve	ribber, river	dub, dove	saber, savor

(B) Artwork: draw mouth diagrams to show the differences in each of the following pairs of phonemes. You can use the diagrams in this chapter as models, but *don't trace them*; there is value in trying to sketch articulator positions on your own.

1. /b/ versus /v/   2. /θ/ versus /s/   3. /s/ versus /ʃ/   4. /g/ versus /ŋ/

(C) Determine whether *th* in each word represents voiceless /θ/ or voiced /ð/:

rhythm   author   theorem   these   smooth   bathe   anthem   brother

(D) Analysis: in older English, voiced fricatives [v ð z] were allophones of /f θ s/ respectively before they split off as distinct phonemes, and that situation left behind numerous alternations. For each word, give another form or derivative of it that shows the switch from [-voice] to [+voice]. Example: *shelf*: verb *shelve* (or plural *shelves*).

thief	advice	use	bath	leaf	proof	knife	north
worth	safe	house	half	belief	excuse	breath	mischief

6.8 /h/: A sound that can get lost. The sound /h/ is classified as a voiceless glottal fricative: you open your mouth (with the velum up), spread the glottis enough to avoid voice, and blow hard through the unobstructed vocal tract. The "friction" is just the sound of eddies of air rushing through: plain aspiration, in other words. Because there is no oral obstruction, some linguists hesitate to call /h/ a true fricative; it is actually vowel-like, as you can verify by comparing the initial sounds of *heat, hate, height, hope,* and *hoot* when you prolong them: the mouth assumes the position of the vowel early on, so that the /h/ is actually like an initial voiceless segment of the vowel. However, it *acts* like a consonant in the numerous languages that have it and it occurs in consonant positions, which is why we call it a fricative. But its main contrasts are not with /f/, /s/, /θ/, and so on but with vowel-initial words that lack this initial aspiration: *heat* versus *eat, hair* versus *air*.

A special quirk of /h/ in English is that it occurs only as the onset of a syllable, either stressed or initial or both; words such as /hɛd/ (*head*) and /əhɛ́d/ (*ahead*) are possible, but not */dɛh/, */dɛhp/, or */dɛ́hə/. Consequently, stress changes can result in loss of /h/, as in the following examples:

- *prohíbit, inhíbit, vehícular,* with /h/; *pròhibítion, ìnhibítion, véhicle* without it.
- *hèlp <u>hím</u>* (emphatic, [hèlp hím]) but *hélp him* (unstressed, [hélpɪm]).
- *fínd <u>hér</u> bóok* (emphatic, [fáind hə́r búk]), *fínd her bóok* (unstressed, [fáindər búk]).

However, Cockney and many other urban British dialects have generalized "aitch-dropping" to all environments: *the 'eat* (for *the heat*), or *Aeow, 'e couldn't find 'is 'at, could 'e?*

Exercise 6.9

(A) Pronounce the following contrasts, listening also to the corresponding CD recording.

heat, eat	*hairy, airy*	*Herman, ermine*
whose, ooze	*hitch, itch*	*holder, older*
who'd, food	*home, foam*	*high, thigh*

(B) As noted in §6.8, English /h/ is limited to certain positions. Study the following words in (1–2); then, in the list of made-up forms phonemically transcribed in (3), judge which ones are possible English words and which ones just do not conform to the rules of English pronunciation.

1. real words: *behind, ahead, hypocrisy, haste, human, rehearsal, dehydrate, cohort*
2. derived forms of real words: *history, prehistory, prehistoric, vehicle, vehicular*
3. made-up forms: /hidʒ/, /əhép/, /vɑht/, /hɑrf/, /lush/, /ðɛh/, /fhump/, /díhæk/, /dihʌk/, /hɛg/, /jhɛg/, /ənhóst/

(C) In older English, a /t/ between a voiceless fricative and a syllabic /n/ dropped out: that is why the letter 't' is silent today in *soften* and *fasten* (cf. its presence in *soft* and *fast*). But many speakers have restored the /t/ in *often* as a SPELLING PRONUN-CIATION, an alteration based on the assumption that spelling indicates the "proper" pronunciation. The word therefore has FREE VARIANTS (see §5.6.5) today: /ɔ́fən/ ~ /ɔ́ftən/.

Consider, then, the case of /h/: a large number of words with an initial silent *h* entered English from French and Spanish. Many speakers interpreted the *h* as /h/ because of spelling pronunciation. Say the following examples, all of them origi-nally /h/-less: in which of them do you actually pronounce the /h/?

humble	hotel	heir	herb	hour	hacienda	hammock
honor, honest	vehicle	heirloom	harangue	homage	horizon	hazard

6.9 Glides /j/ and /w/. The /j/ (called "yod" /jod/) is a palatal glide: the middle of the tongue (with the tip pointing down) glides up toward the palate and then down and

away into another articulation. The sound /w/ (called "wau" /wau/) is a labiovelar glide, requiring coarticulation: the lips are rounded while the back of the tongue glides up toward the velum. In its acoustic quality, /w/ resembles the liquids /r/ (in rounding) and /l/ (in velarization). Because the articulators approach without touching, the glides /j/ and /w/ are also called APPROXIMANTS (§6.2).

Note on symbols

Some linguists use **y** instead of IPA **j** for yod. This practice can cause confusion because **y** in the IPA means the high front rounded vowel of French *tu* [ty] 'you' or German *früh* [fry] 'early.'

Glides are also called SEMIVOWELS because they are vowel-like. In fact, /j/ and /w/ are essentially the same as /i/ and /u/ except in one feature: they are briefer, [-syllabic], whereas each of the corresponding vowels serves as the nucleus of its syllable and is therefore [+syllabic]. One way of learning glides then is to start with high vowels in two-syllable sequences such as [i.á], [u.á], then say them faster, crushing the high vowel against its more open neighbor: → [já], [wá]. Generally, though, learners do not have much trouble acquiring /j/ and /w/ as phonemes because these are common in the rest of the world too. The main problem is that some languages restrict glides' distribution to occurring just before low and mid vowels (i.e., [-high] vowels) or even just low vowels such as /ɑ/. Students may then have trouble saying the /w/ of *wood, woman, woo, wound, wick,* or the distinction in *ear/year, east/yeast,* and may need to practice raising the tongue a little higher than they do for the following high vowel in order to make the difference. In a few other languages, /j/ is raised quite a bit higher to a palatal fricative ([ʝ]) or stop (alveopalatal [dʒ] or palatal [ɟ]) before certain vowels, and in that case there may be problems with English contrasts between /j/ and /dʒ/ as in *yip/gyp, year/jeer, use* (noun)/*juice.*

The /w/ has been very stable in the history of English, but, as in other languages, /j/ has often assimilated a preceding consonant to its palatal position in a process called PALATALIZATION (§4.2.3). In modern English, it is better called ALVEOPALATALIZATION because the /j/ causes alveolars to become alveopalatals. The rule is stated as follows, with V́ = stressed vowel (strong or weak), V̆ = unstressed vowel. (Note again the pervasive influence of stress on English phonology.)

$$\text{tj dj sj zj} \rightarrow \text{tʃ dʒ ʃ ʒ} / \acute{V}\underline{\quad\quad} \text{(n, r)} \ \breve{V}$$

The rule is variable, though. Word-internally, the change has been consummated in words such as *ocean, measure, nature, cordial* that originally had medial /sj zj tj dj/; that is why we see automatic fusion of the /j/ of the suffix *–ure* (as in *fail-ure* /fel+jər/) with the alveolar obstruent in *depart-departure, proceed-procedure, erase-erasure, please-*

Figure 6.l. Alveopalatalization

	Higher (careful) registers	Colloquial registers
not yet, can't you, don't you, eat your peas	-[t j]-	-[tʃ]-
need you, would you, did you	-[d j]-	-[dʒ]-
miss you, this year, I'll pass you	-[s j]-	-[ʃ]-
Please you, as your	-[z j]-	-[ʒ]-

pleasure. In other cases, there is still variation: thus most of us today say *issue* as [íʃu], whereas some retain older [ísju], and one may pronounce *educate* as [édjukèt] or [édʒukèt] (or with reduction, [édʒəkèt]) or vary between them. Across word boundaries—that is, with a /j/ beginning the next word—virtually all speakers vary stylistically, as shown in figure 6.l. Sometimes we hear an intermediate [tʃj], [dʒj], [ʃj], [ʒj] with the glide not fully absorbed, but in one stage or the other, (alveo)palatalization is common on both sides of the Atlantic (and of the Pacific), and to the nonnative listener, it drastically alters the expected sequence of sounds.

Another variable is the sequence /ju/ in words such as *use* or *few*, inaccurately called "long U." In reality, it is a more or less normal /u/ preceded by /j/: compare *ooze* /uz/ versus *use* /juz/, *coot* /kut/ versus *cute* /kjut/, *booty* /búti/ versus *beauty* /bjúti/, *food* /fud/ versus *feud* /fjud/, differing only in the unwritten /j/ of the second member of each pair. (Cf. also *you, yew, ewe,* all /ju/.) After consonants, this /j/ in /ju/ has been falling out as a result of the following rule (its environment generally differs from that of alveopalatalization, so the two do not come into conflict):

$$j \rightarrow \emptyset \ / \ \$C \ \_\_ \ \acute{V}$$

As a result, most speakers have lost it in words such as *lute* (originally /ljut/) and many have also lost it in *dew* /dju/ (thus making it a homophone of *do*). The general distribution is summarized in figure 6.m (based on Wells 1982), but because there is variation within regions too, you should compare your own pronunciation of the examples to see

Figure 6.m. Loss of /j/ in /ju/

after the following consonants in the same syllable:	1. older RP	2. current RP, Australia	3. U.S. south	4. U.S. north and west, Canada	5. East Anglia (in England)
alveopalatals, /r/-, /Cl/- (*chew, juice, rule, blue*)	Ø	Ø	Ø	Ø	Ø
/θ, s, l/- (*enthusiasm, suit, assume, lute*)	j-	Ø	Ø	Ø	Ø
/t, d, n/- (*tune, dew, subdue, new, nuisance*)	j-	j-	j-	Ø	Ø
labials and velars: /p, b, m, f, k/- (*pew, beauty, music, few, cute, view, argue*)	j-	j-	j-	j-	Ø

how far the process has progressed in your own speech. Note the condition "in the same syllable" in the rule and the effect of different syllabication and stress patterns in Dialect 4: *lute* /ljut/, *new* /nju/, and *avenue* /ǽ.və.njù/ have lost their original /j/, but not *value* /vǽl.ju/, *annual* /ǽn.ju.əl/, or *venue* /vέn.ju/.

Exercise 6.10

(A) Pronounce the following contrasts, listening also to the corresponding CD recordings:

1. /w/ versus Ø (no onset) and versus /j/

woozy, oozy	win, in	work, irk	woo, ooh!
wore, oar	woe, owe	woke, oak	well, yell
wander, yonder	wet, yet	wield, yield	we, ye

2. /w/ versus /v/, /w/ versus /r/

wet, vet	wiper, viper	went, vent	wise, vise
wine, vine	worse, verse	wickets, rickets	watt, rot
wed, red	away, array	woe, row	wince, rinse

3. /j/ versus Ø (no onset) and versus /dʒ/

year, ear, jeer	yeast, east	ye, "E"	yin, in, gin
yield, eel	use (verb), ooze	yell, jell	yoke, oak, joke
yam, jam	yet, jet	juice, use (noun)	yellow, jello

(B) Pronounce the postconsonantal /j/ and /w/ in the following words, paying attention to their voicing in set 2. In this latter group, are the glides fully voiced (as in set 1), partly devoiced, or completely devoiced (voiceless)? Use a phonological rule to describe what is happening.

   Set 1: *view, abuse, music, argue*   *dwindle, moiré* /mwaré/
   Set 2: *few, puke, cute, huge*   *tweak, between, thwack, quit, swap*

(C) All of the following words historically had /ju/. Say them to yourself, then *circle* those in which you retain the /j/ in your own speech and <u>underline</u> those that took a different route, alveopalatalization. To what extent does your usage reflect the norms shown in figure 6.m?

suit	amuse	tune	feud	dune	tulip	prelude
sure	human	azure	reduce	beauty	issue	duke
assume	enthusiasm	cute	chew	resume	sumac	tumor
Tuesday	view	news	mature	revenue	refuse	residue
nuisance	tissue	rule	maturation	allure	mildew	residual

(D) One might assume that the (alveo)palatalization rule need not be taught in ESOL classes because the pronunciations that result are "slangy" or improper. Present arguments for and against this position, noting the range of factors that you are appealing to a decision on usage.

(E) Like vowels (§5.6.5), consonants show differences in LEXICAL INCIDENCE, whether as free variation or dialect variants. In the following cases, indicate which is your normal pronunciation of the underlined consonant(s) and compare your responses with those of your classmates:

greasy: /s/ ~ /z/   *without:* /θ/ ~ /ð/   *schedule:* /sk/ ~ /ʃ/   *William:* /lj/ ~ /j/
nephew: /fj/ ~ /vj/   *garden:* /g/ ~ /gj/   *both:* /θ/ ~ /f/   *mirage:* /ʒ/ ~ /dʒ/

(F) Pair work: follow the two-way dictation technique (see Exercise 6.4), preparing a list of five English words using a variety of consonants. Then, in pairs, each dictates his/her list to the other, this time using a *phonetic* transcription in which the listener observes special articulatory details the other used (or expected details the other did *not* use) in his/her articulation of consonants.

6.10 Syllable reprise: How to build an English word. Phonemes are combined to create the words of a language—to some extent the way that ten digits (0–9) are combined to form the identifiers that we call "social security numbers." Imagine a simple language with just three "digits" or phonemes: one consonant, /p/, and two vowels, /ɑ/ and /i/. (No language is so minimal; this is just a thought experiment.) If this language's words can be up to two phonemes in length, then its putative vocabulary will consist of /ɑ/, /i/, /p/, /pɑ/, /pi/, /ɑp/, /iɑ/, /ip/, /ɑɑ/, /ɑi/, /ii/, and so on. Theoretically, we could determine in this way how many combinations of how many phonemes would be needed for the language to have a vocabulary of, say, 500,000 words.

Yet phonemes are not combined randomly. Even in this hypothetical language, it is unlikely that */pp/ would qualify as a word, because as we have seen, some units (consonants) are organized around others (vowels) to form syllables. Sequences like /pp/ do not show that kind of organization, whereas those like /pɑp/ and /pip/ conform to the constraint and therefore constitute possible syllables of a language, and in fact real words of English (*pop, peep*).

Many linguists attribute this consonants-around-vowels constraint to a SONORITY SCALE (or HIERARCHY), which ranks sound types in terms of their relative resonance or sonority (Zwicky 1972). From this scale, given in figure 6.n, two corollaries follow. First, a syllable should have a nucleus that is more sonorous than surrounding units. Thus in *yelping*, /jɛ́lpɪŋ/, the scale defines /ɛ/ and /ɪ/ as more sonorous than their neighbors (check to make sure), so there are two nuclei, and /j/, /lp/, and /ŋ/ sort out as onsets and codas. Second, a syllable's sonority crescendos into the nucleus and then fades, so the sequencing of units inside the onset should reflect *increasing* sonority, and that of

Figure 6.n. The sonority scale

low vowel > mid vowel > high vowel > glide > liquid > nasal > obstruent

decreasing   sonority

the units in the coda should reflect *decreasing* sonority. This is why the /klʌ/- of *club* seems a normal way to begin a syllable and word, and it is also why the reverse sequence -/ʌlk/ of *bulk* seems a well-formed rhyme. But one such as /lkʌb/ should be anomalous unless the /l/ becomes syllabic as a nucleus in its own right, and a sequence such as */wkbhfðʌhθ/ would be unsalvageable, because it lacks the peaks of sonority we expect from the sonority scale.

Yet the sonority scale does not always work. For the word *mile* /mail/, the units line up as they should for a single syllable, yet many speakers "feel" two syllables in it and in fact syllabify the final /l/. Note, too, that the scale does not tell us how to sequence units with the same sonority ranking, for example, two or more obstruents: why does the English onset allow the sequence /st/- (*step*) but not */ts/-, and why does the coda allow -/st/ (*pest*), -/ts/ (*pets*), or even -/sts/ (*pests*)? And why do other languages differ so strongly on such points? It is clear that at least some of the constraints on syllable and word formation are language-specific, not universal.

The study of how a language arranges its phonemes is called PHONOTACTICS, and its role in language learning has been vastly underestimated in textbooks that focus just on individual sounds. You may have no trouble saying sound *A* by itself, but if your native language has different phonotactic constraints from the language you are studying, you may balk when you have to combine *A* with sound *B*, or use *A* in a different position. For example, Spanish speakers have no trouble with /s/ initially (as in English *sea*) or with /sC/ in medial position (*aspirin*). But /sC/ at the beginning of a word is another matter because Spanish phonotactics blocks it there. So when speaking English, Spanish speakers tend to insert /e/ before the cluster to break it up (*spray* → [es.pré]). Because this can cause confusion for pairs like *steam/esteem* and *state/estate*, such students will need to practice holding out an [sː] by itself and then adding the obstruent.

Turnabout is fair play: English speakers have their own phonotactic problems with other languages. They likewise apply EPENTHESIS, or insertion of a sound (usually [ə]), to break up unfamiliar clusters like Spanish /trw/-, Japanese /rj/-, German /kv/-, Greek /mn/-, Czech /ʒl/-, Italian /zb/-, Russian /gd/-, and Swahili /ŋg/-. In fact, initial /ŋ/ can give an English speaker problems even *without* another consonant after it because English disallows /ŋ/ at the beginning of a word, a constraint expressed as *#ŋ-. You can get an idea of the power of phonotactics by saying *ton* /tʌn/ and *tongue* /tʌŋ/ and then reversing their phonemes: you should have no trouble with /nʌt/, but how do you cope with /ŋʌt/? The /ŋʌt/ combination is simply un-English.

Let's now examine in more detail how to build an English word. The maximum syllable structure is shown on the left in figure 6.o, where the numerical indices on "C" are

Figure 6.0. The phonotactics of the English syllable

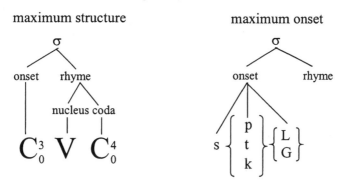

a way of showing the minimum and maximum of a unit. Thus, the onset may have from zero to three consonants (*eye, rye, pry, spry*) and the coda can have up to four (*saw* /sɔ/, *song* /sɔŋ/, *link* /lɪŋk/, *lynx* /lɪŋks/, *glimpsed* /glɪmpst/). But inside each cluster certain constraints prevail, among them the following ones. (Remember that other languages have different preferences on these points.)

1. /ŋ/ cannot begin an English word, nor can nasal clusters of any type (*/mb/-, */dn/-).

2. Voiced fricatives may begin a word singly (although /ʒ/- is unlikely except in loanwords), but not in combination with other consonants (*/ðr/-, */vl/-, */zb/-).

3. Other obstruents may begin a word, but affricates combine with nothing (*/tʃl/-, */bdʒ/-) and most other obstruents only combine with a following liquid or glide: *pray, bray, play, tray, shred, thread, schlep, great, quad* /kwɑd/, *cute* /kjut/ (but not */gd/-, */ks/-, /θp/-, */ʃk/-). The liquid or glide must be at a different place of articulation: thus, /tr dr/- (alveolar + retroflex) in *tread, dread*, but not */tl dl/- (alveolar + alveolar), and although labiovelar /w/ may follow /k/ (*quit*), it does not follow labials /p b f v/.

4. Yet /s/ does join with a following obstruent, always a *voiceless* one (*spill, still, skill, sphere*). Hence, an initial cluster of two obstruents must be /sC̥/ (where C̥ = voiceless consonant). For that reason, if someone says "Give me a [ʃtek]" or "Give me a [θtek]," you will probably interpret that initial bit of friction as /s/ because that is all it *could* be in English.

5. From constraints 4 and 5, it follows that the *only* options in English for a CCC-onset are as shown on the right in figure 6.0 (recall that L = liquids and that G = glides): *splay, spray, screw, stray, spew* /spju/, *squat* /skwɑt/, and so on.

The coda is often the reverse of the onset (cf. -/lk/ as opposed to /kl/-, as already noted), but it allows other combinations such as nasal-obstruent (*band, camp, link, warmth*), fricative-fricative (*fifth*), and almost any combination with final /s z t d/

(*adze=adds* /ædz/, *ranks* /ræŋks/, *ranged* /rendʒd/). In fact, the only way the full potential of four consonants is reached is with an inflectional *-s* or *-(e)d* tacked on, as in *instincts* /ínstìŋkts/ and *glimpsed* /glɪmpst/. Unlike certain other languages, though, English permits /h/ only in an onset, never in the coda, and therefore blocks it from word-final and preconsonantal position (§6.8).

Even in English, certain clusters are adjusted in articulation. An example is -/ns/ in a coda: *tense, rinse, mince, chance, dunce.* Say these words: do you sense a brief stop [t] in the transition between the nasal and the sibilant? Many speakers say *tense* like *tents* /tɛnts/, *mince* like *mints* /mɪnts/, *chance* like *chants* /tʃænts/. The following rule accounts for the epenthesis of this /t/:

Ø → t / n____s

You may find that you similarly insert /d/ in the cluster /nz/, as in *lens* (= *lends*?), *bans* (= *bands*?), *bonanza*, and so on. On the other hand, some obstruent clusters are simplified in casual pronunciation by deleting a consonant: thus, for many if not most speakers, *clothes* /kloðz/ and *fifths* /fɪfθs/ become [kʰloz] and [fɪθs] ~ [fɪfs] in all but the most careful speaking styles.

Just as speakers differ in their pronunciation of consonants and vowels, they also differ in their phonotactics. One such difference in English is in onset clusters with /h/: Old English had several of these (*horse* used to be spelled **hros**, and so pronounced), but they have decreased over time, and today /h/ combines only with glides. Many speakers retain /hj/- in *hue, human, huge* and /hw/ in *why, whack, wheeze* (the spelling *wh-* is the reverse of what it should be and once was), but many others have eliminated even these remnants by dropping the /h/, making the following pairs homophones: *hue/you, which/witch, where/wear, whine/wine, whether/weather.*

Note on symbols

The IPA has an alternative symbol that you may see for /hw/, an inverted *w*: ʍ. But **hw** is a more accurate representation for most speakers who have this sound (a voiceless [w̥] preceded by the "blowing" of aspiration), and the IPA prefers it as a simpler transcription.

Exercise 6.11

(A) In the following list of clusters, decide whether each is phonotactically possible or impossible in English. If it is possible, give a word that illustrates it; if impossible, mark it with an asterisk.

1. In **initial** position:

/bn/	/θr/	/sr/	/sd/	/ʃw/	/pt/	/stw/	/str/
/dv/	/θl/	/fj/	/skj/	/mn/	/hl/	/wh/	/kn/
/pr/	/ðj/	/sf/	/ʒw/	/dʒl/	/skw/	/mj/	/tm/

2. In **final** position:

/mz/	/ŋks/	/pʃ/	/mb/	/ntʃt/	/ndʒ/	/lkt/	/ʃnt/
/ft/	/rvdʒ/	/θs/	/ld/	/ŋd/	/mfs/	/ʒg/	/zz/
/bzd/	/mθ/	/hd/	/rθk/	/vb/	/lsk/	/ðd/	/gd/

(B) Classify each of the following syllables according to whether it is (1) impossible in English (and in that case circle the phonotactic violations), (2) phonotactically possible but happens not to be used as a current word, or (3) is possible and indeed exists as an English word.

/θræʃt/	/straivz/	/ʃrimp/	/hlɔθs/	/bliks/	/flig/	/pfukʃ/	/skjumd/
/gnais/	/mʌltʃ/	/dlʌŋg/	/bwoln/	/bniks/	/θkʊrdʒ/	/blwanʒ/	/vɛkst/
/ʒdrov/	/ŋʊrnd/	/drɛst/	/tsiŋk/	/hjumd/	/ðroz/	/ghosts/	/vlɑrgd/
/rhɑmb/	/morgj/	/ndæŋkt/	/kjubz/	/siksθ/	/mlɑrf/	/sfiŋks/	/dwɔrfs/

(C) Consider **medial** clusters (in the middle of a word). These can consist of more than three consonants because the coda of one syllable meets the onset of the next. Several examples follow. Your job is to think of others, make a general list of allowed (and disallowed) medial clusters, and try to determine the maximum number of consonants that can occur in this position.

- no medial clusters (i.e., no consonants) between syllables: *bias, bio, lion* . . .
- with medial consonants (ambisyllabic or not): *copy, author, very, napkin, asphalt, amber, master, empty, function* . . .

6.11 Teaching pronunciation: Error analysis.

In order to apply one's knowledge of English to the needs of teaching, it is important to be able to perceive and remediate learners' problems precisely. Their performance reflects an evolving transitional system called INTERLANGUAGE (Selinker 1992), intermediate between their first or primary language (L1) and second or target language (L2). Two traditional tools for understanding it are contrastive analysis and error analysis. CONTRASTIVE ANALYSIS (Lado 1957; James 1980) compares L2 and L1 for similarities and differences in order to predict likely problems with L2 and even rank them in difficulty and impact. Although L1 does not cause all problems with L2,[7] its interference in pronunciation is undeniable, and contrastive analysis has been the basis for numerous textbooks focusing on the needs of particular L1 groups (e.g., Grate 1974 for Japanese learners of English). In ESOL classes, though, one may have several L1 groups in the same classroom, each with a different interlanguage phonology, and although manuals such as Nilsen and Nilsen (1973) have offered generalizations about phonemic problems for the most common L1 groups, the teacher may not have the expertise or time to locate contrastive resources for each student's linguistic background.

ERROR ANALYSIS (Richards 1974; James 1998) complements contrastive analysis: instead of predicting problems, it diagnoses them from student performance. One obtains a corpus or set of examples (expanded as needed) of a student's rendition of one or more target units, features, or distinctions and studies them for error types and patterns—in effect reconstructing the apparent rules of L1 from their transfer to L2. The results can be important in deciding on appropriate strategies for remediation. Take, for example, a classroom in which students A and B both pronounce *car* as [kal], and student C pronounces it as [kaː]. The teacher may jump to the conclusion that all of them have trouble with /r/ or that they randomly substitute one sound for another. But now consider a larger corpus of six samples from each speaker:

	car	*rag*	*lag*	*berry*	*belly*	*fry*
A	[kal]	[lag]	[lag]	[bɛ́li]	[bɛ́li]	[flai]
B	[kal]	[ɾag]	[lag]	[bɛ́ɾi]	[bɛ́li]	[flai]
C	[kaː]	[ɹag]	[lag]	[bɛ́ɹi]	[bɛ́li]	[fɹai]

Now three distinct patterns emerge. Speaker A apparently has an L1 with a single liquid, /l/; r-articulations will need to be developed from scratch. B, on the other hand, does have an /r l/ distinction (*rag/lag*, *berry/belly*), but with a rule that neutralizes it in final position (*car*) and in consonant clusters (*fry*). This student has a wholly different challenge: to extend an already existing distinction to two specific environments and to weaken the flap [ɾ] to an approximant so that *berry* is not misinterpreted as *Betty*. Student C, meanwhile, has simply learned British pronunciation, which is perfectly acceptable and needs no intervention at all. In fact, the only problem that all three of these students share is vocalic: an apparent merger of /ɑ/ and /æ/ as [a], although more data would be needed to make sure.

Contrastive analysis and error analysis are not techniques for *how* to teach; but they can be useful tools for understanding the nature of a problem and adapting one's approach to it.

Exercise 6.12

Carry out an error analysis of the following samples, focusing on the identified sounds.

(A) L1 = Chinese; focus: rendition of English consonants, especially liquids and obstruents. (Note: [ẓ] is a voiced retroflex sibilant fricative, like [z] but with the tip curled back as for [ɻ].)

carry [kʰέɹ̥i]   person [pʰɚ̩sn̩]   phrase [f.ɹ̥es]
form [fɔɹm]   number [nʌmbɚ]   comparing [kʰɑmpʰέɹɪŋ]
verb [vɚp]   agree [ɑg.ɹí]   more [moɚ]
plural [pʰ.ɹú.ɹɑl̩]   red [z̪ɛt]   clue [kʰ.ɹu]
rule [z̪ul̩]   glue [g.ɹu]   rug [z̪ʌk]
let [l̥ɛt]   loose [l̥us]   less [l̥ɛs]

(B) Speaker A's L1 = French; Speaker B's L1 = Flemish Dutch. Focus: differences and similarities in how the two speakers treat stress and pronounce the indicated vowels and consonants.

	this	father	thread	third	nerve	sheath
A:	[zis]	[fazέʁ]	[sʁɛd̪]	[sœʁd̪]	[nœʁv]	[ʃis]
B:	[d̪ɪs]	[fád̪əʁ]	[t̪ʁɛt̪]	[t̪œʁt̪]	[nœʁf]	[ʃit̪]

(C) L1 = Japanese; focus: (a) liquids and voiced fricatives (Eng. /z ʒ/), (b) phonotactics, (c) rendition of vowels. Here, the accent mark means higher pitch; [ɸ] is a voiceless bilabial fricative, and [ɯ] is an unrounded [u] (lips spread).

write	[ɾáitɔ]	course	[kɔ́ːsɯ]	fly, fry	[ɸɯɾái]
your	[júɑ]	heart	[háːtɔ]	try	[tɔɾái]
yellow	[jέɾɔ]	sorry	[sóriː]	bell	[béɾɯ]
lesson	[ɾésɔn]	paper	[pέipɑ]	bear	[béɑ]
reason	[ɾíːdzɔn]	sure	[ʃúɑ]	belt	[béɾɯtɔ]
class	[kɯɾásɯ]	grade	[gɯɾέidɔ]	Christmas	[kɯɾísɯmasɯ]
zoo	[dzɯː]	leisure	[ɾédʒɑ]	bees	[bíːdzɯ]

(D) Speaker: L1 = Arabic (Majdi 1983); focus: (a) vowels and (b) consonants and phonotactics.

cat	[kat̪]	cut	[kat̪]	cot	[kat̪]
pen	[feːn]	look	[lʊk]	sin	[sɪn]
pain	[feːn]	Luke	[luːk]	seen	[siːn]
bought	[boːt]	are	[ʔaːɾ]	ice	[ʔaːjɪs]
boat	[boːt]	eat	[ʔiːt]	fine	faːjɪn]

(E) Speaker: L1 = Spanish; focus: (a) voiced stops (including affricates) and fricatives, (b) liquids.

although	[aldó]	very	[béɾi]	goes	[gos]
father	[fáðeɾ]	berry	[béɾi]	leader	[líðeɾ]

there, dare	[d̪eɾ]	trouble, travel	[t̪ɾáβel]	bug	[baɣ]
go there	[god̪éɾ]	T.V.	[t̪iβí]	baggie	[báɣi]
be good	[biɣúð]	invite	[imbáit̪]	agree	[aɣɾí]
these, this	[d̪is]	glove	[glaβ]	major	[méijeʀ]
sandy	[sán̪di]	vibration	[baiβréiʃan]	use, juice	[ɟus]

(F) Error analysis. Speaker: L1 = Spanish; focus: phonotactics.

remind	[ɾimáin]	stress	[est̪rés]	spray	[espréi]
test, tests	[t̪és]	crates	[kreis]	smell	[esmél]
skipped	[eskíp]	New York	[nuɟór]	sixths	[sis]
myths	[mis]	a student	[anest̪úðen]		

NOTES

1. Because the voicing of consonants shows variation (§6.5.1), some phonologists refer to the voiced/voiceless contrast as one of LENIS (weakly articulated) versus FORTIS (forcefully articulated).

2. In older linguistics, velars were sometimes called GUTTURAL, which incorrectly suggests articulation in the throat. "Throat sounds" are quite possible, but are called PHARYNGEALS.

3. For research on phonological universals, see Greenberg (1978), Maddieson (1984), and Ladefoged and Maddieson (1996).

4. In a sentential context at normal tempo, the learner may not hear the difference (just a syllabic [n̩]) between *She would take it* and *She wouldn't take it*. As for syllabic [l̩], recall that it is velarized in this position ([ɫ̩]), so it has the dark resonance of back [o] or [u], and many learners hear it as those vowels: *people* = "pipo," *model* = "motto."

5. Although the raised equals sign is not official in the IPA, it has been approved as the diacritic for 'unaspirated' by the Extensions to the IPA (International Phonetic Association 1999).

6. This formulation of the environment for flapping sounds vague but reflects the facts. In *vánity*, where the /t/ is between unstressed vowels, it is generally flapped but is sometimes heard as a full [t]; in *cíty*, where it is between a stressed and unstressed vowel, it is almost always flapped.

7. See Gass and Selinker 2001 for an evaluation of contrastive analysis and error analysis within second language acquisition theory and research.

Wrap-Up Exercises

(A) Give the symbol (broad transcription) representing the *first* phoneme in:

| 1. chord | 3. sugar | 5. pneumonia | 7. whose | 9. young | 11. phase |
| 2. wrestling | 4. queen | 6. ptomaine | 8. why | 10. germ | 12. through |

(B) Give the symbol (broad transcription) representing the *last* phoneme in:

1. comb	3. bathe	5. strong	7. rough	9. wedge	11. smooth
2. science	4. bath	6. strange	8. rouge	10. of	12. tease

(C) Transcribe the following words phonemically, including a marking of stress when there is more than one syllable. Remember that a *phonemic* representation (/ /) omits details of allophones that might be shown in a narrower transcription. Be careful not to let spelling interfere with your perception of how the word sounds.

1. thirst	5. damage	9. pleasure	13. polish	17. authorize	21. imagine
2. chalk	6. countries	10. tribute	14. cushion	18. vacuum	22. shorter
3. duchy	7. silence	11. recognition	15. museum	19. conscious	23. judge
4. people	8. cupboard	12. colonel	16. breakfast	20. rhythmical	24. banality

(D) Analogies: Study the relationships in each pair of phones and then complete the analogy.

1. [b] is to [m] as [g] is to _____.
2. [d] is to [t] as [dʒ] is to _____.
3. [t] is to [s] as [ʔ] is to _____.
4. [w] is to [w̥] as [v] is to _____.
5. [ʃ] is to [ʒ] as [θ] is to _____.
6. [p] is to [b] as [k] is to _____.

(E) **Это Америка!** (*That's America!*) Vladimir, a Russian acquaintance of yours, is a Moscow anchorman whose TV team has prepared a series on how local governments in the United States deal with urban problems. He is already familiar with well-known names such as New York and Chicago and can figure out from spelling names like Salt Lake City, but he has written you asking how to pronounce the following cities. He knows English and can more or less fill in details like aspiration, type of *r*, and so on, so all he needs is a broad (phonemic) representation, including an indication of stress. You can take for granted his familiarity with IPA; that is fairly standard in other countries for educated professionals in language and journalism, and their English dictionaries almost always use IPA (unlike our dictionaries, which usually do not).

1. Seattle	6. Syracuse	11. Boise	16. Milwaukee
2. Minneapolis	7. Phoenix	12. Tucson	17. Des Moines
3. Raleigh	8. Binghamton	13. Kalamazoo	18. Wheeling
4. Dallas	9. Albuquerque	14. Norfolk	19. Tallahassee
5. Anchorage	10. Cincinnati	15. Baton Rouge	20. San Jose

(F) Review. Read the following passage out loud to practice with phonemic transcription; for certain words, you may have a slightly different pronunciation in your own dialect. Then do the following:

1. Copy it and mark strong and weak stresses throughout the passage.
2. Mark intonations by using curves over the phrases and/or arrows (see chapter 3).
3. Retranscribe this phonemic version **phonetically**, in square brackets, bringing out as much phonetic detail as you can in consonants' allophones, precise articulations, vowel details such as nasalization, and so on. The double vertical bar, ‖, is the IPA's "pause" symbol for breaks in speech.

/ə brif hɪstəri əv ɪŋglɪʃ/

/ɪŋglɪʃ ɪz ðə dʒɜrmænɪk daiəlɛkt əv æŋglosæksən traibz hu kem tu ɪŋglənd ɪŋ ðə fɪfθ sɛntʃəri ‖ðæt ərli vərʒən əv ðə læŋgwədʒ ‖ kɔld old ɪŋglɪʃ ‖ læstəd əŋtɪl ðə nɔrmən ɪnveʒən ɪn tɛn sɪksti sɪks (h)wɪtʃ kəntrɪbjətəd θauzəndz əv frɛntʃ wərdz tu ðə læŋgwədʒ ‖ d(j)ʊrɪŋ ðə mɪdəl edʒəz ðə græmər bəkem sɪmplər luzɪŋ mɛni əv ɪts ɛndɪŋz ænd muvɪŋ tɔrdz ə mɔr fɪkst sɪntæks ‖ bʌt ɪt wəz frəm ðə fɪftinθ θru ði ettinθ sɛntʃəriz (h)wɛn ðə prənʌnsieʃən tʃendʒd ðə most/

🎧(G) Error analysis. Listen to the corresponding CD recording of a nonnative (L1 = Spanish) speaker of English. Focus on special features of his stress and intonation and pronunciation of vowels and consonants, and take notes (with transcriptions of key examples), listening as many times as you need to. Write a summary describing his English and compare your observations with those of your classmates.

(H) Discussion. Dalton and Seidlhofer (1994, 17) give ESOL teachers the following piece of advice: "It is important to emphasize that articulation needs to be experienced to be understood, and that this understanding should lead to an awareness of how sounds are actually pronounced, not simply a technical vocabulary for describing them. There is no point in teachers just telling their students that the consonant in the English word 'fee' is a 'voiceless labio-dental fricative.'" Come up with several ideas about the best way to apply the contents of the chapter you have just finished studying so you can help your students do a better job of pronouncing the consonant sounds of English.

CHAPTER 7

Sounds and Forms That Change and Merge

7.1 English phonemes in (con)text. Chapters 4–6 surveyed the system of English phonemes, together with their chief variants and the rules that produce them. These phonemes are not distributed equally in the language: we have seen phonotactic constraints on their combinations and positions in the word and syllable rules such as reduction that further alter their distribution. To a large extent, then, the question of how important a given distinction may be depends not just on potential minimal pairs but on frequency of occurrence in the language.

There are two ways to compute phonemic frequency. One is LEXICAL FREQUENCY, a phoneme's frequency in the overall vocabulary of the language. This can be determined by tallying its occurrence in all the entries of a dictionary or, as a shortcut, in every *n*th word of a dictionary. The other approach is TEXTUAL FREQUENCY, or how often the phoneme appears in a typical text—a story, a conversation, an essay, and so on. For either approach, a computer can calculate *grapheme* (letter) frequency, but for *phoneme* frequency the tokens to count must come from an analyzed oral sample because phoneme-grapheme correspondences are too irregular (chapter 4) for a computer to identify phonemes reliably from written text. The two types of studies yield different results, for a word as often used as *the* will count only once in a lexical frequency study, but repeatedly in a textual frequency analysis. The latter, of course, reflects natural usage more accurately because we do not use each word only once, as implied by lexical frequency alone.

In figure 7.a, we have digested a famous text, Lincoln's *Gettysburg Address* (1863) as read aloud by one of the authors. His forty phonemes are ranked from most to least frequent in number of tokens (instances).[1] Another text might yield slightly different frequencies, although ranking would not change greatly. It is unlikely, for example, that /ʒ/

Figure 7.a. Text frequency of English phonemes: *The Gettysburg Address*

Total number of phonemic tokens: 900		
1. /ə/ 99 (11%)	14–15. /ɛ/ 25 (2.78%)	28. /m/ 12 (1.33%)
2. /t/ 70 (7.78%)	/ər/ 25 (2.78%)	29. /ɔ/ 9 (1%)
3. /n/ 66 (7.33%)	16. /h/ 22 (2.44%)	30. /ŋ/ 8 (0.89%)
4. /r/ 52 (5.78%)	17–18. /ɑ/ 21 (2.33%)	31. /u/ 7 (0.78%)
5. /d/ 45 (5%)	/f/ 21 (2.33%)	32. /ai/ 6 (0.67%)
6. /ɪ/ 44 (4.89%)	19–20. /o/ 19 (2.11%)	33. /au/ 5 (0.56%)
7. /ð/ 39 (4.33%)	/w/ 19 (2.11%)	34–35. /j/ 4 (0.44%)
8. /l/ 33 (3.6%)	21. /æ/ 17 (1.89%)	/ʊ/ 4 (0.44%)
9–10. /s/ 30 (3.33%)	22–23. /p/ 14 (1.56%)	36. /θ/ 3 (0.33%)
/i/ 30 (3.33%)	/z/ 14 (1.56%)	37–38. /tʃ/ 2 (0.22%)
11. /e/ 28 (3.11%)	24–27. /ʌ/ 13 (1.44%)	/dʒ/ 2 (0.22%)
12–13. /k/ 26 (2.89%)	/b/ 13 (1.44%)	39. /ʒ/ 1 (0.11%)
/v/ 26 (2.89%)	/g/ 13 (1.44%)	40. /oi/ 0 (0.00%)
	/ʃ/ 13 (1.44%)	Consonant-vowel ratio 548:352

would appear in the top ten consonants unless we purposely included words such as *pleasure* and *fusion*. Note that because of reduction, the most common vowel is schwa—a striking indication of the way the language sounds; the least common vowel—in fact it is completely absent from Lincoln's text—is /oi/. As for consonants, the coronals /t d n r l ð s/ clearly dominate English articulation; velars and labials come next, with most alveopalatals last. The /ð/ is particularly common in Lincoln's speech, and in virtually *any* representative sampling of English, because of the frequency of *the, this,* and *that.*

The speaker adopted a fairly slow, deliberate tempo and register in view of the formality and rhythmic cadences of public speaking and the special gravity of the situation and topic. In this kind of speech, articulation tends to be relatively precise, with fairly clear phonemic distinctions. In a lower register, however, phonemic counts become more problematic because adjacent units alter each other more and even fuse together, as we will shortly see in the following sections. (For the acoustic side of the processes described in the following discussion, see the appendix, §8.1.)

7.2 When words change their pronunciation. Both dictionaries and linguistic descriptions focus on the way that a word is pronounced by itself in terms of its component phonemes. Thus, for the word *delete* you see /dɪ.lít/ or /də.lít/, indicating how it might be pronounced in a fairly slow, deliberate tempo, without connecting it to anything else. This is called a CITATION FORM, the way we cite the word when pronouncing it alone—as if in response to the questions "What is this word? How do you say it?"

Yet we seldom speak in single words like this. From age one and a half onward, humans combine words with affixes (suffixes and prefixes) and with other words to form phrases, sentences, conversations, stories, arguments, and speeches. In those longer contexts, a word's pronunciation is affected by its neighbors, sometimes drastically. Add the suffix *-ion* (as in *opin-ion*) to *delete,* and the pronunciation of the /t/ changes to [ʃ], yielding [dɪlíʃən]. Join *delete* with a following pronoun *it* as a verb phrase, and the /t/ again changes, this time to a flap (§6.5.2): [dɪlíɾɪt]. Speed up the tempo and the unstressed vowels become schwas, [dəlíɾət]; speed it up more and now the first schwa drops out to leave a syllabic /l/ (§6.4.3), [dl̩íɾət].

So how exactly do we "say a word"? As we first pointed out in chapter 1, that depends on its context. We now focus on three major contextual factors: word linkage, rhythm, and grammar.

7.3 Changes due to word linkage. When words are joined together into phrases, their consonants come into contact and their vowels may fall at weak positions between the stresses. Especially in a faster articulation, we then adapt their pronunciation by using SANDHI /sʌ́ndi/ versions, a Sanskrit term meaning 'joined forms in connected speech.'

Sometimes sandhi reflects phonological rules that also apply inside a word. Such is the case of a flapped [dəlíɾ]- for *delete* when followed by a vowel (*delete it, delete eleven, delete another one*): the /t/ undergoes the flapping rule across word boundaries just as it does word-internally (*liter, meeting, waited, deleted*). Other cases of English sandhi result from three main processes.

Unstressed vowel deletion: Because schwa is a weak vowel that generally occurs in unstressed positions, it shortens and sometimes drops out altogether in fast articulation. We have seen schwa-dropping inside words (§5.5): *traveler* /trǽvələr/ → [trǽvl̩ər] ~ [trǽvlər]. (Remember that the tilde means 'varying with.') In connected words in fast articulation, the dropping of unstressed vowels is especially notable in cases such as the following:

- sentence-initially: *It seems hard* → [tsimz . . .], *It's pretty bad* → [tsp . . .], *If you'd wait* → [fjud . . .], *about eight* → [baʊɾ . . .], *The milk spoiled* → [ðmɪlk . . .], *except you* → [(k)sɛ̀ptʃú].
- after a stressed vowel: *Go away* → [gòwéi], *I expect it* [àikspɛ́kt- . .]
- between like sounds: *probably* → [prʌ́b(b)li], *this assortment* → [ðɪssóɾʔ- . .]

The technical names for vowel dropping are PROCOPE in an initial syllable, SYNCOPE in a medial one, and APOCOPE in a final one. Note that it can produce clusters like [ðm]- or [tsp]- that are phonotactically blocked (§6.10) in citation forms.

Assimilation: In assimilation, one segment becomes more like its neighbor, or both assimilate to each other. One example is (alveo)palatalization, which assimilates alveolars to a following /j/. We have already noted (§6.9) that this process applied historically inside the word (*issue* /ísju/ → /íʃu/, *nature* /nétjʊr/ → /nétʃər/, *gradual* /grǽdjuəl/ → /grǽdʒuəl/) and variably applies across words today: *miss you* →

[míʃu], *eat yet* → [ítʃɛ̀t], *please you* → [plíʒu]. Other examples show assimilation of voicing and place of articulation:

- (de)voicing: *as fast as Tom* /æz fǽst æz tám/ → [sfǽst əs tám]
- place of articulation: *miss Sherry* /mís ʃɛ́ri/ → [míʃʃɛ́ri], *in case* /ín kés/ → [íŋkéis], *one more* /wʌ́n mór/ → [wʌ́mmór], *said this* /sɛ́d ðìs/ → [sɛ́ḍðìs]
- both voicing and place of articulation: *does she* /dʌ́z ʃi/ → [dʌ́ʃʃi]

Cluster simplification: English permits complex consonant clusters (§6.10), but while a cluster such as /fθs/ in *fifths* may be fully pronounced in a high register, it often simplifies in a lower one: → [fɪfs] ~ [fɪθs]. Simplification also applies when the coda of one word must be articulated with the onset of the next, when vowel deletion and assimilation may kick in as well:

- simplification: *just now* /dʒʌ́st náu/ → [dʒʌ́snáu], *first-born* /fə́rst bórn/ → [fə́sbórn], *don't know* /dònt nó/ → [dòunnóu] → [dòunóu], *let me in* /lɛ́t mi ín/ → [lɛ́mi ín], *give me that* /gív mi ðǽt/ → [gími ðǽt], *must be* /mʌ́st bí/ →[mʌ́s bí]
- simplification and assimilation: *hand made* /hǽnd mɛ́d/ → [hǽn méid] → [hǽmméid]
- vowel deletion, simplification, and assimilation: *Jack and Jill* /dʒǽk ænd dʒíl/ → [dʒǽk n̩ dʒíl] → [dʒǽkŋ̍ dʒíl]

Yet we obviously do not drop *all* unstressed vowels or assimilate or simplify *all* clusters, which is why it is impossible to formulate exact rules for these processes. Much of the speech signal is **redundant** in that some of the sounds do not make a difference in meaning and can be inferred from the context. Therefore, simplification is often a matter of what the speaker can get by with, given a hearer who shares the same lexicon, the same phonemes and rules, the same patterns of articulatory timing, and especially the same *nonlinguistic* context—common focus on the same topic in the same situation. When you reduce *and* to just [n̩] or [ŋ], you will still make yourself understood, because between two nouns (*Jack __ Jill*) the grammar of English makes a conjunction likely, and native speakers and listeners recognize that a syllabic nasal can suffice for the full form of *and* there (it cannot be *but* or *or*). Nor is there a problem with dropping the /t/ in *first-born*, because there is no word /fərs/ with which it might be confused. Strictly speaking, [hǽmméid] for *hand made* might be construed as *ham made,* as in *The ham made a great sandwich*, but in a context like *This cloth was hand-made*, the thought of *ham* would probably not occur to anyone focused on the subject of textiles. (Only linguists and punsters might seize on the ambiguity.)

Matters are different in public speaking, however: newscasters, for example, tend to avoid many of the processes we are describing here because they do not know their listeners and do not share with them a common context or common presuppositions. Even their topic jumps frequently and abruptly from one item to the next, and their information must be condensed to pack as much as possible into each minute, so there is little redundancy. Although broadcasters are sometimes taken as speech models (e.g., the BBC for RP), it is not the case that they speak more "correctly" than the rest of us; rather, they are speaking in a special situation that demands a more precisely delivered articulation than normal conversation does.[2]

Exercise 7.1

Listen to your instructor reading a passage out loud or two friends conversing in English, and then list at least five examples of words whose citation-form pronunciation changed when linked to others in context. Transcribe each one in two ways: (1) its normal citation-form and (2) the sandhi version(s) you heard.

7.4 Changes due to stress. Chapters 1–3 emphasized the role of stress in English pronunciation, and chapter 5 described its effects on vowel articulation. Stressed vowels are stretched out to the point that wobbles in tongue position become diphthongization; unstressed vowels are shortened and relaxed into a central position, undergoing reduction to schwa. The effect of stress is quite pervasive in the language, as we will continue to see in the next section.

7.4.1 Speaking metrically. Languages tend to sort out into two main types according to their rhythmic setting. In STRESS-TIMED languages such as English, German, Danish, and Russian, syllables are organized into groups called FEET containing one strong-stressed syllable plus surrounding unstressed or weak-stressed ones. The strong stresses tend to occur at regular intervals, like the downbeats of measures in music, and their syllables are lengthened or shortened according to the number of unstressed syllables that must be packed into the same foot with them. Thus the /i/ of *sléep* (said as a single word) is rather long; that of *sléepy* is a bit shorter, and that of *sléepily* or *sléep on it* is shorter still. Hence the *syllables* vary in duration, but the foot remains relatively even, and for that reason the term FOOT ISOCHRONY, or 'even timing of feet,' is also used to describe this kind of rhythm. Traditional poets of these languages intentionally regularize the feet for recurrent metrical patterns, as noted in chapters 1–2.

On the other hand, SYLLABLE-TIMED languages such as French, Spanish, Italian, Japanese, Arabic, and Hindi tend to deliver each syllable as a single quick beat. They may have distinctive stress[3] (Italian and Spanish) like English, or may not (Hindi), but this does not result in significant lengthening or shortening, only greater prominence. Their poets organize syllables into recurrent patterns too, not usually on the basis of feet but, instead, on the basis of phrases with the same number of syllables.

The sentences in figure 7.b show the stretching and shortening of stress timing in English, using an approximate musical notation. These sentences consist of two feet (shown as measures), corresponding to the two main stresses—until the addition of another strong-stressed word creates a third foot, as in (d) and (e). The unstressed initial

Figure 7.b. The feet of stress-timing

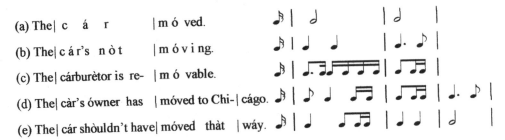

the lies outside the first foot, like a quick pick-up beat in music, and is therefore EXTRA-METRICAL ('outside the meter,' §1.2). Say the sentences to yourself: native speakers vary slightly in the precise way that they fit their syllables in, just as singers differ a little in how they render the same notes of a song, but your reading will probably reveal similar metrical feet, with similar lengthenings of *car* and *move* and similar shortenings of the unstressed syllables. Note, too, the syncopated effect in (d) of starting a foot with a weak-stressed syllable (*càr's ówner*).

By way of contrast, a Spanish version of sentence (b), for example, might be as shown in figure 7.c, with little variation in the fundamental evenness of syllable delivery except merger of the adjacent /e/'s in *se está* in a fast tempo (as shown by the subscript arc in the transcription) and optional lengthening on the last stressed syllable (/bjén/) for intonational highlighting.

Of course, no one speaks like a metronome; rhythm varies according to tempo, degree of excitement, discourse emphasis, phrasal complexity, and other factors. Some phonologists (Cruttenden 1986,25) have therefore expressed doubts about stress timing and syllable timing, and these doubts have filtered down into ESOL literature (Dalton and Seidlhofer 1994, 41). However, there is a strong body of research (e.g., Bond and Fokes 1985; Fokes and Bond 1989) that confirms the distinction as an overall tendency and also as a major factor in how we process speech. Native speakers themselves hear it: Spanish sounds machine-gun-like to English speakers, English sounds jerky to French speakers, and the English of many Hindi speakers sounds like *dot-dot-dot-dot-dot* instead of the expected *di-DUM-di-DUM-di-di-DUM*, and may even be hard to understand despite general phonemic accuracy. Likewise, songs and poetry translated to another language may sound wrong, for the words no longer fit the original meter. Especially convincing is the fact that many of the English processes we will discuss in the

Figure 7.c. Syllable-timing

(b)   El carro no se está moviendo.

/el.ká.ɾo.nó.se͜es.tá.mo.bjén.do/

next section seldom have an equivalent in syllable-timed languages because the rhythmic setting is so different.

Exercise 7.2

(A) Divide the following sentences into feet using vertical bars as foot boundaries; also mark the strong stress of each foot. Circle any initial extrametrical syllables. Review chapter 1 for help.

1. Give me a break.
2. Come to our party tomorrow.
3. You can lead a horse to water, but you cannot make him drink.
4. Once upon a time, there was a prince who had been turned into a frog.
5. A lot of what we have done will have to be done over.
6. A phoneme is the significant unit of a sound system.
7. Two plus the square root of nine is five.
8. Now is the time for all good men to come to the aid of their party.
9. As long as there are songs to sing, I'll be loving you.
10. At the stroke of midnight she abandoned the ball.
11. The rain in Spain falls mainly on the plain.
12. Frankly, Scarlet, I don't give a damn.

(B) Now read the sentences in (A) out loud to yourself, and beat the downbeat of each foot by rapping your knuckles on a table. In which cases do the feet sound slightly irregular and uneven?

(C) Listen to the corresponding exercise on the CD as some of these sentences are read with *syllable-timing*. Then try to describe the impression that this kind of syllable delivery produces.

7.4.2 Crushed words: Weak forms and contractions. Assume you are aghast at the way that someone is doing something. You might shriek *WHÁT ÁRE YÓU DÓING?!*, stressing each word as its own foot as if underscoring it for maximum impact. But this is not the normal way we talk. In the usual pronunciation of this question we retain the stresses only on *what* and *do-*, and fit the other syllables into the two feet with them: |*Whát are you* | *dó-ing?*|. Because of the stress timing, the unstressed syllables are now under pressure to shorten, and as the tempo speeds up, reduction, deletion, and assimilation apply to produce drastic changes in the words of the first foot. Each of the following stages can be heard with increasing speed and informality:

[(h)wát ɑr ju . . .] → [(h)wárər ju . . .] → [(h)wárərjə . . .] →
[(h)wárəjə . . .] → [(h)wátjə . . .] → [(h)wátʃə . . .]

The versions [ə(r)] and [jə] of *are* and *you* are called WEAK FORMS; the full versions [ɑr] and [ju] are, of course, the corresponding STRONG FORMS used under full stress or as citation forms.

We can see a similar progression in the ways to pronounce *car should not have* in example (e) of figure 7.b. In a slow register, this group may be pronounced as two feet, | *cár shòuld* | *nót hàve*|; but in a faster tempo with no emphasis (peak stress, §3.1) on *should not have,* the second foot may merge into the first one, a process known as DEFOOTING:[4]

[kɑ́r ʃʊd nɑt hæv . . .] → [kɑ́r ʃʊdənt həv . . .] → [kɑ́r ʃədn̩təv . . .] → [kɑ́rʃədn̩ə . . .]

Note the crushing of the words *should not have* once they are in the same foot as strong-stressed *car*: they reduce to the weak forms [ʃəd], [ənt ~ n̩t ~ n̩] (spelled -*n't*), and [həv ~ əv ~ ə] (spelled -*'ve*) for *have*. The next example shows a similar defooting: the second foot is incorporated into the first one as tempo speeds up, yielding weak forms of *is, going to,* and *them:*

|*Máry is* | *góing to* | *líke them.*| → |*Máry is going to* | *líke them.*| → [mɛ́rizgənə láikəm]

As illustrated in figure 7.d, most weak forms in English are those pieces of grammatical machinery—auxiliary verbs, pronouns, prepositions, and conjunctions—that can be recovered on the basis of the overall sentence structure and are therefore deemphasized under normal conditions. Note especially the pronunciation differences between plain (affirmative) and negative auxiliary verbs: *is/isn't, would/wouldn't, has/hasn't, had/hadn't, can/can't,* and so on. Except when emphatic (as in *Yes, he ís. He ís coming*), the affirmative form is generally unstressed and therefore reduced or contracted. The negative form has a contracted -*n't* for *not* but its /t/ may be difficult to hear (it becomes a glottal stop [ʔ], §6.5.1, or even drops out), so the most audible difference between negative and affirmative will be the negative form's syllabic nasal [n̩] and its full (unreduced) vowel. In the case of *won't* and *can't,* the vowel tends to be strongly nasalized: [kæ̃nʔ(t)] (with local variants [kẽæ̃ʔ(t)] ~ [kɪ̃ə̃nʔ(t)] ~ [kɑ̃nʔ(t)] ~ [kẽɪ̃nʔ(t)]). Examples:

1. *Dad is leaving* = [dǽd ɪz lívɪŋ] → [dǽdz lívɪŋ].
   Dad is not leaving = [dǽd ɪz nɑ̀t lívɪŋ] → [dǽdɪzn̩ʔ lívɪŋ] or [dǽdznɑ̀ʔlívɪŋ].

2. *We can do it* = [wìkæ̀n dúɪt] → [wìkn̩ dúɪt].
   We can't do it = [wìkǽnt dúɪt] → [wìkæ̃nʔdúət].

If you compare the forms in figure 7.d, you will see that distinct words converge on the same weak form: *have* and *of* = [ə(v)], *is* and *has* = [z], *had* and *did* and *would*

Figure 7.d. Strong and weak forms

auxiliary verbs	*can* [kæn, kən, kn, kŋ, ŋ]	*am* [æm, əm, m̩, m]
	could [kʊd, kəd]	*is* [ɪz, əz, z, s]
	will [wɪl, wəl, əl, l]	*are* [ɑr, ər, r]
	would [wʊd], [wəd], [əd], [d]	*have* [hæv], [həv], [əv], [v]
	do [du], [də]	*has* [hæz], [həz], [əz], [z], [s]
	did [dɪd], [dəd], [əd], [d]	*had* [hæd], [həd], [əd], [d]
	going to [góɪŋ tu], [góənə], [gənə]	*ought to* [ɔ́ttu], [ɔ́ɾə]
pronouns	*he* [hi], [i]	*her* [hər], [ər]
	him [hɪm], [ɪm]	*them* [ðɛm], [ðəm], [əm], [m̩]
	you [ju], [jə]	*your* [jʊr], [jər]
prepositions	*to* [tu], [tə], [ə]	*from* [frʌm], [frəm], [fəm]
	for [fɔr], [fər]	*of* [ɑv], [əv], [ə]
other: conjunc-tions, adverbs, determiners (articles)	*and* [ænd], [ənd], [ən], [n̩], [n]	*some* [sʌm], [səm], [sm̩]
	or [ɔr], [ər]	*because* [bəkɔ́z], [bəkəz], [kəz]
	not [nɑt], [ənt], [ən], [n̩]	*a / an* [e] / [æn], [ə(n)], [n̩]

[(ə)d], *am* and *them* = [əm], *are* and *or* = [ər]. For that reason, some people view weak forms as slovenly or slurred speech that should be avoided. Yet weak forms have been around for a very long time; many of those in use today—and even *more*—are found in Shakespeare. They are therefore well entrenched as part of normal English, and in *context* they produce little or no real confusion.

Remember that pronunciation is linked to grammar, so two speakers with a thorough command of the language have no problem interpreting these fragments in normal "top-down" processing of sounds within the overall context (Dalton and Seidlhofer 1994, 26):

- *a bag* [ə] *corn chips*: a preposition is likely between the two nouns, and of *have, of,* and *a,* only *of* qualifies.
- *he would* [ə] *helped*: *have* fits the context and can combine with the -*ed* form of the second verb, while *of* and *a* cannot.

The following drastic case of sandhi is more complex, but native speakers still process it easily:

- [(h)wádʒə dú]: The first foot [(h)wádʒə] (or, for some, [(h)wʌ́dʒə]) is a nonword, but the stressed syllable is interpretable as *what,* which sets up the expectation of a question. The grammar of this question requires a subject preceded by an auxiliary verb. Subject *you* qualifies as a source of the -[dʒə] but the alveopalatalization rule (§6.9) cannot produce [dʒ] directly from *what you*; a /d/ is needed for that. Because the auxiliary *did* has /d/ as a weak form and fits the context, the pre-crushed sentence must be *What did you do?*

Given the frequency of sandhi in speech, the contractions that appear in the written version of the language (*can't, what'd, she's, I'll,* etc.) are just the tip of the iceberg. To learners of English, however, sandhi forms are baffling. In a sentence such as "No, he could not have seen them," learners expect to hear the citation forms they have studied in class as the "correct" word pronunciations—/no/, /hi/, /kʊd/, /nɑt/, /hæv/, /sin/, /ðɛm/—and so are quite perplexed when they hear an English speaker say, instead, [nóːi | kʊ́ːdnə | síːnəm]. Learners may only perceive *No___could___ seen___*, and therefore misinterpret the utterance or draw a total blank.

Exercise 7.3

(A) Discerning weak forms. On the CD (or from your instructor), you will hear the following sentences read in a normal colloquial style. Imitate the recording/reading and pronounce each sentence yourself. Then mark the feet with vertical bars and transcribe the italicized parts phonetically. Explain the various processes that have produced each weak form.

1. Some *of them are supposed to* give *us a* hand.
2. *Would you* like *some* coffee *and* donuts?
3. She *could not have* known that, *because* she *was not at* home.
4. *Why did he* tell *you that it* bothered *him*?
5. John *will want to* look *for a* new car while *he is* there.
6. They *probably went* up *to the top of the* roof.

(B) Pronounce the following sentence pairs (or listen to your instructor pronounce them) in a colloquial speech style with normal reduced forms. Pinpoint the crucial differences in the italicized portions and transcribe these phonetically.

1. a. Janet *can* swim fast.   b. Janet *can't* swim fast.
2. a. She *has* eaten.   b. She *hasn't* eaten.
3. a. Perhaps he *would* help us.   b. Perhaps he *wouldn't* help us.
4. a. *Would she* like this?   b. *Would he* like this?
5. a. *Is he* back yet?   b. *Is she* back yet?
6. a. Did you *see them* downtown?   b. Did you *see him* downtown?

(C) Pair work: two-way dictation. Prepare a list of three phonemically transcribed sentences in English, consisting of two to three feet each and including weak forms.

Each of you then dictates your list to the other for a *phonetic* transcription that brings out the effects of the kinds of processes we have discussed in this section.

7.5 Changes due to grammar: Morphemes and allomorphs.

A MORPHEME (§2.9) is any minimal unit with its own meaning and patterning. It can be a word by itself, with any number of syllables as long as the word is an indivisible unit—*will, apple, catapult, cucumber, Massachusetts*—or it can be part of a word, such as a stem (the *aud-* of *audible* and *auditory*) or an affix (*re-, in-, -able, -tion, -ness, -ly, -s*). Just as graphemes have allographs and phonemes have allophones, morphemes have ALLO-MORPHS, variants that appear in a different context. Another way of looking at strong and weak forms, then, is to consider them as allomorphs of the same morpheme. Thus /wɪl/ (*She will?*), /əl/ (*Jane'll go*), and /l/ (*I'll go too*) are pronounced differently, but native speakers associate them as forms of the same morpheme, *will*. This is also true of /ɪz/ and /z/ for *is*, /nɑt/ and /ənt/ for *not*, and /ðɛm/ and /əm/ for *them*.

Here are some other examples of allomorphs of the same morpheme:

- The article *a* becomes *an* before a word starting with a vowel phoneme: *a hoe, an hour* /aur/.
- The verb *say* /se/ changes to [sɛ]- before the suffixes /z/ and /d/ (*says, said*).
- *Five* /faiv/ changes to [fɪf]- before the suffix /θ/ (as in *fifth*).
- *History* changes to *histor-* (losing its final /i/) before suffixes like *-ic* and *-ian*.

A common way to show morphological structure is to use a plus, the sign for 'morpheme boundary,' to indicate the juncture or "stitch" between each morpheme, whether in phonemic representation or in conventional orthography. Thus, *fifth* consists of *five+th*, *fifths* is *five+th+s*, *said* is /se+d/, *undesirable* is *un+desir(e)+able*, *historic* is *histor(y)+ic*, and *historians* is *histor(y)+ian+s*. For a fuller representation, the inner structure is shown as a branching tree that subdivides the form into its component parts layer by layer, as in (a-b) in figure 7.e. The same structure can also be shown with a labeled (indexed) bracketing of the parts, as in (c), but although this method is easier on the typesetter, it can be harder on the reader to figure out.

Why our emphasis on grammar here? It is because grammar not only helps us interpret pronunciation, as we saw with weak forms, but may also directly *determine* how (and whether) phonological rules operate. Consider the possible use of weak forms for the italicized words in the following pairs of sentences:

1. a. We're *going to* come.	b. We're *going to* Pittsburgh.
2. a. They *want to* come.	b. Tom's the one they *want to* come.
3. a. They *used to* cook outside a lot.	b. This is the pan I *used to* cook the peas.

If you are like other English speakers (especially Americans), you find it natural to reduce /góɪŋ tu/, /wɔ́nt tu/ (~ /wɑ́nt tu/), and /júzd tu/ all the way to [gənə], [wənə], and [jùstə] in the (a) versions but *not* in the (b) versions on the right. This is because

Figure 7.e. Morphological structure

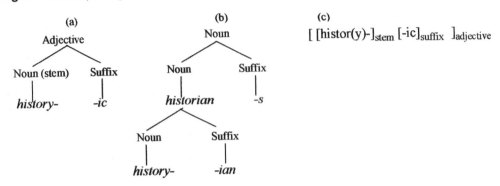

of differences in SYNTAX, that is, sentence structure. In (1.b), *to* begins a separate phrase of direction, and in (2.b) and (3.b) the *to* is preceded by a phrasal gap that resulted from movement of a word out of that position (*they want **Tom** to come, I used **the pan** to cook the peas*). The difference could again be shown with tree structures or by simply using a symbol for the boundary, in this case the IPA's double-bar ‖ meaning 'phrase boundary.' Thus, the (b) sentences might be shown as *We're going ‖ to Pittsburgh, Tom's the one they want ‖ to come, This is the pan I used ‖ to cook potatoes.* Like the morpheme boundary +, the word boundary #, and the foot boundary |, the phrase boundary ‖ may not appear as an audible gap in pronunciation, but it does block the kinds of coalescence and assimilation occurring in the (a) sentences.

The interpenetration of grammar and pronunciation is even stronger in the inflectional system of a language, as we will see in the next section.

Exercise 7.4

(A) Divide the following words into morphemes, using + boundaries, tree structures, or both, as your instructor prefers. A few of these are MONOMORPHEMIC (containing just one morpheme) and therefore indivisible.

1. grandmother	6. twelfths	11. phonemic	16. thermometer
2. yellowishness	7. avenue	12. babysitter	17. impersonality
3. employees	8. tailgating	13. magazine	18. globalization
4. characterized	9. developmental	14. prewashed	19. irreversible
5. unjustifiable	10. rewritten	15. hydroelectricity	20. moisturizer

(B) Using a [fənɛ́rɪk rɛ̀prəzənthéʃn̩] to show pronunciation variants, identify the allomorphs of each morpheme as used in the contexts provided. Do not transcribe the whole form; just the variants of the indicated morpheme. In some cases, the morpheme is "Ø," deleted or unrealized.

Example: *do* /du/: He [dʌ]-es his work, He [dɪ]-d (past) his work, I [do]-n't (present) want it.

1. past participle suffix /d/: *I have play___, I have finish___, I have plant___, I have eat___.*
2. *nature* /nétʃər/: _____al
3. *five* /faiv/: ___ty, *three* /θri/: ____ty
4. *sheep* /ʃip/, _____herd
5. *include* /ɪnklúd/, _____ive
6. *habit* /hǽbɪt/, _____ual
7. *obey* /obé/, _____ient
8. *solve* /sɑlv/, _____tion; *satisfy* /sǽtəsfài/, _____tion

7.6 Phonology in grammar. Morphology, the forms that words take, is subdivided into two areas or (in some theories)[5] two separate components of the linguistic system. INFLECTION is the way in which a word is adapted to carry syntactic information such as number (singular/plural), case (subject/object forms), agreement, and tense. DERIVATION is the set of processes that derive or create related forms in the vocabulary system (or LEXICON). The difference is not always clear, but consider the following forms of *relate*: if you were compiling an English dictionary, which ones would you include in the same entry as the base word, and which ones would you give separate entries to?

relative, relating, relativistic, relation, relates, related, relational, relatability, unrelatability

You probably assigned *relates, related,* and *relating* to *relate,* because they are all inflectional forms of the same verb; the other forms are derived from *relate* but are felt to be distinct words.

7.6.1 Inflectional morphology. English has less inflectional morphology than certain other languages (e.g., Japanese, Latin, Russian, Spanish, Greek, Arabic), but what it has—mainly noun plurals and verb tenses—is illustrative. The traditional assumption seems to be that such forms are learned as wholes without manipulation of their parts. Thus, for languages such as Latin, students are asked to recite full PARADIGMS (sets of forms): for the verb *love,* they chant *amō, amās, amat, amāmus,* and so on. But there is a body of evidence demonstrating that in most cases, humans acquiring their first language do not memorize whole paradigms, but assemble the forms by adding morphemes and then applying general rules to adjust their pronunciation. This is why you have no difficulty in instantly supplying a plural for a noun such as *gleesh*—one gleesh, two gleeshes—even though you have never heard it before, could not have memorized it (we made it up), and have no meaning for it. As we will see, though, the rules that produce such forms demonstrate the impossibility of describing pronunciation without reference to grammar, or grammar without reference to pronunciation.

7.6.2 A case study: English plural formation. In the following discussion, we will focus on plural formation, analyzing the allomorphs of the plural suffix to discover their CONDITIONING, the factors that determine which is used where. Begin with the following set of nouns and say their plurals, paying attention to how you pronounce them:

Set 1: *pig, zoo, lab, sister, cousin, law, lathe, glove, idea, friend, painting, album, cookie*

Although the plurals are spelled with the letter *-s*, what we really add is the voiced phoneme /z/. There is a reason for that. Look at the final phoneme of the stem in these nouns: whether consonant or vowel, it is voiced. This class of nouns is the largest one, so the most general way to represent the English plural suffix is /z/. Thus, the plural of the first word is /pɪg+z/ (the plus sign again indicates a morpheme boundary). Note that there is another suffix, possessive *-'s* as in *the pig's tail,* that is also pronounced as /z/, but it can have a different effect, as we will see later.

Consider the next set of nouns, again saying their plurals out loud (do not whisper):

Set 2: *cat, insect, myth, lake, tulip, cliff, ship, tariff, carrot, reef, asp, mattock, faith*

In this case, the /z/ suffix devoices to [s] in assimilation to the final consonant of the stem, which is voiceless:

/z/ → [-voice] / [-voice] ____#

This devoicing rule is PHONOLOGICALLY CONDITIONED: it is wholly cued by adjacent sounds, without complications from any other factors. As expressed earlier (without further conditions), the rule will apply to the possessive /z/ too, which is just what happens: *the cat's* [kæts] *tail.*

Now assume that English grammar adds the /z/ suffix to the next nouns: what happens?

Set 3: *bush, premise, purpose, ax, college, mirage, rhinoceros, chance, trapeze, bench*

You will note that /z/ stays /z/ in these plurals but that a vowel is inserted—a lax high [ɪ] for some speakers (§5.5), but the slightly lower schwa [ə] for many others. (We will go with the latter.) What cues this insertion? Note that each of these nouns ends in a sibilant (§6.6): /s z ʃ ʒ tʃ dʒ/. Because /z/ is also a sibilant, this would mean two sibilants clustered at the end of the word, for example, "/bʊʃz/" for the plural of *bush*. English phonotactics (§6.10) does not permit two sibilants in the coda, so the solution is an insertion, or EPENTHESIS, of a vowel to separate them:

Ø → ə / sibilant __ sibilant #

or, expressed with features,

$$\emptyset \rightarrow \text{ə} / [+\text{coronal}, +\text{strident}] \underline{\quad} [+\text{coronal}, +\text{strident}] \#$$

Thus, /bʊʃ+z/ changes to [bʊ́ʃəz]. This rule is likewise phonologically conditioned: we apply it on the basis of the sounds alone. If other suffixes create a final sibilant cluster, epenthesis should also occur—which indeed it does with the possessive /z/: *the bush's* [bʊ́ʃəz] *roots*.

The devoicing and epenthesis rules suffice for the majority of English noun plurals, so let's summarize those rules before proceeding to trickier patterns. The grammar of the language attaches /z/ to a noun as the plural marker, feeds this formation to the pronunciation system as an UNDERLYING REPRESENTATION, and the suffix then undergoes two rules to output the correct form. The representation in figure 7.f, called a DERIVATION, shows how this process operates step by step. (The abbreviation *N.A.* means that the rule is ***not applicable*** in this instance.)

As an experiment, repeat the previous derivation for /bʊʃ+z/ but *with rules 1 and 2 in reverse order*, that is, with devoicing applying before schwa-epenthesis. The output, if you trace it step by step, will now be *[bʊ́ʃəs], which is wrong. In some theories of phonology, cases like this one suggest that the rules of language, as mental operations carried out on forms, are ORDERED, just as the series of commands in a computer program must also follow a certain sequence.

Let's now go on to the next noun class; again, pronounce the plurals:

Set 4: *leaf, path, house, knife, life, shelf, hoof, wreath*

The underlying formations /lif+z/, /pæθ+z/, /haus+z/ emerge as [livz pæðz háuzəz]. This time, the problem is not the suffix, which is voiced as it should be after voiced sounds (including the schwa inserted between sibilants in the case of *houses*); rather, it is how the voiceless /f θ s/ that end the stem get voiced to [v ð z]. These nouns apparently undergo a fricative voicing rule:

$$[+\text{continuant}, -\text{sonorant}] \rightarrow [+\text{voice}] / \underline{\quad} + z$$

Figure 7.f. The derivation of English plurals

underlying representation:	/pɪg + z/	/kæt+ z/	/bʊʃ+ z/
1. $\emptyset \rightarrow$ ə / sibilant____sibilant	*N.A.*	*N.A.*	[bʊʃ+əz]
2. /z/ $\rightarrow$ s / [-voice] ____ #	*N.A.*	kæt+ s	*N.A.*
3. Other purely phonetic rules:	pʰɪːg z	kʰæʔt s	[bʊʃ əz]
phonetic output:	[pʰɪːgz]	[kʰæʔts]	[bʊ́ʃəz]

Yet this rule, unlike the others, does *not* apply automatically with phonological conditioning alone, because the possessive /z/ declines to undergo it: *the leaf's* [lifs] *color.*
Hence there is GRAMMATICAL CONDITIONING: to apply the rule correctly, one has to take
into account the grammar of the form, namely that the /z/ is not just any /z/, but a specifically *pluralizing* /z/. In fact, even for plurals, not all fricatives voice before /z/, as we
see in *reefs, masses,* and *myths.* Why *leaves* but *reefs*? There is no clue in either the pronunciation of /lif/ and /rif/ or in their grammar as to why one voices but the other does
not. Speakers simply have to memorize the class of nouns in the lexicon of English that
undergo a special rule here. This complication is called LEXICAL CONDITIONING, meaning that the applicability of the rule depends on the particular word itself: some words
do, other words do not.

Again let's summarize: the underlying representation of the plural morpheme is /z/,
surfacing as three allomorphs [z], [s], [əz] according to whether epenthesis and devoicing apply. Both rules are phonologically conditioned, which is why English speakers
can automatically apply them to pluralize made-up words like *bloog* (→ [blugz]), *blook*
(→ [bluks]), or *blooch* (→ [blútʃəz]). But a third rule, fricative voicing, applies *only*
to plural /z/, not possessive /z/, and *only* in a certain class of nouns; these conditions are
respectively grammatical and lexical. Regardless of whether you acquired English as a
child or whether you studied it as a second language, phonological conditioning was the
easiest type to master because it is straightforward, based on pronunciation and nothing
more. Grammatical conditioning is more complex, requiring you to keep in mind grammatical distinctions when deciding whether to apply a rule or not; and lexical conditioning is the biggest challenge of all, because you can only memorize which
morphemes undergo a special rule. Given the unpredictability of lexical conditioning, it
is not surprising that speakers differ in the words they assign to the affected class: some
include the last two nouns in Set 4 in the fricative voicing group (→ [hʊvz, riðz]),
whereas others let the regular rules apply (→ [hʊfs, riθs]).

Now we proceed to another typical problem. How do you say the plurals of the
next set?

Set 5: *sheep, deer, series, moose, fish, aircraft, Swiss, Japanese*

For these, the plural /z/ is simply dropped: *this sheep is, these sheep are.* The rule
would be:

z → Ø / + ___#

that is, /z/ drops or becomes zero as a word-final suffix; indeed, the suffix is said to be
a ZERO ALLOMORPH in this case. Once again, we encounter grammatical conditioning,
since the possessive /z/ is unaffected (*the sheep's appetite*), and also lexical conditioning, because other nouns with similar pronunciations and grammar retain their plural
suffix (*sheep sheepØ ,* but *heap heaps*). There may, however, be partial SEMANTIC CON-

DITIONING, because if you know that a singular noun ending in -/iz/ refers to a nationality (*Japanese, Chinese, Portuguese,* but not *cheese, freeze, breeze*), you can successfully apply this plural suffix-dropping rule.[6]

Now consider the plurals of the next two sets:

Set 6: *ox, child*

Set 7: *alumnus, vertebra, criterion, analysis, stratum, curriculum, cherub*

In both sets, possessive /z/ comes out as it should: *the ox's* [áksəz] *head, the child's* [tʃaildz] *head, the curriculum's current problems.* But for the plural in Set 6, /z/ is replaced by a special allomorph, /(r)ən/, that is phonetically unrelated to [z, s, əz]. Speakers do not produce it by applying rules to /z/, but by directly replacing /z/ in a special class of nouns, so the change is not only lexically conditioned but IRREGULAR (i.e., not governed by a *rule,* Latin *regula*). As often happens with irregularities, fewer nouns get assigned to an odd group in its transmission across the generations, and today the comparable plurals *eyen, kine,* and *shoon* are archaic, replaced by forms generated by modern rules: *eyes, cows, shoes.* In Set 7, the memorized plural is one that was retained from the Latin, Greek, or Hebrew original: *alumni, vertebrae, criteria, analyses, strata, curricula, cherubim.* But given the cost in memory of lexical conditioning, these plurals gradually succumb to regularization, and probably most speakers today say *curriculums* and *cherubs.* Note also *antenna,* which retains its Latin plural *antennae* for the specialized sense of insect body parts, but has been regularized to *antennas* for radio or TV reception.

But all languages retain some irregularities, as we see in the next group:

Set 8: *mouse, louse, foot, tooth, goose, man, woman*

A plural such as *oxen* at least has an identifiable plural suffix, *ox* + *en*; but for the nouns in Set 8 there is a lexically conditioned vowel change inside the stem to show plurality. A word like [mais] or [wímɪn] is a PORTMANTEAU, a form containing two morphemes (*mouse* + plural, *woman* + plural) that are indivisibly fused. We just have to memorize that the form in question /maus+z/ (= *plural* /z/, but not possessive /z/) is replaced in the plural by the special form *mice* [mais]. Again, variation shows the precariousness of lexical conditioning: some speakers say *mice* for rodents, but regularize it to *mouses* when talking about the input devices for computers.

One more common situation in morphology is illustrated by the final four sets of nouns.

Set 9a: *people*

Set 9b: *scissors, pliers, pants, shorts*

Set 9c: *linguistics, politics, mathematics*

Set 9d: *rice, chalk, furniture, soap, news*

People is obligatorily plural (*people* **are**), despite its zero plural ending;[7] for a singular, we have to switch to a totally unrelated form, *person,* a substitution known as SUPPLETION. The nouns in Set 9b come with a plural /z/ that is pronounced according to the regular rules, but it is "built in": these nouns cannot be used without it and therefore lack a corresponding singular form. Those in Set 9c have a final [s] that confuses learners—is it an allomorph of plural /z/, or not? They tend to arrive at an indeterminate analysis: *politics is? are?*

Finally, the nouns in Set 9d are singular and exempt from normal pluralization: in traditional terms, they are DEFECTIVE in not accepting the plural /z/ suffix or any allomorph thereof. To indicate quantities with them, we have to add phrases such as *two grains of (rice), two pieces (of chalk/furniture), two bars of (soap), two items of (news).* Such nouns are called MASS NOUNS because they refer to undifferentiated substances that cannot be counted directly—which seems like semantic conditioning until you realize that if you have a plate of little green things called *peas,* why not call one of little white things *rices?* The fact that related languages such as French and Spanish also have mass nouns but disagree with English about which ones are assigned to this category only serves to demonstrate the presence of arbitrary lexical conditioning here too.

As we noted earlier, other languages may have more morphology, but the examples we have just provided illustrate the usual kinds of problems, as well as fascinating patterns that are English-specific.

Exercise 7.5

(A) When explaining grammar, many textbook writers view the written language as *the* language, forgetting that speakers acquire a first language as young children from *oral* input. Try to express the rules for English pluralization without ever referring to pronunciation or phonological conditioning. How does doing so complicate the rules?

(B) Give the plural of each of the following nouns and explain the derivation of its pronunciation.

   1. graph   2. bunch   3. thief   4. Lebanese   5. homework

(C) Orthography has its own rules (see chapter 4). Add a /z/ suffix (the plural one in the case of nouns, the present tense —*s* in the case of verbs) to the following words. Express the orthographic rule that applies. To what extent do the spelling changes reflect change in pronunciation?

nouns: *bully, penny, fly, sky, philosophy, day, toy*
verbs: *hurry, carry, apply, try, pay, lay*

(D) Past tense forms of English verbs: Review the step-by-step analysis that we carried out for plural formation, and then analyze past tense formation in the same way, proceeding from one set of verbs to the next. Formulate the rules and apparent conditioning as precisely as possible.

Set 1: *play, beg, accuse, tie, love, expose, pledge, double, stir, reveal, agree, disturb, explain*
Set 2: *punish, reach, stuff, reduce, link, punch, promise, work, cough, panic, worship*
Set 3: *start, elect, remind, hunt, wait, demand, trade, result, wade, want, invite*
Set 4: *keep, leave, feel, mean, deal, sleep, dream, leap*
Set 5: *let, burst, cut, shut, hurt, put, cast, set, bet, fit*
Set 6: *drive, weave, feed, drink, eat, begin, fly, come, sing, know, run, take, hang, hold, find, spit*
Set 7: *go, be*

7.7 The phoneme exchange. In many languages, the vowel and consonant phonemes of a stem tend to stay constant from one form to the next. This is the default case in English too: if you know that *neighbor* is /nébər/, then it is a safe bet that it keeps that pronunciation in *neighbors* and in derivatives like *neighborly, neighborliness,* and *neighborhood.* Likewise, if you know that *public* is /pʌ́blɪk/ (or /pʌ́blək/) and add the suffix *-ly* to it, it seems logical for the /k/ to stay as is, /pʌ́blɪk+li/, unaffected by either the following /l/ or by the intervening morpheme boundary between the two parts. In short, although we expect affixes to show some allomorphy (as in pluralization), we tend to assume INVARIANCE in the main part of a word, its stem.

But phonemes sometimes *do* switch in related forms of a stem. Thus *sane* has /e/, but when you add the noun-creating suffix *-ity*, the vowel changes to /æ/: /sǽnəti/, not */sénəti/. Such switches are MORPHOPHONEMIC CHANGES because they change phonemes under morphological conditions. The switched phonemes (/e/ and /æ/ in this case) are then said to ALTERNATE. Likewise, *-ly* may not affect *public,* but *-ity* does: not the vowel this time, but the consonant, since *publicity* is pronounced /pəblísəti/, not */pəblíkəti/. In this case, /k/ alternates with /s/.

Morphophonemic changes are hard to anticipate because English spelling may mask them—*sane* and *sanity* are both spelled with *san-*, and the stem-final consonant of *public(ity)* is spelled *c* whether its pronunciation is /k/ or /s/. This is no problem for speakers of English who have heard both allomorphs and know that the first has one phoneme where the other has a different one; but to learners—both children learning their first language and older students studying it as a second or foreign language—morphophonemic changes can be the hardest aspects of phonology to control.

Vowels first . . .

7.7.1 Vowel alternations. Although there is no easy way to master alternations, there *are* some recurrent patterns in English that can be brought out, and in the following section we summarize the main ones.[8]

Stress-based alternations: We have seen (chapter 2) that unlike *neighbor-ly, -ness, -hood,* certain suffixes cause stress to shift to another syllable. In that case, the originally stressed vowel tends to reduce to /ə/, whereas a vowel that was originally "submerged" in the mid-central area reemerges as a full vowel (§5.5). An example is *átom,* whose vowels are /æ/ and /ə/, but when the suffix *-ic* pulls stress to the right in *atómic,* the first vowel reduces to /ə/, while the second one now sounds forth as /ɑ́/. The stem acts as if it were "ǽtɑm," with each vowel surfacing in turn depending on stress position. But "ǽtɑm" is not a normal phonemic representation; it underlies both /ǽtəm/ and /ətɑ́m/ but differs from both of the pronounced versions of the stem. Because "ǽtɑm" expresses a morphological generalization at a deeper phonological level, it is sometimes called a MORPHOPHONEMIC REPRESENTATION and is enclosed in double slants, //ǽtɑm//.[9] Obviously, though, you cannot tell from the normal pronunciation of /ǽtəm/ alone what its other vowel is until you hear and learn the form with a different stress pattern, *atómic.* It is true that orthography helps a little: once you have learned that /ǽtəm/ is spelled *atom,* then if stress shifts to the second syllable, the newly-stressed vowel will probably be one that is spelled with an *o.* In *atómic,* /ɑ/ qualifies (chapter 4), whereas /e/, /ai/, /æ/, or others are highly unlikely.

    Laxing: In other formations, the stress stays in the same position, but the addition of a suffix causes the vowel to change, as in *sane/sanity.* There are two generalizations that may be useful in this kind of alternation.

- The alternation usually involves a laxer or less diphthongal vowel, as in /e/ ~ /æ/ in *sanity,* although at a different height—the low front vowel /æ/ in this case.
- This laxing is most common when (a) the vowel is three or more syllables from the end ("trisyllabic laxing"), as in *sánity;* (b) before *-ic,* as in *volcano/volcanic;* and (c) before two or more consonants.

The table in figure 7.g gives more examples, although not all possibilities can be illustrated. The alternations are lexically conditioned, as evidenced by the presence of

- exceptions: the same stressed vowel (unlaxed) is retained in *use/usual, brave/bravery, drape/drapery, pirate/piracy*
- arbitrary variants: *private/privacy* and *obese/obesity* have the expected alternations in traditional British pronunciation but keep the same vowels in American English.

    Since these alternations are so peculiarly English, it may be useful to examine where they came from. Old English had long and short vowels, and toward the end of the Middle English period (1200–1400), the long ones began to migrate, unleashing an

Figure 7.g. Vowel alternations

	≥3 syllables from the end	before -ic	before ≥2 consonants
/e/ ~ /æ/	*sane, sanity*	*volcano, volcanic*	
/ai/ ~ /ɪ/	*divine, divinity*	*cycle, cyclic*	*five, fifth*
/au/ ~ /ʌ/	*pronounce, pronunciation*		*foul, fulsome*
/i/ ~ /ɛ/	*extreme, extremity*	*meter, metric*	*deep, depth; sleep, slept*
/o/ ~ /ɑ/ (RP /ɒ/)	*provoke, provocative*	*tone, tonic*	*nose, nostril*
/u/ ~ /ɑ/ (RP /ɒ/)	*school, scholarly*		*goose, gosling*

upheaval called the Great Vowel Shift. The changes were still underway during Shakespeare's time and have never really stopped (§5.6.3). Figure 7.h summarizes earlier versus later pronunciations. Pronounce each word so that you can appreciate the changes it underwent. First, say the word in medieval fashion by using its older vowel; next, say it the way we do in modern English. Finally, trace the changes that we have mapped out on the accompanying vowel trapezoid.

Some scholars infer that the trigger was /ɑː/ moving forward and crowding /ɛː/ into the /e/ zone: this forced original /eː/ to move up to /iː/, which in turn displaced the original /iː/ (which could not go any higher) to become the diphthong /əi/, then /ai/—with parallel movements in the back vowels. This is the PUSH-CHAIN theory. Others argue for the opposite causality: the high vowels /iː/ and /uː/ diphthongized to /əi/ and /əu/ (the Shakespearean pronunciation, but today /ai/ and /au/), leaving gaps that were filled by the original /eː/ and /oː/, which in turn caused /ɛː/ and /ɔː/ to move up into *their* gaps, and so on. This is the PULL-CHAIN theory.[10]

By whichever chaining, each long vowel ended up in a different position as a tense vowel or diphthong, with two results that distinguish English from many other European languages. First, we continue to *write* these vowels as they were formerly pro-

Figure 7.h. The Great Vowel Shift: From Chaucer to Shakespeare

/iː/: *wife, night, ice, vine* → /əi/ → /ai/

/eː/: *beet, weep, serene* → /i/

/ɛː/: *beat, clean, sea* → /eː/→ /i/

/ɑː/: *name, sane*→ /æː/ → /e/

/uː/: *out, loud, profound,* → /əu/ → /au/

/oː/: *moon, goose, school, who* → /u/

/ɔː/: *loan, home, road, both, stone* → /o/

/au/: *law, sauce, naughty* → /ɔ/

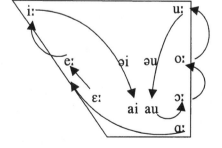

nounced; note for instance the doubled *ee, oo* in *weep* and *moon* for the originally long vowels /eː/ and /oː/. Second, whenever the originally long vowels left behind shortened laxed versions under the conditions described in figure 7.g, we have allomorphs today with different vowels: *divine* with /ai/ but *divinity* with /ɪ/, both originally /iː/, and *sleep* with /i/ and *slept* with /ɛ/, both originally /eː/.

Exercise 7.6

(A) For the three words *melody, algebra,* and *photograph,* give a derived form with a stress change, and transcribe the vowel alternation(s) that result.

(B) For each following group of pairs, identify the vowel alternation (using the table in figure 7.g as a guide) and the condition that triggers the change (if one is apparent to you).

crime, criminal; line, linear; Bible, Biblical	obscene, obscenity; repeat, repetitive
wise, wisdom; wide, width	athlete, athletic; meter, metric
code, codify; omen, ominous; mediocre, mediocrity	mean, meant; deal, dealt; keep, kept
table, tabulate; explain, explanatory	reptile, reptilian
parasite, parasitic	neurosis, neurotic; diagnosis, diagnostic
redeem, redemption	south, southern
penal, penalty	nation, national
holy, holiday	hero, heroism

(C) Give reasons for why such vowel changes (as in B) can be a special challenge for ESOL students. To what extent do you believe that these changes can be taught and practiced?

7.7.2 Consonant alternations. As with vowels, consonant alternations have resulted from 2000 years of changes in English and in the languages from which it obtained much of its vocabulary. There are quite a few of them, and the simplest way to survey the main types is with a list of examples in sets.

   1. *five, fif+th; give, gif+t; twelve, twelf+th; hundred -/d/, hundred+th -/tθ/*
   In these words, a suffix consisting of a voiceless obstruent causes a preceding fricative to assimilate by becoming voiceless. Relatively few words are affected by this change, though, and the -/t/ suffix in *gift* is no longer productive.

   2. *long -/ŋ/, long+er -/ŋg/-, long+est -/ŋg/-; strong -/ŋ/, strong+er -/ŋg/-, strong+est -/ŋg/-*

In adjectives, a final /ŋ/ alternates with /ŋg/, with a stop /g/ appearing when a vowel-initial suffix is added. The change is grammatically conditioned because verbs are exempt: *sing+er, long+er* (one who longs for something) with /ŋ/ only.[11] The underlying representation may be something like //lɔŋg+ər//, with a rule that ordinarily drops the /g/ after /ŋ/ except when it is followed by a vowel in adjectives—and in nouns too, as we see in *prolong* with -/ŋ/ and *pro-longation* with -/ŋg/-.

3. *anger, angr+y; hunger, hungr+y; cylinder, cylindr+ical; enter, entr+ance; center, centr+al*
   In words like these, final /ər/ (= [ɚ] in American English, [ə] in RP) as in *ang<u>er</u>* alternates with consonantal /r/ as in *ang<u>r</u>-y*. There are two ways of accounting for this relationship:

   (a) The underlying representation of *anger* is //ǽŋgər//, with a rule that drops the /ə/ of its /ər/ when a vowel-initial suffix follows—or, what amounts to the same thing, the rule de-syllabifies [ɚ] to consonantal [r] (§6.4.3).
   (b) The underlying representation is //æŋgr//, as in *angr-y,* with a rule that *inserts* /ə/ (or syllabifies /r/ to [ɚ]) when the final /Cr/ cluster ends the word. (Cf. the similar pattern in *simpl-icity* [sɪmplísəti] but *simple* [símpl̩], and *prism-atic* [prɪzmǽtɪk] but *prism* [prízm̩].)

   Which solution correctly describes the structure of English? Each has adherents, but there are formations such as *rubber/rubber-y, burglar/burglar-y, polymer/polymer-ize* in which the /ə/ of /ər/ fails to drop as in solution (a). Either there is lexical conditioning, or solution (b) is preferable. The latter also receives phonotactic support: because English does not permit final clusters of /Cr/, there seems to be a natural reason for why schwa epenthesis applies to break them up (→ [Cər]).

4. *angle, angul+ar; circle, circul+ar; table, tabul+ate; strangle, strangul+ation*
   In the plain form of these words, the stem ends in a syllabic liquid ([l̩]), phonemically /əl/: *angle* = /ǽŋgəl/ (§6.4.3). But when a vowel-initial suffix is added, the stem switches to a longer allomorph with -/jul/- or reduced -/jəl/-. Again, there are two approaches:

   (a) The underlying representation of a stem such as *angle* is //ǽŋgəl//, with a rule that changes its /əl/ to /jul/ when a vowel-initial suffix has been added.
   (b) The underlying representation of the stem instead has /jul/ (*angle* = //ǽŋgjul//), with a rule that changes its /jul/ to /əl/ when it is word-final (not followed by a suffix).

   In this case, both solutions run into exceptions. The form *global* /glóbəl/ does *not* change to **globul-* in suffixed forms like *globalize,* as solution (a) might predict; but likewise the unsuffixed form of *pustular* is *pustule*, not **pustle* as solution (b) would predict. Evidently, then, there is lexical conditioning: whether speakers relate the allomorphs with an /əl/ → /jul/ rule or with a /jul/ → /əl/ rule, they have to memorize which stems do it and which ones do not. There is also grammatical conditioning: the -/jul/- allomorph of the stem appears when a vowel-initial *derivational* suffix is added (one creating a new word with a different part of speech), but not when a vowel-initial *inflectional* suffix is present. This is why *strangle* has *strangul-ation* as the derived noun but simply *strangl-ing* (never **strangul-ing*) as another form of the verb.

5. ***hymn, hymnal; sign, signature; paradigm, paradigmatic; bomb, bombard***
   Words like these have a final "silent consonant" in the plain form, but show an allomorph with that consonant pronounced when a vowel-initial suffix has been added. Thus we have /hɪm/ but /hím<u>n</u>+əl/. Once more, there are two ways of analyzing these alternations:

   (a) The special consonant is *inserted* when a vowel-initial suffix follows: underlying representation //hɪm// → /hɪmn/-.
   (b) The special consonant is present in the underlying representation of the stem, but is *dropped* from pronunciation whenever a vowel is *not* added: //hɪmn//- → /hɪm/.

   The first solution begs the question of *which* consonant is to be inserted in a given stem: /n/? /g/? /b/? The second solution recognizes that the consonant is already there as part of the stem and is deleted for, say, phonotactic reasons because an English syllable cannot end in the clusters /mn/, /gn/, /gm/, or /mb/. The latter solution is a more faithful reflection of the facts.

6a. ***public, public+ity, public+ize; medic(al), medic+ine; electric, electric+ity; analogue (-ous), analog+y; fanatic, fanatic+ism***
   We have already noted the /k/ → /s/ switch in such stems. In a similar way, voiced /g/ as in *analog-* changes to /dʒ/. These two rules are often called VELAR SOFTENING. As you can see, they apply before high front /i/ (*analogy*) and /ɪ/ (*medicine*), although the /ɪ/ can then reduce to schwa if unstressed; but it also occurs before /ai/ (*publicize, analogize*). To this phonological conditioning we must add grammatical conditioning: velar softening only occurs before a suffix boundary (<u>k</u>ick does not become <u>s</u>ick), and specifically before a *derivational* suffix (thus ki<u>ck</u> + ing does not become ki<u>ss</u> + ing either). Hence the underlying representation //pʌ́blɪk+(noun-forming) ɪti// changes regularly to /pʌblísɪti/.

6b. ***private, privac+y; president, presidenc+y; vacant, vacanc+y, galact(ic), galax-y***
   As it turns out, /t/ also undergoes a "softening" rule, changing to /s/ before a derivational suffix beginning with /i/—but in this case, *not* before /ai/: *pri-*

vate/privacy, but *privatize*, not **privacize*. This rule is therefore separate from velar softening, despite the resemblance. Note that /t/ softening is also behind the change of underlying //gælækt+i// → /gǽləksi/, despite being masked by the spelling with *x*.

7. *please, pleas+ure; seize, seiz+ure; rapt, rapt+ure; erase, eras+ure; grand, grand+eur*

   Do these changes seem familiar? We have already encountered them (§6.9) as a rule of ALVEOPALATALIZATION: the alveolar obstruents /t d s z/ fuse with a following /j/ and are then pronounced as /tʃ dʒ ʃ ʒ/. But what is the evidence for an underlying /j/ in *seizure* /síʒər/? Note that although we hear only -/ər/ in these forms, the noun-forming suffix is actually /jər/, as in *fail/failure* /feljər/. This evidence suggests that the underlying representation of what we pronounce as /síʒər/ is actually //siz+jər//, and that the rule of alveopalatalization is obligatory inside a word, as in these forms, though it is optional between words, as in *as you*.

8. *face, fac+ial; part, part+ial; delete, delet+ion; protect, protect+ion; Egypt, Egypt+ian; digest, digest+ion; music, music+ian; cooperate, cooperat+ion; colleague, colleg+ial*

   The alternations in this group seem more complex: we have seen /s/ ~ /ʃ/ as in *face/facial*, but note now /t/ ~ /ʃ/ in *delete/deletion*[12] and /k/ ~ /ʃ/ in *music/musician*. To understand what is happening, we need to find other forms that show the same affixes *without* interaction with the stem-final consonant. Those forms do exist:

   - *centenn+ial* = -/iəl/; *editor, editor+ial* = -/iəl/; *proverb, proverb+ial* -/iəl/
   - *opine, opin+ion* = -/jən/; *rebel, rebell+ion* = -/jən/
   - *Ukraine, Ukrain+ian* = -/iən/; *Brazil Brazil+ian* = -/jən/; *Canada, Canad+ian* = -/iən/; *mammal, mammal+ian* = -/iən/; *Darwin, Darwin+ian* = -/iən/

   The suffix spelled *-ion* for forming nouns is simply -/jən/; the others, though, alternate between a two-syllable allomorph with the vowel /i/ and another version with the glide /j/. There is no obvious reason for why /i/ loses its syllabicity and is glided to /j/ in *Brazilian* but not in *mammalian*, or in *Pennsylvanian* but not in *Ukrainian*. We seem to be dealing with lexical conditioning here: some words change /i/ to /j/, and some do not.[13]

   Thus, the suffixes in these formations begin with /j/ or with an /i/ that can become /j/. With that established, everything else falls into place: the alternations are complex only because they result from multiple rule applications. Assuming the underlying representations //part+iəl// and //mjuzɪk+iən// to show the relationship of *partial* and *musician* to *part* and *music*, we can see in figure 7.i the step-by-step generation of the phonetic output:

Figure 7.i. Rules for allomorphs: A derivation

underlying representation:	//pɑrt + iəl//	//mjuzɪk+ iən//
1. velar softening:	*N.A.*	mjuzɪs+ iən
2. alveolar softening:	pɑrs + iəl	*N.A.*
3. gliding:	pɑrs jəl	mjuzɪs jən
4. alveopalatalization:	pɑrʃəl	mjuzɪʃ ən
5. other purely phonetic rules:	pʰɑrʃl̩	mjuzɪʃn̩
phonetic output:	[pʰɑ́rʃl̩]	[mjuzíʃn̩]

Exercise 7.7

(A) For each of the following words, give a derived form with a morphophonemic change. Identify the alternation, indicate whether it seems to be due to one of the rules described in this section, or to some other change.

1. proceed	4. infant	7. vibrate	10. miracle
2. young	5. twelve	8. commerce	11. divide
3. aroma	6. tempest	9. condemn	12. idiot

(B) Pair work: two-way dictation. Prepare a list of three English pairs showing morphophonemic alternations and perhaps stress changes, for example, *various/-variety*. In pairs, each dictates his/her list to the other for a *phonetic* transcription, and then both discuss the details that they perceived.

7.7.3 Rules, constraints, alternations: How deep does phonology go?
Although several theories have addressed the issues broached in the foregoing sections, we have generally followed the approach of LEXICAL(IST) PHONOLOGY (Kiparsky 1982; Kaisse and Shaw 1985), which posits two types of rules assigned to distinct components. Rules not based purely on phonetic conditioning are called LEXICAL RULES because they apply inside the lexicon as words and forms are assembled. Lexical rules are of two subtypes: Level 1 rules, which depend on lexical or word-specific conditioning, and Level 2 rules, which are based on grammatical conditioning. What we have described as morphophonemic rules and stress assignment rules (for both depend on factors such as part of speech and internal structure) are therefore lexical rules, considered to be part of the vocabulary system rather than belonging to the general phonological component of a language.

Once the lexically adjusted forms are joined together by the syntactic system, the second type of phonological rules applies. These POSTLEXICAL RULES include general processes that apply automatically with phonetic conditioning, for example, aspiration,

Figure 7.j. Lexicalist derivation of the pronunciation of a phrase

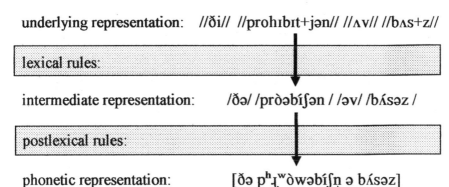

underlying representation: //ði// //prohɪbɪt+jən// //ʌv// //bʌs+z//

lexical rules:

intermediate representation: /ðə/ /pròəbíʃən / /əv/ /bʌ́səz /

postlexical rules:

phonetic representation: [ðə pʰɹ̬ʷòwəbíʃn̩ ə bʌ́səz]

but also including rules of stress adjustment, intonation, reduction, and sandhi that apply to whole phrases. Figure 7.j illustrates these types of rules in the derivation of the pronunciation of the phrase *the prohibition of buses*.

Yet other phonologists have questioned the existence of rules of any kind, and therefore of derivations of the type illustrated in figure 7.j. For example, those who adhere to Optimality Theory (Prince and Smolensky 1993) see pronunciation adjustments as due to resolutions of conflicts between two kinds of constraints: markedness constraints (in favored types of units and combinations of them) and "faithfulness" constraints (in retaining the underlying representation with minimal tampering). Consider the following proposed constraints (Fromkin 2000, 614–41) for English and, presumably, for other languages as well:

1. NOT-TOO-SIMILAR: clusters of similar consonants are not allowed at the beginning or ending of words.
2. RECOVER THE MORPHEME: at least one phoneme in a morpheme's underlying representation must be retained in the phonetic (surface) representation.
3. RETAIN OBSTRUENCY: An underlying phoneme that is an obstruent should remain [-sonorant] on the surface.
4. RETAIN ADJACENCY: Phonemes that are adjacent in the underlying representation should stay adjacent in the surface representation.

The first constraint is phonotactic and is therefore of the markedness type; the other three follow from the tendency toward faithfulness. Now, let us reconsider our earlier analysis of English plurals (§7.6.2). Given the underlying representation (UR) //bʌs+z// for the plural of *bus*, Optimality Theory holds that there are several "candidates" or possible pronunciations a speaker could attempt, and these are depicted as in figure 7.k in a table called a TABLEAU. Each solution for //bʌs+z // happens to violate one of these constraints, as indicated by the asterisks; and as the best or "optimal" solution (shown

Figure 7.k. A tableau for the constraints applying to *buses*

UR = bʌs+z	1. Not-too-similar	2. Recover the morpheme	3. Retain obstruency	4. Retain adjacency
[bʌsz]	*			
[bʌs]		*		
[bʌrz], [bʌnz], [bʌz]...			*	
☞[bʌsəz]				*

by the right-pointing hand in this theory), English speakers adopt the fourth candidate, with an epenthesized vowel creating a separate syllable for the /z/. This means that RETAIN ADJACENCY is ranked lower than the other constraints in English phonology and is therefore overridden to arrive at a pronunciation.

Obviously, a tableau showing why //prohɪbɪt+jən// is pronounced as [pʰɹʷòwəbíʃn̩] will be more complex than one that shows why //bʌsz// emerges as [bʌsəz]. But the principle is the same: like the "Not-too-similar" constraint against pronouncing //bʌsz// "as is," English has phonotactic constraints that disfavor the following:

- [h] between a stressed and unstressed vowel (§6.8)
- the post-stress sequence [tj], whence its resolution as [ʃ] (§6.9)
- nuclei other than [ə] or syllabic nasals or liquids in unstressed syllables (§6.4.3)

The thrust of Optimality Theory is that this language-specific ranking of constraints (rather than a series of phonological rules) is what yields the variety of phonetic and morphophonemic alterations that we observe in different languages.

However, in either theory of phonology—lexical (with rules) or optimal (without rules)—a fundamental question remains: *how deep does phonology go?* A representation such as /prohíbɪt/ is close to the sequence of vocal gestures that we make when articulating this word, aside from details such as /p/-aspiration and /r/-rounding that we add automatically. But we may feel skeptical about the more abstract levels of underlying structure required for explaining alternations like those in this chapter. Is a morphophonemic representation such as //prohɪbɪt +jən// for *prohibition* psychologically real as a fact about the pronunciation of this word? Do we really arrive at this mental representation of the noun in order to connect it to the verb? Are the rules (or constraints) for relating /prohíbɪt/ and /pròəbíʃən/ also real in our knowledge of the sound system of English? Are they part of what a nonnative learner must acquire as well?

The rules or constraints for morphophonemic alternations certainly have a special status, especially when they depend on grammatical and lexical conditioning. Consider the following observations:

1. A representation such as //prohɪbɪt +jən// is never pronounced "as is"—not even as a citation form, in its own foot, unconnected with anything else, freed of normal speaking constraints, not even in the most deliberate, rhythmically slowed and careful register, not even if we say it syl-la-ble by syl-la-ble ("pro, hi, bi, tyon").

2. Morphophonemic rules differ from other kinds of phonological processes. When English speakers study a foreign language, they carry over or TRANSFER (§6.11) rules such as aspiration, vowel lengthening, reduction, schwa-*r* merger, diphthongization, vowel nasalization, /l/ velarization, /r/ rounding, and syllabi-fication of /l/ and nasals. They apply phonotactic rules to simplify clusters that they find odd or insert [ə] in them as English does, and they project English stress rules onto the other language's words. They are usually unaware of trans-ferring these English rules, but the fact that they apply them so automatically (and find it so hard to suppress them) suggests that these rules are a real part of how they learned to speak. Morphophonemic rules such as vowel laxing and velar softening, on the other hand, are seldom transferred in this way to the sec-ond language; they stay behind in the English formations they are attached to.

3. Children quickly master the phonemes of their language(s), sorting them out almost programmatically. Normally, by the time they enter school, their phone-mic system is already in place. This means that for an early-acquired word such as *table,* they had no evidence of anything but the straightforward /tébəl/ as their mental representation of it. Then later (*much* later) in their education, they come across the less common word *tabulate*: do they now mentally revise /tébəl/ to ///tébjul//- in order to relate it to the associated verb? Or do they just add *tabulate* to their mental lexicon as a separate item that is *semantically* related to *table* (and to just one meaning of *table*) but without linking the two to a common phonological representation? To see the extent of this prob-lem, consider the following pairs that also share a resemblance in meaning and pronunciation.

vowel, vocal+ic	*comb, un+kemp+t*	*humble, humil+ity*	*prey, pred+atory*
dig, ditch	*flower, flor+al*	*consume, consump+tion*	*chart, cart+ographer*
inquire, inquis+itive	*bear, bir+th*	*double, dupl+icate*	*candle, chandel+ier*
deceive, decep+tion	*judge, judic+ial*	*revolve, revolu+tion*	*bishop, episcop+al*
move, mob+ility	*die, dea+th*	*money, monet+ary*	*heart, card+iac*

We undoubtedly establish a connection between the meanings in such pairs, and we may even learn from the dictionary that each pair in fact came from the same original root. There is little evidence, though, that we mentally create a common phonological representation for them or deduce the presence of rules or constraints for changing /w/ to /k/ (*vowel/vocalic*), or /g/ to /tʃ/ (*dig/ditch*), or /r/ to /z/ (*inquire/inquisitive*), or /uv/ to /ob/ (*move/mobility*), and so on. Nor do we usually extend the alternations in such pairs to new forms: not even in jest do we coin an adjective *tocalic* for *towel* (*This cloth is tremendously tocalic.*)

Nevertheless, at *some* level, at least for *some* alternations, we do arrive at *some* kind of phonological connection between the forms of *some* morphemes. At a certain point during your school years, you may have heard someone criticize another's remarks as "/ɪnén/" (*inane*). When that speaker went on to speak of the comment's "/ɪnǽnəti/" (*inanity*) and then spoke—with reference to a table of figures—of a better way to "/tǽbjulèt/" the data, you probably had little trouble in recognizing that /ɪnǽnəti/ and /tǽbjulèt/ are built on the same bases as /ɪnén/ and /tébəl/, respectively, and you absorbed those new forms without even thinking about them, factoring out the effects of laxing (§7.7.1) and the /jul/ ~ /əl/ alternation (§7.7.2). Somehow, the phonemic switches seemed a normal part of English and entered your knowledge of how the language operates. Although invariance seems to be the default expectation in language learning, as we noted earlier, allomorphy is not particularly shocking to the human brain, which somehow assimilates it and gets on with the task of communicating.

The problem, then, is not *whether* there is a deeper phonological level than a close-to-the-surface phonemic one, but how learners infer it and how we can explain it. Pending further development of linguistic theory, our current morphophonemic representations and rules will remain a tentative notation for the kinds of relationships that must be accounted for.

7.8 English spelling revisited.

We now return to the question (chapter 4) of why English is spelled the way it is. Though its phonemes have varied over time (currently about forty of them), the twenty-three original graphemes of the Roman alphabet were never enough, so a few additional letters (*j, v, w*) and digraphs (*th, sh, ee, ow*) were created. Even then, different orthographic conventions were introduced by the continuing flood of foreign loanwords; and when spelling froze while phonology continued to evolve, the two kept diverging. We still write the way that English (*knight, one*), French (*crochet, isle*), and Latin (*sign, nation*) were once pronounced.

Although some fairly intricate rules about English orthography can be derived (as in chapter 4), our modern spelling clearly shows a poor degree of fit with actual pronunciation, particularly in the case of vowels. This mismatch greatly complicates the task of the learner, whether native or foreign. Yet after surveying the material in the last three chapters, we can see that from another point of view our orthography is a system that has risen to the task of balancing a strictly phonemic rendering with at least three other important factors.

First, in order to assign to a given word a fixed, recognized spelling that is most convenient for reading and reference, English cannot recognize all of the word's variants. Instead, it singles out the way the word might be pronounced as a citation form and leaves its sandhi and weak forms implicit, aside from a few written contractions.

Second, instead of reflecting the pronunciation of one main cultural center, as French does, the orthography of English has to be a compromise of dialects. It is inconvenient for us to write 'o' in *pot* and 'a' in *par* on the basis of a vowel distinction (§5.6.1) in British English when both are pronounced /ɑ/ in North America; but it is equally inconvenient for English, Australian, and New Zealand speakers to have to learn to write a silent *r* in *par* or *murder* that North Americans, Scots, and Irish need for their pronunciation of the language.

Third, given English morphophonemic and stress-based alternations, there are advantages in using an invariant spelling for each morpheme. *Partial* might be written *parshül* in a phonemic orthography such as TWOR (§4.1), but the spelling *partial* relates its /pɑrʃ/- to the stem *part,* and the spelling of the suffix *-ial* helps the learner infer that when a restressing (chapters 1–2) brings out the "submerged" vowel in that syllable as in *pàrtiálity,* it will probably be /æ/.

In short, English spelling is a mixed phonemic-morphophonemic-multidialectal system for a very complex phonology, and what it shows is not any given speaker's own pronunciation, but a set of underlying pan-English citation forms from which speakers who know the phonetic and morphophonemic rules of the language can infer the variants that arise in context. It is as though we agreed to factor out the effects of the Great Vowel Shift and other changes in order to preserve a common version of the language that can subsume all our modern pronunciations.

Exercise 7.8

(A) List a possible *disadvantage* of reforming each of the following words' spellings as shown.

1. four → foh
2. could have → cooda
3. grammatical → grammaticle
4. fusion → fyuzhun
5. cats and dogs → catsn dogz
6. knowledge → nollij

(B) ESOL students learn much of their vocabulary through reading. Explain and illustrate the ways in which the spellings that they see can impede perception of actual pronunciation, and yet facilitate perception of morphophonemic connections among derived forms of the same word.

7.9 Teaching pronunciation: Sounds in context. For focusing on fluency in context, the traditional teaching techniques have been repetition, oral reading, and memorization. In REPETITION, the instructor models a sentence and students repeat it in imitation. Longer sentences are built up gradually by expansion or backwards build-up.

- Expansion: "Chris is going." (+ to the movies) → "Chris is going to the movies." (+ at seven) → "Chris is going to the movies at seven" (etc.).
- Backwards build-up: "history" (+registered for) → "registered for history" (+my friends) → "my friends registered for history" (etc.).

In ORAL READING, students read sentences or paragraphs out loud, focusing on accuracy with one or several target sounds together with a more nativelike rhythm and intonation. For greater value, the reading is practiced beforehand to enhance delivery. Although some specialists have not hesitated to use sentences they deliberately enriched with a target distinction, for example, *Tomorrow Molly can collect the corrections* for /l/ versus /r/ (Grate 1974, 13), many today prefer culturally authentic material whenever possible. Especially valuable for its realistic dialog is contemporary drama. In READERS' THEATER (Richard-Amato 1988, 143), students present a scene from a play, still reading their script but after thoroughly rehearsing it. They may sit on stools facing the audience when they are in the scene, then turn around when their character exits.

MEMORIZATION OF PASSAGES has long roots in the history of language teaching, but it became a hallmark of audiolingualism, an oral-intensive approach of the mid-twentieth century. A native model presented a dialog that students imitated and practiced until they could recite it correctly from memory. With the shift to communicative language teaching, such dialogs were rejected as inauthentic because conversation is not normally memorized, and "mim-mem" (mimic and memorize) was seen as having little value for developing true proficiency, the ability to communicate spontaneously. But despite its faults, "mim-mem" did seem to hone fluency with articulation, stress, rhythm, and intonation, and there is nothing wrong with memorizing the kinds of things that native speakers themselves learn by memorization, for example, proverbs, poems, songs, tongue-twisters, and jokes.

For auditory discrimination of sounds in context, DICTATION has likewise been widely used. It does not merely check knowledge of spelling, but integrates listening comprehension with grammatical processing of meaning. There are several types (Omaggio-Hadley 1993, 193), but the two main ones are COMPLETE DICTATION, in which students write down the whole sentence, and PARTIAL FILL-IN (or CLOZE), in which they see parts of the sentence on their paper and fill in the missing words. Here is an example focusing on weak forms, which are especially difficult for learners to understand. Note that they must determine that some blanks are *not* to be filled in.

Teacher's script

1. *I'll* give *them* fifty dollars *to* fix *the* door.
2. Who*'s going to* eat *an* orange *with* me?
3. *It's* not *as* late *as you* think; there*'s* still lots *of* time.

Students' printed version (for fill-in)

1. give   fifty   dollars   fix   door
2. Who   eat   orange   me?
3. not   late   think; there   still   lots   time

As a transition to partial fill-in, the students could mark a multiple choice handout while listening, for example, "She would___done it: (a) a, (b) have, (c) of."

Recent works (e.g., Dalton and Seidlhofer 1994 and Celce-Murcia, Brinton, and Goodwin 1996) have explored other modes of practice. For example, another way to focus on weak forms with *-n't* is to use sentences combining impersonal *you* (another problem for some students) with *can/can't* and *should/shouldn't*. The teacher says a series of statements such as "You can [jəkən] use a pencil" and "You can't [jəkʰæʔ] come in here" and students mark their papers appropriately, that is, with a checkmark or an X according to whether the action is permissible or not.

Jazz Chants (Graham 1978) are very effective. These develop sensitivity to stress timing, rhythmic feet, and the weak forms inside them. Students clap or tap the beat while chanting series of refrains such as the following (39) and fitting in the syllables between the beats:

> Hów do you like your cóffee?
>   Bláck! Bláck!
> Hów do you like your téa?
>   With lémon, pléase.

Finally, teachers should keep in mind that pronunciation work can be integrated with form-focused practice. Thus both of the following contextualized activities for grammar practice also set up a likely context for flapping.

- "Carrie and Kelly were college roommates. Describe what they did back then." (The cues—pictures or a word list—feature verbs whose past tense will have a flap, e.g., *date* (→ *dated* [déɾəd]). With a different situation favoring present tense, the focus will be on the allomorphs of the verb inflection *-s*, comparable to those of pluralizing *-s*.
- "Sarah is a little girl who goes around hitting people. Did she hit you? Did she hit Johnny? Didn't she hit the teacher?" This activity's grammatical point is pronominalization, but the processes of flapping, alveopalatalization, and weak forms apply in responses such as "Yes, she *hit her*" and "No, *she didn't hit him*."

On the other hand, for practicing complex alternations such as those in §7.7.1–2, there is little alternative but to set up questions ("If you are *pleased*, then what do you feel?") or word sets (*please, pleasure*) that directly target the change. Because many of these alternations are found in relatively advanced vocabulary, such practice may be inappropriate for lower levels of study.

NOTES

1. This speaker makes a consistent contrast in two areas where others may not: /ɑ/ versus /ɔ/ (§5.6.1) and /hw/ versus /w/ (§6.10; the /h/ of /hw/ accounted for five of the twenty-two tokens of /h/.) He also retains a version of /ɪ/ instead of /ə/ in some unstressed syllables (§5.5). Although weak forms (§7.4.2) were less frequent in this formal register, there was

nonetheless reduction of *and, or, a, the, as, can, that, for, to,* and *shall,* although not categorically, since metrical and rhetorical factors sometimes favored full forms. The sounds /ər/, /ai/, and /au/ were counted as single units; syllabic [l̩], [n̩], [m̩] were counted as /əl/, /ən/, and /əm/ (respectively ten, nineteen, and one of the ninety-nine occurrences of /ə/).

2. Another way of putting this difference is that overly careful pronunciation is HYPERSPEECH, whereas the modifications heard in more casual pronunciation constitute HYPOSPEECH (Lindblom 1990).

3. DISTINCTIVE stress means that stress distinguishes between or contrasts pairs of words, as in English *súbject* versus *subjéct.* In some theories of phonology, stress in such cases has been termed "phonemic."

4. Defooting varies according to register. As long as the basic stress-timed rhythm is maintained, speakers often have several options for foot organization and syllable "crushing" in the continuums we show in this section, and they do not always adopt the most extreme version.

5. See, for example, the version of LEXICAL PHONOLOGY presented by Booij and Rubach (1984).

6. There is also semantic conditioning in the subrule that says that *fishes* is appropriate if it refers to *types* of fish. As might be expected, subtle details such as this one are not always fully acquired by many speakers.

7. As with *fishes,* there is a subrule here: *peoples* is acceptable for referring to ethnic or cultural groups (*the peoples of the Pacific*).

8. See Kreidler (1989), chapter 14 for another treatment of these vowel alternations.

9. For this deeper level of structure, others use vertical bars |ætɑm|, curly braces {ætɑm}, or slashes /ætɑm/. Linguists generally agree that there is a more abstract level of phonology reflecting the units of morphology but have varied in their theories for it. Here, we retain the traditional term MORPHOPHONEMIC (MORPHOPHONOLOGICAL is a synonym) without committing ourselves to any particular theoretical elaboration of the notion.

10. See Jespersen (1928: I, 231–48) for an early staking out of positions in this debate. It continues today.

11. But some nonstandard varieties in both Britain and the United States have the /g/ in verb derivatives too: /síŋgə(r)/ instead of /síŋər/.

12. We assume you see that in *delete/deletion* there is a process that changes /t/ to /ʃ/, not one that changes /ʃ/ to /t/. A pair such as *demolish/demolition,* both with /ʃ/, demonstrates that a /ʃ/ → /t/ rule is unlikely in this formation.

13. This wavering between /i/ and /j/ in such affixes has been going on for centuries in English; see Jespersen (1928). We noted it in chapter 4 as a spelling problem for sibilants; see especially §4.2.3.

Wrap-Up Exercises

(A) More weak forms: the following sentences have strong-stressed versus weak- or null-stressed versions of the same italicized word. Read them out loud, with reduced forms where appropriate, and transcribe the two versions of the word.

1. Whát's she lóoking *fór*? — She's lóoking *for* the scíssors.
2. Do you réally *wánt tó*? — Yés, I *want to* trý it.
3. *Wóuld* he líke this? — Yés, he *would* líke it a lót.
4. I'd sáy it *is* prétty hárd. — Yés, it *ís*.
5. He *can* dó it if he tríes. — Yés, he *cán*.

(B) Grammar and pronunciation: in each of the following cases, transcribe the weak form that the words in parentheses share, indicate the full word that is meant, and explain why it is likelier in the context.

1. You shouldn't (*have, of*) bothered.
2. I think I'll have the hamburger (*and, in, an*) fries.
3. Your book wasn't as expensive (*has, as*) mine.
4. He said he (*had, would*) finish (*it, at*) home.
5. She (*is, has*) visiting (*are, or, our*) mother.
6. Most (*have, of*) them (*are, or, her*) good (*and, in, an*) math.

(C) In the following sentences, circle the words that are likely to be pronounced with a weak or sandhi form, and then indicate in a phonetic transcription exactly how they change in context.

1. You have got to get better soon.
2. I could have been home by now.
3. It would not have mattered.
4. Why did you tell him that it does not work?
5. You ought to wait until he gets back from class.
6. We used to be afraid of them.
7. He has to learn how to fend for himself.
8. I am supposed to tell her tomorrow.
9. Pat and Cary are going to pay me back in a couple of days.
10. They could not find the right kind of wrench or pliers.

(D) Mark each sentence in the following dialogs like this: (1) put a vertical bar |
between the feet, (2) mark each foot's peak stress by double underlining the peak-stressed syllable, (3) inside each foot place the IPA's mark for 'linked,' a subscript arc ‿, between the final sound of one word and the initial sound of the next, and (4) circle the parts of the sentence that are likely to have sandhi and/or weak forms, including contractions. Then read everything out loud.

Dialog 1: In the store

1. CLERK: Hello, may I help you?
2. CARL: No thanks, we're just looking.
3. BERT: Hey, check out these shirts; they're reduced to twenty-nine fifty.

4. CARL: Have they got any in a large?
5. BERT: Yeah, here is a green one.
6. CARL: Whoa, this says 100 percent Dacron and that stuff can feel pretty hot. It's cotton or nothing for me. Come on, let's go to another store.

Dialog 2: A phone call to an academic advisor

1. SMITH: Hello?
2. CAROL: May I speak with Professor Smith?
3. SMITH: Speaking.
4. CAROL: Hi, this is Carol Anderson. I need some help with my registration for next semester. Will you be in this afternoon?
5. SMITH: Sure, Carol. From three to five.
6. CAROL: Good, then how about four o'clock?
7. SMITH: That will be fine. I will put you down for four.
8. CAROL: Fine. I will see you then. Goodbye.
9. SMITH: Bye.

(E) Discussion: many students who began studying English in their home countries before coming to the United States or other countries where it is spoken natively often show surprise or even disapproval toward the more colloquial speech that they are hearing and being taught. They may tell their instructor that they were taught to pronounce *better* with a /t/ sound, not /d/ (referring to the flap); or to pronounce their vowels distinctly (referring to reduction); or to avoid contractions (implicitly, all the weak forms discussed in this chapter) as "slang." How would you respond to such statements from your students?

(F) Project: listen to (or record a sample of) the speech of a speaker of English whose proficiency in English is different from your own. How many contractions and weak forms do you hear? Compare this speaker's frequency of contractions and weak forms with the way that you would pronounce the same sentences. Is there also a difference in tempo and rhythm? How might these factors affect the frequency you have observed?

(G) Working with a long selection. Here are some of the many things you can do with the following story, "The Piece of Pecan Pie":

1. Read all or part of it out loud.
2. Listen to all or part of it on the CD, observing and describing special features of the speaker's rendition that seem different from your own.
3. Write out selected parts of it in phonemic and then phonetic transcription.
4. Mark all or part of it for strong stress and weak stress.
5. Write falling, rising, curved, and flat lines to describe the selection's intonation.

The Piece of Pecan Pie

1. Jessica Moulton Beasley had really had it up to here with Death. Why—she had asked herself repeatedly these last seven years—couldn't Death behave rationally, logically, intelligently, prudently? Jessica had just turned fifty-four when she became a widow. Her husband, Jerry, had never been sick a day in his life. Yet all of a sudden, Wham!, there he was, dead of his very first heart attack on the floor of the YMCA locker room right after playing his usual game of basketball. But the problem was no longer the poor dead Jerry or even the purgatorial years of pain and loneliness that followed his death. What had really made Jessica's existence so very bitter these last seven years were the ongoing troubles of Mother Beasley. At the time of her son's precipitous heart attack she was eighty years old and her health was already failing. And what failing! Was there any infirmity that poor Mother Beasley didn't know? Arthritis, bunions, cataracts, diphtheria, elephantiasis, aftosa fever, gangrene—old Mother Beasley had suffered them all. But what really worried Jessica about her mother-in-law was the always-dreaded Alzheimer's disease, the "scourge of the superannuated," as people called it. Mother Beasley was already getting "very forgetful" around the time of Jerry's death; indeed, the poor dear lady never fully understood that her beloved son, the apple of her eye, was actually dead. At first she asked for him constantly, and eventually Jessica dealt with the problem by assuring her that Jerry had been detained "in Memphis on business" but would return "tomorrow or the day after" and had phoned just that morning to let her know how much he cared. That always made Mother happy.

2. Mother Beasley had moved in with Jessica and Jerry two years before the latter's death, and at first there were no problems: the old lady had her own bedroom and bath in the back of the house, and she was even able to help out in the kitchen from time to time. But after Jerry's death the Alzheimer's got worse, and Jessica was forced to hire a day nurse to "watch over" Mother Beasley from eight to five. (To supplement the inadequate insurance money that was paid when Jerry died, Jessica had gone to work as a bookkeeper in a real estate office.) And then there came a time when the poor sick mother-in-law became so demented—and at times so violent, despite her arthritis and the many other ailments—that Jessica simply had to insist that at least one of her three daughters be there from five to midnight to "help out with Grandma." But it was very hard for Samantha, Judith, or Heather to do so, as all of them had their own families to care for. What's more, all three worked outside the home—Samantha as a nurse, Judy as a teacher, and Heather as a social worker. So Jessica eventually hired a second or "night" nurse, which just about depleted her bank account. But even with this added help it was all that she could do to cope with Mother Beasley, who was completely irrational by then. Finally Jessica gave up: she sold the house and moved her mother-in-law into the best nursing home she

could afford with the money from the house plus the old lady's Social Security and Medicare. The "home" was hardly the number one in the metro Atlanta area, but it would have to do. For two years, Jessica visited Mother Beasley every day, if only to check on the state of her health. Poor old Mother Beasley no longer recognized anyone, and spent her days either sleeping or fighting with the nursing staff, which barely tolerated her. There then came a time when Mother Beasley no longer fought with anyone, as she had lost her ability to speak, couldn't walk, and had almost forgotten how to eat, despite Jessica's best efforts to coax her into taking "just one more spoonful of this delicious chicken soup, Mother dear."

3. But at last it was over. At 9:57 P.M. on the fourth of January, Mother Beasley breathed her last. Jessica was at her bedside when Death entered the room. He hardly looked the way he'd been drawn or painted by artists since the beginning of time. For one thing he didn't carry a scythe. For another thing, he was hardly old or thin, but looked, instead, like a well-fed middle-aged accountant drinking whiskey in the club car of a commuter train on his way back home from an office in the city. One could only tell that Death was Death because of his total transparency: you could see straight through him, for his large round body was just an outline or a sketch. But Death indeed was deadly—it took him less than a second to wave a pudgy paw over Mother Beasley's thin drawn face and Poof!, end of story. Yet it wasn't quite the end of the story for her long-suffering daughter-in-law, who had a bone to pick with this particular grim reaper. "Now you just listen to me, Death. Aren't you aware of all the advances of modern medicine and how difficult they make it for people to die these days? I mean, get a life! If we humans keep inventing new ways to prolong our existence, then Death has got to come up with new ways to make it shorter. Do you really think it was any Sunday school picnic for my poor mother-in-law to lie there crippled and demented for years and years? Are you aware that at age sixty-one I'm now financially dependent on my overburdened daughters, their husbands, and the taxpayers of the state of Georgia? It's time you learn how to speed up the dying process, you lousy rotten good-for-nothing procrastinator!"

4. Death agreed. "I feel your pain, Jessica. But you know I've got only one trick in my book."
"Well how's about your agreeing to come back when I'm good and ready for you? Like, say, oh, maybe fifteen years from now, unless I give you a call before then?"
"But it's so much easier to murder a person who isn't all that old. Look how quickly I offed your husband. I think I'll kill you now."

5. Thinking fast, Jessica reached into her large brown tote bag and took out a carefully wrapped pecan pie, which she'd been planning to give to the staff nurses for services rendered. "Mr. Death, I just **know** how hard you've been working today and I reckon you haven't even had a chance to eat your supper. So the

very least I can do is let you have a big old slice of pie! I'll just wash off this plate of Mother Beasley's and serve you some."

6. Death's mouth immediately began to water. "Why how'd you ever know that I was hungry? And there's **nothing** I love more than a nice piece of pie à la mode!" Death smacked his lips and quickly devoured one slice of the pie along with the two scoops of the thick rich vanilla ice cream that mysteriously materialized when Jessica waved her hand. "Another helping, Mr. Death?" "Why I think I will," the Reaper responded. "And I don't know **where** you got that ice cream but it sure is good!" Three scoops of the cool creamy white stuff accompanied the second piece of pie, which was twice the size of the first. "That was gooooood!" panted Death. "Just a tiny little bit more, Death dear?" "Well I really **shouldn't**," drooled Death, "but this pie and that ice cream are **so** good that I just **can't** say no!" Jessica forked over a third helping, every bit as large as the second. And a **fourth** helping, and a **fifth** helping, until Death's transparent body outline had expanded well beyond the arms of his chair. The pie pan was clean as a whistle and the ice cream container looked as if someone had licked it with their tongue.

7. Jessica abruptly stood up, gathered her belongings, and began to leave the room. At this, Death gave a quick low moan. "But when am I going to see you again, Mrs. Beasley?" "You mean when are you going to see some more of my pecan pie!" "Well, yeah, uh, it really was very good, but it's you and not the pie. I mean, um, oh damn, I just can't speak. What I'm trying to say is that I think I'm in love with you." Jessica smiled. "Can I see you again sometime real soon?" "Why you most certainly can, Mr. Death!" "Please call me Arthur." "And **you** must call **me Jessica**!" "Yes, yes, yes! Anything you say, dear Jessica! But please let me know where I can find you." "Why certainly, Arthur. I live in the basement apartment at 3046 E. Veranda Lane, and my phone number is 306–1736. You drop on by, you hear?"

8. And so there began a lengthy and pleasant relationship based on Jessica's delicious Southern cooking. As long as Jessica still had the mind and the strength to cook, Death would spare her; but the minute her wits and her body finally failed her, Death—by now totally in her debt—could be counted on to do her just one last little favor.

CHAPTER 8

Appendix

This appendix contains additional resources: a section on acoustic phonetics (§8.1), the official chart of the IPA (§8.2),[1] and a summary of *PEASBA*'s database and CD (§8.3).

For further phonetics study, the instructor might supplement the coverage of English phonology in *PEASBA* with works such as Ladefoged 2000 and Whitley 2003. The former is a practical survey of general phonetics; the latter is a multimedia phonetics encyclopedia that combines a comprehensive symbol guide with a description of all known speech sounds, with recordings, diagrams, spectrograms, and indications of frequency in the world's languages.

8.1 Acoustic phonetics. Whereas articulatory phonetics focuses on the production of sounds, acoustic phonetics looks at the basis for their perception. A sound is a wave of compression and rarefaction that moves outward from a vibrating object (the vocal cords, a reed, a string, or tuning fork) through a medium such as air. It is depicted as a sine curve, as shown in figure 8.a.

Figure 8.a. A sound wave

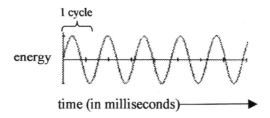

Figure 8.b. Sound waves differing in loudness and pitch

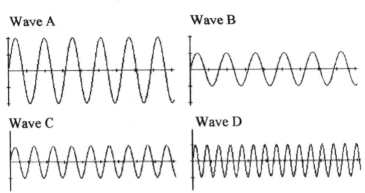

Wave A Wave B

Wave C Wave D

The FREQUENCY of vibration is the number of cycles per second (horizontal or *x*-axis), that is, how many times the object vibrates per unit of time, and is what our ears perceive as pitch (§3.2). Thus figure 8.a shows a sound wave of five cycles in eight milliseconds, or 5/8 of a cycle per millisecond, which works out to 625 cycles per second (cps). The energy of the sound (vertical or *y*-axis) is its AMPLITUDE ('bigness') or energy of vibration, what we hear as volume (§1.1) or relative loudness. Thus in figure 8.b Wave A has the same frequency of vibration (same pitch) as B, but is more energetic or louder than B. On the other hand, C and D have the same amplitude (energy/volume) as B, but are increasingly higher in pitch—wave C is higher-pitched than B, and D is higher-pitched than C. Unless the source of the sound continues vibrating at the same frequency and amplitude, the sound wave loses energy, trails off, and becomes inaudible.

The pitch of the vocal cords acquires overtones or RESONANCE in passing through the oral and nasal cavities. The position of the tongue and lips shapes that resonance (§5.1–2), just as different bottles produce distinct resonance when you blow across their openings. For the vowel [i], the tongue takes a high front position, forming a small "bottle" (the oral cavity) in front of itself but a fairly large one behind (the pharynx). For the back vowel [u], in contrast, the area in front of the retracted tongue is bigger and extended by lip rounding, so this "bottle" resonates at a lower pitch. You can check the difference in oral resonance by turning off your voice (to subtract the pitch of the vocal cords' own vibration), and by then whispering, or by thumping your throat (just above the larynx), while setting your mouth for various vowel positions.

There are several tools for analyzing voice and resonance, but the most useful one is the SOUND SPECTROGRAPH, which was formerly a machine and is now simply a program that runs on a computer to analyze a digitized sound sample. It displays an image called a SPECTROGRAM, with the *x*-axis indicating the passage of time in seconds or milliseconds and the *y*-axis depicting resonance frequency in cycles per second, cps (also called

Figure 8.c. Sample vowel spectrograms

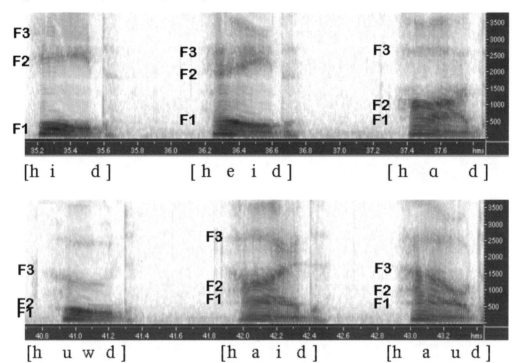

Hertz, or Hz). The details of that image can then be studied and analyzed for the basis of vowel and consonant perception.

For sonorants (vowels, nasals, liquids, glides), a spectrogram shows resonance concentrated at dark horizontal bands of energy called FORMANTS. There are three pertinent formants for speech analysis, numbered from bottom up as F(ormant) 1, F2, and F3. F1 correlates in part to pharyngeal resonance; F2 reflects resonance in the oral cavity in front of the tongue, and F3 reflects resonance elsewhere in the head. (Another band often appears at the bottom of the spectrogram, underneath F1, but it shows voicing rather than resonance.) Vowels are characterized by the positions of F1 and F2, as illustrated in figure 8.c for *heed, hayed, hod, who'd, hide,* and *how'd.* Thus for the vowel /i/, F1 lies at about 250 Hz (see scale on the right side of the spectrogram), while F2 is at about 2,300 Hz. For some of these vowels, the formants shift during articulation, indicating changing tongue and lip position, that is, diphthongization (§5.4.2–3). For this speaker, the spectrograms show slight diphthongization of /e/ (*hayed*) and /u/ (*who'd*), but sharper gliding of /ai/ (*hide*) and /au/ (*how'd*).

Nasals (§6.4.2) have a well-defined F1 and F3, although fainter than for vowels, whereas liquids (§6.4.1) and glides are vowel-like but shorter, as shown in figure 8.d for

Figure 8.d. Some sonorant spectrograms

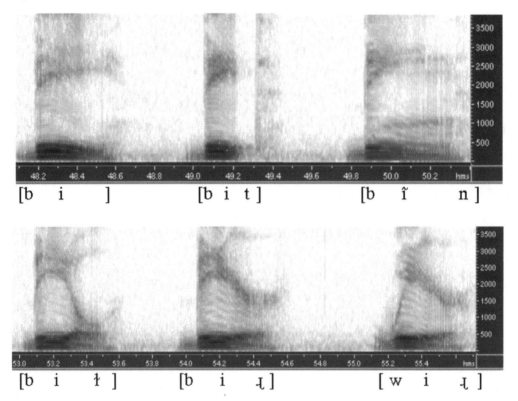

[b   i   ]   [b i t]   [b   ĩ   n]

[b   i   ł]   [b   i   ɻ]   [w   i   ɻ]

bean, Beale, beer, we're. In the same spectrogram, you also see differences in length
(§5.4) on the *x*-axis: compare *beat* (/i/ before a voiceless stop) with the longer duration
of the vowel in *bee* and *bean*.

Obstruents lack resonance and therefore formants; they are simply noise in the case
of fricatives (§6.6–7), and silence in the case of stops. The spectrogram in figure 8.e
compares the fricative noise of /s θ f ʃ/, apparent as fuzzy vertical swaths at the beginning of *sin, thin, fin,* and *shin.* Note the special intensity of the sibilants, which differ in
that the hiss is concentrated at higher frequencies for /s/ than for /ʃ/. The noise for non-
sibilants /f/ and /θ/ is weaker and acoustically very similar. As illustrated by figure 8.c,
/h/ shows as a weakly fricative beginning of the following vowel. Stops, on the other
hand, appear as gaps in the surrounding sound. Figure 8.f compares *attáck* (or *a táck*)
with *áttic*: note the rather sizable gap (about 1/10 of a second) for the first /t/ and its
noisy aspirated release (§6.5.1), as opposed to the much briefer gap for the flapped allophone in *áttic.* The /b/ of *rebel* shows voicing and a shorter duration than a voiceless
stop. The only indication of the stop's place of articulation is a slight warping of an adjacent sonorant's formants as the tongue or lips move into or out of the stop position. For

Figure 8.e. Fricative spectrograms

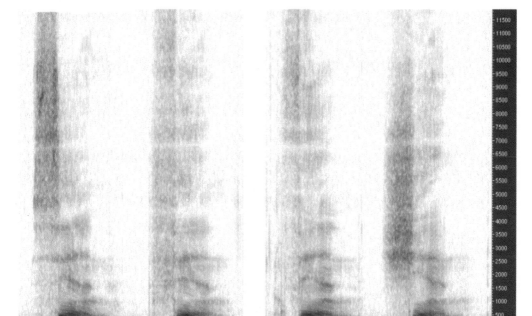

[s ɪ n]   [θ ɪ n]   [f ɪ n]   [ʃ ɪ n]

prevocalic stops, a bilabial shows as a relatively low start of F2 and F3 (note the /ɛ/ of *I rebel* in figure 8.f), an alveolar as a start of F2 at about 1,700–1,800 Hz, and a velar as a high start of F2. In short, spectrograms confirm that what we hear is not the stop itself, but its perturbation of adjacent resonance.

Spectrograms also provide evidence for suprasegmentals. Strong stress appears in the greater intensity (energy, loudness) of a vowel: note in figure 8.f the greater blackness of the vowel formants of the stressed syllables in *attáck* versus *áttic*, and *a rébel* versus *I rebél*. In *I rebél*, the stressed syllable is also longer. Pitch can likewise be analyzed from a spectrogram. At some resolutions, the resonance shows vertical lines called *striations*, each one indicating a vibration of the vocal cords. Note in figure 8.f that these striations are closer together in the stressed syllables, meaning more vibrations per unit of time and therefore higher pitch (↗), while at the end of the utterances, the striations spread apart, meaning a decreasing frequency and therefore a descending intonation (↘).

The full-sentence example in figure 8.g, *When is he going to tell her the bad news?*, illustrates some of the processes discussed in chapter 7. There is stress-timing: the unstressed syllables are shortened, contracted, and even dropped, whereas stressed ones are correspondingly lengthened. Sandhi and weak forms emerge (*when's he* and *gonna*), and the /h/ of *he* and *her* disappears. Note the intonation again: in the final syllable

Figure 8.f. Stops, stress, and pitch on spectrograms

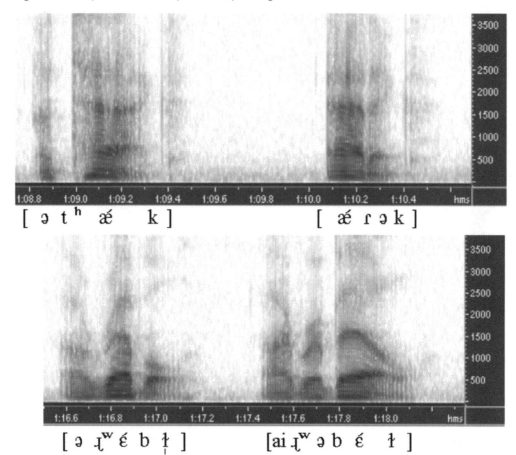

(*news*) the striations crowd close together and then spread apart, indicating that the pitch rises and then falls.

This has been a brief introduction to acoustic phonetics, but it may suffice to illustrate the usefulness of a visual display of sound. Sometimes the ear cannot discern details of interest: was that stop aspirated, or flapped? Was that vowel diphthongized, and longer than others? Did intonation rise, or fall? Spectrographic analysis offers valuable evidence for answering such questions, and it poses others of its own. For example, full-sentence displays such as figure 8.g demonstrate that there is no separation of words, or syllables, or even phonemes in speech; adjacent sonorants, in particular, merge into a continuous blur. Therefore how do we perceive in the stream of speech the units to be processed for meaning? However this is done, it is clearly not on the basis of hearing

Figure 8.g. Rhythm and sandhi on a spectrogram

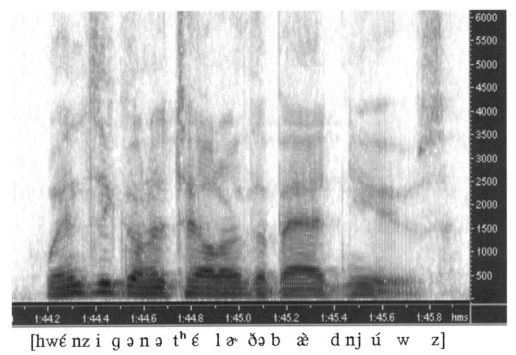

[hwέ nz i g ə n ə tʰ έ l ɚ ðɘ b ǽ d nj ú w z]

discrete sounds. And that is a point that teachers need to keep in mind: we may *think* that we are modeling the units of pronunciation, but what students hear is an indistinct smear of sound—at least until they are processing the language more efficiently.

8.2. The International Phonetic Alphabet. The current IPA chart is given in figure 8.h for reference in using this book. It is reprinted with permission from the International Phonetic Association;[2] see also the IPA website, www.arts.gla.ac.uk/IPA/ipa.html. For a summary of the development of the IPA and of phonological transcription in general, see Whitley (2003).

Figure 8.h. The International Phonetic Alphabet (revised to 1993)

THE INTERNATIONAL PHONETIC ALPHABET (revised to 1993)

8.3. *PEASBA*'s **CD: Recordings and Corpus.** The CD in this book contains two types of materials. First, there are recordings of the examples and exercises marked with an earphones symbol (🎧) in the text. These are playable on most personal computers and on regular CD players. The track listing follows.

Track	Location in Book	Time
Track 1	Exercise 1.3 (B)	1:17
Track 2	My Car (chap. 1)	2:08
Track 3	Exercise 1.6	1:22
Track 4	Wrap-up exercise, end of chap. 1	2:32
Track 5	Chap. 3 examples	9:46
Track 6	Exercise 3.2 (A)	0:38
Track 7	Exercise 3.2 (B)	0:56
Track 8	Exercise 3.2 (C)	1:32
Track 9	Exercise 3.5 (A)	0:53
Track 10	Exercise 3.6 (A)	0:27
Track 11	Exercise 3.6 (B)	1:31
Track 12	Exercise 5.2 (A)	0:48
Track 13	Exercise 5.3 (A)	2:41
Track 14	Exercise 5.4 (A)	1:01
Track 15	Exercise 5.5 (A)	2:34
Track 16	Exercise 5.6 (A)	0:56
Track 17	Exercise 5.7	0:55
Track 18	Exercise 5.8 (A)	1:09
Track 19	Wrap-up exercise I, end of chap. 5	1:31
Track 20	Exercise 6.3 (A)	0:56
Track 21	Exercise 6.5 (A)	1:01
Track 22	Exercise 6.7 (A)	3:56
Track 23	Exercise 6.8 (A)	5:08
Track 24	Exercise 6.9 (A)	0:39
Track 25	Exercise 6.10 (A)	2:34
Track 26	Wrap-up exercise G, end of chap. 6	2:25
Track 27	Exercise 7.2 (C)	1:28
Track 28	Exercise 7.3 (A)	1:04
Track 29	Wrap-up exercise G, end of chap. 7	9:55

Second, the CD has a folder of data files called **Corpus** that served as the basis for many of the statistics cited in the book. To open them, insert the CD in your computer, shut down its CD player if it pops up in response to the sound files, then access your CD drive. Open the CD and double-click on the folder **Corpus**. The files in it are data lists, explained in the following section, in an enriched text (**.rtf**) format that can be

Figure 8.i. The data files in the Corpus

^R-FON.rtf	04-ULT.rtf	07.rtf	-AU-FON.rtf	-OO-FON.rtf
01.rtf	05.rtf	07-ANT.rtf	-CHV-FON.rtf	PEN.rtf
02.rtf	05-ANT.rtf	07-PEN.rtf	COMPOUND.rtf	PRE.rtf
02-PEN.rtf	05-PEN.rtf	07-PRE.rtf	CORPUS.rtf	QUI.rtf
02-ULT.rtf	05-PRE.rtf	07-QUI.rtf	-EE-FON.rtf	SEX.rtf
03.rtf	05-QUI.rtf	08.rtf	-E-FON.rtf	sibspell.rtf
03-ANT.rtf	05-ULT.rtf	08-ANT.rtf	ER-spell.rtf	-U-FON.rtf
03-PEN.rtf	06.rtf	08-PRE.rtf	FONAPERC.rtf	ULT.rtf
03-ULT.rtf	06-ANT.rtf	08-QUI.rtf	FONATHON.rtf	-UU-FON.rtf
04.rtf	06-PEN.rtf	-AE-FON.rtf	-I-FON.rtf	WORDFAM1.rtf
04-ANT.rtf	06-PRE.rtf	-A-FON.rtf	-II-FON.rtf	WORDFAM2.rtf
04-PEN.rtf	06-QUI.rtf	-AI-FON.rtf	-O-FON.rtf	Z-spell.rtf
04-PRE.rtf	06-SEX.rtf	ANT.rtf	-OI-FON.rtf	

opened and read by most word processing programs. In Microsoft Windows, the contents should appear as shown in figure 8.i.

These files are of several types, explained later in this section:

- word lists by number of syllables: "03," "04," and so on.
- word lists by stress pattern: "03-ANT," "03-PEN," and so on.
- word lists by stressed vowel: "-^R.FON," "-AE-FON," and so on.
- combined lists by stressed vowel and stress pattern: "CORPUS" and "FONATHON" (note: the latter uses a small font; set your word processor's zoom control at higher magnification). "FONAPERC" is a summary of statistics from the FONATHON.
- lists of word families by endings: "WORDFAM1," "WORDFAM2."
- lists of compounds (left- vs. right-stressing): "COMPOUNDS."
- lists of words that spell certain phonemes various ways: "er-spell," "Z-spell," "sibspell."

All are based on a unique statistical analysis of all the entries (25,108) of an entire dictionary, the 655-page "English-Spanish" section of Carvajal and Horwood (1996). This dictionary was chosen because of the length of its English corpus, which was neither too long to prevent each lexical item from being entered manually and keyed appropriately into a computerizable database over a reasonable period of time, nor too short for an adequate representation of the lexicon of English.[3]

As is apparent in chapters 1–2, a key element of our approach was a lexical classification based on stress patterns. To prepare the database, all 25,108 items were entered and keyed according to number of syllables (02, 03, 04, etc.) and stress position (*ulti*-mate, *pen*ultimate, *ante*penultimate, *pre*-antepenultimate, *quin*tultimate, *sex*ultimate;

Figure 8.j. Stress and syllable categories in the Corpus

	By number of syllables (01, 02, 03 ...) →							
By stress placement (ult, pen, ant ...)	01-ult	02-ult	03-ult	04-ult	05-ult			
		02-pen	03-pen	04-pen	05-pen	06-pen	07-pen	
			03-ant	04-ant	05-ant	06-ant	07-ant	08-ant
				04-pre	05-pre	06-pre	07-pre	08-pre
					05-qui	06-qui	07-qui	08-qui
						06-sex		

see §2.1). The twenty-seven categories that resulted from this classification are summarized in figure 8.j, and form the basis for the corresponding lists in the Corpus.

Entries were also sorted by lexical families to permit an analysis of factors, such as part of speech, word ending, and compounding patterns that affect stress shifts, and were sorted by their strong-stressed vowel to bring out generalizations by vowel type (e.g., tense vs. lax). Because phonetic symbols would have required special fonts, the following substitutes were adopted in the file names and in certain files. (Some of the files also use the differential symbol ∂ for /ə/.)

^r: /ər/	AU: /au/	I: /ɪ/	OO: /o/
AE: /æ/	CHV or Ω: /ʌ/	II: /i/	U: /ʊ/
A: /ɑ/	EE: /e/	OI: /oi/	UU: /u/
AI: /ai/	E: /ɛ/	O or _: /ɔ/	∂ or ¶: /ə/

As made clear by the statistics in chapter 4, the data were also analyzed by grapheme-phoneme correspondences, and some of the resulting files are likewise included in the Corpus folder. (See figure 8.i.)

The files on the CD provide readers with an invaluable reference guide to the great variety of syllable-length and stress-pattern types that characterize English, and will enable students using *PEASBA* to quickly access lexical families that stress a common root as well as those that don't. Given the extent to which English vowel pronunciation is determined by stress position, all these reference files constitute an indispensable complement to any textbook that wishes to take seriously a new, metric-centered and corpus-based approach to the teaching of English pronunciation.

NOTES

1. For IPA computer fonts that can be used with this book, instructors and students may go to the website of SIL International, which offers a self-installing set that can be downloaded (free, at this writing): **www.sil.org/computing/fonts/encore-ipa.html**.

2. The IPA permits (with no limitations or licensing restrictions and at no change in the form of a license fee or royalties) third parties to use (copy, publicly display, publicly perform, publish/distribute, and create derivative works based thereon) the IPA symbols and IPA charts as part of or in products such as books and software/hardware as long as the third party acknowledges the International Phonetic Association as the copyright owner of the International Phonetic Alphabet and the IPA charts.

3. The program used to order and analyze the data for *PEASBA* was written in the "C" programming language by Ralph W. Ewton Jr., emeritus, Department of Computer Science, The University of Texas at El Paso. This language allows users to comb the base to key in the search criteria and then produce the data that match the specifications.

GLOSSARY

This glossary lists key notions for reference, but does not include certain terms that are defined in context in this book for limited purposes but are subsequently little used.

absent stress: lack of stress.

acoustic phonetics: the study of speech from the perspective of how it sounds and is perceived.

adverbial clause: a clause beginning with an adverbial conjunction (*when, before, if, while, so, because*, etc.) inside a larger sentence.

affix: a prefix or suffix.

affricate: a stop released as a fricative.

allograph: a variant of a grapheme.

allomorph: a variant of a morpheme.

allomorphy: the presence of multiple forms of the same morpheme.

allophone: a variant of a phoneme.

alternation: a systematic variation between two phonemes, one in one form of a word and another in a different form.

alveolar: pronounced on the alveolar ridge (gum ridge behind the upper teeth).

alveopalatal (also called *postalveolar* and *palatoalveolar*): pronounced with the tip close to the upper teeth and alveolar ridge and the blade up close to the forward part of the palate.

alveopalatalization: the change of alveolar /t d s n/ to alveopalatals before /j/.

ambisyllabic: belonging to two syllables as the coda of one and the onset of the next.

anapest (adjective *anapestic*): a foot consisting of two unstressed syllables followed by a stressed one.

antepenult, or **ant** (adjective *antepenultimate*): the third syllable from the end of a word.

apex (adjective *apical*, prefix *apico-*): the tip of the tongue.

appositive: an element that renames the immediately preceding noun.

approximant: a sound in which articulators approach each other without contact; essentially the same as *glide* (although some phoneticians also include laterals as approximants).

aspirated (noun *aspiration*): released with "puff of air" due to delayed voicing.

assimilation (verb *assimilate*): a process in which a sound becomes more like its neighbor(s).

autosegmental phonology: a school that regards features of suprasegmentals and phonemes as operating on levels (tiers) that are autonomous from the vowel and consonant segments.

back: describing a sound made in the back of the oral cavity.

base (base word): the main word (root) from which others in its family are formed.

bilabial: pronounced with both lips.

bisegmental: referring to a sound analyzed as a sequence of two phonemes instead of one.

bisyllabic: consisting of two syllables.

bounded: referring to feet that are limited in the number of syllables they usually embrace; referring to languages that impose such constraints.

broad: describing a transcription that records only the essential features of pronunciation; loosely synonymous with *phonemic* or *phonological*; opposite: *narrow*.

central: pronounced in the middle of the oral cavity; neither front nor back.

checked: describing vowels that generally must be followed by a consonant; opposite: *free* (or *unchecked*).

citation form: the pronunciation a word tends to have when "cited" as a word and carefully pronounced by itself.

clipping: the dropping of unstressed syllables from a word to leave a shortened one- or two-syllable version.

closed syllable: one with a coda (i.e., "closed" by one or more consonant phonemes).

cluster: a group of adjacent consonants.

coda: the end of a syllable, consisting of a consonant or consonant cluster.

complementary: describing a distribution in which two units (e.g., allophones) occur in different positions; opposite: *contrastive*.

compound: a tightly bound combination (written as one word or several, with hyphens or without) of two or more lexical components each of which can stand alone as separate words.

conditioned: describing a change that occurs only under certain conditions. *Phonological* conditioning refers to suprasegmentals or adjacent sounds; *grammatical* conditioning is the effect of part of speech and inflectional features; *lexical* conditioning is the limitation to certain classes of words.

consonant: a class of sounds used with vowels to form syllables; includes stops, fricatives, nasals, liquids, and in some classifications, glides.

constituent unit: each grouping of units at successive levels in the organization of a compound or phrase.

contrastive analysis: a procedure that compares two languages to determine their similarities and differences and to predict possible problems when speakers of one study the other.

contrastive: (1) describing units or features that contrast distinct words; synonym: *distinctive*. (2) describing a distribution in which two units (especially phonemes) occur in the same positions and there contrast distinct words; opposite: *complementary*.

coronal: made with the front part of the tongue.

dactyl (adjective *dactylic*): a foot made up of a stressed syllable followed by two unstressed ones.

deictic: a word that points at something in the context: *this, that, here, then, now*.

defooting: merger of two adjacent feet into one in faster tempos of speaking.

dental: made with the tongue on the upper teeth.

derivation: (1) a type of morphology for altering the meaning or syntactic category of the base word; opposite: *inflection*. (2) a representation of the successive applications of rules to generate phonetic output from an underlying form.

devoiced: describing a sound that has lost its voicing in a specific environment (position).

diacritic: a mark (accent, macron, breve, tilde, umlaut, etc.) added to a primary character to indicate a modification of its pronunciation.

digraph: a two-letter combination that represents a single sound.

diphthong (adjective *diphthongized*): a complex vowel in which tongue and/or lip position change during articulation; a combination of a vowel and a glide.

diphthongization: addition of a gliding movement to a vowel's articulation.

discontinuous: referring to a unit (e.g., a digraph) in two parts, separated by other material.

discourse: the overall conversation or composition in which a given word or sentence is used.

disyllable: a word of two syllables; opposites: *monosyllable, polysyllable*.

dorsum: the back of the tongue; dorsal: pronounced with the dorsum.

downstep: a drop to a lower musical key in mid-sentence to introduce a parenthetical element.

enumeration: listing of elements (e.g., *bread, butter, coffee, tea*).

epenthesis: insertion of a sound, usually to facilitate pronunciation.

error analysis: a procedure that determines the sources of language acquisition problems by examining a corpus of errors from learners.

extrametrical: describing a syllable that lies outside the regular feet of a sequence of syllables.

family: a group of related words formed on the same base.

feature: a property that is either present or absent from a unit in its contrasts with other units.

flap: a sound in which the articulator weakly strikes a place of articulation.

flooding: a technique in which students are bombarded with examples of words that illustrate a particular point and conform to a specific pattern.

foot: a unit of rhythm or meter consisting of a strong-stressed syllable with neighboring weak- or null-stressed syllables. Note: the term is used with some ambiguity in linguistics: strictly speaking, a *metric* foot, as in chapter 2, contains only one stressed syllable (strong or weak), whereas a *rhythmic* foot, as in chapter 7, is a potentially longer unit that may contain weak-stressed syllables along with one strong-stressed one.

formant: a band of resonance at a certain frequency in a spectrogram.

free: (in reference to vowels) able to occur at the end of a syllable without a consonant coda.

free variation: a situation in which either of two phonemes may be used in a word without changing its meaning, yielding alternative pronunciations.

fricative: a consonant that continues (without being stopped) and is characterized by air stream turbulence (friction).

front: pronounced in the front of the mouth.

function words: words such as articles (*a, the*), auxiliary verbs (*be, can, will, have*), prepositions (*at, of, to*), conjunctions (*and, or*), and pronouns (*her, him, it, them*) that mainly carry out grammatical functions in the sentence and (except when emphasized) tend to lose their stress and be pronounced together with an adjacent stressed word.

functional load: the relative number of words that a given phonemic contrast distinguishes.

geminate (in reference to phonemes or graphemes): doubled.

glide: a semivowel; a sound in which the tongue and/or lips quickly slide into and out of a position. Unlike vowels, glides are nonsyllabic (do not form the nucleus of a syllable).

glottal: referring to the glottis; made in the larynx with a certain configuration of the vocal cords.

glottaling: the change of /t/ to a glottal stop, [ʔ].

glottis: the opening between the vocal cords.

grapheme: a unit of a writing system; a letter, numeral, punctuation mark, or other written mark ($, %, &, etc.), as opposed to a phoneme of a pronunciation system.

high: pronounced with the body of the tongue in a high position, close to the roof of the mouth; synonym (in reference to vowels): *close*.

homographs: words that are written the same way despite a difference in pronunciation.

homophones (homonyms): distinct words that happen to be pronounced the same way.

iamb (adjective *iambic*): a foot made up of an unstressed syllable followed by a stressed one.

inflection: (1) a type of morphology used to show grammatical features such as tense, number, gender, and case. (2) (in reference to the voice) intonation.

info(rmation) unit: a sentence (or part thereof) centered on a peak stress, corresponding to a point of information being made within the discourse.

interlanguage: the transitional system of second language learners, intermediate between their native language and the target language.

intervocalic: occurring between vowels.

intonation: a melody or characteristic series of pitches applied over a whole utterance.

labial: made with the lips.

labiodental: made with the upper teeth and lower lip.

labiovelar: made with constrictions between the lips and between the dorsum and the velum.

laminal (or prefix *lamino-*): made with the blade of the tongue, not just the tip.

larynx (adjective *laryngeal*): the voice box; the top cartilage of the trachea, containing the vocal cords.

lateral: made over the sides of the tongue.

lax: pronounced with a relatively relaxed musculature that, in the case of vowels, causes the tongue position to sink in slightly for a more open oral channel.

left-headed: describing a foot with its "head" (strong-stressed) syllable at the left.

left-stressing: referring to a compound with the primary or peak stress on its left element.

length: duration (of a sound or syllable).

lexical incidence: distribution of a unit in the lexicon (especially in reference to dialects that share the same phonemes but differ slightly in their preference for them in certain words).

lexical rules: rules that do not apply generally, but are limited to particular morphological formations.

lexicon (adjective *lexical*): the vocabulary; the total set of words and forms of a language.

liquids: sonorant consonants that are not nasals or glides; /l/ and /r/ sounds.

loanword: a nonnative word, one that was borrowed from another language.

low: pronounced with the body of the tongue in a lowered position; synonym (in reference to vowels): *open*.

medial: referring to the middle of a word (as opposed to initial and final positions).

metricalism (metrical theory): an approach to suprasegmentals that emphasizes the relative strength of a syllable at successively higher levels of organization such as the foot.

mid: pronounced with the body of the tongue neither raised nor lowered.

minimal pair: a pair of words whose pronunciations differ in only one phoneme.

monomorphemic: describing a word that consists of a single morpheme.

monophthong: a simple vowel with a relatively steady pronunciation; opposite: *diphthong*.

monosyllable (adjective *monosyllabic*): a word consisting of just one syllable.

morpheme: a minimal subunit of a word; a stem, prefix, or suffix.

morphology: the system of word formation and word inflection in a language.

morphophonemic: referring to rules or forms in which phonemes are adjusted according to grammatical conditions.

multisyllabic: synonym of *polysyllabic*.

nasal (verb *nasalize*): pronounced by lowering the velum to pass the air stream through the nose and add nasal resonance (nasality).

natural class: a group of related sounds that act similarly in the rules of the language.

neutralization (verb *neutralize*): the cancellation of a distinction or contrast in a given situation.

nucleus: the main, most sonorous part of a syllable (normally a vowel).

null stress (adjective *null-stressed*, or *unstressed*): lacking strong or weak stress.

obstruent: a consonant resulting from complete or partial obstruction of the air stream; a stop or fricative; opposite: *sonorant*.

onset: the beginning of a syllable, consisting of one or more consonants (if present).

open syllable: one that ends in a vowel, without a closing consonant (coda).

Optimality Theory: a linguistic theory that views adjustments of form and pronunciation as due to resolutions of constraint violations rather than application of rules.

orthography (adjective *orthographic*): spelling (of words); the writing system of a language.

oxytone: a word stressed on its last syllable.

palatal (verb *palatalize*): made on or close to the (hard) palate.

paradigm: the full set of forms a word has (e.g., the full conjugation of a verb).

paroxytone: a word stressed on its penult.

part of speech: the syntactic category of a word: verb, noun, adjective, adverb, and so on.

peak stress: stress heightened by greater loudness, pitch, and sometimes length, used to emphasize or contrast a word in a phrase or sentence.

penult, or **pen**: (adjective *penultimate*): the next-to-last syllable of a word.

perfect fit: an orthographic situation in which each phoneme would be written with a single grapheme, and each grapheme would represent only one phoneme.

pharynx (adjective *pharyngeal*): the upper throat, particularly the area behind the tongue.

phone (adjective *phonetic*): any speech sound, regardless of whether it is a phoneme.

phoneme (adjective *phonemic*): an underlying phonological unit (often with allophones) that contrasts with other such units to distinguish the words of a language.

phonemic representation: a broad transcription that factors out nondistinctive details.

phonetic representation: a detailed (narrow) transcription that includes features that may not be distinctive.

phonetics: the study of the articulation and perception of speech sounds.

phonics: an approach to teaching reading and writing that emphasizes phoneme-grapheme correspondences.

phonology: the sound system of a language, including its phonemes, rules, and suprasegmentals.

phonotactics: principles for how a language assembles phonemes into words, and constraints against certain combinations.

phrase: a group of words consisting of a head word and its modifiers and forming a syntactic unit (e.g., noun phrase, verb phrase).

pitch: the tone (relative highness/lowness) of a sound, due to the frequency of vibration.

polysyllable (adjective *polysyllabic*): describing a word consisting of several syllables.

portmanteau: a word that merges two morphemes into a single indivisible form.

postlexical rule: a surface-level phonetic rule that applies generally, without regard to morphological conditions.

postvocalic: occurring after a vowel.

pre-antepenultimate, or **pre**: the fourth syllable from the end of a word.

preglottalized: describing a consonant pronounced with a glottal stop before it.

present stress: the occurrence of stress (strong or weak) on a vowel or syllable.

prevocalic: occurring before a vowel.

proparoxytone: a word stressed on its third syllable from the end.

quintultimate, or **qui**: the fifth syllable from the end of a word.

reduction (verb *reduce*): a process that neutralizes the distinctions of vowels so that they converge on the same articulation, usually (but not always) in the absence of stress.

reduplication: an orthographic rule that doubles a letter in a given environment.

register: speech level or style of speaking, ranging from high (formal) to low (casual), indicated by relative tempo and carefulness.

retroflex: pronounced with the tip of the tongue curled up and slightly back toward the palate.

r-ful/*r*-less: describing a dialect division in English resulting from loss of /r/ in a coda ("*r*-less") in varieties such as RP as opposed to its retention ("*r*-ful") in most American varieties.

rhotic: (1) referring to /r/-sounds in general. (2) *r*-ful.

rhyme: the syllable nucleus together with a coda (if present); that part of a syllable that is felt to rhyme with other syllables.

right-headed: describing a foot with its "head" (strong-stressed) syllable at the right.

right-stressing: referring to a compound whose primary or peak stress is on its right element.

rounded: pronounced with the lips constricted; opposite: *unrounded*, or *spread*.

RP: Received Pronunciation, the favored pronunciation of standard southern British English.

sandhi: processes that merge adjacent words in connected speech, or the forms that then result.

schwa: a very lax mid-central vowel, resulting in English from reduction of more distinct vowels.

selection question: a question that gives a choice of alternatives; synonym: *choice question*.

semivowel: a glide, so called because it is intermediate between vowels and consonants.

sexultimate, or **sex**: the sixth syllable from the end of a word.

shifter ending: an ending that causes stress to change to another syllable.

sibilant: a fricative or affricate that sounds "hissy" because of high-frequency turbulence resulting from a grooved tongue surface.

skip-a-syllable rule (or alternating stress rule): a tendency to alternate stressed syllables with unstressed ones, avoiding adjacent stresses or a long sequence of null stresses.

smoothing: a process that simplifies a diphthong, resulting in less tongue movement and perhaps a monophthong.

softening: a change of a velar to an alveolar, or of an alveolar to an alveopalatal.

sonorants: generally voiced sounds with resonance (vowels, liquids, nasals, glides); opposite: *obstruents*.

spectrograph: a machine or program that analyzes sound as an image (*spectrogram*) showing resonance frequencies.

spelling pronunciation: a change of a word's pronunciation to make it conform to the orthography, due to the belief that the latter reflects the "correct" way of saying it.

spondee (adjective *spondaic*): a foot made up of two stressed syllables.

stop: a consonant in which the articulators completely block the air stream; synonym (for most kinds of stops): *plosive*.

stress (adjective *stressed*): the greater prominence or loudness that a vowel or syllable exhibits within a word, in at least two degrees: strong/weak (or primary/secondary).

stress relocation: movement of peak stress to an element that ordinarily would not receive it, for emphasis or contrast.

stress-timing: a speaking rhythm based on rather evenly paced stresses, with unstressed syllables shortened to fit into feet organized around the strong stresses; also known as foot isochrony.

suppletion: the replacement of a given formation with a special phonologically unrelated form.

suprasegmentals: features regarded as being above the consonant and vowel segments: stress, pitch, and (in some analyses) length.

syllabic: (1) referring to a syllable. (2) carrying the beat of a syllable and serving as its nucleus.

syllabication (verb *syllabify*): division of a word into its syllables.

syllable: a unit consisting of a nucleus (usually a vowel) with its associated consonants.

syllable-timing: a kind of speaking rhythm based on a chaining together of syllables with about the same length (duration).

syntax: principles for joining words in a certain order to form phrases and sentences.

tableau: a representation comparing possible outputs and the constraints they violate.

tag: an element added onto the end of the sentence (or sometimes at the beginning or in mid-sentence), typically set off by commas or a break in intonation.

tense: pronounced with a relatively tauter musculature that, in the case of vowels, causes the tongue to rise slightly for a more closed oral channel.

trill: a kind of /r/ sound in which an articulator (apex, lips, or uvula) is forced to vibrate by an increased air stream.

triphthong: a three-part vowel consisting of one main tongue position with two gliding movements.

trisyllabic: consisting of three syllables.

trochee (adjective *trochaic*): a foot made up of a stressed syllable followed by an unstressed one.

ultimate, or **ult**: the last syllable of a word (or its only syllable).

unbounded: referring to feet that are not fixed in their number of syllables but can embrace an entire word; referring to languages with such feet.

underlying representation: an abstract representation of pronunciation that differs from a strictly phonetic transcription in reflecting deeper phonological and morphological relationships.

universals: properties, constraints, or units that are found in all languages.

upstep: a jump upward in intonation to resume the main idea after a parenthetical element.

uvula (adjective: *uvular*): the appendage hanging down from the back of the velum.

variable rule: a rule whose frequency of application varies according to sociolinguistic factors such as style (register) and social class.

velum (adjective: *velar*): the soft palate, extending behind the (hard) palate; velarized: pronounced with a secondary articulation at the velum.

vocal cords: two muscular bands in the larynx, controlled by the arytenoid cartilages, that can be spread apart or brought together for voice; synonym: *vocal folds*.

vocalization: weakening of the articulation of liquids so that they become more vowel-like.

vocative: a label (name, nickname, title) used to directly address or call out to a person.

voice (adjective *voiced*): vibration of the vocal cords.

voicing onset time (VOT): the relative lag between release of a voiceless consonant and the beginning of voice for a following vowel.

voiceless: pronounced with the vocal cords spread apart instead of vibrating; opposite: *voiced*.

volume: loudness of a sound, due to the forcefulness (energy) of vibration; synonym: *amplitude*.

vowel: a sound with strong oral (and sometimes nasal) resonance that serves as the nucleus of a syllable and lacks the constriction of a consonant.

wau: the labiovelar glide /w/.

weak forms: reduced and often shorted (contracted) forms of words that are used when they are unstressed and merged with adjacent stressed words as sandhi.

WH-content question (or *wh*-question): a question that begins with an interrogative word such as *who, what, when, why,* or *how.*

yes-no question: a question that requests verification of information rather than conveying it, typically answered with *yes* or *no.*

yod: the palatal glide /j/.

zero allomorph: a case in which a morpheme that should be present is not pronounced.

REFERENCES

Allen, Edward David, and Rebecca M. Valette. 1977. *Classroom techniques: Foreign languages and English as a second language.* San Diego: Harcourt Brace Jovanovich.

Avery, Peter, and Susan Ehrlich. 1992. *Teaching American English pronunciation.* Oxford: Oxford University Press.

Beckman, Mary E., and Janet Pierrehumbert. 1986. Intonation structure in Japanese and English. *Phonology Yearbook* 3:255–309.

Bolinger, Dwight. 1978. *Intonation across languages: Universals of human language,* Vol. 2, *Phonology,* ed. Joseph Greenberg, 471–524. Stanford, Calif.: Stanford University Press.

Bond, Z. S., and Joann Fokes. 1985. Non-native patterns of English syllable timing. *Journal of Phonetics* 13:407–20.

Booij, Geert, and Jerzy Rubach. 1984. Morphological and prosodic domains in lexical phonology. *Phonology Yearbook* 1:1–28.

Bowen, J. Donald. 1972. *Patterns of English pronunciation.* Rowley, Mass.: Newbury House.

Brazil, David. 1985. Phonology: Intonation in discourse. In *Handbook of discourse,* ed. by Teun A. Van Dijk, vol. 2: 57–75. London: Academic Press.

Carvajal, Carol Styles, and Jane Horwood. 1996. *The Oxford Spanish-English dictionary: New international edition.* Oxford: Oxford University Press.

Celce-Murcia, Marianne, Donna M. Brinton, and Janet M. Goodwin. 1996. *Teaching pronunciation: A reference for teachers of English to speakers of other languages.* Cambridge, UK: Cambridge University Press.

Chafe, Wallace. 1980. *The pear stories III: Advances in discourse processes.* Norwood, N.J.: Ablex.

Chao, Yuen-Ren. 1934 [1957]. The Nonuniqueness of phonemic solutions of phonetic systems. *Bulletin of the Institute of History and Philology, Academia Sinica* 4, no. 4:363–97. Reprinted in Martin Joos (ed.), *Readings in linguistics I.* 4th ed. Chicago: University of Chicago Press.

Chomsky, Noam, and Morris Halle. 1968. *The sound pattern of English.* New York: Harper and Row.

Clark, John, and Colin Yallop. 1995. *An introduction to phonetics and phonology.* 2d ed. Oxford UK: Blackwell.

Coulthard, Malcolm. 1985. *Discourse analysis*. New York: Longman.

Cruttenden, Alan. 1986. *Intonation*. Cambridge UK: Cambridge University Press.

Dalbor, John. 1989. *Spanish pronunciation: Theory and practice*. New York: Holt, Rinehart and Winston.

Dalton, Christiane, and Barbara Seidlhofer. 1994. *Pronunciation*. Oxford: Oxford University Press.

Dewey, Godfrey. 1970. *Relative frequency of English spellings*. New York: Teachers College Press, Columbia University.

Dickerson, Wayne B. 1975. Decomposition of orthographic word classes. *Linguistics* 163:19–34.

———. 1977. Assigning stress to multi-suffixed words: Applications for TESL. *ITL: Review of Applied Linguistics* 36:71–88.

———. 1978. English orthography: A guide to word stress and vowel quality. *IRAL* 16:127–47.

———. 1985. The invisible Y: A case for spelling in pronunciation learning. *TESOL Quarterly* 19:303–16.

———. 1990. Morphology via orthography: A visual approach to oral decisions. *Applied Linguistics* 11:238–52.

Dickerson, Wayne B., and Rebecca H. Finney. 1978. Spelling in TESOL: Stress cues to vowel quality. *TESOL Quarterly* 12:163–75.

Fokes, Joann, and Z. S. Bond. 1989. The vowels of stressed and unstressed syllables in nonnative English. *Language Learning* 39:341–73.

Fries, Charles C. 1945. *Teaching and learning English as a foreign language*. Ann Arbor: University of Michigan Press.

Fromkin, Victoria, ed. 2000. *Linguistics: An introduction to linguistic theory*. Malden, Mass.: Blackwell Publishers.

Fromkin, Victoria, and Robert Rodman. 1998. *An introduction to language*. 6th ed. Fort Worth, Tex.: Harcourt, Brace.

Gass, Susan, and Larry Selinker. 2001. *Second language acquisition: An introductory course*. Mahwah, N.J.: Lawrence Erlbaum Associates.

Gimson, A. C. 1962. *An introduction to the pronunciation of English*. London: Edward Arnold.

Gleason, H. A. 1967. *Descriptive linguistics*. New York: Holt, Rinehart and Winston.

Goldsmith, John. 1976. An overview of autosegmental phonology. *Linguistic Analysis* 2, no. 1.

Graham, Carolyn. 1978. *Jazz chants*. New York: Oxford University Press.

———. 1992. *Singing, chanting, telling tales: Arts in the language classroom*. New York: Harcourt Brace.

Grate, Harriette Gordon. 1974. *English pronunciation exercises for Japanese students*. New York: Regents.

Greenberg, Joseph, ed. 1978. *Universals of human language*. Vol. 2, *Phonology*. Stanford, Calif.: Stanford University Press.

Gussenhoven, Carlos, and Haike Jacobs. 1998. *Understanding phonology*. London: Arnold.

Hayes, Bruce. 1981. A metrical theory of stress rules. Ph.D. diss., Massachusetts Institute of Technology. Bloomington: Indiana University Linguistics Club.

———. 1985. Iambic and trochaic rhythm in stress rules. *Berkeley Linguistics Society* 13:429–46.

Hogg, Richard, and C. B. McCully. 1987. *Metrical phonology: A coursebook*. Cambridge, UK: Cambridge University Press.

International Phonetic Association. 1999. *Handbook of the International Phonetic Association*. Cambridge, UK: Cambridge University Press.

James, Carl. 1980. *Contrastive analysis*. London: Longman.

———. 1998. *Errors in language learning and use: Exploring error analysis*. New York: Longman.

Jespersen, Otto. 1928. *A modern English grammar on historical principles*. Heidelberg: Carl Winters Universitätsbuchhandlung.

Jones, Daniel. 1950. *The phoneme: Its nature and use*. Cambridge, UK: W. Heffer and Sons.

Kaisse, Ellen M., and Patricia A. Shaw. 1985. On the theory of lexical phonology. *Phonology Yearbook* 2:1–30.

Kenyon, John S., and Thomas A. Knott. 1953. *A pronouncing dictionary of American English*. Springfield, Mass.: Merriam Company.

Kiparsky, Paul. 1982. From cyclic phonology to lexical phonology. In *The structure of phonological representations*, part 2, ed. H. Van der Hulst and N. Smith. Dordrecht, 131–76. The Netherlands: Foris.

Knowles, Phillip L., and Ruth A. Sasaki. 1980. *Story squares: Fluency in English as a second language*. Cambridge, Mass.: Winthrop Publishers.

Kreidler, Charles. 1989. *The pronunciation of English: A course book in phonology*. Oxford: Basil Blackwell.

Labov, William. 1972. The internal evolution of linguistic rules. In *Linguistic change and generative theory*, ed. Robert P. Stockwell and Ronald Macaulay, 101–71. Bloomington: Indiana University Press.

Ladd, D. Robert. 1986. Intonational phrasing: The case for recursive prosodic structure. *Phonology Yearbook* 3:311–40.

Ladefoged, Peter. 2000. *A course in phonetics*. 4th ed. Cambridge, Mass.: International Thomson.

Ladefoged, Peter, and Ian Maddieson. 1996. *The sounds of the world's languages*. Oxford: Blackwell.

Lado, Robert. 1957. *Language across cultures*. Ann Arbor: University of Michigan Press.

Lass, Roger. 1984. *Phonology: An introduction to basic concepts*. Cambridge, UK: Cambridge University Press.

Lee, W. R. 1979. *Language teaching games*. Oxford: Oxford University Press.

Lehnert, Martin. 1971. *Rückläufiges Wörterbuch der englischen Gegenwartssprache / Reverse dictionary of present-day English.* Leipzig, Germany: VEB Verlag Enzyklopädie.

Liberman, Mark, and Alan Prince. 1977. On stress and linguistic rhythm. *Linguistic Inquiry* 8:249–336.

Lindblom, B. 1990. Explaining phonetic variation: A sketch of the H&H Theory. In *Speech production and speech modelling,* ed. W. J. Hardcastle and A. Marchal, 403–39. Dordrecht: Kluwer.

Maddieson, Ian. 1984. *Patterns of sounds.* Cambridge, UK: Cambridge University Press.

Majdi, Basim. 1983. Teaching English phonology in Iraq: Problems and possible solutions. M.A. thesis, West Virginia University.

Nilsen, Don L. F., and Alleen Pace Nilsen. 1973. *Pronunciation contrasts in English.* New York: Regents.

O'Grady, William, Michael Dobrovolsky, and Mark Aronoff. 1997. *Contemporary linguistics: An introduction.* 3d ed. New York: St. Martin's Press.

Omaggio-Hadley, Alice. 1993. *Teaching language in context.* 2d ed. Boston: Heinle and Heinle.

Pike, Kenneth. 1947. *Phonemics: A technique for reducing languages to writing.* Ann Arbor: University of Michigan Press.

Prince, Alan, and Paul Smolensky. 1993. *Optimality theory: Constraint interaction in generative grammar.* New Brunswick, N.J.: Technical Reports of the Rutgers Center for Cognitive Science.

Richard-Amato, Patricia. 1988. *Making it happen: Interaction in the second language classroom from theory to practice.* New York: Longman.

Richards, Jack C., ed. 1974. *Error analysis: Perspectives on second language acquisition.* London: Longman.

Selinker, Larry. 1992. *Rediscovering interlanguage.* New York: Longman.

Trager, George, and Henry Lee Smith Jr. 1951. *Outline of English structure.* Norman, Okla.: Battenburg Press.

Viëtor, Wilhelm. 1894. *Elemente der phonetik des Deutschen, Englischen und Französischen.* 3d ed. Leipzig: Reisland.

Wells, J. C. 1982. *Accents of English.* Cambridge, UK: Cambridge University Press.

Whitley, M. Stanley. 2003. *Phonicon: A multimedia digital encyclopedia of the sounds of the world's languages.* On CD-ROM; co-producer Bakhit Kourmanov. Dallas: SIL International.

Zwicky, Arnold. 1972. Note on a phonological hierarchy in English. In *Linguistic change and generative theory,* ed. Robert P. Stockwell and Ronald Macaulay, 275–301. Bloomington: Indiana University Press.

INDEX

acoustic phonetics: Appendix (8.1)

adverbial clauses: intonation 3.6.3

affixation: effect on stress position 2.2.3–2.9

allomorphs, allomorphy: 7.5–7.7.2

alternating (skip-a-syllable) stress rule: 1.4, 2.13.3

alternations (morphophonemic): 1.4, 5.5, 7.7–7.7.2

alveopalatalization of /t d s z/: 6.9, 7.7.2. *See also* palatalization of /t d s z/

anapest: 1.3

articulation (place/manner) 6.2.2–3

aspiration: 6.2.4, 6.5.1

assimilation: 6.4.2, 7.3; as a problem in orthography 4.2

autosegmental phonology: intonation 3.7; assimilation 6.4.2

backwards buildup (teaching technique) 2.15, 7.9

base word (of a family): 2.4

bisyllabic words: stress patterns 2.7, 2.11

bounded/unbounded: 1.2

breaking (of vowels): 5.4.2

checked/free vowels: 1.4, 6.1

citation forms: 7.2

clipping: 1.5

closed/open syllables: 1.4; effect on stress 2.7, 2.11.1, 2.13.2–3

cloze (partial fill—in): 7.9

clusters (of consonants): 6.10; simplification 7.3

compounds: stress patterns 2.11.2, 3.3–3.3.3

conditioning (phonological, grammatical, lexical:) 7.6.2

consonants: spelling 4.2–4.2.6; English system 6.3; articulation 6.2–6.2.4, 6.4.1–6.9; teaching 5.9; morphophonemic alternations 7.7.2; acoustic analysis 8.1

constituent (units): of compounds and phrases 3.3.2

constraints: 6.10, 7.7.3

context: effect on articulation 7.3

contractions: 7.4.2

contrast: as a use of peak stress 3.1

contrastive analysis: 6.11

Corpus (database used in *PEASBA*): Appendix (8.3)

dactyl: 1.3

defooting: 7.4.3

delateralization of /l/: 6.4.1

derivation: word formation 7.6; series of rule applications 7.6.2

diacritics: 4.3

dialect variation: in stress position 2.10; in vowels 5.6–5.6.5, in consonants 6.4.1–6.9; and orthography 4.1, 7.8

dictation: as a teaching technique 7.9

dictionaries: transcription in 5.8

digraphs: 4.1; discontinuous 4.3

diphthong: 1.4, 5.4.3; smoothed diphthongs 5.6.4

diphthongization: of /i e o u/ 5.4.2, in /ai oi au/ 5.4.3, of other vowels 5.6.2–3

discourse: impact on peak stress 3.1, 3.4; and intonation 3.5.1; effect on articulation 7.2–3.

distribution (complementary/contrastive): 5.1

downstep/upstep: 3.6.4

drag strip (teaching technique): 2.15

drumsticks (teaching technique): 1.6

emphasis: as a use of peak stress 3.1

endings: effect on stress position 2.5, 2.7

enumeration (listing): intonation 3.6.1

epenthesis: 6.10; in plurals 7.6.2

error analysis: 6.11

extrametrical: 1.2, 7.4.1

families (of words): and stress position 2.3–5

features: of vowels 5.7; of consonants 6.2.2–3

flapping: 6.5.2

flooding (teaching technique): 2.15, 4.15

Fluency Squares: 5.9

foot: metric 1.2; in speech rhythm 7.4.1; types (spondee, trochee, iamb, etc.) 1.3

four-plus words (words of four or more syllables): stress patterns 2.9, 2.13

free variation: 5.6.5

frequency: of word types by stressed syllable 2.1; of spellings for phonemes 4.2–4.4.3; of phonemes in text: 7.1; in sound waves 8.1

functional load: 5.5

glides: 6.9

glottaling: 6.5.1

grammar: role in phonology 7.4.3, 7.5–6; combining with pronunciation in teaching 7.9

grapheme: vs. phoneme 2.14, 4.1

Great Vowel Shift: 7.7.1; effect on spelling 4.1

greetings and farewells: intonation 3.5.3

iamb: 1.3

inflection: 7.6

information: info(rmation) units and peak stress 3.4; new information and peak stress 3.4

information gap activities: 5.9

interlanguage: 6.11

International Phonetic Alphabet: 1.4; Appendix (8.2)

intonation: 3.2; and emotional reactions 3.5.1–2; falls, rises, rise-falls, fall-rises in statements, questions, commands 3.5–3.6.2; in greetings/farewells 3.5.3; in enumeration 3.6; in tags 3.6.3; in complex sentences and parentheticals 3.6.3; approaches 3.7; teaching 3.8

irregularity (in morphology): 7.6.2

Jazz Chants: 7.9

left-headed feet: 1.2, 1.4; left-stressed compounds 3.3.1–3

length: as part of peak stress 3.1; of vowels 5.4, 5.4.2; of syllables according to rhythm 7.4.1

lexical incidence, differences in: 5.6.5

lexical(ist) phonology: 7.7.3

liquids: 6.2.3, 6.4.1

loanwords: effect on English stress 1.5, 2.7; effects on spelling 4.1–2, 4.4.1

manner of articulation: 6.2.3

melodic line: *See* intonation

memorization: for fluency 7.9

metric foot: *See* foot

metrical theory: 1.2

minimal pairs: 5.1; use in teaching 5.9

monosyllabicity: as a trend in English 1.5

morphemes: and stress 2.9; and morphology 7.5–7

morphophonemic changes (alternations) and representations: 7.7–7.7.1

nasalization: 5.1, 6.4.2

nasals: 6.4.2

neutralization: of tense/lax 5.4.2; of /t d/ 6.5.2

null stress: 1.1; effect on vowels 1.4, 5.3, 5.5, 6.4.3, 7.3

obstruents: 6.2.3

Optimality Theory: 7.7.3

oral reading: 7.9

orthography: 4.1; consonants 4.2–4.2.6; vowels 4.3–4.4.2; teaching 4.5; as a mixed system 7.8

oxytones: 2.1

palatalization of /t d s z/: 6.9; as spelling problem 4.2.3

parenthetical expressions: intonation 3.6.3

paroxytones: 2.1

part of speech: effect on stress position 2.2.2, 2.5, 2.7

peak stress: characteristics and functions 3.1; on affixes 2.13.4; in compounds 3.3–3.3.1; info units in a sentence 3.4; for new information 3.4

phoneme: 5.3

phonics: vs. look–say approach 4.1

phonological rules: 5.7, 7.6.2–7.7.3

phonotactics: 6.10; role in rules or constraints 7.6.2, 7.7.3

phrases: vs. compounds in stress location 3.3.1–2; linkage of phonemes in phrases 7.3

pitch: in stress 1.1; in peak stress 3.1; in intonation 3.2; in compounds 3.3.3; of sound wave 8.1. *See also* intonation

place of articulation: 6.2.2

pluralization: 4.2.5, 7.6.2

prefixes: effect on stress 2.6–8, 2.13.3

preglottalization: 6.5.1

proparoxytones: 2.1

questions: intonation 3.5.1, 3.6.2

r-dropping, *r*-less/*r*-ful dialects: 5.4.4, 6.4.1

reduction: with null stress 2.14; problems in spelling 4.4–4.4.1; effects on vowel pronunciation and alternations 5.4–5

redundancy: 7.3

reduplication (consonant letter doubling): 4.2

register: 1.4; effect on weak vs. null stress 2.10, 2.11.2, 2.13.3; effect on weak forms 7.4.2

repetition (in modeling pronunciation): 7.9

rhotics: 6.4.1

rhythm (stress/syllable timing): 7.4.1

right-headed feet: 1.2, 1.4; right-stressed compounds 3.3.1–3

Romance languages: effect on English stress 2.7. *See also* loanwords

rounding (lip rounding): 5.2, 6.4.1

rules: orthographic 4; phonological 5.7, 6.4.1–6.5.2, 6.9–10, 7.6.2–7.7.3

sandhi: 7.3, 7.4.3

schwa: 1.4; spelling 2.14; articulation 5.3; frequency 6.1; in alternations 1.4, 5.5; schwa-drop 2.14, 5.5, 6.4.3, 7.3

semivowels: *See* glides

shifts in stress: 2.4; shifter endings 2.5; effect of prefixes 2.8

sibilants: 6.6; spelling 4.2.2–6; acoustic analysis 8.1

skip-a-syllable (alternating) stress rule: 1.4, 2, 2.12, 2.13.4

smoothed diphthongs: 5.6.4

sonorants: 6.2.3; acoustic analysis 8.1

sonority scale (hierarchy): 6.10

spectrograms, spectrograph: 8.1

spelling: 4; and morphophonemics: 7.8. *See also* orthography

spondee: 1.3

statements: intonation 3.5.1

stops: types 6.2.3; voicing, aspiration, flapping, preglottalization 6.5–6.5.2

stress: definition and degrees (strong/weak/ null) 1.1; leftward movement 2.1; placement (position) chap. 2; relocation 3.1, 3.5.1; in the rhythm of speech 7.4.1; in vowel alternations 7.7.1; teaching 1.6, 2.15. *See also* strong stress; weak stress

stress equivocation (teaching technique): 2.15

strong stress: 1.1; placement in other languages 2.1; placement in English chap. 2; retention/shift in word families 2.3–5

suffixes: effect on stress 2.4–7; allomorphs of 7.6.2; effect on a stem 7.7.1–2

suppletion: 7.6.2

suprasegmentals: 1.2; acoustic analysis 8.1

syllable: in feet 1.3; stress position (ult, pen, ant, pre, qui, sex) 2.1, 2.2.1, 2.7–13; syllable structure, syllabication 6.1, 6.10; syllabic nasals and liquids 6.4.3

syntax: effect on weak forms 7.5

tag (comments, vocatives, questions): intonation of 3.6.3

teaching/practicing: of stress 1.6, 2.15; of peak stress and intonation 3.8; of orthography 4.5; of phoneme distinctions 5.9; of linked forms in context 7.9

tempo: as part of register 1.4; effect on pronunciation 7.2, 7.4.1–2

tense/lax vowels: 1.4; 5.4.2

timing: of voice 6.5.1; of rhythm (stress- vs. syllable-timing) 7.4.1

tonette (for teaching purposes, use of): 3.8

Total Physical Response: 5.9

transcription: broad vs. narrow 5.1

transfer: 6.11, 7.7.3

trisyllabic words: stress patterns 2.8, 2.12

trochee: 1.3

underlying representation: 7.6.2
universals: 6.3
variable rules: 5.7
velarization of /l/: 6.4.1
vocalization (of liquids): 6.4–6.4.1
voice (voiced/voiceless) 6.2; voice onset time
    (VOT) 6.5.1; voiceless vowels 5.5; effect
    on plural allomorphs 7.6.2
vowels: and stress 1.4, 2.11.1; spelling 4.3;
    vowel systems 4.3, 5.3; pronunciation 5;

different analyses 5.8; alternations 1.4, 5.5,
    7.7.1; teaching 5.9; acoustic analysis 8.1
weak forms: 7.4.3; acoustic analysis 8.1
weak stress: 1.4; placement (position)
    2.10–13; multiple weak stresses 2.13.2
whistling (teaching technique): 1.6
yod (and yod loss in /ju/): 6.9; spelling
    4.2.1–3
zero allomorph: 7.6.2